Beginning Perl for Bioinformatics

James D. Tisdall

O'REILLY®

Beijing · Cambridge · Farnham · Köln · Paris · Sebastopol · Taipei · Tokyo

Beginning Perl for Bioinformatics
by James D. Tisdall

Published by O'Reilly Media, Inc., 1005 Gravenstein Highway North,
Sebastopol, CA 95472.

O'Reilly Media, Inc. books may be purchased for educational, business, or sales promotional use. On-line editions are also available for most titles (*safari.oreilly.com*). For more information contact our corporate/institutional sales department: (800) 998-9938 or *corporate@oreilly.com*.

Editor:	Lorrie LeJeune
Production Editor:	Mary Anne Weeks Mayo
Cover Designer:	Ellie Volckhausen
Interior Designer:	Melanie Wang

Printing History:

October 2001:	First Edition.

 This book uses RepKover™, a durable and flexible lay-flat binding.

ISBN: 0-596-00080-4
ISBN13: 978-0-596-0080-6
[M]   [02/07]

Table of Contents

Preface

What Is Bioinformatics?

Biological data is proliferating rapidly. Public databases such as GenBank and the Protein Data Bank have been growing exponentially for some time now. With the advent of the World Wide Web and fast Internet connections, the data contained in these databases and a great many special-purpose programs can be accessed quickly, easily, and cheaply from any location in the world. As a consequence, computer-based tools now play an increasingly critical role in the advancement of biological research.

Bioinformatics, a rapidly evolving discipline, is the application of computational tools and techniques to the management and analysis of biological data. The term bioinformatics is relatively new, and as defined here, it encroaches on such terms as "computational biology" and others. The use of computers in biology research predates the term bioinformatics by many years. For example, the determination of 3D protein structure from X-ray crystallographic data has long relied on computer analysis. In this book I refer to the use of computers in biological research as bioinformatics. It's important to be aware, however, that others may make different distinctions between the terms. In particular, bioinformatics is often the term used when referring to the data and the techniques used in large-scale sequencing and analysis of entire genomes, such as *C. elegans*, *Arabidopsis*, and *Homo sapiens*.

What Bioinformatics Can Do

Here's a short example of bioinformatics in action. Let's say you have discovered a very interesting segment of mouse DNA and you suspect it may hold a clue to the development of fatal brain tumors in humans. After sequencing the DNA, you perform a search of GenBank and other data sources using web-based sequence alignment tools such as BLAST. Although you find a few related sequences, you don't get a direct match or any information that indicates a link to the brain tumors you suspect exist. You know that the public genetic databases are growing daily and rapidly. You would like to perform your searches every day, comparing the results to the previous searches, to see if anything new appears in the databases. But this could take an hour or two each day! Luckily, you know Perl. With a day's work, you write a program (using the Bioperl module among other things) that automatically conducts a daily BLAST search of GenBank for your DNA sequence, compares the results with the previous day's results, and sends you email if there has been any change. This program is so useful that you start running it for other sequences as well, and your colleagues also start using it. Within a few months, your day's worth of work has saved many weeks of work for your community. This example is taken from real life. There are now existing programs you can use for this purpose, even web sites where you can submit your DNA sequence and your email address, and they'll do all the work for you!

This is only a small example of what happens when you apply the power of computation to a biological problem. This is bioinformatics.

About This Book

This book is a tutorial for biologists on how to program, and is designed for beginning programmers. The examples and exercises with only a few exceptions use biological data. The book's goal is twofold: it teaches programming skills and applies them to interesting biological areas.

I want to get you up and programming as quickly and painlessly as possible. I aim for simplicity of explanation, not completeness of coverage. I don't always strictly define the programming concepts, because formal definitions can be distracting.

The Perl language makes it possible to start writing real programs quickly. As you continue reading this book and the online Perl documentation, you'll fill in the details, learn better ways of doing things, and improve your understanding of programming concepts.

Depending on your style of learning, you can approach this material in different ways. One way, as the King gravely said to Alice, is to "Begin at the beginning and go on till you come to the end: then stop." (This line from *Alice in Wonderland* is often used as a whimsical definition of an algorithm.) The material is organized to be read in this fashion, as a narrative.

Another approach is to get the programs into your computer, run them, see what they do, and perhaps try to alter this or that in the program to see what effect your changes have. This may be combined with a quick skim of the text of the chapter. This is a common approach used by programmers when learning a new language. Basically, you learn by imitation, looking at actual programs.

Anyone wishing to learn Perl programming for bioinformatics should try the exercises found at the end of most chapters. They are given in approximate order of difficulty, and some of the higher-numbered exercises are fairly challenging and may be appropriate for classroom projects. Because there's more than one way to do things in Perl, there is no one correct answer to an exercise. If you're a beginning programmer, and you manage to solve an exercise in any way whatsoever, you've succeeded at that exercise. My suggested solutions to the exercises may be found at *http://www.oreilly.com/catalog/begperlbio*.

I hope that the material in this book will serve not only as a practical tutorial, but also as a first step to a research program if you decide that bioinformatics is a promising research direction in itself, or as an adjunct to ongoing investigations.

Who This Book Is For

This book is a practical introduction to programming for biologists.

Programming skills are now in strong demand in biology research and development. Historically, programming has not often been viewed as a critical skill for biologists at the bench. However, recent trends in biology have made computer analysis of large amounts of data central to many research programs. This book is intended as a hands-on, one-volume course for the busy biologist to acquire practical bioinformatics programming abilities. So, if you are a biologist who needs to learn programming, this book is for you. Its goal is to teach you how to write useful and practical bioinformatics programs as quickly and as painlessly as possible.

This book introduces programming as an important new laboratory skill; it presents a programming tutorial that includes a collection of "protocols," or programming techniques, that can be immediately useful in the lab. But its primary purpose is to teach programming, not to build a comprehensive toolkit.

There is a real blending of skills and approaches between the laboratory bench and computer programming. Many people do indeed find themselves shifting from running gels to writing Perl in the course of a day—or a career—in biology research. Of course, programming is its own discipline with its own methods and terminology, and so must be approached on its own terms. But there is cross-fertilization going on (if you'll pardon the metaphor between the two disciplines).

This book's exercises are of varying difficulty for those using it as a class textbook or for self study. (Almost) all examples and exercises are based on real biological problems, and this book will give you a good introduction to the most common bioinformatics programming problems and the most common computer-based biological data.

This book's web site, *http://www.oreilly.com/catalog/begperlbio*, includes all the program code in the book for convenient download, including the exercises and solutions, plus errata and other information.*

Why Should I Learn to Program?

Since many researchers who describe their work as "bioinformatics" don't program at all, but rather, use programs written by others, it's tempting to ask, "Do I really need to learn programming to do bioinformatics?" At one level, the answer is no, you don't. You can accomplish quite a bit using existing tools, and there are books and documentation available to help you learn those tools. But at another, higher level, the answer to the question changes. What happens when you want to do something a preexisting tool doesn't do? What happens when you can't find a tool to accomplish a particular task, and you can't find someone to write it for you?

At that point, you need to learn to program. And even if you still rely mainly on existing programs and tools, it can be worthwhile to learn enough to write small programs. Small programs can be incredibly useful. For example, with a bit of practice, you can learn to write programs that run other programs and spare yourself hours sitting in front of the computer doing things by hand.

Many scientists start out writing small programs and find that they really like programming. As a programmer, you never need to worry about finding the right tools for your needs; you can write them yourself. This book will get you started.

Structure of This Book

There are thirteen chapters and two appendixes in this book. The following provides a brief introduction:

Chapter 1, *Biology and Computer Science*
    This chapter covers some key concepts in molecular biology, as well as how biology and computer science fit together.

Chapter 2, *Getting Started with Perl*
    This chapter shows you how to get Perl up and running on your computer.

Chapter 3, *The Art of Programming*
    Chapter 3 provides an overview as to how programmers accomplish their jobs. Some of the most important practical strategies good programmers use are explained, and where to find answers to questions that arise while you are

---

* *Program code*, or simply *code*, means a computer program—the actual Perl language commands a programmer writes in a file.

programming is carefully laid out. These ideas are made concrete by brief narrative case studies that show how programmers, given a problem, find its solution.

Chapter 4, *Sequences and Strings*

In Chapter 4 you start writing Perl programs with DNA and proteins. The programs transcribe DNA to RNA, concatenate sequences, make the reverse complement of DNA, read sequences data from files, and more.

Chapter 5, *Motifs and Loops*

This chapter continues demonstrating the basics of the Perl language with programs that search for motifs in DNA or protein, interact with users at the keyboard, write data to files, use loops and conditional tests, use regular expressions, and operate on strings and arrays.

Chapter 6, *Subroutines and Bugs*

This chapter extends the basic knowledge of Perl in two main directions: subroutines, which are an important way to structure programs, and the use of the Perl debugger, which can examine in detail a running Perl program.

Chapter 7, *Mutations and Randomization*

Genetic mutations, fundamental to biology, are modelled as random events using the random number generator in Perl. This chapter uses random numbers to generate DNA sequence data sets, and to repeatedly mutate DNA sequence. Loops, subroutines, and lexical scoping are also discussed.

Chapter 8, *The Genetic Code*

This chapter shows how to translate DNA to proteins, using the genetic code. It also covers a good bit more of the Perl programming language, such as the hash data type, sorted and unsorted arrays, binary search, relational databases, and DBM, and how to handle FASTA formatted sequence data.

Chapter 9, *Restriction Maps and Regular Expressions*

This chapter contains an introduction to Perl regular expressions. The main focus of the chapter is the development of a program to calculate a restriction map for a DNA sequence.

Chapter 10, *GenBank*

The Genetic Sequence Data Bank (GenBank) is central to modern biology and bioinformatics. In this chapter, you learn how to write programs to extract information from GenBank files and libraries. You will also make a database to create your own rapid access lookups on a GenBank library.

Chapter 11, *Protein Data Bank*

This chapter develops a program that can parse Protein Data Bank (PDB) files. Some interesting Perl techniques are encountered while doing so, such as finding and iterating over lots of files and controlling other bioinformatics programs from a Perl program.

Chapter 12, *BLAST*

Chapter 12 develops some code to parse a BLAST output file. Also mentioned are the Bioperl project and its BLAST parser, and some additional ways to format output in Perl.

Chapter 13, *Further Topics*

Chapter 13 looks ahead to topics beyond the scope of this book.

Appendix A, *Resources*

Collected here are resources for Perl and for bioinformatics programming, such as books and Internet sites.

Appendix B, *Perl Summary*

This is a summary of the parts of Perl covered in this book, plus a little more.

Conventions Used in This Book

The following conventions are used in this book:

Italic

Used for commands, filenames, directory names, variables, modules, URLs, and for the first use of a term

`Constant width`

Used in code examples and to show the output of commands

This icon designates a note, which is an important aside to the nearby text.

This icon designates a warning relating to the nearby text.

Comments and Questions

Please address comments and questions concerning this book to the publisher:

O'Reilly & Associates, Inc.
1005 Gravenstein Highway North
Sebastopol, CA 95472
(800) 998-9938 (in the United States or Canada)
(707) 829-0515 (international/local)
(707) 829-0104 (fax)

There is a web page for this book, which lists errata, examples, or any additional information. You can access this page at:

http://www.oreilly.com/catalog/begperlbio

To comment or ask technical questions about this book, send email to:

bookquestions@oreilly.com

For more information about books, conferences, Resource Centers, and the O'Reilly Network, see the O'Reilly web site at:

http://www.oreilly.com

Acknowledgments

I would like to thank my editor, Lorrie LeJeune, and everyone at O'Reilly & Associates for their skill, enthusiasm, support, and patience; and my technical reviewers Cynthia Gibas, Joel Greshock, Ian Korf, Andrew Martin, Jon Orwant, and Clay Shirky, for their helpful and detailed reviews. I also thank M. Immaculada Barrasa, Michael Caudy, Muhammad Muquit, and Nat Torkington for their excellent help with particular chapters.

Thanks also to James Watson, whose classic book *The Molecular Biology of the Gene* first got me interested in biology; Larry Wall for inventing and developing Perl; and my colleagues at Bell Laboratories in Murray Hill, NJ, for teaching me computer science. Thanks to Beverly Emmanuel, David Searls, and the late Chris Overton, who started the Computational Biology and Informatics Laboratory in the Human Genome Project for Chromosome 22 at the University of Pennsylvania and Children's Hospital of Philadelphia. They gave me my first bioinformatics job. Thanks to Mitch Marcus of Bell Labs and the Department of Computer and Information Science at UPenn who insisted that I borrow his copy of *Programming Perl* and try it out. I'd also like to thank my colleagues at Mercator Genetics and The Fox Chase Cancer Center for supporting my work in bioinformatics.

Finally, I'd like to thank my friends for encouraging my writing; and especially my parents Edward and Geraldine, my siblings Judi, John, and Thom, my wife Elizabeth, and my children Rose, Eamon, and Joe.

## CHAPTER 1

Biology and Computer Science

One of the most exciting things about being involved in computer programming and biology is that both fields are rich in new techniques and results.

Of course, biology is an old science, but many of the most interesting directions in biological research are based on recent techniques and ideas. The modern science of genetics, which has earned a prominent place in modern biology, is just about 100 years old, dating from the widespread acknowledgement of Mendel's work. The elucidation of the structure of deoxyribonucleic acid (DNA) and the first protein structure are about 50 years old, and the polymerase chain reaction (PCR) technique of cloning DNA is almost 20 years old. The last decade saw the launching and completion of the Human Genome Project that revealed the totality of human genes and much more. Today, we're in a golden age of biological research—a point in human history of great medical, scientific, and philosophical importance.

Computer science is relatively new. Algorithms have been around since ancient times (Euclid), and the interest in computing machinery is also antique (Pascal's mechanical calculator, for instance, or Babbage's steam-driven inventions of the 19th century). But programming was really born about 50 years ago, at the same time as construction of the first large, programmable, digital/electronic (the ENIAC) computers. Programming has grown very rapidly to the present day. The Internet is about 20 years old, as are personal computers; the Web is about 10 years old. Today, our communications, transportation, agricultural, financial, government, business, artistic, and of course, scientific endeavors are closely tied to computers and their programming.

This rapid and recent growth gives the field of computer programming a certain excitement and requires that its professional practitioners keep on their toes. In a way, programming represents procedural knowledge—the knowledge of how to do things—and one way to look at the importance of computers in our society and our history is to see the enormous growth in procedural knowledge that the use of computers has occasioned. We're also seeing the concepts of computation and algorithm being adopted widely, for instance, in the arts and in the law, and of course in the sciences. The computer has become the ruling metaphor for explaining things in general. Certainly, it's tempting to think of a cell's molecular biology in terms of a special kind of computing machinery.

Similarly, the remarkable discoveries in biology have found an echo in computer science. There are evolutionary programs, neural networks, simulated annealing, and more. The exchange of ideas and metaphors between the fields of biology and computer science is, in itself, a spur to discovery (although the dangers of using an improper metaphor are also real).

The Organization of DNA

It's necessary to review some of the very basic concepts and terminology of DNA and proteins at this point. This review is for the benefit of the nonbiologist; if you're a biologist you can skip the next two sections.

DNA is a polymer composed of four molecules, usually called *bases* or *nucleotides*. Their names and one-letter abbreviations are adenine (A), cytosine (C), guanine (G), and thymine (T).* (See Chapter 4 for more about how DNA is represented as computer data.) The bases joined end to end to form a single strand of DNA.

In the cell, DNA usually appears in a double-stranded form, with two strands wrapped around each other in the famous double helix shape. The two strands of the double helix have matching bases, known as the *base pairs*. An A on one strand is always opposite a T on the other strand, and a G is always paired with a C.

There is also an orientation to the strands. One end of a nucleotide is called the 5' (five prime) end, and the other is called the 3' (three prime) end. When nucleotides join to make a single strand of DNA, they always connect the 5' end of one to the 3' end of the other. Furthermore, when the cell uses the DNA, as in transcribing it to RNA, it does so base by base from the 5' to the 3' direction. So, when DNA is written, it's done so left to right on the page, corresponding to the 5' to 3' orientation of the bases. An encoded gene can appear on either strand, so it's important to look at both strands when searching or analyzing DNA.

When two strands are joined in a double helix (as in Figure 1-1), the two strands have opposite orientations. That is, the 5' to 3' orientation of one strand runs in an opposite direction as the 5' to 3' orientation of the other strand. So at each end of the double helix, one strand has a 3' end; the other has a 5' end.

Because the base pairs are always matched A-T and C-G and the orientation of the strands are the reverse of each other, the term *reverse complement* describes the relationship of the bases of the two strands. It's "reverse" because the orientations are

---

* These names come from where they were originally found: the glands, the cell, guano, and the thymus.

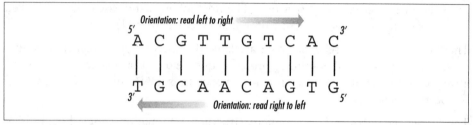

Figure 1-1. Two strands of DNA

reversed, and "complement" because the bases always pair to their complementary bases, A to T and C to G.

Given these facts and a single strand of DNA, it's easy to figure what the matching strand would be in the double helix. Simply change all bases to their complements: A to T, T to A, C to G, and G to C. Then, since DNA is written in the 5' to 3' direction, after complementing the DNA, write it in reverse.

GenBank, the Genetic Sequence Data Bank (*http://www.ncbi.nlm.nih.gov*), contains most known sequence data. We'll take a closer look at GenBank in Chapter 10.

The Organization of Proteins

Proteins are somewhat similar to DNA. They are also polymers, long strings made up of a small number of simple molecules. As DNA is composed of four nucleotides, so proteins are composed of 20 amino acids. These amino acids may occur in any order. See Table 4-2 for the names and one- and three-letter abbreviations for the amino acids.

Amino acids are composed of an amino group, a carboxyl group and a sidechain. They form a chemical bond, called a peptide bond, between the amino group and the carboxyl group of adjacent amino acids. Each of the 20 amino acids has a different sidechain, which protrudes from the backbone. The chemical properties of the sidechains are important in determining the properties of the protein.

Proteins usually have a more complex 3D structure than DNA. The peptide bonds have a great deal of rotational freedom, which allows proteins to form many 3D structures. Instead of DNA's double helix, proteins tend to fold up in a variety of different shapes and are composed of one or more strands of amino acids assembled together.* The sequence of amino acids along the strand is called the *primary structure*. The coiling in on itself into local structures such as helices, beta-strands, and

---

* I try to avoid most of the potentially confusing biology in this text in order to concentrate on learning Perl, but I can't help mentioning at this point that DNA also has a more complex 3D structure. It can appear as one-stranded, two-stranded, and three-stranded forms, and it is also coiled and recoiled into a small space during most of the life of the cell.

turns, is called the *secondary structure*. The final foldings and assemblies are called the *tertiary* and *quaternary* structure of proteins (see Chapter 11).

There is more primary sequence data available than secondary or higher structural data. In fact, a great deal of primary protein sequence data is available (since it is relatively easy to identify primary protein sequence from DNA, of which a great deal has been sequenced).

The Protein Data Bank (PDB) contains structural information about thousands of proteins, the accumulated knowledge of decades of work. We'll look at the PDB in Chapter 10, but you may want to get a headstart by visiting the PDB web site (*http://www.rcsb.org/pdb/*) to become familiar with this essential bioinformatics resource.

In Silico

Recently, the new term *in silico* has become a common reference to biological studies carried out in the computer, joining the traditional terms *in vivo* and *in vitro* to describe the location of experimental studies.

For nonbiologists, *in vitro* means "in glass," that is, in the test tube; *in vivo* means "in life," that is, in a living organism. The term *in silico* stems from the fact that most computer chips are made primarily of silicon. Personally, I prefer a term such as *in algorithmo*, since there are plenty of ways to compute that don't involve silicon, such as the intriguing processes of DNA computing, quantum computing, optical computing, and more.

The large amount of biological data available online has brought biological research to a situation somewhat similar to physics and astronomy. Those sciences have found that experiments in modern equipment produce huge amounts of data, and the computer isn't only invaluable but necessary for exploring the data. Indeed, it's become possible to simulate experiments entirely in the computer. For instance, an early use of computer simulation in physics was in modeling the acoustics of a concert hall and then experimenting with the results by changing the design of the hall— clearly a much cheaper way to experiment than by building dozens of concert halls!

A similar trend has been occurring in biology since computers were first invented, but this trend has sharply accelerated in recent years with the Human Genome Project and the sequencing of the DNA of many organisms. The experimental data that has to be collected, searched, and analyzed is often far too large for the unaided biologist, who is now forced to rely on computers to manage the information.

Beyond the storage and retrieval of biological data, it's now possible to study living systems through computer simulation. There are standard and accepted studies done routinely on computers that access the genes of humans and of several other organisms. When the sequence of some DNA is determined, it can be stored in the computer, and programs can be written to identify restriction sites, perform restriction digests and create restriction maps (see Chapter 9). Similarly, gene-finding programs can take sequenced DNA and identify putative exons and introns. (Not perfectly, as of this writing, and results differ for different organisms.) Models of cellular processes exist in which it is possible to study for example, the effect of a change in the regulation of a gene.

Today, microarray technology (incorporating glass slides spotted with thousands of samples that can be probed, usually with the aid of robotics) can assess the levels of expression of thousands of genes with one laboratory run. Computers are helping to unravel the complex interactions between genes. We hope to find, for example, all sets of genes related by virtue of their protein products as part of a biochemical pathway in the cell. Microarrays generate a large volume of data. This data needs to be stored, compared with other experimental data, and analyzed on the computer.

On my first day as a programmer at Bell Labs Research, my boss told me that his simulations could now be computed so fast—overnight—that it was creating a problem for him. There wasn't enough time to think about the last simulation! Nevertheless, and despite all the attendant headaches and pitfalls of computers, their use to simulate experiments is proving to be beneficial in biology.

Limits to Computation

Some of the most interesting results of computer science demonstrate certain limits to human knowledge. There are many open problems in biology, and one hopes that applying more computer power to them may help solve them. But this isn't always possible, because some problems can be shown to be *unsolvable*; that is, they can't be solved by any program. Furthermore, some problems may be solvable, but as the size of the problem grows, they get practically impossible to solve. These problems are called *intractable*, or *NP-complete*. Even a million computers, each a million times more powerful than the most powerful computer existing today, could take perhaps a billion years to compute the answer to such an intractable problem.

Now the chances are that you're not going to get stung by an unsolvable or intractable problem. It can happen, but it's relatively rare. I mention them more as a point of interest than as a practical concern to the beginning programmer. But as you attempt more complex programs down the road, these limitations, and especially the intractable nature of several biological problems, can have a practical impact on your programming efforts.

CHAPTER 2
Getting Started with Perl

Perl is a popular programming language that's extensively used in areas such as bio-informatics and web programming. Perl has become popular with biologists because it's so well-suited to several bioinformatics tasks.

Perl is also an application, just like any other application you might install on your computer. It is available (at no cost) and runs on all the operating systems found in the average biology lab (Unix and Linux, Macintosh, Windows, VMS, and more).* The Perl application on your computer takes a Perl language program (such as one of the programs you will write in this book), translates it into instructions the computer can understand, and runs (or "executes") it.

So, the word *Perl* refers both to the language in which you will write programs and to the application on your computer that runs those programs. You can always tell from context which meaning is being used.

Every computer language such as Perl needs to have a translator application (called an interpreter or compiler) that can turn programs into instructions the computer can actually run. So the Perl application is often referred to as the Perl interpreter, and it includes a Perl compiler as well. You will often see Perl programs referred to as Perl scripts or Perl code. The terms program, application, script, and executable are somewhat interchangeable. I refer to them as "programs" in this book.

A Low and Long Learning Curve

A nice thing about Perl is that you can learn to write programs fairly quickly; in essence, Perl has a *low learning curve*. This means you can get started easily, without having to master a large body of information before writing useful programs.

---

* An *operating system* manages the running of programs and other basic services that a computer provides, such as how files are stored.

Perl provides different styles of writing programs. Since these are beyond the scope of this book, I won't go into details, except to mention the popular style called imperative programming that you'll learn in this book. The equally popular style called object-oriented programming is also well-supported in Perl. Other styles of programming include functional programming and logic programming.

Although you can get started quickly, learning all of Perl will certainly take awhile, if that's your goal. Most people learn the basics, as presented in this book, and then learn additional topics as needed.

Let's get a few elementary definitions out of the way:

What is a computer program?

It's a set of instructions written in a particular programming language that can be read by the computer. A program can be as simple as the following Perl language program to print some DNA sequence data onto the computer screen:

```
print 'ACCTGGTAACCCGGAGATTCCAGCT';
```

The Perl language programs are written and saved in files, which are ways of saving any kind of data (not only programs) on a computer. Files are organized hierarchically in groups called folders on Macintosh or Windows systems or directories in Unix or Linux systems. The terms folder and directory will be used interchangeably.

What is a programming language?

It's a carefully defined set of rules for how to write computer programs. By learning the rules of the language, you can write programs that will run on your computer. Programming languages are similar to our own natural, or spoken languages, such as English, but are more strictly defined and specific to certain computer systems. With a little bit of training, it's not difficult to read or write computer programs. In this book you'll write in Perl; there are many other programming languages.

A program that a programmer writes is also called source code, or just source or code. The source code has to be turned into machine language, a special language the computer can run. It's hard to write or read a machine language program because it's all binary numbers; it's often called a *binary executable*. You use the Perl interpreter (or compiler) to turn a Perl program into a running program, as you'll see later in this chapter.

What is a computer?

Well, ...

Okay, silly question. It's that machine you buy in computer stores. But actually, it's important to have a clear idea of what kind of machine a computer is. Essentially, a computer is a machine that can run many different programs. This is the fundamental flexibility and adaptability that makes the computer such a useful and general-purpose tool. It's *programmable*; you will learn how to program it using the Perl programming language.

Perl's Benefits

The following sections illustrate some of Perl's strong points.

Ease of Programming

Computer languages differ in which things they make easy. By "easy" I mean easy for a programmer to program. Perl has certain features that simplifies several common bioinformatics tasks. It can deal with information in ASCII text files or flat files, which are exactly the kinds of files in which much important biological data appears, in the GenBank and PDB databases, among others. (See the discussion of ASCII in Chapter 4; Genbank and PDB are the subjects in Chapter 10 and Chapter 11.) Perl makes it easy to process and manipulate long sequences such as DNA and proteins. Perl makes it convenient to write a program that controls one or more other programs. As a final example, Perl is used to put biology research labs, and their results, on their own dynamic web sites. Perl does all this and more.

Although Perl is a language that's remarkably suited to bioinformatics, it isn't the only choice nor is it always the best choice. Other programming languages such as C and Java are also used in bioinformatics. The choice of language depends on the problem to be programmed, the skills of the programmers, and the available system.

Rapid Prototyping

Another important benefit of using Perl for biological research is the speed with which a programmer can write a typical Perl program (referred to as *rapid prototyping*). Many problems can be solved in far fewer lines of Perl code than in C or Java. This has been important to its success in research. In a research environment there are frequent needs for programs that do something new, that are needed only once or occasionally, or that need to be frequently modified. In Perl, you can often toss such a program off in a few minutes or a few hours work, and the research can proceed. This rapid prototyping ability is often a key consideration when choosing Perl for a job. It is common to find programmers familiar with both Perl and C who claim that Perl is five to ten times faster to program in than C. The difference can be critical in the typical understaffed research lab.

Portability, Speed, and Program Maintenance

Portability means how many types of computer systems the language can run on. Perl has no problems there, as it's available for virtually all modern computers found in biology labs. If you write a DNA analyzer in Perl on your Mac, then move it to a Windows computer, you'll find it usually runs as is or with only minor retrofitting.

Speed means the speed with which the program runs. Here Perl is pretty good but not the best. For speed of execution, the usual language of choice is C. A program written in C typically runs two or more times faster than the comparable Perl program. (There are ways of speeding up Perl with compilers and such, but still... .)

In many organizations, programs are first written in Perl, and then only the programs that absolutely need to have maximum speed are rewritten in C. The fact is, maximum speed is only occasionally an important consideration.

Programming is relatively expensive to do: it takes time, and skilled personnel. It's labor-intensive. On the other hand, computers and computer time (often called CPU time after the central processing unit) are relatively inexpensive. Most desktop computers sit idle for a large part of the day, anyway. So it's usually best to let the computer do the work, and save the programmer's time. Unless your program absolutely must run in say, four seconds instead of ten seconds, you're okay with Perl.

Program maintenance is the general activity of keeping everything working: such activities as adding features to a program, extending it to handle more types of input, porting it to run on other computer systems, fixing bugs, and so forth. Programs take a certain amount of time, effort and cost to write, but successful programs end up costing more to maintain than they did to write in the first place. It's important to write in a language, and in a style, that makes maintenance relatively easy, and Perl allows you to do so. (You can write obscure, hard-to-maintain code in Perl, as in other languages, but I'll give you pointers on how to make your code easy for other programmers to read.)

Versions of Perl

Perl, like almost all popular software, has gone through much growth and change over the course of its nearly 15-year life. The authors—Larry Wall and a large group of cohorts—publish new versions periodically. These new versions have been carefully designed to support most programs written under old versions, but occasionally some major new features are added that don't work with older versions of Perl.

This book assumes you have Perl Version 5 or higher installed. If you have Perl installed on your computer, it's likely Perl 5, but it's best to check. On a Unix or Linux system, or from an MS-DOS or MacOS X command window, the perl -v command displays the version number, in my case, Version 5.6.1. The number 5.6.1 is "bigger" than 5; that means it's okay. If you get a smaller number (very likely 4.036), you have to install a recent version of Perl to enable the majority of programs in this book to run as shown.

What about future versions? Perl is always evolving, and Perl Version 6 is on the horizon. Will the code in this book still work in Perl 6? The answer is yes. Although

Perl 6 is going to add some new things to the language, it should have no trouble with the Perl 5 code in this book.

Installing Perl on Your Computer

The following sections provide pointers for installing Perl on the most common types of computer systems.

Perl May Already Be Installed!

Many computers—especially Unix and Linux computers—come with Perl already installed. (Note that Unix and Linux are essentially the same kind of operating system; Linux is a clone, or functional copy, of a Unix system.) So first check to see if Perl is already there. On Unix and Linux, type the following at a command prompt:

```
$ perl -v
```

If Perl is already installed, you'll see a message like the one I get on my Linux machine:

```
This is perl, v5.6.1 built for i686-linux

Copyright 1987-2001, Larry Wall

Perl may be copied only under the terms of either the Artistic License or the
GNU General Public License, which may be found in the Perl 5 source kit.

Complete documentation for Perl, including FAQ lists, should be found on
this system using 'man perl' or 'perldoc perl'.  If you have access to the
Internet, point your browser at http://www.perl.com/, the Perl Home Page.
```

If Perl isn't installed, you'll get a message like this:

```
perl: command not found
```

If you get this message, and you're on a shared Unix system at a university or business, be sure to check with the system administrator, because Perl may indeed be installed, but your environment may not be set to find it. (Or, the system administrator may say, "You need Perl? Okay, I'll install it for you.")

On Windows or Macintosh, look at the program menus, or use the *find* program to search for perl. You can also try typing perl -v, at an MS-DOS command window or at a shell window on the MacOS X. (Note that the MacOS X is a Unix system!)

No Internet Access?

If you don't have Internet access, you can take your computer to a friend who has access and connect long enough to install Perl. You can also use a Zip drive or burn a CD from a friend's computer to bring the Perl software to your computer. There are commercial shrink-wrapped CDs of Perl available from several sources (ask at your local software store) and several books such as O'Reilly's *Perl Resource Kits,* include CDs with Perl.

Apart from installing Perl, you don't need Internet access for everything in this book. If you want to do the exercises while commuting on the train, or whatever, it can certainly be done. Apart from installing Perl, the main use of the Internet for this book is to download its examples from the book's web site without having to type them; to download and try the exercises; to explore biological data from various biological databases; and to access Perl documentation, if it's not installed on your machine.

Know that if you want to do bioinformatics, the Internet is a practical necessity. You can learn programming fundamentals from this book without an Internet connection, but you will need Internet access to download bioinformatics software and data.

Downloading

Perl is an application, so downloading and installing it on your computer is pretty much the same as installing any other application.

The web site that serves as a central jumping off point for all things Perl is *http://www.perl.com/.* The main page has a Downloads clickable button that guides you to everything you need to install Perl on your computer. At the Downloads page, there's a Getting Help link and other links. So even if the information in this book becomes outdated, you can visit the Perl site and find all you need to install Perl.

Downloading and installing Perl is usually quite easy, in fact, the majority of the time it's perfectly painless. However, sometimes you may have to put some effort into getting it to work. If you're new at programming, and you run into difficulties, you should ask for help from a professional computer programmer, administrator, teacher, or someone in your lab who already programs in Perl.

So, in a nutshell, here are the basic steps for installing Perl on your computer:

1. Check to see if Perl is already installed; if so, check the that version is at least Perl 5.
2. Get Internet access and go to the Perl home page at *http://www.perl.com/.*
3. Go to the Downloads page and determine which distribution of Perl to download.
4. Download the correct Perl distribution.
5. Install the distribution on your computer.

Binary Versus Source Code

When downloading from the *http://www.perl.com* site, you need to choose between binary or source-code distributions of Perl. The best choice for installing Perl on your computer is to get an already made binary version of the program, because it's the easiest to install. However, if no binary is available, or if you want to control the various options of your Perl installation, you can get the source code for Perl, which is itself written in the C programming language. You then compile it using a C compiler. But try to find a binary for your particular computer's operating system; compiling from source code can be complicated for beginners.

Installation

The next sections provide specific installation instructions for specific platforms.

Unix and Linux

If Perl isn't installed on your Unix or Linux machine, first try to find a binary to install. At the Downloads page of *http://www.perl.com*, you'll see the subheading Binary Distributions. Select Unix or Linux, and then see if your particular flavor of operating system has a binary available. Several versions are available, and the website instructions should be enough to get Perl installed once you've downloaded the binary. Most versions of Linux maintain up-to-date Perl binaries on their web sites. For instance, if you have a Red Hat Linux system, you need to identify which version of the system you have (by typing uname -a) and then get the appropriate *rpm* file to download and install. Red Hat has an *rpm* for Perl that Red Hat Linux users can install by typing:

```
rpm -Uvh perl.rpm
```

(the actual name of the *perl.rpm* file varies).

If no binary version of Perl is available for your flavor of Unix or Linux, you must compile Perl from its source code. In this case, starting from the Perl web page, click on the Downloads button and then select Source Code Distribution. The source code has an *INSTALL* file with instructions that guide you through the process of downloading the source code, installing it on your system, compiling the source code into a binary, and finally installing the binary.

As mentioned previously, compiling from source code is a considerably longer process than installing an already made binary, and requires a bit more reading of instructions, but it usually works quite well. You will need a C compiler on your computer to install from source code. Nowadays, some Unix systems ship without a complete C compiler. Linux will always have the free C compiler called *gcc* installed, and you can also install *gcc* on any Unix (or Windows, or Mac) system that lacks a C compiler.

Macintosh

The MacPerl installation steps are clearly explained on the MacPerl web page, *http://www.macperl.com/* (which you can also get to from the Perl web page and its Downloads button). Here's a very brief overview.

From the MacPerl page, click on Get MacPerl, and follow the directions to download the application. It will appear on your desktop. Double-click it to unstuff it. If you don't have Alladin Stuffit Expander (most Macs already do), this won't work, and you'll have to go to *http://www.alladinsys.com* to download and install Stuffit.

MacPerl can be installed as a standalone application under the MacOS Finder or as a tool under the Macintosh Programmer's Workbench; you will probably want the standalone application. Perl Version 5 is available for MacOS 7.0 and later. Details about which Perl version is available for your particular hardware and MacOS version are available at the MacPerl web page.

Windows

Several binaries for different Windows versions are available. Since Windows is closely coupled with Intel 32-bit chips, these binaries are often called Wintel or Win32 binaries. The current standard Perl distribution is ActivePerl from ActiveState, at *http://www.activestate.com/ActivePerl/*, where you can find complete installation directions. You can also get to ActivePerl via the Downloads button from the Perl web site. Under the subheading Binary Distributions, go to Perl for Win32, and then click on the ActivePerl site.

From the ActiveState web site's ActivePerl page, click the Downloads button. You can then download the Windows-Intel binary. Note that installing it requires a program called Windows Installer, which is available at ActivePerl if it's not already on your computer.

How to Run Perl Programs

The details of how to run Perl vary depending on your operating system. The instructions that come with your Perl installation contain all you need to know. I'll give short summaries here, just enough to get you started.

Unix or Linux

On Unix or Linux, you usually run Perl programs from the command line. If you're in the same directory as the program, you can run a Perl program in a file called *this_program* by typing perl this_program. If you're not in the same directory, you may have to give the pathname of the program, for example:

```
perl /usr/local/bin/this_program
```

Usually, you set the first line of *this_program* to have the correct pathname for Perl on your system, because different machines may have installed Perl in different directories. On my computer, I use the following as the first line of my Perl programs:

```
#!/usr/bin/perl
```

You can type which perl to find the pathname where Perl is installed on your system.

You can make the program executable using the *chmod* program: for instance, you can type:

```
chmod 755 this_program
```

If you've set the first line correctly and used *chmod*, you can just type the name of the Perl program to run it. So, if you're in the same directory as the program, you can type ./this_program. If the program is in a directory that's included in your $PATH or $path variable, you can type this_program.*

If your Perl program doesn't run, the error messages you get from the shell in the command window may be confusing. For instance, the *bash* shell on my Linux system gives the error message:

```
bash: ./my_program: No such file or directory
```

in two cases: if there really is no program called *my_program* in the current directory or if the first line of *my_program* has incorrectly given the location of Perl. Watch for that, especially when running programs from CPAN (see Appendix A), which may have different pathnames for Perl embedded in their first lines. Also, if you type my_program, you may get this error message:

```
bash: my_program: command not found
```

which means that the operating system can't find the program. But it's there in your current directory! The problem is probably that your $PATH or $path variable doesn't include the current directory, and so the system isn't even looking in the current directory for the program. In this case, change the $PATH or $path variable (depending on which shell you're using), or just type ./my_program instead of my_program.

Macs

On Macs, the recommended way to save Perl programs is as "droplets"; the MacPerl documentation gives the simple instructions. Basically, you open the Perl program with the MacPerl application and then choose Save As and select the Type option Droplet.

You can drag and drop a file onto a droplet in order to use the file as input (via the @ARGV array—see the discussion in Chapter 6).

---

* $PATH is the variable used for the *sh*, *bash*, and *ksh* shells; $path is used for *csh* and *tcsh*.

The new MacOS X is a Unix system on which you have the option of running Perl programs from the command line as described earlier for Unix and Linux systems.

Windows

On Windows systems, it's usual to associate the filename extension *.pl* with Perl programs. This is done as part of the Perl installation process, which modifies the registry settings to include this file association. You can then launch *this_program.pl* by typing this_program in an MS-DOS command window or by typing perl this_program.pl. Windows has a PATH variable specifying folders in which the system looks for programs, and this is modified by the Perl installation process to include the path to the folder for the Perl application, usually *c:\perl*. If you're trying to run a Perl program that isn't installed in a folder known to the PATH variable, you can type the complete pathname to the program, for instance *perl c:\windows\desktop\ my_program.pl*.

Text Editors

Now that you've set up your computer and installed Perl, you need to select and learn the basics of a text editor. A *text editor* is used to type documents, such as programs, and to save the contents of those documents into files. So to write a Perl program, you need to use a text editor. This can be a medium-sized learning job if you have never used an editor before, although some text editors are easy to learn. Here are some examples of the most popular editors, arranged by operating-system type:

Unix or Linux
> *vi* and *emacs* are complex (but very good) editors. *pico*, *xedit*, and several others (*nedit*, *gedit*, *kedit*) are easy to use and simple to learn but less powerful. There is also a free, Microsoft Word-compatible editor included in StarOffice (but be sure to save your files as ASCII or text-only).

Macintosh
> The built-in editor that comes with MacPerl is fine. There is also a nice commercial editor called BBEdit that is optimized for Perl, as well as a freeware version called BBEdit Lite. You can also use the Alpha shareware editor or Microsoft Word (be sure to save as ASCII text only).

Windows
> Notepad works satisfactorily and may already be familiar; Microsoft Word is also usable, but always save as ASCII or text-only. Emacs on Windows is highly recommended for Perl programming on Windows-based computers, but it's a little complicated to learn. There are many other editors as well; I use a free version of the Unix editor *vi* called *vim* that has been ported to Windows.

Many other text editors are available. Most computers come with a choice of several editors. (Many programmers try their hand at writing an editor or extending an already existing editor at some point in their careers, so the choices are truly legion.)

Some editors are very simple to learn and use. Others have a huge variety of features, their own instruction books and discussion groups and web sites and so on, and can take quite a while to learn. If you're a new programmer, pick an easy one and save yourself the headache. Later, if you feel adventurous, you can graduate to a fancier editor with features that can speed your work. Not sure what is available on your computer? Ask for help from a programmer or another user, or consult the documentation that came with your computer system.

Finding Help

Make sure you have the necessary documentation. If you installed Perl as outlined earlier, documentation is installed as part of the general Perl installation, and the instructions that come with your Perl distribution explain how to get the documentation. There is also excellent online documentation; look for it at the Perl home page.

Programming resources are places to look for answers to programming questions. Perl resources are essential to doing Perl programming. Check out Appendix A to learn where to find resources such as books, online documentation, working programs, newsgroups, archives, journals, and conferences.

As you get involved in programming, you will learn the most important books, web sites, Internet newsgroups and their searchable archives, local gurus (experts in the subject at hand), and program documentation. This includes programming manuals (printed or online) and frequently asked question (FAQs).

Most languages have a standard document set that includes the whole story about the language definition and use. Perl's is included with the program as the online manual. Although programming manuals often suffer from poor writing, it's best to be prepared to dig into them. A well-honed ability to skim is a great asset. The Perl manual isn't bad; its main problem is that, as with most manuals, all the details are there, so it can be a bit overwhelming at first. However, the Perl documentation does a decent job of helping the beginner navigate, by means of tutorial documents.

Finally, I urge you, the beginning programmer, to find some experienced Perl programmer who can answer the occasional question. This may be your teacher or teaching assistant in a course, a coworker, someone down at the local computer store, or someone replying to your posting on an online newsgroup (there are newsgroups specifically for Perl beginners). Chances are that an occasional conversation with an experienced user can save you many hours of chasing deadends during your initial learning stages. Many programmers are happy to lend a hand or offer advice to beginners, there's a friendly and collegial atmosphere that prevails in the programming community.

Be warned, however: experts can become irritated at people who continually pose questions whose answers are readily available in FAQs and other standard documentation. You might sometimes see the advice to RTFM—acronym for Read The F(ine) Manual—in response to such questions. So do a little checking around in the FAQs before repeatedly asking for someone's valuable time.

(I can't resist the occasional anecdote.) At my first programming job, which I took to learn programming, I was stumped by a problem for which there seemed to be no obvious solution. I approached the person who had been cited as the best programmer in the laboratory. I carefully explained my predicament as he patiently listened. When I was done, he smiled and advised, "Be a man. Do it yourself." I was crestfallen and retired in confusion. But as it turned out, his advice was given with tongue in cheek, and he later approached me and gave me pointers that led to a solution.

CHAPTER 3

The Art of Programming

This chapter provides an overview of how programmers accomplish their jobs. If you already have Perl installed, and you want to get started writing programs for bioinformatics, feel free to skip ahead to Chapter 4.

Just as visitors to a biology lab tend to have a clueless awe of "all those test tubes," so the newcomer to programming may regard the world of the programmer as a kind of arcane black box full of weird terminology and abstruse skills. So, to make the whole enterprise a little more congenial, let's take a short tour of some important realities that affect all programmers. Two of the most important are practical strategies that good programmers use and where to go to find answers to questions that arise while you are programming. Using a couple of brief narrative case studies, we'll look at how programmers find solutions to problems. Appendix A lists some of the best Perl and bioinformatics resources to help you solve your particular problems.

Individual Approaches to Programming

What's the best way to learn programming? The answer depends on what you hope to accomplish. There are several ways to get started. You can:

- Take classes of many different kinds
- Read a tutorial book like this one
- Get the programming manuals and plunge in
- Be tutored by a programmer
- Identify a program you need
- Try any and all of the above until you've managed to write the program

The answer also depends on how you choose to learn. Some people prefer classes, because the information is often presented in a well-organized way, and questions can be answered by the teacher. Others learn best with self-paced study.

Some things about learning to program are common to all these approaches. If you've never programmed at all, the information in the following sections is a "heads-up" about what's ahead.

Edit—Run—Revise (and Save)

The most important thing about programming is that it's a hands-on learning activity such as dancing, playing music, cooking, or some other family-oriented activity. You can read about it, but you can't actually do it until you actually do it.

While learning to program in Perl, you need to read about how Perl works, as you will in the chapters that follow. You also need to look at plenty of examples of programs. But you especially need to attempt to write your own programs, as you are asked to do in the exercises at the end of the later chapters. Only this kind of direct experience will make you a programmer.

So I want to give you an overview of the most important tasks involved in writing programs, to help you approach your first programs with a clearer idea of what's really involved.

What exactly will you be doing at the computer? The bulk of a programmer's work involves the steps of writing or revising a program in an editor, then running the program and watching how it behaves, and on the basis of that behavior going back and revising the program again. A typical programmer spends more than half of his or her time editing the program.

Saves and Backups

Once you have even a few lines of code written, it's important to save it. In fact, you should always remember to save a version of your program at regular intervals during editing, so if you make a bunch of edits and the computer crashes, you don't lose hours of work. Also, make sure you back up your work on another disk. Hard disks fail, and when yours does, the information on it will be lost. Therefore it's essential to make regular (daily) backups of your work onto some other medium—tape, floppy disk, Zip disk, another hard disk, writable CD—whatever, just so you won't lose all your work if a disk failure occurs.

In addition to backups of your disks, it's also a good idea to save a dated version of your program at regular intervals. This will allow you to go back to an earlier version of your program should that prove necessary.

It's also a good idea to make sure the backups you're making actually work. So, for instance, if you're backing up to a tape drive, try restoring the files from your tape drive every once in a while, just to make sure that the software and the tapes themselves are all working. You may also want to print out ("make a hardcopy") of your programs at regular intervals for extra insurance against system failures. Finally, it's good policy to keep the backups somewhere away from the computer, so in case of fire or other disaster, the backups will be safe.

Error Messages

Fixing errors is an essential step in writing programs. After you've written and edited a program, the next step is to run it to see if it works. Very often, you'll find that you've made some typographical error, like forgetting to put in a semicolon. As a result, your program isn't valid, and you'll get various error messages from the system. You then have to read the error messages and reedit your program to repair the offending code.

These error messages are sometimes rather cryptic. In the event of an error, the Perl interpreter may have some trouble knowing exactly where you went wrong. It may only recognize that there is something wrong. So it guesses where the problem is, and in the process, it may give you some extraneous information.

The most important thing about using error messages is to look at the first one or two error messages and ignore the rest; fix the top problems, and try running the program again. Error messages are often verbose and can run on for several pages. Just ignore everything but the first errors reported. Another important point is that the line numbers reported in those first error messages are usually right. Sometimes they're off by a line, and they're rarely way off. Later on, we'll practice generating and reading error messages.

Debugging

Perhaps your edits created a valid program, and the Perl interpreter reads in your program and runs it. You find, however, that the program isn't doing what you want it to do. Now you have to go back, look at the program, and try to figure out what's wrong.

Perhaps you made a simple mistake, such as adding instead of subtracting. You may have misread the documentation, and you're using the language the wrong way (reread the documentation). You may simply have an inadequate plan for accomplishing your goal (rethink your strategy and reprogram that part of the code). Sometimes you can't see what's wrong, and you have to look elsewhere (try searching newsgroup archives or FAQs or asking colleagues for help).

For errors that are difficult to find, there are programs called *debuggers* that allow you to run the program step by step, looking at everything that's happening in the program. (Chapter 6 takes an in-depth look at Perl's debugger.)

There are other tools and techniques you can use. For instance, you can examine your program by adding print statements that print out intermediate values or results. There are also special helper programs that can observe your program while it's running and then report about it, telling you, for instance, about where the program is spending most of its time. These tools, and others like them, are essential to programming, and you need to learn how to use them.

An Environment of Programs

Programming is an exercise in problem solving. It's an iterative, gradual process. Although it can be done by one person alone, it's often a social activity (this surprises many newcomers). It requires developing specific problem-solving skills and learning a few tools. Programming is sometimes tricky and can be frustrating. On the other hand, for those with an aptitude, there's a great sense of satisfaction that comes from building a working program.

Computer programs can be many things, from barely useful, to aesthetically and intellectually stimulating, to important generators of new knowledge. They can be beautiful. (They can also be destructive, stupid, silly, or vicious; they are human creations, after all.) Because writing a program is an iterative, building, gradual process, there can be real satisfaction in seeing the work unfold from simple beginnings to complete structures. For the beginning student, this gradual unfolding of a new program mirrors the gradual mastery of the language.

As our culture began writing and accumulating programs in the middle of the 20th century, a programming environment began to develop. Gradually, we've been accumulating a substantial body of procedural knowledge. Programs often reflect the fact that they swim in waters populated by many other programs, and beginning programmers can expect to learn a lot from this environment.

Open Source Programs

As programming has become important in the world, it has also become economically valuable. As a result, the source code for many programs is kept hidden to protect commercial assets and stymie the competition.

However, the source code for many of the best and most used programs are freely available for anyone to examine. Freely available source code is called *open source*. (There are various kinds of copyrights that may attach to open source program code, but they all allow anyone to examine the source code.) The open source movement treats program source code in a similar manner to the way scientists publish their results: publicly and open to unfettered examination and discussion.

The source code for these programs can be a wonderful place for the beginning programmer to learn how professional programmers write. The programs available in open source include the Perl interpreter and a large amount of Perl code, the Linux operating system, the Apache web server, the Netscape web browser, the *sendmail* mail transfer agent, and much more.

Programming Strategies

In order to give you, the beginning programmer, an idea of how programming is done, let's see how an experienced programmer goes about solving problems by giving a couple of instructive case studies.

Imagine that you want to count all the regulatory elements* in a large chunk of DNA that you just got from the sequencing lab. You're a professional bioinformatics programmer. What do you do? There are two possible solutions: find a program or write one yourself.

It's likely there is already a perfectly good, working, and maybe even free program that does exactly what you need. Very often, you can find exactly what you need on the Web and avoid the cost and expense of reinventing the wheel. This is programming at its best—minimal work for maximal effect. It's the classic case of the experimentalist's adage: a day in the library can save you six months in the lab.

An important part of the art of programming is to keep aware of collections of programs that are available. Then you can simply use the code if it does exactly what you need, or you can take an existing program and alter it to suit your own needs. Of course, copyright laws must be observed, but much is available at no cost, especially to educational and nonprofit organizations. Most Perl module code has a copyright, but you are allowed to use it and modify it given certain restrictions. Details are available at the Perl web site and with the particular modules.

How do you find this wonderful, free, and already existing program? The Perl community has an organized collection of such programming code at the Comprehensive Perl Archive Network (CPAN) web site, *http://www.CPAN.org*. Try exploring: you'll find it's organized by topic, so it's possible to quickly find, for example, web, statistics, or graphics programs. In our case, you will find the Bioperl module, which includes several useful bioinformatics functions. A *module* is a collection of Perl code that can be easily loaded and used by your Perl programs.

The most useful kinds of code are convenient libraries or modules that package a suite of functions. These packages offer a great deal of flexibility in creating new programs. Although you still have to program, the job may be only a small fraction of the work of writing the whole program from scratch. For instance, to continue our example of looking for regulatory elements, your search may turn up a convenient module that lists the regulatory elements plus code that takes a list of elements and searches for them in a DNA library. Then all you have to do is combine the existing code, provide the DNA library, and with a little bit of programming, you're done.

---

* A regulatory element is a stretch of DNA used by the cell in the control of a coding region, helping to determine if and when it's used to create a protein.

There are lots of other places to look for already existing code. You can search the Internet with your favorite search engines. You can browse collections of links for bioinformatics, looking for programs. You can also search the other sources we've already covered, such as newsgroups, relevant experts, etc.

If you haven't hit paydirt yet, and you know that the program will take a significant amount of time to write yourself, you may want to search the literature in the library, and perhaps enlist the aid of a librarian. You can search Medline for articles about regulatory elements, since often an article will advertise code (an actual program in a language like Perl) that the authors will forward. You can consult conference proceedings, books, and journals. Conferences and trade shows are also great places to look around, meet people, and ask questions.

In many cases you succeed, and despite the effort involved, you saved yourself and your laboratory days, weeks, or months of effort.

However, one big warning about modifying existing code: depending on how much alteration is required, it can sometimes be more difficult to modify existing code than to write a whole program from scratch. Why? Well, depending on who wrote the program, it may be difficult just to see what the different parts of the code do. You can't make modifications if you can't understand what methods the program uses in the first place. (We'll talk more about writing readable code, and the importance of comments in code, later.) This factor alone accounts for a large part of the expense of programming; many programs can't be easily read, or understood, so they can't be maintained. Also, testing the program may be difficult for various reasons, and it may take a lot of time and effort to assure yourself that your modifications are working correctly.

Okay, let's say that you spent three days looking for an existing program, and there really wasn't anything available. (Well, there was one program, but it cost $30,000 which is way outside your budget, and your local programming expert was too busy to write one for you.) So you absolutely have to write the program yourself.

How do you start from scratch and come up with a program that counts the regulatory elements in some DNA? Read on.

The Programming Process

You've been assigned to write a program that counts the regulatory elements in DNA. If you've never programmed you probably have no idea of how to start. Let's talk about what you need to know to write the program.

Here's a summary of the steps we'll cover:

1. Identify the required inputs, such as data or information given by the user.
2. Make an overall design for the program, including the general method—the algorithm—by which the program computes the output.

3. Decide how the outputs will print; for example, to files or displayed graphically.

4. Refine the overall design by specifying more detail.

5. Write the Perl program code.

These steps may be different for shorter or longer programs, but this is the general approach you will take for most of your programming.

The Design Phase

First, you need to conceive a plan for how the program is going to work. This is the overall design of the program and an important step that's usually done before the actual writing of the program begins. Programs are often compared to kitchen recipes, in that they are specific instructions on how to accomplish some task. For instance, you need an idea of what inputs and outputs the program will have. In our example, the input would be the new DNA. You then need a strategy for how the program will do the necessary computing to calculate the desired output from the input.

In our example, the program first needs to collect information from the user: namely, where is the DNA? (This information can be the name of a file that contains the computer representation of the DNA sequence.) The program needs to allow the user to type in the name of a datafile, maybe from the computer screen or from a web page. Then the program has to check if the file exists (and complain if not, as might happen, for instance, if the user misspelled the name) and finally open the file and read in the DNA before continuing.

This simple step deserves some comment. You can put the DNA directly into the program code and avoid having to write this whole part of the program. But by designing the program to read in the DNA, it's more useful, because you won't have to rewrite the program every time you get some new DNA. It's a simple, even obvious idea, but very powerful.

The data your program uses to compute is called the *input*. Input can come from files, from other programs, from users running the program, from forms filled out on web sites, from email messages, and so forth. Most programs read in some form of input; some programs don't.

Let's add the list of regulatory elements to the actual program code. You can ask for a file that contains this list, as we did with the DNA, and have the program be capable of searching different lists of regulatory elements. However, in this case, the list you will use isn't going to change, so why bother the user with inputting the name of another file?

Now that we have the DNA and the list of regulatory elements you have to decide in general terms how the program is actually going to search for each regulatory element in the DNA. This step is obviously the critical one, so make sure you get it right. For instance, you want the program to run quickly enough, if the speed of the program is an important consideration.

This is the problem of choosing the correct algorithm for the job. An algorithm is a design for computing a problem (I'll say more about it in a minute). For instance, you may decide to take each regulatory element in turn and search through the DNA from beginning to end for that element before going on to the next one. Or perhaps you may decide to go through the DNA only once, and at each position check each of the regulatory elements to see if it is present. Is there be any advantage to one way or the other? Can you sort the list of regulatory elements so your search can proceed more quickly? For now, let's just say that your choice of algorithm is important.

The final part of the design is to provide some form of output for the results. Perhaps you want the results displayed on a web page, as a simple list on the computer screen, in a printable file, or perhaps all of the above. At this stage, you may need to ask the user for a filename to save the output.

This brings up the problem of how to display results. This question is actually a critically important one. The ideal solution is to display the results in a way that shows the user at a glance the salient features of the computation. You can use graphics, color, maps, little bouncing balls over the unexpected result: there are many options. A program that outputs results that are hard to read is clearly not doing a good job. In fact, output that makes the salient results hard to find or understand can completely negate all the effort you put into writing an elegant program. Enough said for now.

There are several strategies employed by programmers to help create good overall designs. Usually, any program but the smallest is written in several small but interconnecting parts. (We'll see lots of this as we proceed in later chapters.) What will the parts be, and how will they interconnect? The field of software engineering addresses these kinds of issues. At this point I only want to point out that they are very important and mention some of the ways programmers address the need for design.

There are many design methodologies; each have their dedicated adherents. The best approach is to learn what is available and use the best methodology for the job at hand. For instance, in this book I'm teaching a style of programming called *imperative programming*, relying on dividing a problem into interacting *procedures* or *subroutines* (see Chapter 6), known as *structured design*. Another popular style is called *object-oriented programming*, which is also supported by Perl.

If you're working in a large group of programmers on a big project, the design phase can be very formal and may even be done by different people than the programmers themselves. On the other end of the scale, you will find solitary programmers who just start writing, developing a plan as they write the code. There is no one best way that works for everyone. But no matter how you approach it, as a beginner you still need to have some sort of design in mind before you start writing code.

Algorithms

An *algorithm* is the design, or plan, for the computation done by a computer program. (It's actually a tricky term to define, outside of a formal mathematical system, but this is a reasonable definition.) An algorithm is implemented by coding it in a specific computer language, but the algorithm is the idea of the computation. It's often well represented in pseudocode, which gives the idea of a program without actually being a real computer program.

Most programs do simple things. They get filenames from users, open the files, and read in the data. They perform simple calculations and display the results. These are the types of algorithms you'll learn here.

However, the science of algorithms is a deep and fruitful one, with many important implications for bioinformatics. Algorithms can be designed to find new ways of analyzing biological data and of discovering new scientific results. There are certainly many problems in biology whose solutions could be, and will be, substantially advanced by inventing new algorithms.

The science of algorithms includes many clever techniques. As a beginning programmer, you needn't worry about them just yet. At this stage, an introductory chapter in a beginning tutorial on programming, it's not reasonable to go into details about algorithmic methods. Your first task is just to learn how to write in some programming language. But if you keep at it, you'll start to learn the techniques. A decent textbook to keep around as a reference is a good investment for a serious programmer (see Appendix A).

In the current example that counts regulatory elements in DNA, I suggest a way of proceeding. Take each regulatory element in turn, and search through the DNA for it, before proceeding to the next regulatory element. Other algorithms are also possible; in fact, this is one example from the general problem called *string matching*, which is one of the most important for bioinformatics, and the study of which has resulted in a variety of clever algorithms.

Algorithms are usually grouped by such problems or by technique, and there is a wealth of material available. For the practical programmer, some of the most valuable materials are collections of algorithms written in specific languages, that can be incorporated into your programs. Use Appendix A as a starting place. Using the collections of code and books given there, it's possible to incorporate many algorithmic techniques in your Perl code with relative ease.

Pseudocode and Code

Now you have an overall design, including input, algorithm, and output. How do you actually turn this general idea into a design for a program?

A common implementation strategy is to begin by writing what is called pseudo-code. *Pseudocode* is an informal program, in which there are no details, and formal syntax isn't followed.* It doesn't actually run as a program; its purpose is to flesh out an idea of the overall design of a program in a quick and informal way.

For example, in an actual Perl program you might write a bit of code called a subroutine (see Chapter 6), in this case, a subroutine that gets an answer from a user typing at the keyboard. Such a subroutine may look like this:

```
sub getanswer {
    print "Type in your answer here :";
    my $answer  = <STDIN>;
    chomp $answer;
    return $answer;
}
```

But in pseudocode, you might just say:

```
getanswer
```

and worry about the details later.

Here's an example of pseudocode for the program I've been discussing:

```
get the name of DNAfile from the user

read in the DNA from the DNAfile

for each regulatory element
    if element is in DNA, then
        add one to the count

print count
```

Comments

Comments are parts of Perl source code that are used as an aid to understanding what the program does. Anything from a # sign to the end of a line is considered a comment and is ignored by the Perl interpreter. (The exception is the first line of many Perl programs, which looks something like this: #!/usr/bin/perl; see the section "Command Interpretation" in Chapter 4.)

---

* *Syntax* refers to the rules of grammar. English syntax decrees, "Go to school" not "School go to." Programming languages also have syntax rules.

Comments are of considerable importance in keeping code useful. They typically include a discussion of the overall purpose and design of the program, examples of how to use the program, and detailed notes interspersed throughout the code explaining why that code is there and what it does. In general, a good programmer writes good comments as an integral part of the program. You'll see comments in all the programming examples in this book.

This is important: your code has to be readable by humans as well as computers.

Comments can also be useful when debugging misbehaving programs. If you're having trouble figuring out where a program is going wrong, you can try to selectively comment out different parts of the code. If you find a section that, when commented out, removes the problem, you can then narrow down the part you've commented out until you have a fairly short section of code in which you know where the problem is. This is often a useful debugging approach.

Comments can be used when you turn pseudocode into Perl source code. Pseudocode is not Perl code, so the Perl interpreter will complain about any pseudocode that is not commented out. You can *comment out* the pseudocode by placing # signs at the beginning of all pseudocode lines:

```
#get the name of DNAfile from the user

#read in the DNA from the DNAfile

#for each regulatory element
#     if element is in DNA, then
#            add one to the count

#print count
```

As you expand your pseudocode design into Perl code, you can uncomment the Perl code by removing the # signs. In this way you may have a mixture of Perl and pseudocode, but you can run and test the Perl parts; the Perl interpreter simply ignores commented-out lines.

You can even leave the complete pseudocode design, commented out, intact in the program. This leaves an outline of the program's design that may come in handy when you or someone else tries to read or modify the code.

We've now reached the point where we're ready for actual Perl programming. In Chapter 4 you will learn Perl syntax and begin programming in Perl. As you do, remember the initial phase of designing your program, followed by the cycle you will spend most of your time in: editing the program, running the program, and revising the program.

## CHAPTER 4

Sequences and Strings

In this chapter you will begin to write Perl programs that manipulate biological sequence data, that is, DNA and proteins. Once you have the sequences in the computer, you'll start writing programs that do the following with the sequence data:

- Transcribe DNA to RNA
- Concatenate sequences
- Make the reverse complement of sequences
- Read sequence data from files

You'll also write programs that give information about your sequences. How GC-rich is your DNA? How hydrophobic is your protein? You'll see programming techniques you can use to answer these and similar questions.

The Perl skills you will learn in this chapter involve the basics of the language. Here are some of those basics:

- Scalar variables
- Array variables
- String operations such as substitution and translation
- Reading data from files

Representing Sequence Data

The majority of this book deals with manipulating symbols that represent the biological sequences of DNA and proteins. The symbols used in bioinformatics to represent these sequences are the same symbols biologists have been using in the literature for this same purpose.

As stated earlier, DNA is composed of four building blocks: the nucleic acids, also called nucleotides or bases. Proteins are composed of 20 building blocks, the amino acids, also called residues. Fragments of proteins are called peptides. Both DNA and proteins are essentially polymers, made from their building blocks attached end to end. So it's possible to summarize the structure of a DNA molecule or protein by simply giving the sequence of bases or amino acids.

These are brief definitions; I'm assuming you are either already familiar with them or are willing to consult an introductory textbook on molecular biology for more specific details. Table 4-1 shows bases; add a sugar and you get the nucleotides adenosine, guanosine, cytidine, thymidine, and uridine. You can further add a phosphate and get the nucleotides adenylic acid, guanylic acid, cytidylic acid, thymidylic acid, and uridylic acid. A *nucleic acid* is a chemically linked sequence of nucleotides. A *peptide* is a small number of joined amino acids; a longer chain is a *polypeptide*. A *protein* is a biologically functional unit made of one or more polypeptides. A *residue* is an amino acid in a polypeptide chain.

For expediency, the names of the nucleic acids and the amino acids are often represented as one- or three-letter codes, as shown in Tables 4-1 and 4-2. (This book mostly uses the one-letter codes for amino acids.)

Table 4-1. Standard IUB/IUPAC nucleic acid codes

Code	Nucleic Acid(s)
A	Adenine
C	Cytosine
G	Guanine
T	Thymine
U	Uracil
M	A or C (amino)
R	A or G (purine)
W	A or T (weak)
S	C or G (strong)
Y	C or T (pyrimidine)
K	G or T (keto)
V	A or C or G
H	A or C or T
D	A or G or T
B	C or G or T
N	A or G or C or T (any)

Table 4-2. Standard IUB/IUPAC amino acid codes

One-letter code	Amino acid	Three-letter code
A	Alanine	Ala
B	Aspartic acid or Asparagine	Asx

Table 4-2. Standard IUB/IUPAC amino acid codes (continued)

One-letter code	Amino acid	Three-letter code
C	Cysteine	Cys
D	Aspartic acid	Asp
E	Glutamic acid	Glu
F	Phenylalanine	Phe
G	Glycine	Gly
H	Histidine	His
I	Isoleucine	Ile
K	Lysine	Lys
L	Leucine	Leu
M	Methionine	Met
N	Asparagine	Asn
P	Proline	Pro
Q	Glutamine	Gln
R	Arginine	Arg
S	Serine	Ser
T	Threonine	Thr
V	Valine	Val
W	Tryptophan	Trp
X	Unknown	Xxx
Y	Tyrosine	Tyr
Z	Glutamic acid or Glutamine	Glx

The nucleic acid codes in Table 4-1 include letters for the four basic nucleic acids; they also define single letters for all possible groups of two, three, or four nucleic acids. In most cases in this book, I use only A, C, G, T, U, and N. The letters A, C, G, and T represent the nucleic acids for DNA. U replaces T when DNA is transcribed into ribonucleic acid (RNA). N is the common representation for "unknown," as when a sequencer can't determine a base with certainty. Later on, in Chapter 9, we'll need the other codes, for groups of nucleic acids, when programming restriction maps. Note that the lowercase versions of these single-letter codes is also used on occasion, frequently for DNA, rarely for protein.

The computer-science terminology is a little different from the biology terminology for the codes in Tables 4-1 and 4-2. In computer-science parlance, these tables define two *alphabets*, finite sets of symbols that can make strings. A sequence of symbols is called a *string*. For instance, this sentence is a string. A language is a (finite or infinite) set of strings. In this book, the languages are mainly DNA and protein sequence data. You often hear bioinformaticians referring to an actual sequence of DNA or protein as a "string," as opposed to its representation as sequence data. This is an example of the terminologies of the two disciplines crossing over into one another.

As you've seen in the tables, we'll be representing data as simple letters, just as written on a page. But computers actually use additional codes to represent simple letters. You won't have to worry much about this; just remember that when using your text editor to save as ASCII, or plain text.

ASCII is a way for computers to store textual (and control) data in their memory. Then when a program such as a text editor reads the data, and it knows it's reading ASCII, it can actually draw the letters on the screen in a recognizable fashion because it's programmed to know that particular code. So the bottom line is: ASCII is a code to represent text on a computer.*

A Program to Store a DNA Sequence

Let's write a small program that stores some DNA in a variable and prints it to the screen. The DNA is written in the usual fashion, as a string made of the letters A, C, G, and T, and we'll call the variable $DNA. In other words, $DNA is the name of the DNA sequence data used in the program. Note that in Perl, a variable is really the name for some data you wish to use. The name gives you full access to the data. Example 4-1 shows the entire program.

Example 4-1. Putting DNA into the computer

```
#!/usr/bin/perl -w
# Storing DNA in a variable, and printing it out

# First we store the DNA in a variable called $DNA
$DNA = 'ACGGGAGGACGGGAAAATTACTACGGCATTAGC';

# Next, we print the DNA onto the screen
print $DNA;

# Finally, we'll specifically tell the program to exit.
exit;
```

Using what you've already learned about text editors and running Perl programs in Chapter 2, enter the code (or copy it from the book's web site) and save it to a file. Remember to save the program as ASCII or text-only format, or Perl may have trouble reading the resulting file.

The second step is to run the program. The details of how to run a program depend on the type of computer you have (see Chapter 2). Let's say the program is on your

---

* A new character encoding called *Unicode*, which can handle all the symbols in all the world's languages, is becoming widely accepted and is supported by Perl as well.

computer in a file called *example4-1*. As you recall from Chapter 2, if you are running this program on Unix or Linux, you type the following in a shell window:

```
perl example4-1
```

On a Mac, open the file with the MacPerl application and save it as a droplet, then just double-click on the droplet. On Windows, type the following in an MS-DOS command window:

```
perl example4 -1
```

If you've successfully run the program, you'll see the output printed on your computer screen.

Control Flow

Example 4-1 illustrates many of the ideas all our Perl programs will rely on. One of these ideas is *control flow*, or the order in which the statements in the program are executed by the computer.

Every program starts at the first line and executes the statements one after the other until it reaches the end, unless it is explicitly told to do otherwise. Example 4-1 simply proceeds from top to bottom, with no detours.

In later chapters, you'll learn how programs can control the flow of execution.

Comments Revisited

Now let's take a look at the parts of Example 4-1. You'll notice lots of blank lines. They're there to make the program easy for a human to read. Next, notice the comments that begin with the # sign. Remember from Chapter 3 that when Perl runs, it throws these away along with the blank lines. In fact, to Perl, the following is exactly the same program as Example 4-1:

```
#!/usr/bin/perl -w
$DNA = 'ACGGGAGGACGGGAAAATTACTACGGCATTAGC'; print $DNA; exit;
```

In Example 4-1, I've made liberal use of comments. Comments at the beginning of code can make it clear what the program is for, who wrote it, and present other information that can be helpful when someone needs to understand the code. Comments also explain what each section of the code is for and sometimes give explanations on how the code achieves its goals.

It's tempting to belabor the point about the importance of comments. Suffice it to say that in most university-level, computer-science class assignments, the program without comments typically gets a low or failing grade; also, the programmer on the job who doesn't comment code is liable to have a short and unsuccessful career.

Command Interpretation

Because it starts with a # sign, the first line of the program looks like a comment, but it doesn't seem like a very informative comment:

```
#!/usr/bin/perl -w
```

This is a special line called command interpretation that tells the computer running Unix and Linux that this is a Perl program. It may look slightly different on different computers. On some machines, it's also unnecessary because the computer recognizes Perl from other information. A Windows machine is usually configured to assume that any program ending in *.pl* is a Perl program. In Unix or Linux, a Windows command window, or a MacOS X shell, you can type `perl my_program`, and your Perl program `my_program` won't need the special line. However, it's commonly used, so we'll have it at start all our programs.

Notice that the first line of code uses a flag -w. The "w" stands for warnings, and it causes Perl to print messages in case of an error. Very often the error message suggests the line number where it thinks the error began. Sometimes the line number is wrong, but the error is usually on or just before the line the message suggests. Later in the book, you'll also see the statement use `warnings` as an alternative to -w.

Statements

The next line of Example 4-1 stores the DNA in a variable:

```
$DNA = 'ACGGGAGGACGGGAAAATTACTACGGCATTAGC';
```

This is a very common, very important thing to do in a computer language, so let's take a leisurely look at it. You'll see some basic features about Perl and about programming languages in general, so this is a good place to stop skimming and actually read.

This line of code is called a *statement*. In Perl, statements end in a semicolon (;). The use of the semicolon is similar to the use of the period in the English language.

To be more accurate, this line of code is an *assignment* statement. Its purpose in this program is to store some DNA into a variable called $DNA. There are several fundamental things happening here as you will see in the next sections.

Variables

First, let's look at the variable $DNA. Its name is somewhat arbitrary. You can pick another name for it, and the program behaves the same way. For instance, if you replace the two lines:

```
$DNA = 'ACGGGAGGACGGGAAAATTACTACGGCATTAGC';

print $DNA;
```

with these:

```
$A_poem_by_Seamus_Heaney = 'ACGGGAGGACGGGAAAATTACTACGGCATTAGC';

print $A_poem_by_Seamus_Heaney;
```

the program behaves in exactly the same way, printing out the DNA to the computer screen. The point is that the names of variables in a computer program are your choice. (Within certain restrictions: in Perl, a variable name must be composed from upper- or lowercase letters, digits, and the underscore _ character. Also the first character must not be a digit.)

This is another important point along the same lines as the remarks I've already made about using blank lines and comments to make your code more easily read by humans. The computer attaches no meaning to the use of the variable name $DNA instead of $A_poem_by_Seamus_Heaney, but whoever reads the program certainly will. One name makes perfect sense, clearly indicates what the variable is for in the program, and eases the chore of understanding the program. The other name makes it unclear what the program is doing or what the variable is for. Using well-chosen variable names is part of what's called self-documenting code. You'll still need comments, but perhaps not as many, if you pick your variable names well.

You've noticed that the variable name $DNA starts with dollar sign. In Perl this kind of variable is called a *scalar* variable, which is a variable that holds a single item of data. Scalar variables are used for such data as strings or various kinds of numbers (e.g., the string hello or numbers such as 25, 6.234, 3.5E10, -0.8373). A scalar variable holds just one item of data at a time.

Strings

In Example 4-1, the scalar variable $DNA is holding some DNA, represented in the usual way by the letters A, C, G, and T. As stated earlier, in computer science a sequence of letters is called a string. In Perl you designate a string by putting it in quotes. You can use single quotes, as in Example 4-1, or double quotes. (You'll learn the difference later.) The DNA is thus represented by:

```
'ACGGGAGGACGGGAAAATTACTACGGCATTAGC'
```

Assignment

In Perl, to set a variable to a certain value, you use the = sign. The = sign is called the *assignment operator*. In Example 4-1, the value:

```
'ACGGGAGGACGGGAAAATTACTACGGCATTAGC'
```

is assigned to the variable $DNA. After the assignment, you can use the name of the variable to get the value, as in the print statement in Example 4-1.

The order of the parts is important in an assignment statement. The value assigned to something appears to the right of the assignment operator. The variable that is assigned a value is always to the left of the assignment operator. In programming manuals, you sometimes come across the terms *lvalue* and *rvalue* to refer to the left and right sides of the assignment operator.

This use of the = sign has a long history in programming languages. However, it can be a source of confusion: for instance, in most mathematics, using = means that the two things on either side of the sign are equal. So it's important to note that in Perl, the = sign doesn't mean equality. It assigns a value to a variable. (Later, we'll see how to represent equality.)

So, to summarize what we've learned so far about this statement:

```
$DNA = 'ACGGGAGGACGGGAAAATTACTACGGCATTAGC';
```

It's an assignment statement that sets the value of the scalar variable $DNA to a string representing some DNA.

Print

The statement:

```
print $DNA;
```

prints ACGGGAGGACGGGAAAATTACTACGGCATTAGC out to the computer screen. Notice that the print statement deals with scalar variables by printing out their values—in this case, the string that the variable $DNA contains. You'll see more about printing later.

Exit

Finally, the statement exit; tells the computer to exit the program. Perl doesn't require an exit statement at the end of a program; once you get to the end, the program exits automatically. But it doesn't hurt to put one in, and it clearly indicates the program is over. You'll see other programs that exit if something goes wrong before the program normally finishes, so the exit statement is definitely useful.

Concatenating DNA Fragments

Now we'll make a simple modification of Example 4-1 to show how to concatenate two DNA fragments. *Concatenation* is attaching something to the end of something else. A biologist is well aware that joining DNA sequences is a common task in the biology lab, for instance when a clone is inserted into a cell vector or when splicing exons together during the expression of a gene. Many bioinformatics software packages have to deal with such operations; hence its choice as an example.

Example 4-2 demonstrates a few more things to do with strings, variables, and print statements.

Example 4-2. Concatenating DNA

```perl
#!/usr/bin/perl -w
# Concatenating DNA

# Store two DNA fragments into two variables called $DNA1 and $DNA2
$DNA1 = 'ACGGGAGGACGGGAAAATTACTACGGCATTAGC';
$DNA2 = 'ATAGTGCCGTGAGAGTGATGTAGTA';

# Print the DNA onto the screen
print "Here are the original two DNA fragments:\n\n";

print $DNA1, "\n";

print $DNA2, "\n\n";

# Concatenate the DNA fragments into a third variable and print them
# Using "string interpolation"
$DNA3 = "$DNA1$DNA2";

print "Here is the concatenation of the first two fragments (version 1):\n\n";

print "$DNA3\n\n";

# An alternative way using the "dot operator":
# Concatenate the DNA fragments into a third variable and print them
$DNA3 = $DNA1 . $DNA2;

print "Here is the concatenation of the first two fragments (version 2):\n\n";

print "$DNA3\n\n";

# Print the same thing without using the variable $DNA3
print "Here is the concatenation of the first two fragments (version 3):\n\n";

print $DNA1, $DNA2, "\n";

exit;
```

As you can see, there are three variables here, $DNA1, $DNA2, and $DNA3. I've added print statements for a running commentary, so that the output of the program that appears on the computer screen makes more sense and isn't simply some DNA fragments one after the other.

Here's what the output of Example 4-2 looks like:

```
Here are the original two DNA fragments:

ACGGGAGGACGGGAAAATTACTACGGCATTAGC
ATAGTGCCGTGAGAGTGATGTAGTA

Here is the concatenation of the first two fragments (version 1):
```

```
ACGGGAGGACGGGAAAATTACTACGGCATTAGCATAGTGCCGTGAGAGTGATGTAGTA
```

Here is the concatenation of the first two fragments (version 2):

```
ACGGGAGGACGGGAAAATTACTACGGCATTAGCATAGTGCCGTGAGAGTGATGTAGTA
```

Here is the concatenation of the first two fragments (version 3):

```
ACGGGAGGACGGGAAAATTACTACGGCATTAGCATAGTGCCGTGAGAGTGATGTAGTA
```

Example 4-2 has many similarities to Example 4-1. Let's look at the differences. To start with, the print statements have some extra, unintuitive parts:

```
print $DNA1, "\n";
```

```
print $DNA2, "\n\n";
```

The print statements have variables containing the DNA, as before, but now they also have a comma and then "\n" or "\n\n". These are instructions to print newlines. A *newline* is invisible on the page or screen, but it tells the computer to go on to the beginning of the next line for subsequent printing. One newline, "\n", simply positions you at the beginning of the next line. Two new lines, "\n\n", moves to the next line and then positions you at the beginning of the line after that, leaving a blank line in between.

Look at the code for Example 4-2 and to make sure you see what these newline directives do to the output. A blank line is a line with nothing printed on it. Depending on your operating system, it may be just a newline character or a combination formfeed and carriage return (in which cases, it may also be called an empty line), or it may include nonprinting whitespace characters such as spaces and tabs. Notice that the newlines are enclosed in double quotes, which means they are parts of strings. (Here's one difference between single and double quotes, as mentioned earlier: "\n" prints a newline; '\n' prints \n as written.)

Notice the comma in the print statement. A comma separates items in a list. The print statement prints all the items that are listed. Simple as that.

Now let's look at the statement that concatenates the two DNA fragments $DNA1 and $DNA2 into the variable $DNA3:

```
$DNA3 = "$DNA1$DNA2";
```

The assignment to $DNA3 is just a typical assignment as you saw in Example 4-1, a variable name followed by the = sign, followed by a value to be assigned.

The value to the right of the assignment statement is a string enclosed in double quotes. The double quotes allow the variables in the string to be replaced with their values. This is called *string interpolation.*[*] So, in effect, the string here is just the DNA of variable $DNA1, followed directly by the DNA of variable $DNA2. That concatenation of the two DNA fragments is then assigned to variable $DNA3.

After assigning the concatenated DNA to variable $DNA3, you print it out, followed by a blank line:

```
print "$DNA3\n\n";
```

One of the Perl catch phrases is, "There's more than one way to do it." So, the next part of the program shows another way to concatenate two strings, using the dot operator. The dot operator, when placed between two strings, creates a single string that concatenates the two original strings. So the line:

```
$DNA3 = $DNA1 . $DNA2;
```

illustrates the use of this operator.

 An operator in a computer language takes some arguments—in this case, the strings $DNA1 and $DNA2—and does something to them, returning a value—in this case, the concatenated string placed in the variable $DNA3. The most familiar operators from arithmetic—plus, minus, multiply, and divide—are all operators that take two numbers as arguments and return a number as a value.

Finally, just to exercise the different parts of the language, let's accomplish the same concatenation using only the print statement:

```
print $DNA1, $DNA2, "\n";
```

Here the print statement has three parts, separated by commas: the two DNA fragments in the two variables and a newline. You can achieve the same result with the following print statement:

```
print "$DNA1$DNA2\n";
```

Maybe the Perl slogan should be, "There are more than two ways to do it."

Before leaving this section, let's look ahead to other uses of Perl variables. You've seen the use of variables to hold strings of DNA sequence data. There are other types of data, and programming languages need variables for them, too. In Perl, a scalar variable such as $DNA can hold a string, an integer, a floating-point number (with a decimal point), a boolean (true or false) value, and more. When it's required, Perl figures out what kind of data is in the variable. For now, try adding the following

---

[*] There are occasions when you might add curly braces during string interpolation. The extra curly braces make sure the variable names aren't confused with anything else in the double-quoted string. For example, if you had variable $prefix and tried to interpolate it into the string I am $prefixinterested, Perl might not recognize the variable, confusing it with a nonexistent variable $prefixinterested. But the string I am ${prefix}interested is unambiguous to Perl.

lines to Example 4-1 or Example 4-2, storing a number in a scalar variable and printing it out:

```
$number = 17;
print $number,"\n";
```

Transcription: DNA to RNA

A large part of what you, the Perl bioinformatics programmer, will spend your time doing amounts to variations on the same theme as Examples 4-1 and 4-2. You'll get some data, be it DNA, proteins, GenBank entries, or what have you; you'll manipulate the data; and you'll print out some results.

Example 4-3 is another program that manipulates DNA; it transcribes DNA to RNA. In the cell, this transcription of DNA to RNA is the outcome of the workings of a delicate, complex, and error-correcting molecular machinery.* Here it's a simple substitution. When DNA is transcribed to RNA, all the T's are changed to U's, and that's all that our program needs to know.†

Example 4-3. Transcribing DNA into RNA

```
#!/usr/bin/perl -w
# Transcribing DNA into RNA

# The DNA
$DNA = 'ACGGGAGGACGGGAAAATTACTACGGCATTAGC';

# Print the DNA onto the screen
print "Here is the starting DNA:\n\n";

print "$DNA\n\n";

# Transcribe the DNA to RNA by substituting all T's with U's.
$RNA = $DNA;

$RNA =~ s/T/U/g;

# Print the RNA onto the screen
print "Here is the result of transcribing the DNA to RNA:\n\n";

print "$RNA\n";

# Exit the program.
exit;
```

---

* Briefly, the coding DNA strand is the reverse complement of the other strand, which is used as a template to synthesize its reverse complement as RNA, with T's replaced as U's. With the two reverse complements, this is the same as the coding strand with the T→U replacement.

† We're ignoring the mechanism of the splicing out of introns, obviously. The T stands for thymine; the U stands for uracil.

Here's the output of Example 4-3:

```
Here is the starting DNA:

ACGGGAGGACGGGAAAATTACTACGGCATTAGC

Here is the result of transcribing the DNA to RNA:

ACGGGAGGACGGGAAAAUUACUACGGCAUUAGC
```

This short program introduces an important part of Perl: the ability to easily manipulate text data such as a string of DNA. The manipulations can be of many different sorts: translation, reversal, substitution, deletions, reordering, and so on. This facility of Perl is one of the main reasons for its success in bioinformatics and among programmers in general.

First, the program makes a copy of the DNA, placing it in a variable called $RNA:

```
$RNA = $DNA;
```

Note that after this statement is executed, there's a variable called $RNA that actually contains DNA.* Remember this is perfectly legal—you can call variables anything you like—but it is potentially confusing to have inaccurate variable names. Now in this case, the copy is preceded with informative comments and followed immediately with a statement that indeed causes the variable $RNA to contain RNA, so it's all right. Here's a way to prevent $RNA from containing anything except RNA:

```
($RNA = $DNA) =~ s/T/U/g;
```

In Example 4-3, the transcription happens in this statement:

```
$RNA =~ s/T/U/g;
```

There are two new items in this statement: the binding operator (=~) and the substitute command s/T/U/g.

The *binding operator* =~ is used, obviously enough, on variables containing strings; here the variable $RNA contains DNA sequence data. The binding operator means "apply the operation on the right to the string in the variable on the left."

The *substitution operator*, shown in Figure 4-1, requires a little more explanation. The different parts of the command are separated (or delimited) by the forward slash. First, the s indicates this is a substitution. After the first / comes a T, which represents the element in the string that will be substituted. After the second / comes a U, which represents the element that's going to replace the T. Finally, after the third / comes g. This g stands for "global" and is one of several possible modifiers that can

---

* Recall the discussion in the earlier section "Assignment" about the importance of the order of the parts in an assignment statement. Here, the value of $DNA, that is, the DNA sequence data that has been stored in the $DNA variable, is being assigned to the variable $RNA. If you had written $DNA = $RNA;, the value of the $RNA variable (which is empty) would have been assigned to the $DNA variable, in effect wiping out the DNA sequence data in that variable and leaving two empty variables.

appear in this part of the statement. Global means "make this substitution through-out the entire string," that is to say, everywhere possible in the string.

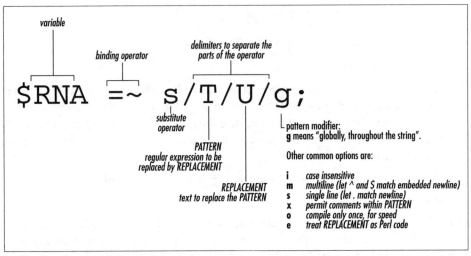

Figure 4-1. The substitution operator

Thus, the meaning of the statement is: "substitute all T's for U's in the string data stored in the variable $RNA."

The substitution operator is an example of the use of regular expressions. Regular expressions are the key to text manipulation, one of the most powerful features of Perl as you'll see in later chapters.

Using the Perl Documentation

A Perl programmer's most important resource is the Perl documentation. It should be installed on your computer, and it may also be found on the Internet at the Perl site. The Perl documentation may come in slightly different forms on your computer system, but the web version is the same for everybody. That's the version I refer to in this book. See the references in Appendix A for more discussion about different sources of Perl documentation.

Just to try it out, let's look up the print operator. First, open your web browser, and go to *http://www.perl.com*. Then click on the Documentation link. Select "Perl's Buil-tin Functions" and then "Alphabetical Listing of Perl's Functions". You'll see a rather lengthy alphabetical listing of Perl's functions. Once you've found this page, you may want to bookmark it in your browser, as you may find yourself turning to it frequently. Now click on Print to view the print operator.

Check out the examples they give to see how the language feature is actually used. This is usually the quickest way to extract what you need to know.

Once you've got the documentation on your screen, you may find that reading it answers some questions but raises others. The documentation tends to give the entire story in a concise form, and this can be daunting for beginners. For instance, the documentation for the print function starts out: "Prints a string or a comma-separated list of strings. Returns TRUE if successful." But then comes a bunch of gibberish (or so it seems at this point in your learning curve!) Filehandles? Output streams? List context?

All this information is necessary in documentation; after all, you need to get the whole story somewhere! Usually you can ignore what doesn't make sense.

The Perl documentation also includes several tutorials that can be a great help in learning Perl. They occasionally assume more than a beginner's knowledge about programming languages, but you may find them very useful. Exploring the documentation is a great way to get up to speed on the Perl language.

Calculating the Reverse Complement in Perl

As you recall from Chapter 1, a DNA polymer is composed of nucleotides. Given the close relationship between the two strands of DNA in a double helix, it turns out that it's pretty straightforward to write a program that, given one strand, prints out the other. Such a calculation is an important part of many bioinformatics applications. For instance, when searching a database with some query DNA, it is common to automatically search for the reverse complement of the query as well, since you may have in hand the opposite strand of some known gene.

Without further ado, here's Example 4-4, which uses a few new Perl features. As you'll see, it first tries one method, which fails, and then tries another method, which succeeds.

Example 4-4. Calculating the reverse complement of a strand of DNA

```
#!/usr/bin/perl -w
# Calculating the reverse complement of a strand of DNA

# The DNA
$DNA = 'ACGGGAGGACGGGAAAATTACTACGGCATTAGC';

# Print the DNA onto the screen
print "Here is the starting DNA:\n\n";

print "$DNA\n\n";

# Calculate the reverse complement
#  Warning: this attempt will fail!
#
# First, copy the DNA into new variable $revcom
# (short for REVerse COMplement)
```

Example 4-4. Calculating the reverse complement of a strand of DNA (continued)

```perl
# Notice that variable names can use lowercase letters like
# "revcom" as well as uppercase like "DNA".  In fact,
# lowercase is more common.
#
# It doesn't matter if we first reverse the string and then
# do the complementation; or if we first do the complementation
# and then reverse the string.  Same result each time.
# So when we make the copy we'll do the reverse in the same statement.
#

$revcom = reverse $DNA;

#
# Next substitute all bases by their complements,
# A->T, T->A, G->C, C->G
#

$revcom =~ s/A/T/g;
$revcom =~ s/T/A/g;
$revcom =~ s/G/C/g;
$revcom =~ s/C/G/g;

# Print the reverse complement DNA onto the screen
print "Here is the reverse complement DNA:\n\n";

print "$revcom\n";

#
# Oh-oh, that didn't work right!
# Our reverse complement should have all the bases in it, since the
# original DNA had all the bases—but ours only has A and G!
#
# Do you see why?
#
# The problem is that the first two substitute commands above change
# all the A's to T's (so there are no A's) and then all the
# T's to A's (so all the original A's and T's are all now A's).
# Same thing happens to the G's and C's all turning into G's.
#

print "\nThat was a bad algorithm, and the reverse complement was wrong!\n";
print "Try again ... \n\n";

# Make a new copy of the DNA (see why we saved the original?)
$revcom = reverse $DNA;

# See the text for a discussion of tr///
$revcom =~ tr/ACGTacgt/TGCAtgca/;

# Print the reverse complement DNA onto the screen
print "Here is the reverse complement DNA:\n\n";
```

Example 4-4. Calculating the reverse complement of a strand of DNA (continued)

```
print "$revcom\n";

print "\nThis time it worked!\n\n";

exit;
```

Here's what the output of Example 4-4 should look like on your screen:

```
Here is the starting DNA:

ACGGGAGGACGGGAAAATTACTACGGCATTAGC

Here is the reverse complement DNA:

GGAAAAGGGGAAGAAAAAAAGGGGAGGAGGGGA

That was a bad algorithm, and the reverse complement was wrong!
Try again ...

Here is the reverse complement DNA:

GCTAATGCCGTAGTAATTTTCCCGTCCTCCCGT

This time it worked!
```

You can check if two strands of DNA are reverse complements of each other by reading one left to right, and the other right to left, that is, by starting at different ends. Then compare each pair of bases as you read the two strands: they should always be paired C to G and A to T.

Just by reading in a few characters from the starting DNA and the reverse complement DNA from the first attempt, you'll see the that first attempt at calculating the reverse complement failed. It was a bad algorithm.

This is a taste of what you'll sometimes experience as you program. You'll write a program to accomplish a job and then find it didn't work as you expected. In this case, we used parts of the language we already knew and tried to stretch them to handle a new problem. Only they weren't quite up to the job. What went wrong?

You'll find that this kind of experience becomes familiar: you write some code, and it doesn't work! So you either fix the syntax (that's usually the easy part and can be done from the clues the error messages provide), or you think about the problem some more, find why the program failed, and then try to devise a new and successful way. Often this requires browsing the language documentation, looking for the details of how the language works and hoping to find a feature that fixes the problem. If it can be solved on a computer, you can solve it using Perl. The trick is, how exactly?

In Example 4-4, the first attempt to calculate the reverse complement failed. Each base in the string was translated as a whole, using four substitutions in a global fashion. Another way is needed. You could march though the DNA left to right, look at each base one at a time, make the change to the complement, and then look at the next base in the DNA, marching on to the end of the string. Then just reverse the string, and you're done. In fact, this is a perfectly good method, and it's not hard to do in Perl, although it requires some parts of the language not found until Chapter 5.

However, in this case, the tr operator—which stands for transliterate or translation—is exactly suited for this task. It looks like the substitute command, with the three forward slashes separating the different parts.

tr does exactly what's needed; it translates a set of characters into new characters, all at once. Figure 4-2 shows how it works: the set of characters to be translated are between the first two forward slashes. The set of characters that replaces the originals are between the second and third forward slashes. Each character in the first set is translated into the character at the same position in the second set. For instance, in Example 4-4, C is the second character in the first set, so it's translated into the second character of the second set, namely, G. Finally, since DNA sequence data can use upper- or lowercase letters (even though in this program the DNA is in uppercase only), both cases are included in the tr statement in Example 4-4.

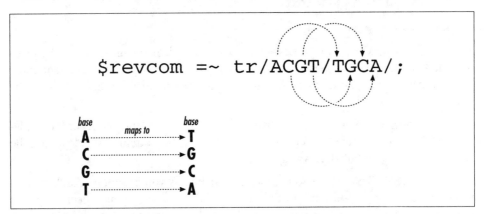

Figure 4-2. The tr statement

The reverse function also does exactly what's needed, with a minimum of fuss. It's designed to reverse the order of elements, including strings as seen in Example 4-4.

Proteins, Files, and Arrays

So far we've been writing programs with DNA sequence data. Now we'll also include the equally important protein sequence data. Here's an overview of what is covered in the following sections:

- How to use protein sequence data in a Perl program
- How to read protein sequence data in from a file
- Arrays in the Perl language

For the rest of the chapter, both protein and DNA sequence data are used.

Reading Proteins in Files

Programs interact with files on a computer disk. These files can be on hard disk, CD, floppy disk, Zip drive, magnetic tape—any kind of permanent storage.

Let's take a look at how to read protein sequence data from a file. First, create a file on your computer (use your text editor) and put some protein sequence data into it. Call the file *NM_021964fragment.pep* (you can download it from this book's web site). You will be using the following data (part of the human zinc finger protein NM_021964):

```
MNIDDKLEGLFLKCGGIDEMQSSRTMVVMGGVSGQSTVSGELQD
SVLQDRSMPHQEILAADEVLQESEMRQQDMISHDELMVHEETVKNDEEQMETHERLPQ
GLQYALNVPISVKQEITFTDVSEQLMRDKKQIR
```

You can use any name, except one that's already in use in the same folder.

Just as well-chosen variable names can be critical to understanding a program, well-chosen file and folder names can also be critical. If you have a project that generates lots of computer files, you need to carefully consider how to name and organize the files and folders. This is as true for individual researchers as for large, multi-national teams. It's important to put some effort into assigning informative names to files.

The filename *NM_021964fragment.pep* is taken from the GenBank ID of the record where this protein is found. It also indicates the fragmentary nature of the data and contains the filename extension *.pep* to remind you that the file contains peptide or protein sequence data. Of course, some other scheme might work better for you; the point is to get some idea of what's in the file without having to look into it.

Now that you've created or downloaded a file with protein sequence data in it, let's develop a program that reads the protein sequence data from the file and stores it into a variable. Example 4-5 shows a first attempt, which will be added to as we progress.

Example 4-5. Reading protein sequence data from a file

```
#!/usr/bin/perl -w
# Reading protein sequence data from a file

# The filename of the file containing the protein sequence data
$proteinfilename = 'NM_021964fragment.pep';

# First we have to "open" the file, and associate
```

Example 4-5. Reading protein sequence data from a file (continued)

```
# a "filehandle" with it.  We choose the filehandle
# PROTEINFILE for readability.
open(PROTEINFILE, $proteinfilename);

# Now we do the actual reading of the protein sequence data from the file,
# by using the angle brackets < and > to get the input from the
# filehandle.  We store the data into our variable $protein.
$protein = <PROTEINFILE>;

# Now that we've got our data, we can close the file.
close PROTEINFILE;

# Print the protein onto the screen
print "Here is the protein:\n\n";

print $protein;

exit;
```

Here's the output of Example 4-5:

```
Here is the protein:

MNIDDKLEGLFLKCGGIDEMQSSRTMVVMGGVSGQSTVSGELQD
```

Notice that only the first line of the file prints out. I'll show why in a moment.

Let's look at Example 4-5 in more detail. After putting a filename into the variable $proteinfilename, the file is opened with the following statement:

```
open(PROTEINFILE, $proteinfilename);
```

After opening the file, you can do various things with it, such as reading, writing, searching, going to a specific location in the file, erasing everything in the file, and so on. Notice that the program assumes the file named in the variable $proteinfilename exists and can be opened. You'll see in a little bit how to check for that, but here's something to try: change the name of the filename in $proteinfilename so that there's no file of that name on your computer, and then run the program. You'll get some error messages if the file doesn't exist.

If you look at the documentation for the open function, you'll see many options. Mostly, they enable you to specify exactly what the file will be used for after it's opened.

Let's examine the term PROTEINFILE, which is called a *filehandle*. With filehandles, it's not important to understand what they really are. They're just things you use when you're dealing with files. They don't have to have capital letters, but it's a widely followed convention. After the open statement assigns a filehandle, all the interaction with a file is done by naming the filehandle.

The data is actually read in to the program with the statement:

```
$protein = <PROTEINFILE>;
```

Why is the filehandle PROTEINFILE enclosed within angle brackets? These angle brackets are called *input operators*; a filehandle within angle brackets is how you bring in data from some source outside the program. Here, we're reading the file called *NM_021964fragment.pep* whose name is stored in variable $proteinfilename, and which has a filehandle associated with it by the open statement. The data is being stored in the variable $protein and then printed out.

However, as you've already noticed, only the first line of this multiline file is printed out. Why? Because there are a few more things to learn about reading in files.

There are several ways to read in a whole file. Example 4-6 shows one way.

Example 4-6. Reading protein sequence data from a file, take 2

```perl
#!/usr/bin/perl -w
# Reading protein sequence data from a file, take 2

# The filename of the file containing the protein sequence data
$proteinfilename = 'NM_021964fragment.pep';

# First we have to "open" the file, and associate
# a "filehandle" with it.  We choose the filehandle
# PROTEINFILE for readability.
open(PROTEINFILE, $proteinfilename);

# Now we do the actual reading of the protein sequence data from the file,
# by using the angle brackets < and > to get the input from the
# filehandle.  We store the data into our variable $protein.
#
# Since the file has three lines, and since the read only is
# returning one line, we'll read a line and print it, three times.

# First line
$protein = <PROTEINFILE>;

# Print the protein onto the screen
print "\nHere is the first line of the protein file:\n\n";

print $protein;

# Second line
$protein = <PROTEINFILE>;

# Print the protein onto the screen
print "\nHere is the second line of the protein file:\n\n";

print $protein;

# Third line
```

Example 4-6. Reading protein sequence data from a file, take 2 (continued)

```
$protein = <PROTEINFILE>;

# Print the protein onto the screen
print "\nHere is the third line of the protein file:\n\n";

print $protein;

# Now that we've got our data, we can close the file.
close PROTEINFILE;

exit;
```

Here's the output of Example 4-6:

```
Here is the first line of the protein file:

MNIDDKLEGLFLKCGGIDEMQSSRTMVVMGGVSGQSTVSGELQD

Here is the second line of the protein file:

SVLQDRSMPHQEILAADEVLQESEMRQQDMISHDELMVHEETVKNDEEQMETHERLPQ

Here is the third line of the protein file:

GLQYALNVPISVKQEITFTDVSEQLMRDKKQIR
```

The interesting thing about this program is that it shows how reading from a file works. Every time you read into a scalar variable such as $protein, the next line of the file is read. Something is remembering where the previous read was and is picking it up from there.

On the other hand, the drawbacks of this program are obvious. Having to write a few lines of code for each line of an input file isn't convenient. However, there are two Perl features that can handle this nicely: arrays (in the next section) and loops (in Chapter 5).

Arrays

In computer languages an *array* is a variable that stores multiple scalar values. The values can be numbers, strings, or, in this case, lines of an input file of protein sequence data. Let's examine how they can be used. Example 4-7 shows how to use an array to read all the lines of an input file.

Example 4-7. Reading protein sequence data from a file, take 3

```
#!/usr/bin/perl -w
# Reading protein sequence data from a file, take 3

# The filename of the file containing the protein sequence data
```

Example 4-7. Reading protein sequence data from a file, take 3 (continued)

```
$proteinfilename = 'NM_021964fragment.pep';

# First we have to "open" the file
open(PROTEINFILE, $proteinfilename);

# Read the protein sequence data from the file, and store it
# into the array variable @protein
@protein = <PROTEINFILE>;

# Print the protein onto the screen
print @protein;

# Close the file.
close PROTEINFILE;

exit;
```

Here's the output of Example 4-7:

```
MNIDDKLEGLFLKCGGIDEMQSSRTMVVMGGVSGQSTVSGELQD
SVLQDRSMPHQEILAADEVLQESEMRQQDMISHDELMVHEETVKNDEEQMETHERLPQ
GLQYALNVPISVKQEITFTDVSEQLMRDKKQIR
```

which, as you can see, is exactly the data that's in the file. Success!

The convenience of this is clear—just one line to read all the data into the program.

Notice that the array variable starts with an at sign (@) rather than the dollar sign ($) scalar variables begin with. Also notice that the print function can handle arrays as well as scalar variables. Arrays are used a lot in Perl, so you will see plenty of array examples as the book continues.

An array is a variable that can hold many scalar values. Each item or element is a scalar value that can be referenced by giving its position in the array (its subscript or offset). Let's look at some examples of arrays and their most common operations. We'll define an array @bases that holds the four bases A, C, G, and T. Then we'll apply some of the most common array operators.

Here's a piece of code that demonstrates how to initialize an array and how to use subscripts to access the individual elements of an array:

```
# Here's one way to declare an array, initialized with a list of four scalar values.
@bases = ('A', 'C', 'G', 'T');

# Now we'll print each element of the array
print "Here are the array elements:";
print "\nFirst element: ";
print $bases[0];
print "\nSecond element: ";
print $bases[1];
print "\nThird element: ";
print $bases[2];
```

```
print "\nFourth element: ";
print $bases[3];
```

This code snippet prints out:

```
First element: A
Second element: C
Third element: G
Fourth element: T
```

You can print the elements one a after another like this:

```
@bases = ('A', 'C', 'G', 'T');
print "\n\nHere are the array elements: ";
print @bases;
```

which produces the output:

```
Here are the array elements: ACGT
```

You can also print the elements separated by spaces (notice the double quotes in the print statement):

```
@bases = ('A', 'C', 'G', 'T');
print "\n\nHere are the array elements: ";
print "@bases";
```

which produces the output:

```
Here are the array elements: A C G T
```

You can take an element off the end of an array with pop:

```
@bases = ('A', 'C', 'G', 'T');
$base1 = pop @bases;
print "Here's the element removed from the end: ";
print $base1, "\n\n";
print "Here's the remaining array of bases: ";
print "@bases";
```

which produces the output:

```
Here's the element removed from the end: T

Here's the remaining array of bases: A C G
```

You can take a base off of the beginning of the array with shift:

```
@bases = ('A', 'C', 'G', 'T');
$base2 = shift @bases;
print "Here's an element removed from the beginning: ";
print $base2, "\n\n";
print "Here's the remaining array of bases: ";
print "@bases";
```

which produces the output:

```
Here's an element removed from the beginning: A

Here's the remaining array of bases: C G T
```

You can put an element at the beginning of the array with unshift:

```
@bases = ('A', 'C', 'G', 'T');
$base1 = pop @bases;
unshift (@bases, $base1);
print "Here's the element from the end put on the beginning: ";
print "@bases\n\n";
```

which produces the output:

```
Here's the element from the end put on the beginning: T A C G
```

You can put an element on the end of the array with push:

```
@bases = ('A', 'C', 'G', 'T');
$base2 = shift @bases;
push (@bases, $base2);
print "Here's the element from the beginning put on the end: ";
print "@bases\n\n";
```

which produces the output:

```
Here's the element from the beginning put on the end: C G T A
```

You can reverse the array:

```
@bases = ('A', 'C', 'G', 'T');
@reverse = reverse @bases;
print "Here's the array in reverse: ";
print "@reverse\n\n";
```

which produces the output:

```
Here's the array in reverse: T G C A
```

You can get the length of an array:

```
@bases = ('A', 'C', 'G', 'T');
print "Here's the length of the array: ";
print scalar @bases, "\n";
```

which produces the output:

```
Here's the length of the array: 4
```

Here's how to insert an element at an arbitrary place in an array using the Perl splice function:

```
@bases = ('A', 'C', 'G', 'T');
splice ( @bases, 2, 0, 'X');
print "Here's the array with an element inserted after the 2nd element: ";
print "@bases\n";
```

which produces the output:

```
Here's the array with an element inserted after the 2nd element: A C X G T
```

Scalar and List Context

Many Perl operations behave differently depending on the context in which they are used. Perl has *scalar context* and *list context*; both are listed in Example 4-8.

Example 4-8. Scalar context and list context

```
#!/usr/bin/perl -w
# Demonstration of "scalar context" and "list context"

@bases = ('A', 'C', 'G', 'T');

print "@bases\n";

$a = @bases;

print $a, "\n";

($a) = @bases;

print $a, "\n";

exit;
```

Here's the output of Example 4-8:

```
A C G T
4
A
```

First, Example 4-8 declares an array of the four bases. Then the assignment statement tries to assign an array (which is a kind of list) to a scalar variable $a:

```
$a = @bases;
```

In this kind of *scalar context*, an array evaluates to the size of the array, that is, the number of elements in the array. The scalar context is supplied by the scalar variable on the left side of the statement.

Next, Example 4-8 tries to assign an array (to repeat, a kind of list) to another list, in this case, having just one variable, $a:

```
($a) = @bases;
```

In this kind of *list context*, an array evaluates to a list of its elements. The list context is supplied by the list in parentheses on the left side of the statement. If there aren't enough variables on the left side to assign to, only part of the array gets assigned to variables. This behavior of Perl pops up in many situations; by design, many features of Perl behave differently depending on whether they are in scalar or list context. See Appendix B for more about scalar and list content.

Now you've seen the use of strings and arrays to hold sequence and file data, and learned the basic syntax of Perl, including variables, assignment, printing, and

---

reading files. You've transcribed DNA to RNA and calculated the reverse complement of a strand of DNA. By the end of Chapter 5, you'll have covered the essentials of Perl programming.

Exercises

Exercise 4.1

Explore the sensitivity of programming languages to errors of syntax. Try removing the semicolon from the end of any statement of one of our working programs and examining the error messages that result, if any. Try changing other syntactical items: add a parenthesis or a curly brace; misspell "print" or some other reserved word; just type in, or delete, anything. Programmers get used to seeing such errors; even after getting to know the language well, it is still common to have some syntax errors as you gradually add code to a program. Notice how one error can lead to many lines of error reporting. Is Perl accurately reporting the line where the error is?

Exercise 4.2

Write a program that stores an integer in a variable and then prints it out.

Exercise 4.3

Write a program that prints DNA (which could be in upper- or lowercase originally) in lowercase (acgt); write another that prints the DNA in uppercase (ACGT). Use the function tr///.

Exercise 4.4

Do the same thing as Exercise 4.3, but use the string directives \U and \L for upper- and lowercase. For instance, print "\U$DNA" prints the data in $DNA in uppercase.

Exercise 4.5

Sometimes information flows from RNA to DNA. Write a program to reverse transcribe RNA to DNA.

Exercise 4.6

Read two files of data, and print the contents of the first followed by the contents of the second.

Exercise 4.7

This is a more difficult exercise. Write a program to read a file, and then print its lines in reverse order, the last line first. Or you may want to look up the functions push, pop, shift, and unshift, and choose one or more of them to accomplish this exercise. You may want to look ahead to Chapter 5 so you can use a loop in this program, but this may not be necessary depending on the approach you take. Or, you may want to use reverse on an array of lines.

CHAPTER 5

Motifs and Loops

This chapter continues demonstrating the basics of the Perl language begun in Chapter 4. By the end of the chapter, you will know how to:

- Search for motifs in DNA or protein
- Interact with users at the keyboard
- Write data to files
- Use loops
- Use basic regular expressions
- Take different actions depending on the outcome of conditional tests
- Examine sequence data in detail by operating on strings and arrays

These topics, in addition to what you learned in Chapter 4, will give you the skills necessary to begin to write useful bioinformatics programs; in this chapter, you will learn to write a program that looks for motifs in sequence data.

Flow Control

Flow control is the order in which the statements of a program are executed. A program executes from the first statement at the top of the program to the last statement at the bottom, in order, unless told to do otherwise. There are two ways to tell a program to do otherwise: conditional statements and loops. A *conditional statement* executes a group of statements only if the conditional test succeeds; otherwise, it just skips the group of statements. A *loop* repeats a group of statements until an associated test fails.

Conditional Statements

Let's take another look at the open statement. Recall that if you try to open a nonexistent file, you get error messages. You can test for the existence of a file explicitly, before trying to open it. In fact, such tests are among the most powerful features of computer languages. The if, if-else, and unless conditional statements are three such testing mechanisms in Perl.

The main feature of these kinds of constructs is the testing for a conditional. A conditional evaluates to a true or false value. If the conditional is true, the statements following are executed; if the conditional is false, they are skipped (or vice versa).

However, "What is truth?" It's a question that programming languages may answer in slightly different ways.

This section contains a few examples that demonstrate some of Perl's conditionals. The true-false condition in each example is equality between two numbers. Notice that equality of numbers is represented by two equal signs ==, because the single equal sign = is already used for assignment to a variable.

 Confusion between = for assignment and == for numeric equality is a frequent programming bug, so watch for it!

The following examples demonstrate whether the conditional will evaluate to true or false. You don't ordinarily have much use for such simple tests. Usually you test the values that have been read into variables or the return value of function calls—things you don't necessarily know beforehand.

The if statement with a true conditional:

```
if( 1 == 1) {

    print "1 equals 1\n\n";
}
```

produces the output:

```
1 equals 1
```

The test is 1 == 1, or, in English, "Does 1 equal 1?" Since it does, the conditional evaluates to true, the statement associated with the if statement is executed, and a message is printed out.

You can also just say:

```
if( 1) {
    print "1 evaluates to true\n\n";
}
```

which produces the output:

```
1 evaluates to true
```

The if statement with a false conditional:

```
if( 1 == 0) {
    print "1 equals 0\n\n";
}
```

produces no output! The test is 1 == 0 or, in English, "Does 1 equal 0?" Since it doesn't, the conditional evaluates to false, the statements associated with the if statement aren't executed, and no message is printed out.

You can also just say:

```
if( 0 ) {
    print "0 evaluates to true\n\n";
}
```

which produces no output, since 0 evaluates to false, so the statements associated with the if statement are skipped entirely.

There's another way to write short if statements that mirrors how the English language works. In English, you can say, equivalently, "If you build it, they will come" or "They will come if you build it." Not to be outdone, Perl also allows you to put the if after the action:

```
print "1 equals 1\n\n" if (1 == 1);
```

which does the same thing as the first example in this section and prints out:

```
1 equals 1
```

Now, let's look at an if-else statement with a true conditional:

```
if( 1 == 1) {
    print "1 equals 1\n\n";
} else {
    print "1 does not equal 1\n\n";
}
```

which produces the output:

```
1 equals 1
```

The if-else does one thing if the test evaluates to true and another if the test evaluates to false. Here is if-else with a false conditional:

```
if( 1 == 0) {
    print "1 equals 0\n\n";
} else {
    print "1 does not equal 0\n\n";
}
```

which produces the output:

```
1 does not equal 0
```

The final example is unless—the opposite of if. It works like the English word "unless": e.g., "Unless you study Russian literature, you are ignorant of Chekov." If the conditional evaluates to true, no action is taken; if it evaluates to false, the associated statements are executed. If "you study Russian literature" is false, "you are ignorant of Chekov."

```
unless( 1 == 0) {
    print "1 does not equal 0\n\n";
}
```

produces the output:

```
1 does not equal 0
```

Conditional tests and matching braces

Two more comments are in order about these statements and their conditional tests.

First, there are several tests that can be used in the conditional part of these statements. In addition to numeric *equality* == as in the previous example, you can also test for inequality !=, greater than >, less than <, and more.

Similarly, you can test for string equality using the eq operator: if two strings are the same, it's true. There are also file test operators that allow you to test if a file exists, is empty, if permissions are set a certain way, and so on (see Appendix B). One common test is just a variable name: if the variable contains zero, it's considered false; any other number evaluates to true. If the variable contains a nonempty string, it evaluates to true; the empty string, designated by "" or '', is false.

Second, notice that the statements that follow the conditional are enclosed within a matching pair of curly braces. These statements within curly braces are called a *block* and arise frequently in Perl.* Matching pairs of parentheses, brackets, or braces, i.e., (), [], <>, and {}, are common programming features. Having the same number of left and right braces in the right places is essential for a Perl program to run correctly.

Matching braces are easy to lose track of, so don't be surprised if you miss some and get error messages when you try to run the program. This is a common syntax error; you have to go back and find the missing brace. As code gets more complex, it can be a challenge to figure out where the matching braces are wrong and how to fix them. Even if the braces are in the right place, it can be hard to figure out what statements are grouped together when you're reading code. You can avoid this problem by writing code that doesn't try to do too much on any one line and uses indentation to further highlight the blocks of code (see the later section "Code Layout").†

Back to the conditional statements. The if-else also has an if-elsif-else form, as in Example 5-1. The conditionals, first the if and then the elsifs, are evaluated in turn, and as soon as one evaluates to true, its block is executed, and the rest of the conditionals are ignored. If none of the conditionals evaluates to true, the else block is executed if there is one—it's optional.

Example 5-1. if-elsif-else

```
#!/usr/bin/perl -w
# if-elsif-else
```

---

* As something of an oddity, the last statement within a block doesn't need a semicolon after it.

† Some text editors help you find a matching brace (for instance, in the *vi* editor, hitting the percent key % over a parenthesis bounces you to the matching parenthesis).

Example 5-1. if-elsif-else (continued)

```
$word = 'MNIDDKL';

# if-elsif-else conditionals
if($word eq 'QSTVSGE') {

    print "QSTVSGE\n";

} elsif($word eq 'MRQQDMISHDEL') {

    print "MRQQDMISHDEL\n";

} elsif ( $word eq 'MNIDDKL' ) {

    print "MNIDDKL—the magic word!\n";

} else {

    print "Is \"$word\" a peptide? This program is not sure.\n";

}

exit;
```

Notice the \" in the else block's print statement; it lets you print a double-quote sign (") within a double-quoted string. The backslash character tells Perl to treat the following " as the sign itself and not interpret it as the marker for the end of the string. Also note the use of eq to check for equality between strings.

Example 5-1 gives the output:

```
MNIDDKL—the magic word!
```

Loops

A *loop* allows you to repeatedly execute a block of statements enclosed within matching curly braces. There are several ways to loop in Perl: while loops, for loops, foreach loops, and more. Example 5-2 (from Chapter 4) displays the while loop and how it's used while reading protein sequence data in from a file.

Example 5-2. Reading protein sequence data from a file, take 4

```
#!/usr/bin/perl -w
# Reading protein sequence data from a file, take 4

# The filename of the file containing the protein sequence data
$proteinfilename = 'NM_021964fragment.pep';

# First we have to "open" the file, and in case the
# open fails, print an error message and exit the program.
unless ( open(PROTEINFILE, $proteinfilename) ) {
```

```
    print "Could not open file $proteinfilename!\n";
    exit;
}

# Read the protein sequence data from the file in a "while" loop,
# printing each line as it is read.
while( $protein = <PROTEINFILE> ) {

    print "  ######  Here is the next line of the file:\n";

    print $protein;
}

# Close the file.
close PROTEINFILE;

exit;
```

Here's the output of Example 5-2:

```
    ######  Here is the next line of the file:
    MNIDDKLEGLFLKCGGIDEMQSSRTMVVMGGVSGQSTVSGELQD
    ######  Here is the next line of the file:
    SVLQDRSMPHQEILAADEVLQESEMRQQDMISHDELMVHEETVKNDEEQMETHERLPQ
    ######  Here is the next line of the file:
    GLQYALNVPISVKQEITFTDVSEQLMRDKKQIR
```

In the while loop, notice how the variable $protein is assigned each time through the loop to the next line of the file. In Perl, an assignment returns the value of the assignment. Here, the test is whether the assignment succeeds in reading another line. If there is another line to read in, the assignment occurs, the conditional is true, the new line is stored in the variable $protein, and the block with the two print statements is executed. If there are no more lines, the assignment is undefined, the conditional is false, and the program skips the block with the two print statements, quits the while loop, and continues to the following parts of the program (in this case, the close and exit functions).

open and unless

The open call is a system call, because to open a file, Perl must ask for the file from the operating system. The operating system may be a version of Unix or Linux, a Microsoft Windows versions, one of the Apple Macintosh operating systems, and so on. Files are managed by the operating system and can be accessed only by it.

It's a good habit to check for the success or failure of system calls, especially when opening files. If a system call fails, and you're not checking for it, your program will continue, perhaps attempting to read or write to a file you couldn't open in the first place. You should always check for failure and let the user of the program know right away when a file can't be opened. Often you may want to exit the program on failure or try to open a different file.

In Example 5-2, the open system call is part of the test of the unless conditional.

unless is the opposite of if. Just as in English you can say "do the statements in the block if the condition is true"; you can also say the opposite, "do the statements in the block unless the condition is true." The open system call gives you a true value if it successfully opens the file; so here, in the conditional test of the unless statement, if the open call fails, the statements in the block are performed, the program prints an error message, and then exits.

To sum up, conditionals and loops are simple ideas and not difficult to learn in Perl. They are among the most powerful features of programming languages. Conditionals allow you to tailor a program to several alternatives, and in that way, make decisions based on the type of input it gets. They are responsible for a large part of whatever artificial intelligence there is in a computer program. Loops harness the speed of the computer so that in a few lines of code, you can handle large amounts of input or continually iterate and refine a computation.

Code Layout

Once you start using loops and conditional statements, you need to think seriously about formatting. You have many options when formatting Perl code on the page. Compare these variant ways of formatting an if statement inside a while loop:

Format A
```
    while ( $alive ) {
        if ( $needs_nutrients ) {
            print "Cell needs nutrients\n";
        }
    }
```
Format B
```
    while ( $alive )
    {
        if ( $needs_nutrients )
        {
            print "Cell needs nutrients\n";
        }
    }
```
Format C
```
        while ( $alive )
          {
            if ( $needs_nutrients )
    {
        print "Cell needs nutrients\n";
    }
    }
```

Format D
```
    while($alive){if($needs_nutrients){print "Cell needs nutrients\n";}}
```
These code fragments are equivalent as far as the Perl interpreter is concerned. That's because Perl doesn't rely on how the statements are laid out on the lines; Perl cares only about the correct order of the syntactical elements. Some elements need some whitespace (such as spaces, tabs, or newlines) between them to make them distinct, but in general, Perl doesn't restrict how you use whitespace to lay out your code.

Formats A nd B are common ways to lay out code. They both make the program structure clear to the human reading it. Notice how the statements that have a block associated with them—the while and if statements—line up the curly braces and indent the statements within the blocks. These layouts make clear the extent of the block associated with the statements. (This can be critical for long, complicated blocks.) The statements inside the blocks are indented, for which you normally use the Tab key or groups of four or eight spaces. (Many text editors allow you to insert spaces when you hit the Tab key, or you can instruct them to set the tab stops at four, eight, or whatever number of spaces.) The overall structure of the program becomes clearer this way; you can easily see which statements are grouped in a block and associated with a given loop or conditional. Personally, I prefer the layout in Format A, although I'm also perfectly happy with Format B.

Format C is an example of badly formatted code. The flow control of the code isn't clear; for instance, it's hard to see if the print statement is in the block of the while statement.

Format D demonstrates how hard it is to read code with essentially no formatting, even a simple fragment like this.

The Perl style guide, available from the main Perl manual page or from the command line by typing:
```
    perldoc perlstyle
```
has some recommendations and some suggestions for ways to write readable code. However, they are not rules, and you may use your own judgment as to the formatting practices that work best for you.

Finding Motifs

One of the most common things we do in bioinformatics is to look for *motifs*, short segments of DNA or protein that are of particular interest. They may be regulatory elements of DNA or short stretches of protein that are known to be conserved across many species. (The PROSITE web site at *http://www.expasy.ch/prosite/* has extensive information about protein motifs.)

The motifs you look for in biological sequences are usually not one specific sequence. They may have several variants—for example, positions in which it doesn't matter which base or residue is present. They may have variant lengths as well. They can often be represented as regular expressions, which you'll see more of in the discussion following Example 5-3, in Chapter 9, and elsewhere in the book.

Perl has a handy set of features for finding things in strings. This, as much as anything, has made it a popular language for bioinformatics. Example 5-3 introduces this string-searching capability; it does something genuinely useful, and similar programs are used all the time in biology research. It does the following:

- Reads in protein sequence data from a file
- Puts all the sequence data into one string for easy searching
- Looks for motifs the user types in at the keyboard

Example 5-3. Searching for motifs

```perl
#!/usr/bin/perl -w
# Searching for motifs

# Ask the user for the filename of the file containing
# the protein sequence data, and collect it from the keyboard
print "Please type the filename of the protein sequence data: ";

$proteinfilename = <STDIN>;

# Remove the newline from the protein filename
chomp $proteinfilename;

# open the file, or exit
unless ( open(PROTEINFILE, $proteinfilename) ) {

    print "Cannot open file \"$proteinfilename\"\n\n";
    exit;
}

# Read the protein sequence data from the file, and store it
# into the array variable @protein
@protein = <PROTEINFILE>;

# Close the file - we've read all the data into @protein now.
close PROTEINFILE;

# Put the protein sequence data into a single string, as it's easier
# to search for a motif in a string than in an array of
# lines (what if the motif occurs over a line break?)
$protein = join( '', @protein);

# Remove whitespace
$protein =~ s/\s//g;

# In a loop, ask the user for a motif, search for the motif,
# and report if it was found.
# Exit if no motif is entered.
```

Example 5-3. Searching for motifs (continued)

```
do {
    print "Enter a motif to search for: ";

    $motif = <STDIN>;

    # Remove the newline at the end of $motif

    chomp $motif;

    # Look for the motif

    if ( $protein =~ /$motif/ ) {

        print "I found it!\n\n";

    } else {

        print "I couldn\'t find it.\n\n";
    }

# exit on an empty user input
} until ( $motif =~ /^\s*$/ );

# exit the program
exit;
```

Here's some typical output from Example 5-3:

```
Please type the filename of the protein sequence data: NM_021964fragment.pep
Enter a motif to search for: SVLQ
I found it!

Enter a motif to search for: jkl
I couldn't find it.

Enter a motif to search for: QDSV
I found it!

Enter a motif to search for: HERLPQGLQ
I found it!

Enter a motif to search for:
I couldn't find it.
```

As you see from the output, this program finds motifs that the user types in at the keyboard. With such a program, you no longer have to search manually through potentially huge amounts of data. The computer does the work and does it much faster and more accurately than a human.

It'd be nice if this program not only reported it found the motif but at what position. You'll see how this can be accomplished in Chapter 9. An exercise in that chapter challenges you to modify this program so that it reports the positions of the motifs.

The following sections examine and discuss the parts of Example 5-3 that are new:

- Getting user input from the keyboard
- Joining lines of a file into a single scalar variable
- Regular expressions and character classes
- do-until loops
- Pattern matching

Getting User Input from the Keyboard

You first saw filehandles in Example 4-5. In Example 5-3 (as was true in Example 4-5), a filehandle and the angle bracket input operator are used to read in data from an opened file into an array, like so:

```
@protein = <PROTEINFILE>;
```

Perl uses the same syntax to get input that is typed by the user at the keyboard. In Example 5-3, a special filehandle called STDIN (short for standard input), is used for this purpose, as in this line that collects a filename from the user:

```
$proteinfilename = <STDIN>;
```

So, a filehandle can be associated with a file; it can also be associated with the keyboard where the user types responses to questions the program asks.

If the variable you're using to save the input is a scalar variable starts with a dollar sign $), as in this fragment, only one line is read, which is almost always what you want in this case.

In Example 5-3, the user is requested to enter the filename of a file containing protein sequence data. After getting a filename in this fashion, there's one more step before you can open the file. When the user types in a filename and sends a newline by hitting the Enter key (also known as the Return key), the filename also gets a newline character at the end as it is stored in the variable. This newline is not part of the filename and has to be removed before the open system call will work. The Perl function chomp removes newlines (or its cousins linefeeds and carriage returns) from the end of a string. (The older function chop removes the last character, no matter what it is; this caused trouble, so chomp was introduced and is almost always preferred.)

So this part of Perl requires a little bit extra: removing the newline from the input collected from the user at the keyboard. Try commenting out the chomp function, and you'll see that the open fails, because no filename has a newline at the end. (Operating systems have rules as to which characters are allowed in filenames.)

Turning Arrays into Scalars with join

It's common to find protein sequence data broken into short segments of 80 or so characters each. The reason is simple: when data is printed out on paper or displayed on the screen, it needs to be broken up into lines that fit into the space. Having your data broken into segments, however, is inconvenient for your Perl program. What if you're searching for a motif that's split by a newline character? Your program won't find it. In fact, some of the motifs searched for in Example 5-3 are split by line breaks. In Perl you deal with this sort of segmented data with the Perl function join. In Example 5-3 join collapses an array @protein by combining all the lines of data into a single string stored in a new scalar variable $protein:

```
$protein = join( '', @protein);
```

You specify a string to be placed between the elements of the array as they're joined. In this case, you specify the empty string to be placed between the lines of the input file. The empty string is represented with the pair of single quotes '' (double quotes "" also serve).

Recall that in Example 4-2, I introduced several equivalent ways to concatenate two fragments of DNA. The use of the join function is very similar. It takes the scalar values that are the elements of the array and concatenates them into a single scalar value. Recall the following statement from Example 4-2, which is one of the equivalent ways to concatenate two strings:

```
$DNA3 = $DNA1 . $DNA2;
```

Another way to accomplish the same concatenation uses the join function:

```
$DNA3 = join( "", ($DNA1, $DNA2) );
```

In this version, instead of giving an array name, I specify a list of scalar elements:

```
($DNA1, $DNA2)
```

do-until Loops

There's a new kind of loop in Example 5-3, the do-until loop, which first executes a block and then does a conditional test. Sometimes this is more convenient than the usual order in which you test first, then do the block if the test succeeds. Here, you want to prompt the user, get the user's input, search for the motif, and report the results. Before doing it again, you check the conditional test to see if the user has input an empty line. This means that the user has no more motifs to look for, so you exit the loop.

Regular Expressions

Regular expressions let you easily manipulate strings of all sorts, such as DNA and protein sequence data. What's great about regular expressions is that if there's something you want to do with a string, you usually can do it with Perl regular expressions.

Some regular expressions are very simple. For instance, you can just use the exact text of what you're searching for as a regular expression: if I was looking for the word "bioinformatics" in the text of this book, I could use the regular expression:

```
/bioinformatics/
```

Some regular expressions can be more complex, however. In this section, I'll explain their use in Example 5-3.

Regular expressions and character classes

Regular expressions are ways of matching one or more strings using special wildcard-like operators. Regular expressions can be as simple as a word, which matches the word itself, or they can be complex and made to match a large set of different words (or even every word!).

After you join the protein sequence data into the scalar variable $protein in Example 5-3, you also need to remove newlines and anything else that's not sequence data. This can include numbers on the lines, comments, informational or "header" lines, and so on. In this case, you want to remove newlines and any spaces or tabs that might be invisibly present. The following line of code in Example 5-3 removes this whitespace:

```
$protein =~ s/\s//g;
```

The sequence data in the scalar variable $protein is altered by this statement. You first saw the binding operator =~ and the substitute function s/// back in Example 4-3, where they were used to change one character into another. Here, they're used a little differently. You substitute any one of a set of whitespace characters, represented by \s with nothing and by the lack of anything between the second and third forward slashes. In other words, you delete any of a set of whitespace characters, which is done globally throughout the string by virtue of the g at the end of the statement.

The \s is one of several metasymbols. You've already seen the metasymbol \n. The \s metasymbol matches any space, tab, newline, carriage return, or formfeed. \s can also be written as:

```
[ \t\n\f\r]
```

This expression is an example of a character class and is enclosed in square brackets. A character class matches one character, any one of the characters named within the square brackets. A space is just typed as a space; other whitespace characters have their own metasymbols: \t for tab, \n for newline, \f for formfeed, and \r for carriage return. A carriage return causes the next character to be written at the beginning of the line, and a formfeed advances to the next line. The two of them together amount to the same thing as a newline character.

Each s/// command I've detailed has some kind of regular expression between the first two forward slashes /. You've seen single letters as the C in s/C/G/g in that position. The C is an example of a valid regular expression.

There's another use of regular expressions in Example 5-3. The line of code:

```
if ( $motif =~ /^\s*$/ ) {
```

is, in English, testing for a blank line in the variable $motif. If the user input is nothing except for perhaps some whitespace, represented as \s*, the match succeeds, and the program exits. The whole regular expression is:

```
/^\s*$/
```

which translates as: match a string that, from the beginning (indicated by the ^), is zero or more (indicated by the *) whitespace characters (indicated by the \s) until the end of the string (indicated by the $).

If this seems somewhat cryptic, just hang in there and you'll soon get familiar with the terminology. Regular expressions are a great way to manipulate sequence and other text-based data, and Perl is particularly good at making regular expressions relatively easy to use, powerful, and flexible. Many of the references in Appendix A contain material on regular expressions, and there's a concise summary in Appendix B.

Pattern matching with =~ and regular expressions

The actual search for the motif happens in this line from Example 5-3:

```
if ( $protein =~ /$motif/ ) {
```

Here, the binding operator =~ searches for the regular expression stored as the value of the variable $motif in the protein $protein. Using this feature, you can interpolate the value of a variable into a string match. (Interpolation in Perl strings means inserting the value of a variable into a string, as you first saw in Example 4-2 when you were concatenating strings). The actual motif, that is, the value of the string variable $motif, is your regular expression. The simplest regular expressions are just strings of characters, such as the motif AQQK, for example.

You can use Example 5-3 to play with some more features of regular expressions. You can type in any regular expression to search for in the protein. Try starting up the program, referring to the documentation on regular expressions, and play! Here are some examples of typing in regular expressions:

- Search for an A followed by a D or S, followed by a V:

```
Enter a motif to search for: A[DS]V
I couldn't find it.
```

- Search for K, N, zero or more D's, and two or more E's (note that {2,} means "two or more"):

```
Enter a motif to search for: KND*E{2,}
I found it!
```

- Search for two E's, followed by anything, followed by another two E's:

```
Enter a motif to search for: EE.*EE
I found it!
```

In that last search, notice that a period stands for any character except a newline, and ".*" stands for zero or more such characters. (If you want to actually match a period, you have to escape it with a backslash.)

Counting Nucleotides

There are many things you might want to know about a piece of DNA. Is it coding or noncoding?* Does it contain a regulatory element? Is it related to some other known DNA, and if so, how? How many of each of the four nucleotides does the DNA contain? In fact, in some species the coding regions have a specific nucleotide bias, so this last question can be important in finding the genes. Also, different species have different patterns of nucleotide usage. So counting nucleotides can be interesting and useful.

In the following sections are two programs, Examples 5-4 and 5-6, that make a count of each type of nucleotide in some DNA. They introduce a few new parts of Perl:

- "Exploding" a string
- Looking at specific locations in strings
- Iterating over an array
- Iterating over the length of a string

To get the count of each type of nucleotide in some DNA, you have to look at each base, see what it is, and then keep four counts, one for each nucleotide. We'll do this in two ways:

- Explode the DNA into an array of single bases, and iterate over the array (that is, deal with the elements of the array one by one)
- Use the substr Perl function to iterate over the positions in the string of DNA while counting

---

* Coding DNA is DNA that codes for a protein, that is, it is part of a gene. In many organisms, including humans, a large part of the DNA is noncoding—not part of genes and doesn't code for proteins. In humans, about 98–99% of DNA is noncoding.

First, let's start with some pseudocode of the task. Afterwards, we'll make more detailed pseudocode, and finally write the Perl program for both approaches.

The following pseudocode describes generally what is needed:

```
for each base in the DNA
    if base is A
        count_of_A = count_of_A + 1
    if base is C
        count_of_C = count_of_C + 1
    if base is G
        count_of_G = count_of_G + 1
    if base is T
        count_of_T = count_of_T + 1
done

print count_of_A, count_of_C, count_of_G, count_of_T
```

As you can see, this is a pretty simple idea, mirroring what you'd do by hand if you had to. (If you want to count the relative frequencies of the bases in all human genes, you can't do it by hand—there are too many of them—and you have to use such a program. Thus bioinformatics.) Now let's see how it can be coded in Perl.

Exploding Strings into Arrays

Let's say you decide to explode the string of DNA into an array. By *explode* I mean separating out each letter in the string—sort of like blowing the string into bits. In other words, the letters representing the bases of the DNA in the string are separated, and each letter becomes its own scalar value in an array. Then you can look at the array elements (each of which is a single character) one by one, making the count as you go along. This is the inverse of the join function in the section "Turning Arrays into Scalars with join," which takes an array of strings and makes a single scalar value out of them. (After exploding a string into an array, you could then join the array back into an identical string using join, if you so desire.)

I'm also adding to this version of the pseudocode the instructions to get the DNA from a file and manipulate that file data until it's a single string of DNA sequence. So first, you join the data from the array of lines of the original file data, clean it up by removing whitespace until only sequence is left, and then explode it back into an array. But, of course, the point is that the last array has exactly what is needed, the data in a convenient form to use in the counting loop. Instead of an array of lines, with newlines and possibly other unwanted characters, there's an exact array of the individual bases.

```
read in the DNA from a file

join the lines of the file into a single string $DNA
```

```
# make an array out of the bases of $DNA
@DNA = explode $DNA

# initialize the counts
count_of_A = 0
count_of_C = 0
count_of_G = 0
count_of_T = 0

for each base in @DNA

    if base is A
        count_of_A = count_of_A + 1
    if base is C
        count_of_C = count_of_C + 1
    if base is G
        count_of_G = count_of_G + 1
    if base is T
        count_of_T = count_of_T + 1
done

    print count_of_A, count_of_C, count_of_G, count_of_T
```

As promised, this version of the pseudocode is a bit more detailed. It suggests a method to look at each of the bases by exploding the string of DNA into an array of single characters. It also initializes the counts to zero to ensure they start off right. It's easier to see what's happening if you spell out the initialization in the program, and it can prevent certain kinds of errors from creeping into your code. (It's not a rule, however; sometimes, you may prefer to leave the values of variables undefined until they are used.) Perl assumes that an uninitialized variable has the value 0 if you try to use it as a number, for instance by adding another number to it. But you'll most likely get a warning if that is the case.

We now have a design for the program, let's turn it into Perl code. Example 5-4 is a workable program; you'll see other ways to accomplish the same task more quickly as you proceed in this chapter, but speed is not the main concern at this point.

Example 5-4. Determining frequency of nucleotides

```
#!/usr/bin/perl -w
# Determining frequency of nucleotides

# Get the name of the file with the DNA sequence data
print "Please type the filename of the DNA sequence data: ";

$dna_filename = <STDIN>;

# Remove the newline from the DNA filename
chomp $dna_filename;

# open the file, or exit
unless ( open(DNAFILE, $dna_filename) ) {
```

Example 5-4. Determining frequency of nucleotides (continued)

```perl
    print "Cannot open file \"$dna_filename\"\n\n";
    exit;
}

# Read the DNA sequence data from the file, and store it
# into the array variable @DNA
@DNA = <DNAFILE>;

# Close the file
close DNAFILE;

# From the lines of the DNA file,
# put the DNA sequence data into a single string.
$DNA = join( '', @DNA);

# Remove whitespace
$DNA =~ s/\s//g;

# Now explode the DNA into an array where each letter of the
# original string is now an element in the array.
# This will make it easy to look at each position.
# Notice that we're reusing the variable @DNA for this purpose.
@DNA = split( '', $DNA );

# Initialize the counts.
# Notice that we can use scalar variables to hold numbers.
$count_of_A = 0;
$count_of_C = 0;
$count_of_G = 0;
$count_of_T = 0;
$errors     = 0;

# In a loop, look at each base in turn, determine which of the
# four types of nucleotides it is, and increment the
# appropriate count.
foreach $base (@DNA) {

    if      ( $base eq 'A' ) {
        ++$count_of_A;
    } elsif ( $base eq 'C' ) {
        ++$count_of_C;
    } elsif ( $base eq 'G' ) {
        ++$count_of_G;
    } elsif ( $base eq 'T' ) {
        ++$count_of_T;
    } else {
        print "!!!!!!!!! Error - I don\'t recognize this base: $base\n";
        ++$errors;
    }
}
```

Example 5-4. Determining frequency of nucleotides (continued)

```
# print the results
print "A = $count_of_A\n";
print "C = $count_of_C\n";
print "G = $count_of_G\n";
print "T = $count_of_T\n";
print "errors = $errors\n";

# exit the program
exit;
```

To demonstrate Example 5-4, I have created the following small file of DNA and called it *small.dna*:

```
AAAAAAAAAAAAAAGGGGGGGGTTTTCCCCCCCC
CCCCCGTCGTAGTAAAGTATGCAGTAGCVG
CCCCCCCCCCGGGGGGGGGAAAAAAAAAAAAAAAAATTTTTTAT
AAACG
```

The file *small.dna* can be typed into your computer using your favorite text editor, or you can download it from this book's web site.

Notice that there is a V in the file, an error.[*] Here is the output of Example 5-4:

```
Please type the filename of the DNA sequence data: small.dna
!!!!!!!! Error - I don't recognize this base: V

A = 40
C = 27
G = 24
T = 17
errors = 1
```

Now let's look at the new stuff in this program. Opening and reading the sequence data is the same as previous programs. The first new thing is at this line:

```
@DNA = split( '', $DNA);
```

which the comments say will explode the string $DNA into an array of single characters @DNA.

split is the companion to join, and it's a good idea to take a little while to look over the documentation for these two commands. Calling split with an empty string as the first argument causes the string to explode into individual characters; that's just what we want.[†]

Next, there are five scalar variables initialized to 0, the variables $count_of_A and so forth. *Initializing* means assigning an initial value, in this case, the value 0.

---

[*] Files of DNA sequence data sometimes include such characters as N, meaning "some undetermined base," or other special characters. You sometimes have to look at the documentation for the source, say an ABI sequencer or a GenBank file or whatever, to discover which characters are used and what they mean.

[†] As you'll see in the documentation for the split function, the first argument can be any regular expression, such as /\s+/ (one or more adjacent whitespace characters.)

Example 5-4 illustrates the concepts of *type* and *initialization*. The type of a variable determines what kind of data it can hold, for instance, strings or numbers. Up to now we've been using scalar variables such as $DNA to store strings of letters such as A, C, G, and T. Example 5-4 shows that you can also use scalar variables to store numbers. For example, the variable $count_of_A keeps a running count of the character A.

Scalar variables can store integers (0, 1, -1, 2, -2, ...), decimal or floating-point numbers such as 6.544, and numbers in scientific notation such as 6.544E6, which translates as 6.544×10^6, or 6,544000. (See Appendix B for more details on types of numbers.)

In Example 5-4, the variables $count_of_A through $count_of_T are initialized to 0. *Initializing* a variable means giving it a value after it's declared. If you don't initialize your variables, they assume the value of 'undef'. In Perl, an undefined variable is 0 if it is asked for in numerical context; it's an empty string if used in a string operation. Although Perl programmers often choose not to initialize variables, it's a critical step in many other languages. In C for instance, uninitialized variables have unpredictable values. This can wreak havoc with your output. You should get in the habit of initializing variables; it makes the program easier to read and maintain, and that's important.

To *declare* a variable means to specify its name and other attributes such as an initial value and a scope (for scoping, see Chapter 6 and the discussion of my variables). Many languages require you to declare all variables before using them. For this book, up to now, declarations have been an unnecessary complication. The next chapter begins to require declarations. In Perl, you may declare a variable's scope (see Chapter 6 and the discussion of my variables) in addition to an initial value. Many languages also require you to declare the type of a variable, for example "integer," or "string," but Perl does not.

Perl is written to be smart about what's in a scalar variable. For instance, you can assign the number 1234 (without quotes) to a variable, or you can assign the string '1234' (with quotes). Perl treats the variable as a string for printing, and as a number for using in arithmetic operations, without your having to worry about it. Example 5-5 demonstrates this ability. In other words, Perl isn't strict about specifying the type of data a variable is used for.

Example 5-5. Demonstration of Perl's built-in knowledge about numbers and strings

```
#!/usr/bin/perl -w
# Demonstration of Perl's built-in knowledge about numbers and strings

$num = 1234;

$str = '1234';
```

Example 5-5. Demonstration of Perl's built-in knowledge about numbers and strings (continued)

```
# print the variables
print $num, " ", $str, "\n";

# add the variables as numbers
$num_or_str = $num + $str;

print $num_or_str, "\n";

# concatenate the variables as strings
$num_or_str = $num . $str;

print $num_or_str, "\n";

exit;
```

Example 5-5 produces the output:

```
1234 1234
2468
12341234
```

Example 5-5 illustrates the smart way Perl determines the datatype of a scalar variable, whether it's a string or a number, and whether you're trying to add or subtract it like a number or concatenate it like a string. Perl behaves accordingly, which makes your job as a programmer a little bit easier; Perl "does the right thing" for you.

Next is a new kind of loop, the foreach loop. This loop works over the elements of an array. The line:

```
foreach $base (@DNA) {
```

loops over the elements of the array @DNA, and each time through the loop, the scalar variable $base (or whatever name you choose) is set to the next element of the array.

The body of the loop checks for each base and increments the count for that base if found. There are four ways to add 1 to a number in Perl. Here, you put a ++ in front of the variable, like this:

```
++$count;
```

You can also put the ++ after the variable:

```
$count++;
```

You can spell it out like this, a combination of adding and assignment:

```
$count = $count + 1;
```

or, as a shorthand of that, you can say:

```
$count += 1;
```

Almost an embarrassment of riches. The plus-plus (++) notation is convenient for incrementing counts, as we're doing here. The plus-equals (+=) notation saves some typing and is very popular for adding other numbers besides 1.

The foreach loop in Example 5-5 could have been written like this:

```
foreach (@DNA) {

    if      ( /A/ ) {
        ++$count_of_A;
    } elsif ( /C/ ) {
        ++$count_of_C;
    } elsif ( /G/ ) {
        ++$count_of_G;
    } elsif ( /T/ ) {
        ++$count_of_T;
    } else {
        print "!!!!!!!! Error - I don\'t recognize this base: ";
        print;
        print "\n";
        ++$errors;
    }
}
```

This version of the foreach loop:

```
foreach (@DNA) {
```

doesn't have a scalar value. In a foreach loop, if you don't specify a scalar variable to hold the scalars that are being read from the array ($base served that function in the version of this loop in Example 5-4), Perl uses the special variable $_.

Furthermore, many Perl built-in functions operate on this special variable if no argument is provided to them. Here, the conditional tests are simply patterns; Perl assumes you're doing a pattern match on the $_ variable, so it behaves as if you had said $_ =~ /A/, for instance. Finally, in the error message, the statement print; prints the value of the $_ variable.

This special variable $_ that doesn't have to be named appears in many Perl programs, although I don't use it extensively in this book.

Operating on Strings

It's not necessary to explode a string into an array in order to look at each character. In fact, sometimes you'd want to avoid that. A large string takes up a large amount of memory in your computer. So does a large array. When you explode a string into an array, the original string is still there, and you also have to make a copy of each character for the elements of the new array you're creating. If you have a large string, that already uses a good portion of available memory, creating an additional array can cause you to run out of memory. When you run out of memory, your computer performs poorly; it can slow to a crawl, crash, or freeze ("hang"). These haven't been worrisome considerations up to now, but if you use large data sets (such as the human genome), you have to take these things into account.

So let's say you'd like to avoid making a copy of the DNA sequence data into another variable. Is there a way to just look at the string $DNA and count the bases from it directly? Yes. Here's some pseudocode, followed by a Perl program:

```
read in the DNA from a file

join the lines of the file into a single string of $DNA

# initialize the counts
count_of_A = 0
count_of_C = 0
count_of_G = 0
count_of_T = 0

for each base at each position in $DNA

    if base is A
        count_of_A = count_of_A + 1
    if base is C
        count_of_C = count_of_C + 1
    if base is G
        count_of_G = count_of_G + 1
    if base is T
        count_of_T = count_of_T + 1
done

print count_of_A, count_of_C, count_of_G, count_of_T
```

Example 5-6 shows a program that examines each base in a string of DNA.

Example 5-6. Determining frequency of nucleotides, take 2

```perl
#!/usr/bin/perl -w
# Determining frequency of nucleotides, take 2

# Get the DNA sequence data
print "Please type the filename of the DNA sequence data: ";

$dna_filename = <STDIN>;

chomp $dna_filename;

# Does the file exist?
unless ( -e $dna_filename) {

    print "File \"$dna_filename\" doesn\'t seem to exist!!\n";
    exit;
}

# Can we open the file?
unless ( open(DNAFILE, $dna_filename) ) {

    print "Cannot open file \"$dna_filename\"\n\n";
    exit;
```

Example 5-6. Determining frequency of nucleotides, take 2 (continued)

```
}

@DNA = <DNAFILE>;

close DNAFILE;

$DNA = join( '', @DNA);

# Remove whitespace
$DNA =~ s/\s//g;

# Initialize the counts.
# Notice that we can use scalar variables to hold numbers.
$count_of_A = 0;
$count_of_C = 0;
$count_of_G = 0;
$count_of_T = 0;
$errors    = 0;

# In a loop, look at each base in turn, determine which of the
# four types of nucleotides it is, and increment the
# appropriate count.
for ( $position = 0 ; $position < length $DNA ; ++$position ) {

    $base = substr($DNA, $position, 1);

    if     ( $base eq 'A' ) {
        ++$count_of_A;
    } elsif ( $base eq 'C' ) {
        ++$count_of_C;
    } elsif ( $base eq 'G' ) {
        ++$count_of_G;
    } elsif ( $base eq 'T' ) {
        ++$count_of_T;
    } else {
        print "!!!!!!!! Error - I don\'t recognize this base: $base\n";
        ++$errors;
    }
}

# print the results
print "A = $count_of_A\n";
print "C = $count_of_C\n";
print "G = $count_of_G\n";
print "T = $count_of_T\n";
print "errors = $errors\n";

# exit the program
exit;
```

Here's the output of Example 5-6:

```
Please type the filename of the DNA sequence data: small.dna
!!!!!!!! Error - I don't recognize this base: V
A = 40
C = 27
G = 24
T = 17
errors = 1
```

In Example 5-6, I added a line of code to see if the file exists:

```
unless ( -e $dna_filename) {
```

There are file test operators for several conditions; see Appendix B or Perl documentation under -X. Note that files have several attributes, such as size, permission, location in the filesystem, and type of file, and that many of these things can be tested for easily with the file test operators.

Notice, also, that I have kept the detailed comments about the regular expression, because regular expressions can be hard to read, and a little commenting here helps a reader to skim the code.

Everything else is familiar, until you hit the for loop; it requires a little explanation:

```
for ( $position = 0 ; $position < length $DNA ; ++$position ) {

    # the statements in the block
}
```

This for loop is the equivalent of this while loop:

```
$position = 0;

while( $position < length $DNA ) {

    # the same statements in the block, plus ...

    ++$position;
}
```

Take a moment and compare these two loops. You'll see the same statements but in different locations.

As you can see, the for loop brings the initialization and increment of a counter ($position) into the loop statement, whereas in the while loop, they are separate statements. In the for loop, both the initialization and the increment statement are placed between parentheses, whereas you find only the conditional test in the while loop. In the for loop, you can put initializations before the first semicolon and increment statements after the second semicolon. The initialization statement is done just once before starting the loop, and the increment statement is done at the end of each iteration through the block before going back to the conditional test. It's really just a shorthand for the equivalent while loop as just shown.

The conditional test checks to see if the position reached in the string is less than the length of the string. It uses the `length` Perl function. Obviously, you don't want to check characters beyond the length of the string. But a word is in order here about the numbering of positions in strings and arrays.

By default, Perl assumes that a string begins at position 0 and its last character is at a position that's numbered one less than the length of the string. Why do it this way instead of numbering the positions from 1 up to and including the length of the string? There are reasons, but they're somewhat abstruse; see the documentation for enlightenment. If it's any comfort, many other programming languages make the same choice. (However, many do it the intuitive way, starting at 1. Ah well.)

This way of numbering is important to biologists because they are used to numbering sequences beginning with 1, not with 0 the way Perl does it. You sometimes have to add 1 to a position before printing out results so they'll make sense to nonprogrammers. It's mildly annoying, but you'll get used to it.

The same holds true for numbering the elements of an array. The first element of an array is element 0; the last is element $length-1.

Anyway, you see that the conditional test evaluates to `true` while the value of `$position` is length-1 or less and fails when `$position` reaches the same value as the length of the string. For example, say you have a string that contains the text "see-ing". This has a length of six characters. The "s" is at position 0, and the "g" is at position 5, which is one less than the string length 6.

Back in the block, you call the `substr` function to look into the string:

```
$base = substr($DNA, $position, 1);
```

This is a fairly general-purpose function for working with strings; you can also insert and delete things. Here, you look at just one character, so you call `substr` on the string $DNA, ask it to look in position `$position` for one character, and save the result in scalar variable $base. Then you proceed to accumulate the count as in the preceding version of the program, Example 5-4.

Writing to Files

Example 5-7 shows one more way to count nucleotides in a string of DNA. It uses a Perl trick that was designed with exactly this kind of job in mind. It puts a global regular expression search in the test for a `while` loop, and as you'll see, it's a compact way of counting characters in a string.

One of the nice things about Perl is that if you need to do something fairly regularly, the language has probably got a relatively succinct way to do it. (The downside of this is that Perl has a lot of things about it to learn.)

The results of Example 5-7, besides being printed to the screen, will also be written to a file. The code that accomplishes this writing to a file is as follows:

```
# Also write the results to a file called "countbase"
$outputfile = "countbase";

unless ( open(COUNTBASE, ">$outputfile") ) {

    print "Cannot open file \"$outputfile\" to write to!!\n\n";
    exit;
}

print COUNTBASE "A=$a C=$c G=$g T=$t errors=$e\n";

close(COUNTBASE);
```

As you see, to write to a file, you do an open call, just as when reading from a file, but with a difference: you prepend a greater-than sign > to the filename. The filehandle becomes a first argument to a print statement (but without a comma following it). This makes the print statement direct its output into the file.*

Example 5-7 is the third version of the Perl program that examines each base in a string of DNA.

Example 5-7. Determining frequency of nucleotides, take 3

```
#!/usr/bin/perl -w
# Determining frequency of nucleotides, take 3

# Get the DNA sequence data
print "Please type the filename of the DNA sequence data: ";

$dna_filename = <STDIN>;

chomp $dna_filename;

# Does the file exist?
unless ( -e $dna_filename) {

    print "File \"$dna_filename\" doesn\'t seem to exist!!\n";
    exit;
}

# Can we open the file?
unless ( open(DNAFILE, $dna_filename) ) {
```

---

* In this case, if the file already exists, it's emptied out first. It's possible to specify several other behaviors, such as appending to a file. As mentioned earlier, the Perl documentation has all the details of the open function, which sets the options for reading from, and writing to, files as well as other actions.

Example 5-7. Determining frequency of nucleotides, take 3 (continued)

```
    print "Cannot open file \"$dna_filename\"\n\n";
    exit;
}

@DNA = <DNAFILE>;

close DNAFILE;

$DNA = join( '', @DNA);

# Remove whitespace
$DNA =~ s/\s//g;

# Initialize the counts.
# Notice that we can use scalar variables to hold numbers.
$a = 0; $c = 0; $g = 0; $t = 0; $e = 0;

# Use a regular expression "trick", and five while loops,
#   to find the counts of the four bases plus errors
while($DNA =~ /a/ig){$a++}
while($DNA =~ /c/ig){$c++}
while($DNA =~ /g/ig){$g++}
while($DNA =~ /t/ig){$t++}
while($DNA =~ /[^acgt]/ig){$e++}

print "A=$a C=$c G=$g T=$t errors=$e\n";

# Also write the results to a file called "countbase"
$outputfile = "countbase";

unless ( open(COUNTBASE, ">$outputfile") ) {

    print "Cannot open file \"$outputfile\" to write to!!\n\n";
    exit;
}

print COUNTBASE "A=$a C=$c G=$g T=$t errors=$e\n";

close(COUNTBASE);

# exit the program
exit;
```

Example 5-7 looks like this when you run it:

```
Please type the filename of the DNA sequence data: small.dna
A=40 C=27 G=24 T=17 errors=1
```

The output file *countbase* has the following contents after you run Example 5-7:

```
A=40 C=27 G=24 T=17 errors=1
```

The while loop:

```
while($dna =~ /a/ig){$a++}
```

has as its conditional test, within the parentheses, a string-matching expression:

```
$dna =~ /a/ig
```

This expression is looking for the regular expression /a/, that is, the letter a. Since it has the i modifier, it's a case-insensitive match, which means it matches a or A. It also has the global modifier, which means match all the a's in the string. (Without the global modifier, it just keeps returning true every time through the loop, if there is an "a" in $dna.)

Now, this string-matching expression, in the context of a while loop, causes the while loop to execute its block on every match of the regular expression. So, append the one-statement block:

```
{$a++}
```

to increment the counter at each match of the regular expression; in other words, you're counting all the a's.

One other point should be made about this third version of the program. You'll notice some of the statements have been changed and shortened this time around. Some variables have shorter names, some statements are lined up on one line, and the print statement at the end is more concise. These are just alternative ways of writing. As you program, you'll find yourself experimenting with different approaches: try some on for size.

The way to count bases in this third version is flexible; for instance, it allows you to count non-ACGT characters without specifying them individually. In later chapters, you'll use those while loops to good effect. However, there's an even faster way to count bases. You can use the tr transliteration function from Chapter 4; it's faster, which is helpful if you have a lot of DNA to count:

```
$a = ($dna =~ tr/Aa//);
$c = ($dna =~ tr/Cc//);
$g = ($dna =~ tr/Gg//);
$t = ($dna =~ tr/Tt//);
```

The tr function returns the count of the specified characters it finds in the string, and if the set of replacement characters is empty, it doesn't actually change the string. So it makes a good character counter. Notice that with tr, you have to spell out the upper- and lowercase letters. Also, because tr doesn't accept character classes, there's no direct way to count nonbases. You could, however, say:

```
$basecount = ($dna = ~ tr/ACGTacgt//);
$ nonbase = (length $dna) - $basecount)
```

The program however, runs faster using tr than using the while loops of Example 5-7.

You may find it a bit much to have three (really, four) versions of this base-counting program, especially since much of the code in each version is identical. The only part of the program that really changed was the part that did the counting of the bases. Wouldn't it have been convenient to have a way to just alter the part that counts the bases? In Chapter 6, you'll see how subroutines allow you to partition your programs in just such a way.

Exercises

Exercise 5.1

Use a loop to write a nonhalting program. The conditional must always evaluate to true, every time through the loop. Note that some systems will catch that you're in an infinite loop and will stop the program automatically. You will stop your program differently, depending on which operating system you use. Ctrl-C works on Unix and Linux, a Windows MS-DOS command window, or a MacOS X shell window.

Exercise 5.2

Prompt the user to enter two (short) strings of DNA. Concatenate the two strings of DNA by appending the second to the first using the .= assignment operator. Print the two strings as concatenated, and then print the second string lined up over its copy at the end of the concatenated strings. For example, if the input strings are AAAA and TTTT, print:

```
AAAATTTT
    TTTT
```

Exercise 5.3

Write a program that prints all the numbers from 1 to 100. Your program should have much fewer than 100 lines of code!

Exercise 5.4

Write a program to calculate the reverse complement of a strand of DNA. Do not use the s/// or the tr functions. Use the substr function, and examine each base one at a time in the original while you build up the reverse complement. (Hint: you might find it easier to examine the original right to left, rather than left to right, although either is possible.)

Exercise 5.5

Write a program to report on the percentage of hydrophobic amino acids in a protein sequence. (To find which amino acids are hydrophobic, consult any introductory text on proteins, molecular biology, or cell biology. You will find information sources in Appendix A.)

Exercise 5.6

Write a program that checks if two strings given as arguments are reverse complements of each other. Use the Perl built-in functions split, pop, shift, and eq (eq actually an operator).

Exercise 5.7

Write a program to report how GC-rich some sequence is. (In other words, just give the percentage of G and C in the DNA.)

Exercise 5.8

Modify Example 5-3 to not only find motifs by regular expressions but to print out the motif that was found. For example, if you search, using regular expressions, for the motif EE.*EE, your program should print EETVKNDEE. You can use the special variable $&. After a successful pattern match, this special variable is set to hold the pattern that was matched.

Exercise 5.9

Write a program that switches two bases in a DNA string at specified positions. (Hint: you can use the Perl functions substr or slice.

Exercise 5.10

Write a program that writes a temporary file and then deletes it. The unlink function removes a file: just say, for example:

```
unlink "tmpfile";
```

but also check to see if unlink is successful.

## CHAPTER 6

Subroutines and Bugs

In this chapter you'll extend your basic knowledge in two directions:

- Subroutines
- Using the Perl debugger

Subroutines are an important way to structure programs. You'll use them in Chapter 7, where you'll learn how to use randomization to simulate the mutation of DNA. The Perl debugger examines a program's behavior in "slow motion" and helps you find those pesky bugs.

Subroutines

Subroutines are an important way to organize a program and are used in all major programming languages.

A *subroutine* wraps up a bit of code, gives the code a name, and provides a way to pass in some values for its calculations and then report back the results. The rest of the program can then use the subroutine's code just by calling its name, giving the needed values to pass in to the subroutine code and then collecting the results. This use or "invocation" of a subroutine is commonly referred to as *calling* the subroutine. You can think of a subroutine as a program within a program; just as you run programs to get results, so your programs call subroutines to get results. Once you have a subroutine, you can use it in a program simply by knowing which values to pass in and what kind of values to expect it to pass out.

Advantages of Subroutines

Subroutines provide several benefits. They endow programs with abstraction, modularization, and the ability to create large programs by organizing the code into manageable chunks with defined inputs and outputs.

Say you need to calculate something, for instance the mean of a distribution at several places in a program or in several different programs. By writing this calculation as a subroutine, you can write it once, and then call it whenever you need it, thus making your program:

- Shorter, since you're reusing the code.
- Easier to test, since you can test the subroutine separately.
- Easier to understand, since it reduces clutter and better organizes programs.
- More reliable, since you have less code when you reuse subroutines, so there are fewer opportunities for something to go wrong.
- Faster to write, since you may, for example, have already written some subroutines that handle basic statistics and can just call the one that calculates the mean without having to write it again. Or better yet, you found a good statistics library someone else wrote, and you never had to write it at all.

There is another subtle, yet powerful idea at work here. Subroutines can themselves call other subroutines, that is, a subroutine can use another subroutine for help in its calculations.* By writing a set of subroutines, each of which does one or a few things well, you can combine them in various ways to make new subroutines. You can then combine the new subroutines, and so on, and the end result can be large and flexible programming systems. Decomposing problems into sets of subroutines that can be conveniently combined allows you to create environments that can grow and adapt to changing conditions with a minimum of effort.

The trick of all this is in how you partition the code into subroutines. You want subroutines that encapsulate something that will be generally useful, and not just called once (although that sometimes can be useful too). There are various rules of thumb: a subroutine should do one thing well, and it should be no more than a page or two of code. These are not real rules, and exceptions are frequent, but they can help you divide your code into manageable chunks, suitable for subroutines.

Writing Subroutines

Let's look at how subroutines are used and then at how they're defined.

To use a subroutine, you pass data into the subroutine as *arguments*, and then you collect the return value(s) of the subroutine. For example, say you want a subroutine that, given some DNA, appends "ACGT" to the end of the DNA and returns the new, longer DNA. Let's call the subroutine addACGT. In Perl, you usually call a

---

* Subroutines can even call themselves, and this so-called recursion can be an elegant way to compute (see Chapter 11).

subroutine by typing its name, followed by a parenthesized list of arguments (if any). For example, here's a call to addACGT with the one argument $dna:

```
addACGT($dna);
```

When calling a subroutine, older versions of Perl required starting the name of a subroutine with the & (ampersand) character. It's still okay to do so (e.g., : &addACGT), but these days the ampersand is usually omitted.*

Example 6-1 demonstrates a subroutine that shows in detail how this works.

Example 6-1. A subroutine to append ACGT to DNA

```
#!/usr/bin/perl -w
# A program with a subroutine to append ACGT to DNA

# The original DNA
$dna = 'CGACGTCTTCTCAGGCGA';

# The call to the subroutine "addACGT".
# The argument being passed in is $dna; the result is saved in $longer_dna
$longer_dna = addACGT($dna);

print "I added ACGT to $dna and got $longer_dna\n\n";

exit;

################################################################################
# Subroutines for Example 6-1
################################################################################

# Here is the definition for subroutine "addACGT"

sub addACGT {
    my($dna) = @_;

    $dna .= 'ACGT';
    return $dna;
}
```

Example 6-1 produces the following output:

```
I added ACGT to CGACGTCTTCTCAGGCGA and got CGACGTCTTCTCAGGCGAACGT
```

We'll now look at this code to see how subroutines are defined and used in a Perl program.

The first thing to notice, taking the large view, is that the program now has two sections. The first section starts from the beginning of the program and ends with the

---

* There are times, even in the newer versions of Perl, when an ampersand is required; you'll see one such case in Chapter 11, in the section, "Processing Many Files," which describes the *File::Find* module. (See also the defined and undef functions in the documentation or the *perlref* manpage).

exit command. Following that (and announced by a blizzard of comments for easy reading) is a section for subroutine definitions, in this case, only the one definition for subroutine addACGT. It is common to place all subroutine definitions together at the end of a program, for ease in reading. Usually they're listed alphabetically or in some other convenient way.

Actually, it is legal to put the subroutine definitions almost anywhere in a program. This is because Perl first scans through the code and does things like check the syntax and learn subroutine definitions, before it starts to run the program. In particular, subroutine definitions can come after the point in the code where you use them (not necessarily before, which many people assume is the rule), and they don't have to be grouped together but can be scattered throughout the code. But our method of collecting them together at the end can make reading a program much easier. The possible exception is when a small subroutine is used in one section of code, as sometimes happens with the sort function, for instance. In this case having the definition right there can save the reader paging back and forth between the subroutine definition and its use. Usually, it's more convenient to read the program without the subroutine definitions, to get the overall flow of the program first, and then go back and look into the subroutines, if necessary.

As you see, Example 6-1 is very simple. It first stores some DNA into the variable $dna and then passes that variable as an argument to the subroutine call, which looks like this: addACGT($dna). The subroutine is called by its name, followed by parentheses containing the arguments to the subroutine. There may be no arguments, or if more than one, they are separated by commas. The value returned by the subroutine can be saved; in this program the value is saved in a variable called $longer_dna, which is then printed, and the program exits.

The part of the program from the beginning to the exit statement is called variously the *main program* or the *main body* of the program. By looking over this section of the code, you can see what happens from the beginning to the end of the program without looking into the details of the subroutines.

Now that you've looked over the main program of Example 6-1, it's time to look at the subroutine definition and how it uses the principal of scoping.

Scoping and Subroutines

A subroutine is defined by the *reserved word*[*] for subroutine definitions, sub; the subroutine's name, in this case, addACGT; and a *block*, enclosed in a pair of matching curly braces. This is the same kind of block seen earlier in loops and conditional statements that groups statements together.

---

[*] A reserved word is a fundamental, defined word in the Perl language, such as if, while, foreach, or sub.

In Example 6-1, the name of the subroutine is addACGT, and the block is everything after the name. Here is the subroutine definition again:

```
sub addACGT {
    my($dna) = @_;

    $dna .= 'ACGT';
    return $dna;
}
```

Now let's look into the block of the subroutine.

A subroutine is like a separate helper program for the main program, and it needs to have its own variables. You will use two types of variables in your subroutines in this book:[*]

- Arguments passed in to the subroutine
- Other variables declared with my and restricted to the scope of the subroutine

Arguments are the values given to a subroutine when it is used, or called. The values of the arguments are passed into the subroutine by means of the special variable @_, as you'll see in the next section.

Other variables a subroutine might use must be protected from interacting with variables in other parts of the program, so they have effect only within the subroutine's own scope. This is accomplished by declaring them as my variables, as will be explained shortly.

Finally, most subroutines return their results via the return function. This can return a single scalar as in return $dna; in our subroutine addACGT, in a list of scalars as in return ($dna1, $dna2);, in an array as in return @lines;, and more.

Arguments

To *call* a subroutine means to type its name and give it appropriate arguments and, usually, collect its results. *Arguments*, sometimes called *parameters*, usually contain the data that the subroutine computes on. In Example 6-1, this is the call of the subroutine addACGT with the argument $dna:

```
$longer_dna = addACGT($dna);
```

The essential point is that whenever you, the programmer, want to use a subroutine, you can call it with whatever argument(s) it is designed to accept and with which you need to compute (in this case, whatever DNA that needs ACGT appended to it) and the value of each argument appears in the subroutine in the @_ array.

---

[*] In the subroutines in this book, we won't use global variables, which can be seen by both the main program and the subroutines; nor will we use variables declared with local, which provides a different kind of scoping restriction than my.

When you call a subroutine with certain arguments, the names of the arguments you provide in the call are not important inside the subroutine. Only the values of those arguments that are actually passed inside the subroutine are important. The subroutine typically collects the values from the @_ array and assigns them to new variables that may or may not have the same names as the variables with which you called the subroutine. The only thing preserved is the order of the values, not the names of the variables containing the values.

Here's how it works. The first line in the subroutine's block is:

```
my($dna) = @_;
```

The values of the arguments from the call of the subroutine are passed into the subroutine in the special array variable @_. You know it's an array because it starts with the @ character. It has the brief name "_", and it's a special array variable that comes predefined in Perl programs. (It's not a name you should pick for your own arrays.) The array @_ contains all the scalar values passed into the subroutine. These scalar values are the values of the arguments to the subroutine. In this case, there is one scalar value: the string of DNA that's the value of the variable $dna passed in as an argument.

If the subroutine has more arguments—for instance one argument for DNA, one for the associated protein, and one for the name of the gene—they are all passed in and assigned to my variables inside the subroutine:

```
my($dna,$protein,$name_of_gene) = @_;
```

If there are no arguments, just omit that statement in the subroutine.

After the statement:

```
my($dna) = @_;
```

executes in the subroutine, the passed-in value is assigned to the subroutine's variable $dna. The next section explains why this is a new variable specific to the subroutine. The subroutine's variable can be called anything; it certainly doesn't have to be the same name as the argument, as it happens to be in this example. What's cool about scoping is that it doesn't matter if it is or not.

Beware the common mistake of forgetting the @_ array when naming your arguments in a subroutine, that is, using the statement:

```
my($dna);
```

instead of:

```
my($dna) = @_;
```

If you make this mistake, the values of the arguments won't appear in your subroutine, even though their names are declared.

Scoping

By keeping all variables a subroutine uses active only within the subroutine, you can make it safe to call the subroutines from anywhere. You make the variables specific only to the subroutine by declaring them as my variables. my is a keyword defined in Perl that limits variables to the block in which they are used (in this case, the block is the subroutine).*

Hiding variables and making them local to only a restricted part of a program, is called *scoping*. In Perl, using my variables is known as *lexical scoping,* and it's an essential part of modularizing your programs.

You declare that a variable is a my variable like this:

```
my($x);
```

or:

```
my $x ;
```

or, combining the declaration with an initialization to a value:

```
my($x) = '49';
```

or, if you're collecting an argument within a subroutine:

```
my($x) = @_;
```

Once a variable is declared in this fashion, it exists only until the end of the block it was declared in. So in a subroutine, if you declare all your variables like this (both the arguments and any other variables), they are active only in the subroutine. If any variable has the same name as another variable elsewhere in the program, you don't have to worry, because the my declaration actually creates a new variable, active only in the enclosing block, and any other variable of the same name used elsewhere outside the block is kept separate.

The example that showed collecting an argument in a subroutine uses parentheses around the variable. Because @_ is an array, the parentheses around the new variables put them in array context and ensure that they are initialized correctly (see Chapter 4).

 Always declare all your variables in your subroutines—even those variables that don't come in as arguments with the my construct (Unless you're using global variables, which we're not.).

Why use scoping? Example 6-2 shows the trouble that can happen when you don't. Recall that one of the advantages of subroutines is writing a useful bit of code once

---

* There are different models of scoping; my implements a type called *lexical scoping*, also known as *static scoping*. Another method is available in Perl via the *local* construct, but you almost always want to use my.

and then using it whenever you need it. Example 6-2 is a program that has a variable in the main program with the same name as a variable in a subroutine it calls. This can easily happen if you write the subroutine at a time other than the main program (say six months later) or if you call a subroutine someone else wrote.

Example 6-2. The pitfalls of not using my variables

```perl
#!/usr/bin/perl -w
# Illustrating the pitfalls of not using my variables

$dna = 'AAAAA';

$result = A_to_T($dna);

print "I changed all the A's in $dna to T's and got $result\n\n";

exit;

##########################################################################
# Subroutines
##########################################################################
sub A_to_T {
    my($input) = @_;

    $dna = $input;

    $dna =~ s/A/T/g;

    return $dna;
}
```

Example 6-2 gives the following output:

```
I changed all the A's in TTTTT to T's and got TTTTT
```

What was expected was this output:

```
I changed all the A's in AAAAA to T's and got TTTTT
```

You can get by this expected output by changing the definition of subroutine A_to_T to the following, in which the variable $dna in the subroutine is declared as a my variable:

```perl
sub A_to_T {
    my($input) = @_;

    my($dna) = $input;

    $dna =~ s/A/T/g;

    return $dna;
}
```

Where exactly did Example 6-2 go wrong? When the program entered the subroutine, and used the variable $dna to calculate the string with A's changed to T's, the Perl language saw that there was already a variable $dna being used in the main part of the program and just kept using it. When the program returned from the subroutine and got to the print statement, it was still using the same (the one and only) variable $dna. So, when it printed the results, the variable $dna, instead of having the original DNA in it, had the altered DNA that had been computed in the subroutine.

Now this sort of thing can happen a lot. Programmers tend to use certain names for variables a great deal: the usual suspects are names such as $tmp, $temp, $x, $a, $number, $variable, $var, $array, $input, $output, $result, $data, $file, $filename, and so on. Bioinformaticians are quite fond of $dna, $protein, $motif, $sequence, and the like. As you start using libraries of subroutines from other people and as your programs get larger, it's much easier—and a whole lot safer—to let the Perl language worry about avoiding the problem of name collisions.

In fact, from now on we're going to stop using undeclared variables. From this point forward, all our variables, even those in the main program, will be declared with my. You can enforce this discipline by adding the following directive to your programs:

```
use strict;
```

which has the effect of insisting that your programs have all their variables declared as my variables.

Lest you rail at this seemingly unnecessary complication to your coding, compared to the simpler and happier days of Chapters 4 and 5, you should know that many languages require declarations for all their variables. The fact that in Perl you don't have to enforce strict scoping is handy when you're writing short programs, for example, or when you're trying to teach programming without hitting the students with a thousand details at the beginning.

Another benefit you get from strict scoping happens if you accidently misspell a variable name while writing a program. If the variables aren't being declared, Perl creates a new variable with the (misspelled) name. The program may not work correctly, and it may be hard to find where the problem is. By strictly scoping the program, any misspelled variables are also undeclared, and Perl complains about it, saving you hours or days of hair-pulling and bad language.

Finally, let's recap how scoping, arguments, and subroutines work by taking another look at Example 6-1. The subroutine is called by writing its name addACGT, passing it the argument $dna, and collecting results (if any) by assignment to $longer_dna:

```
$longer_dna = addACGT($dna);
```

The first line in the subroutine gets the value of the argument from the special variable @_, and stores it in its own variable called $dna, which can't be seen outside the subroutine because it uses my. Even though the original variable outside the subroutine is also called $dna, the variable called $dna within the subroutine is an entirely new variable (with the same name) that belongs only to the subroutine due to the use of my. This new variable is in effect only during the time the program is in the subroutine. Notice in the output from the print statement at the end of Example 6-2 that even though a variable called $dna is lengthened inside the subroutine, the original variable, $dna, outside the subroutine isn't changed.

Command-Line Arguments and Arrays

Example 6-3 is another program that uses subroutines. You use the command line to give the program information it needs (such as filenames, or strings of DNA) without having to interactively answer the program's prompts. This is useful if you're scheduling a program to run at a time when you won't be there, for instance.

Example 6-3 also shows a little more about using arrays. You'll see how to use subscripts to access a specific element of an array.

For command-line programs, you type the name of the program, followed by the arguments to the program, if any, and then hit the Enter (or Return) key to start the program running. In Example 6-3, when the user types the program name, she follows that with the argument, which, in this case, is just the string of DNA in which she'll count the G's. So the program is called and returns an answer like so:

```
% perl example6-3.pl AAGGGGTTTCCC

The DNA AAGGGGTTTCCC has 4 G's in it!
```

Of course, many programs come with a graphical user interface (GUI). This gives the program some or all of the computer screen and usually includes such things as menus, buttons, and places to type in values to set parameters from the keyboard.

However, many programs are run from a command line. Even the newer MacOS X, which is built on top of Unix, now provides a command line. (Although most Windows users don't use the MS-DOS command window much, it's still useful, e.g., for running Perl programs.) As already mentioned, running a program noninteractively, passing parameters in as command-line arguments, allows you to run the program automatically, say in the middle of the night when no one is actually sitting at the computer.

Example 6-3 counts the number of G's in a string of DNA.

Example 6-3. Counting the G's in some DNA on the command line

```
#!/usr/bin/perl -w
# Counting the number of G's in some DNA on the command line

use strict;

# Collect the DNA from the arguments on the command line
#   when the user calls the program.
```

Example 6-3. Counting the G's in some DNA on the command line (continued)

```perl
# If no arguments are given, print a USAGE statement and exit.

# $0 is a special variable that has the name of the program.
my($USAGE) = "$0 DNA\n\n";

# @ARGV is an array containing all command-line arguments.
#
# If it is empty, the test will fail and the print USAGE and exit
#    statements will be called.
unless(@ARGV) {
    print $USAGE;
    exit;
}

# Read in the DNA from the argument on the command line.
my($dna) = $ARGV[0];

# Call the subroutine that does the real work, and collect the result.
my($num_of_Gs) = countG ( $dna );

# Report the result and exit.
print "\nThe DNA $dna has $num_of_Gs G\'s in it!\n\n";

exit;

###########################################################################
# Subroutines for Example 6-3
###########################################################################

sub countG {
    # return a count of the number of G's in the argument $dna

    # initialize arguments and variables
    my($dna) = @_;

    my($count) = 0;

    # Use the fourth method of counting nucleotides in DNA, as shown in
    # Chapter Four, "Motifs and Loops"
    $count = ( $dna =~ tr/Gg//);

    return $count;
}
```

Now let's look at how this program works, while examining and explaining the new features. For starters, notice the new line:

```perl
use strict;
```

which I will use from now on to ensure all variables are declared with my, thus enforcing lexical scoping.

Perl has some special variables it sets so you can easily use the arguments from the command line. Every Perl program has an array variable @ARGV that contains any command-line arguments. Also, there's a special variable called $0 (a zero) that has the name of the program as it was called from the command line.

Notice in Example 6-3 that an informative message is defined in the variable $USAGE and that it begins with the value of the variable $0, followed an indication of the arguments the program needs. This is a common practice; if the user doesn't give the program what it needs, which is determined by some kind of test, the program prints information about how to properly use it and exits.

In fact, this program does check to see if any arguments were typed on the command line. It checks if @ARGV has anything in it, in which case it evaluates to true; or if it is completely empty, in which case it evaluates to false. If you want the program to require an argument be given, you can use the unless conditional, and if @ARGV is empty, to print out the $USAGE statement and exit the program:

```
unless(@ARGV) {
    print $USAGE;
    exit;
}
```

The next bit of code shows something new about arrays, namely, how to extract one element from an array, as referenced by a subscript. In other words, it shows how to get at the first, fourth, or whichever element. The code in Example 6-3 shows how to extract the first element, which as you've seen, is numbered 0:

```
my($dna) = $ARGV[0];
```

Now you already know there is a first element, since you've just tested to make sure the array isn't empty. You get the first element of array @ARGV by changing the @ to a $ and appending square brackets containing the desired subscript; 0 for the first element, 1 for the second element, and so on. This syntax indicates that since you're now looking at just one element of the array, and it's a scalar variable, you use the dollar sign, as you would any other scalar variables.

In Example 6-3, you copy this first (and only) element of the command-line array @ARGV into the variable $dna.

Finally comes the call to the subroutine, which contains nothing new but fulfills a dream from the final paragraph of Chapter 5:

```
my($num_of_Gs) = countG ( $dna );
```

Passing Data to Subroutines

When you start parsing GenBank, PDB, and BLAST files in later chapters, you'll need more complicated arguments to your subroutines to hold the several fields of data you'll parse out of the records. These next sections explain the way it's done in

Perl. You can skim this section and return for a closer read when you get to Chapter 10.

Subroutines: Pass by Value

So far, all our subroutines have had fairly simple arguments. The values of these arguments are copied and passed to the subroutines, and whatever happens to those values in the subroutine doesn't affect the values of the arguments in the main program. This is called *pass by value* or *call by value*. For example:

```
#!/usr/bin/perl -w
# Example of pass-by-value (a.k.a. call-by-value)

use strict;

my $i = 2;

simple_sub($i);

print "In main program, after the subroutine call, \$i equals $i\n\n";

exit;

################################################################################
# Subroutines
################################################################################
sub simple_sub {

    my($i) = @_;

    $i += 100;

    print "In subroutine simple_sub, \$i equals $i\n\n";
}
```

This gives the following output:

```
In subroutine simple_sub, $i equals 102

In main program, after the subroutine call, $i equals 2
```

Subroutines: Pass by Reference

If you have more complicated arguments, say a mixture of scalars, arrays, and hashes, Perl often cannot distinguish between them. Perl passes all arguments into the subroutine as a single array, the special @_ array. If there are arrays or hashes as arguments, their elements get "flattened" out into this single @_ array in the subroutine. Here's an example:

```
#!/usr/bin/perl -w
# Example of problem of pass-by-value with two arrays
```

```
use strict;

my @i = ('1', '2', '3');
my @j = ('a', 'b', 'c');

print "In main program before calling subroutine: i = " . "@i\n";
print "In main program before calling subroutine: j = " . "@j\n";

reference_sub(@i, @j);

print "In main program after calling subroutine: i = " . "@i\n";
print "In main program after calling subroutine: j = " . "@j\n";

exit;

###############################################################################
# Subroutines
###############################################################################

sub reference_sub {

    my(@i, @j) = @_;

    print "In subroutine : i = " . "@i\n";
    print "In subroutine : j = " . "@j\n";

    push(@i, '4');

    shift(@j);
}
```

The following output illustrates the problem of this approach:

```
In main program before calling subroutine: i = 1 2 3
In main program before calling subroutine: j = a b c
In subroutine : i = 1 2 3 a b c
In subroutine : j =
In main program after calling subroutine: i = 1 2 3
In main program after calling subroutine: j = a b c
```

As you see, in the subroutine all the elements of @i and @j were grouped into one @_ array. All distinction between the two arrays you started with was lost in the subroutine. When you try to get the two arrays back in the statement:

```
my(@i, @j) = @_;
```

Perl assigns everything to the first array, @i. This behavior makes passing multiple arrays into subroutines somewhat dicey.

Also, as usual, the original arrays in the main program were not affected by the subroutine, since you used lexical scoping (my variables).

To get around this problem, you can pass arguments into subroutines in a style called *pass by reference* or *call by reference*. Using pass by reference, you can pass a subroutine any collection of scalars, arrays, hashes, and more, and the subroutine can distinguish between them. There is a price to pay: the resulting code looks a little more complex. But the payoff is often well worth it.

There is one big difference in the behavior of arguments that are passed by reference. When argument variables are passed in this fashion, anything you do to the values of the argument variables in the subroutine also affects the values of the arguments in the main program.

To call a subroutine that has its arguments passed by reference, you call it the same way as before, with one difference: you must preface the argument names with a backslash. In the example of pass by reference in this section, the subroutine call is accomplished like so:

```
reference_sub(\@i, \@j);
```

As you see here, the arguments are two arrays, and, to preserve the distinction between them as they are passed into the reference_sub subroutine, they are passed by reference by prepending their names with a backslash.

Within the subroutine, there are a few changes. First, the arguments are collected from the @_ array, and saved as scalar variables. This is because a reference is a special kind of data that is stored in a scalar variable, no matter whether it's a reference to a scalar, an array, a hash, or other. The example collects its arguments as follows:

```
my($i, $j) = @_;
```

reading them from the @_ array as scalars.

The subroutine has to do one more thing with these referenced arguments. When it uses them, it has to dereference them. To dereference a referenced argument, you have to prepend the reference with the symbol that shows what kind of variable it is: a $ for a scalar, @ for an array, % for a hash. So these variables have two symbols before their name—reading left to right, their usual symbol and then a $ that indicates the variable is a reference. The lines:

```
push(@$i, '4');
shift(@$j);
```

in the following subroutine are the ones that manipulate the arguments. The push adds an element '4' to the end of the @i array, and the shift removes the first element from the @j array. Because these arrays have been passed by reference, their names in the subroutine are @$i and @$j. (If you want to look at the third element of the @j array, which normally is $j[2], you'd say $$j[2].)

Whatever changes you make to the arguments in the subroutine also take effect in the main program. This is because the references are references to the actual arguments; they are not copies of their values as in pass by value. So, as you see in the example, after calling the subroutine, the arrays in the main program have been altered accordingly:

```
#!/usr/bin/perl
# Example of pass-by-reference (a.k.a. call-by-reference)

use strict;
use warnings;

my @i = ('1', '2', '3');
my @j = ('a', 'b', 'c');

print "In main program before calling subroutine: i = " . "@i\n";
print "In main program before calling subroutine: j = " . "@j\n";

reference_sub(\@i, \@j);

print "In main program after calling subroutine: i = " . "@i\n";
print "In main program after calling subroutine: j = " . "@j\n";

exit;

##############################################################################
# Subroutines
##############################################################################

sub reference_sub {
    my($i, $j) = @_;

    print "In subroutine : i = " . "@$i\n";
    print "In subroutine : j = " . "@$j\n";

    push(@$i, '4');
    shift(@$j);
}
```

This gives the following output:

```
In main program before calling subroutine: i = 1 2 3
In main program before calling subroutine: j = a b c
In subroutine : i = 1 2 3
In subroutine : j = a b c
In main program after calling subroutine: i = 1 2 3 4
In main program after calling subroutine: j = b c
```

The subroutine can now distinguish between the two arrays passed on as arguments. The changes that were made inside the subroutine to the variables remain in effect after the subroutine has ended, and you've returned to the main program. This is the essential characteristic of pass by reference.

Modules and Libraries of Subroutines

As you start to build a collection of subroutines, you'll find that you're copying them a lot from existing programs and pasting them into new programs. The subroutines then appear in multiple program. This makes the listings of your program code a bit verbose and repetitive. It also makes modifying a subroutine more complicated because you have to modify all the copies.

In short, subroutines are great, but if you have to keep copying them into each new program you write, it gets tiresome. So it's time to start collecting subroutines into the handy files called *modules* or *libraries*.

Here's how it works. You put all your reusable subroutines into a separate file. (Or, as you keep writing more and more code, and things get complicated, you may want to organize them into several files.) Then you just name the file in your program and presto: the subroutine's definitions all get read in, just as if they were in your program. To do this, you use the Perl built-in function use, which reads in the subroutine library file.

Let's call this module *BeginPerlBioinfo.pm*. You can put all your subroutine definitions into it, just as they appear in the program code. Then you can create the module by typing in the subroutine definitions as you read the book; or, more easily, it can be downloaded from the book's web site. But there is one thing to remember when creating or adding to a module: *the last line in a module must be* 1; *or it won't work*. This 1; should be the last line of the *.pm* file, not part of the last subroutine. If you forget this, you'll get an error message something like:

```
BeginPerlBioinfo.pm did not return a true value at jkl line 14.
BEGIN failed--compilation aborted at jkl line 14.
```

Now, to use any of the subroutines in *BeginPerlBioinfo.pm*, you just have to put the following statement in your code, near the top (near the use strict statement):

```
use BeginPerlBioinfo;
```

Note that *.pm* is left off the name on purpose: that's how Perl handles the names of modules.

There's one last thing to know about using modules to load in subroutines: the Perl program needs to know where to find the module. If you're doing all your work in one folder, everything should work okay. If Perl complains about not being able to find *BeginPerlBioinfo.pm*, give full pathname information to the module. If the full pathname is */home/tisdall/book/BeginPerlBioinfo.pm*, then use this in your program:

```
use lib '/home/tisdall/book';
use BeginPerlBioinfo;
```

There are other ways to tell Perl where to look for modules; consult the Perl documentation for use.

Beginning in Chapter 8, I'll define subroutines and show the code, but you'll be putting them into your module and typing:

```
use BeginPerlBioinfo;
```

This module is also available for download at this book's web site.

Fixing Bugs in Your Code

Now let's talk about what to do when your program is having trouble.

A program can go wrong in any number of ways. Maybe it won't run at all. A look at the error messages, especially the first line or two of the error messages, usually leads you to the problem, which will be somewhere in the syntax, and its solution, which will be to use the correct syntax (e.g., matching braces or ending each statement with a semicolon).

Your program may run but not behave as you planned. Then you have some problem with the logic of the program. Perhaps at some point, you've zigged when you should have zagged, like adding instead of subtracting or using the assignment operator = when you meant to test for equality between two numbers with ==. Or, the problem could be that you just have a poor design to accomplish your task, and it's only when you actually try it out that the flaw becomes evident.

However, sometimes the problem is not obvious, and you have to resort to the heavy artillery.

Fortunately, Perl has several ways to help you find and fix bugs in your programs. The use of the statements use strict; and use warnings; should become a habit, as you can catch many errors with them. The Perl debugger gives you complete freedom to examine a program in detail as it runs.

use warnings; and use strict;

In general, it's not too hard to tell when the syntax of a program is wrong because the Perl interpreter will produce error messages that usually lead you right to the problem. It's much harder to tell when the program is doing something you didn't really want. Many such problems can be caught if you turn on the warnings and enforce the strict use of declarations.

You have probably noticed that all the programs in this book up until now start with the command interpreter line:

```
#!/usr/bin/perl -w
```

That -w turns on Perl's warnings and attempts to find potential problems in your code and then to warn you about them. It finds common problems such as variables that are declared more than once, and so on, things that are not syntax errors but that can lead to bugs.

Another way to turn on warnings is to add the following statement near the top of the program:

```
use warnings;
```

The statement use warnings; may not be available on your version of Perl, if it's an old one. So if your Perl complains about it, take it out and use the -w command instead, either on the command interpreter line, or from the command line:

```
$ perl -w my_program
```

However, use warnings; is a bit more portable between different operating systems. So, from now on, that's the way I'll turn on warnings in my code. Another important helper you should use is the following statement placed near the top of your program (next to use warnings;):

```
use strict;
```

As mentioned previously, this forces you to declare your variables. (It has some options, that are beyond the scope of this book.) It finds misspelled variables, undeclared variables that may be interfering with other parts of the program, and so on.

 It's best to always use both use strict; and use warnings; when writing your Perl code.

Fixing Bugs with Comments and Print Statements

Sometimes you can identify misbehaving code by selectively commenting out sections of the program until you find the part that seems to cause the problem. You can also add print statements at suspicious parts of a misbehaving program to check what certain variables are doing. Both of these are time-honored programming techniques, and they work well in almost any programming language.

Commenting out sections of code can be particularly helpful when the error messages that you get from Perl don't point you directly at the offending line. This happens occasionally. When it does happen you may, by trial and error, discover that commenting out a small section of code causes the error messages to go away; then you know where the error is occurring.

Adding print statements can also be a quick way to pinpoint a problem, especially if you already have some idea of where the problem is. As a novice programmer, however, you may find that using the Perl debugger is easier than adding print statements. In the debugger, you can easily set print statements at any line. For instance, the following debugger command says to print the values of $i and $k before line 48:

```
a 48 print "$i $k\n"
```

Once you learn how to do it, this method is generally faster and easier than editing the Perl program and adding print statements by hand. Using this method is partly a matter of taste, since some extremely good Perl programmers prefer to do it the old-fashioned way, by adding print statements.

The Perl Debugger

My favorite way to deal with nonobvious bugs in my programs is to use the Perl debugger. The problem with bugs in code is that once a program starts running, all you can see is the output; you can't see the steps a program is taking. The Perl debugger lets you examine your program in detail, step by step, and almost always can lead you quickly to the problem. You'll also find that it's easy to use with a little practice.

There are situations the Perl debugger can't handle well: interacting processes that depend on timing considerations, for instance. The debugger can examine only one program at a time, and while examining, it stops the program, so timing considerations with other processes go right out the window.

For most purposes, the Perl debugger is a great, essential, programming tool. This section introduces its most important features.

A program with bugs

Example 6-4 has some bugs we can examine. It's supposed to take a sequence and two bases, and output everything from those two bases to the end of the sequence (if it can find them in the sequence). The two bases can be given as an argument, or if no argument is given, the program uses the bases TA by default.

There is one new thing in Example 6-4. The next statement affects the control flow in a loop. It immediately returns the control flow to the next iteration of the loop, skipping whatever else would have followed. Also, you may want to recall $_, which we discussed back in Example 5-5 in the context of a foreach loop.

Example 6-4. A program with a bug or two

```perl
#!/usr/bin/perl
# A program with a bug or two
#
# An optional argument, for where to start printing the sequence,
#  is a two-base subsequence.
#
# Print everything from the subsequence ( or TA if no subsequence
# is given as an argument) to the end of the DNA.

# declare and initialize variables
my $dna = 'CGACGTCTTCTAAGGCGA';
my @dna;
my $receivingcommittment;
my $previousbase = '';

my$subsequence = '';

if (@ARGV) {
    my$subsequence = $ARGV[0];
```

Example 6-4. A program with a bug or two (continued)

```
}else{
    $subsequence = 'TA';
}

my $base1 = substr($subsequence, 0, 1);
my $base2 = substr($subsequence, 1, 1);

# explode DNA
@dna = split ( '', $dna );

######### Pseudocode of the following loop:
#
# If you've received a committment, print the base and continue.  Otherwise:
#
# If the previous base was $base1, and this base is $base2, print them.
#   You have now received a committment to print the rest of the string.
#
# At each loop, save the previous base.

foreach (@dna) {
    if ($receivingcommittment) {
        print;
        next;
    } elsif ($previousbase eq $base1) {
        if ( /$base2/ ) {
            print $base1, $base2;
            $receivingcommitment = 1;
        }
    }
    $previousbase = $_;
}

print "\n";

exit;
```

Here's the output of two runs of Example 6-1:

```
$ perl example 6-4 AA

$ perl example 6-4
TA
```

Huh? It should have printed out AAGGCGA when called with the argument AA, and TAAGGCGA when called with no arguments. There must be a bug in this program. But, if you look it over, there isn't anything obviously wrong. It's time to fire up the debugger. What follows is an actual debugging session on Example 6-4, interspersed with comments to explain what's happening and why.

How to start and stop the debugger

The debugger runs interactively, and you control it from the keyboard.* The most common way to start it is by giving the –*d* switch to Perl at the command line. Since you're using buggy Example 6-4 to demonstrate the debugger, here's how to start that program:

```
perl -d example6-4
```

Alternatively, you could have added a –*d* flag to the command interpreter:

```
#!/usr/bin/perl -d
```

On systems such as Unix and Linux where command interpretation works, this starts the debugger automatically.

To stop the debugger, simply type q.

Debugger command summary

First, let's try to find the bug in Example 6-4 when it's called with no arguments:

```
$ perl -d example6-4
Default die handler restored.

Loading DB routines from perl5db.pl version 1.07
Editor support available.

Enter h or 'h h' for help, or 'man perldebug' for more help.

main::(example6-4:11):    my $dna = 'CGACGTCTTCTAAGGCGA';
  DB<1>
```

Let's stop right here at the beginning and look at a few things. After some messages, which may not mean a whole lot right now, you get the excellent information that the commands h and h h give more help. Let's try h h:

```
DB<1> h h
List/search source lines:                Control script execution:
  l [ln|sub]  List source code             T           Stack trace
  - or .      List previous/current line   s [expr]    Single step [in expr]
  w [line]    List around line             n [expr]    Next, steps over subs
  f filename  View source in file          <CR/Enter>  Repeat last n or s
  /pattern/ ?patt?  Search forw/backw      r           Return from subroutine
  v           Show versions of modules     c [ln|sub]  Continue until position
Debugger controls:                         L           List break/watch/actions
  O [...]     Set debugger options         t [expr]    Toggle trace [trace expr]
  <[<]|{[{]|>[>] [cmd] Do pre/post-prompt  b [ln|event|sub] [cnd] Set breakpoint
  ! [N|pat]   Redo a previous command      d [ln] or D Delete a/all breakpoints
  H [-num]    Display last num commands    a [ln] cmd  Do cmd before line
  = [a val]   Define/list an alias         W expr      Add a watch expression
```

* You also can run it automatically to produce a trace of the program in a file.

```
h [db_cmd]  Get help on command      A or W      Delete all actions/watch
|[|]db_cmd  Send output to pager      ![!] syscmd Run cmd in a subprocess
q or ^D     Quit                      R           Attempt a restart
Data Examination:      expr    Execute perl code, also see: s,n,t expr
  x|m expr      Evals expr in list context, dumps the result or lists methods.
  p expr        Print expression (uses script's current package).
  S [[!]pat]    List subroutine names [not] matching pattern
  V [Pk [Vars]] List Variables in Package.  Vars can be ~pattern or !pattern.
  X [Vars]      Same as "V current_package [Vars]".
For more help, type h cmd_letter, or run man perldebug for all docs.
  DB<2>
```

It's a bit hard to read, but you have a concise summary of the debugger commands. You can also use the h command, which gives several screens worth of information. The | h command displays those several pages one at a time; the pipe at the beginning of a debugger command pipes the output through a pager, which typically advances a page when you hit the spacebar on your keyboard. You should try those out. Right now, however, let's focus on a few of the most useful commands. But remember that typing h *command* can give you help about the command.

Stepping through statements with the debugger

Back to the immediate problem. When you started up the debugger, you saw that it stopped on the first line of real Perl code:

```
main::(example6-4:11):    my $dna = 'CGACGTCTTCTAAGGCGA';
```

There's an important point about the debugger you should understand right away. It shows the line it's about to execute, not the line it just executed.

So really, Example 6-4 hasn't done anything yet. You can see from the command summary that p tells the debugger to print out values. If you ask it to print the value of $dna, you'll find:

```
DB<2> p $dna

DB<3>
```

It didn't show anything because there's nothing to show; it hasn't even seen the variable $dna yet. So you should execute the statement. There are two commands to use: n or s both execute the statement being displayed. (The difference is that n or "next" skips the plunge into a subroutine call, treating it like a single statement; s or "single step" enters a subroutine and single step you through that code as well.) Once you've given one of these commands, you can just hit Enter to repeat the same command.

Since there aren't any subroutines, you needn't worry about choosing between n and s, so let's use n:

```
DB<3> n
main::(example6-4:12):    my @dna;
  DB<3>
```

This shows the next line (you can see the line numbers of the Perl program at the end of the prompt). If you wish to see more lines, the w or "window" command will serve:

```
    DB<3> w
9
10   # declare and initialize variables
11:  my $dna = 'CGACGTCTTCTAAGGCGA';
12==>my @dna;
13:  my $receivingcommittment;
14:  my $previousbase = '';
15
16:  my $subsequence = '';
17
18:  if (@ARGV) {
    DB<3>
```

The current line—the line that will be executed next—is highlighted with an arrow (==>).

The w seems like a useful thing. Let's get more information about it with the help command h w:

```
    DB<3> h w
w [line]        List window around line.
    DB<4>
```

Actually, there's more—hitting w repeatedly keeps showing more of the program; a minus sign backs up a screen. But enough of that.

Now that $dna has been declared and initialized, the program seems wrong on the first statement:

```
    DB<4> p $dna
CGACGTCTTCTAAGGCGA
    DB<5>
```

That's exactly what was expected. There's no bug, so let's continue examining the lines, printing out values here and there:

```
    DB<5> n
main::(example6-4:13):my $receivingcommittment;
    DB<5> n
main::(example6-4:14):my $previousbase = '';
    DB<5> n
main::(example6-4:16):my $subsequence = '';
    DB<5> n
main::(example6-4:18):if (@ARGV) {
    DB<5> p @ARGV

    DB<6> w
15
16:  my $subsequence = '';
17
18==>if (@ARGV) {
```

```
19:       my $subsequence = $ARGV[0];
20    }else{
21:       $subsequence = 'TA';
22    }
23
24: my $base1 = substr($subsequence, 0, 1);
  DB<6> n
main::(example6-4:21):     $subsequence = 'TA';
  DB<6> n
main::(example6-4:24):my $base1 = substr($subsequence, 0, 1);
  DB<6> p $subsequence
TA
  DB<7> n
main::(example6-4:25):my $base2 = substr($subsequence, 1, 1);
  DB<7> n
main::(example6-4:28):@dna = split ( '', $dna );
  DB<7> p $base1
T
  DB<8> p $base2
A
  DB<9>
```

So far, everything is as expected; the default subsequence TA is being used, and the $base1 and $base2 variables are set to T and A, the first and second bases of the subsequence. Let's continue:

```
  DB<9> n
main::(example6-4:39):     foreach (@dna) {
  DB<9> p @dna
CGACGTCTTCTAAGGCGA
  DB<10> p "@dna"
C G A C G T C T T C T A A G G C G A
  DB<11>
```

This shows a trick with Perl and printing arrays: normally they are printed without any spacing between the elements, but enclosing an array in double quotes in a print statement causes it to be displayed with spaces between the elements.

Again, everything seems okay, and we're about to enter a loop. Let's look at the whole loop first:

```
  DB<11> w
36    #
37    # At each loop, save the previous base.
38
39==>foreach (@dna) {
40:       if ($receivingcommittment) {
41:           print;
42:           next;
43        } elsif ($previousbase eq $base1) {
44:           if ( /$base2/ ) {
45:               print $base1, $base2;
  DB<11> w
43        } elsif ($previousbase eq $base1) {
```

```
44:          if ( /$base2/ ) {
45:              print $base1, $base2;
46:              $recievingcommitment = 1;
47              }
48          }
49:      $previousbase = $_;
50   }
51
52: print "\n";
  DB<11>
```

Despite the few repeated lines resulting from the w command, you can see the whole loop. Now you know something in here is going wrong: when you tested the program without giving it an argument, as it's running now, it took the default argument TA, and so far it seemed okay. However, all it actually did in your test was to print out the TA when it was supposed to print out everything in the string starting with the first occurrence of TA. What's going wrong?

Setting breakpoints

To figure out what's wrong, you can set a breakpoint in your code. A *breakpoint* is a spot in your program where you tell the debugger to stop execution so you can poke around in the code. The Perl debugger lets you set breakpoints in various ways. They let you run the program, stopping only to examine it when a statement with a breakpoint is reached. That way, you don't have to step through every line of code. (If you have 5,000 lines of code, and the error happens when you hit a line of code that's first used when you're reading the 12,000th line of input, you'll be happy about this feature.)

Notice that the part of this loop that prints out the rest of the string, once the starting two bases have been found, is the if block starting at line 40:

```
if ($receivingcommittment) {
    print;
    next;
}
```

Let's look at that $receivingcommittment variable.

Here's one way to do this. Let's set a breakpoint at line 40. Type b 40 and then c to continue, and the program proceeds until it hits line 40:

```
  DB<11> b 40
  DB<12> c
main::(example6-4:40):      if ($receivingcommittment) {
  DB<12> p
C
  DB<12>
```

The last command, p, prints out the element from the @dna array you reached in the foreach loop. Since you didn't specify a variable for the loop, it used the default $_ variable. Many Perl commands such as print or pattern matching operate on the default $_ variable if no other variable is given. (It's the cousin of the @_ default array subroutines used to hold their parameters.) So the p debugger command shows that you're operating on C from the @dna array, which is the first character.

All well and good. But it would be good to have the program break when the variable $receivingcommittment has a change in its value, and then single step from there, to see why the program isn't printing out the rest of the string. Recall that this variable is the flag whose change tells the program to print the rest of the string. First let's delete all other breakpoints:

```
DB<12> D
Deleting all breakpoints...
```

You can "watch" the variable with W like so:

```
DB<12> W $receivingcommittment
DB<13> c
TA
Debugged program terminated.  Use q to quit or R to restart,
    use O inhibit_exit to avoid stopping after program termination,
    h q, h R or h O to get additional info.
DB<13>
```

Wait a minute! The W command should indicate when $receivingcommittment changes value. But when the program continued running with the c command, it ran to the end, meaning that $receivingcommittment never changed value. So let's start up the program again and break on the line that changes its value:

```
DB<13> R
Warning: some settings and command-line options may be lost!
Default die handler restored.

Loading DB routines from perl5db.pl version 1.07
Editor support available.

Enter h or 'h h' for help, or 'man perldebug' for more help.

main::(example6-4:11):my $dna = 'CGACGTCTTCTAAGGCGA';
  DB<13> w 45
42:            next;
43        } elsif ($previousbase eq $base1) {
44:            if ( /$base2/ ) {
45:                print $base1, $base2;
46:                $recievingcommitment = 1;
47            }
48        }
49:        $previousbase = $_;
50    }
51
  DB<14> b 46
  DB<15> c
TAmain::(example6-4:46):            $recievingcommitment = 1;
  DB<15> n
```

```
main::(example6-4:49):    $previousbase = $_;
  DB<15> p $receivingcommittment

DB<16>
```

Huh? The code says it's assigning the variable a value of 1, but after you execute the code, with the n and try to print out the value, it doesn't print anything.

If you stare harder at the program, you see that at line 66 you misspelled $receivingcommittment as $recievingcommitment. That explains everything; fix it and run it again:

```
$ perl example6-4
TAAGGCGA
```

Success!

Fixing another bug

Now, did that fix the other bug when you ran Example 6-4 with an argument?

```
$ perl example6-4 AA
GACGTCTTCTAAGGCGA
```

Again, huh? You expected AAGGCGA. Can there be another bug in the program? Let's try the debugger again:

```
$ perl -d example6-4 AA
Default die handler restored.

Loading DB routines from perl5db.pl version 1.07
Editor support available.

Enter h or 'h h' for help, or 'man perldebug' for more help.

main::(example6-4:11):my $dna = 'CGACGTCTTCTAAGGCGA';
  DB<1> n
main::(example6-4:12):my @dna;
  DB<1> n
main::(example6-4:13):my $receivingcommittment;
  DB<1> n
main::(example6-4:14):my $previousbase = '';
  DB<1> n
main::(example6-4:16):my $subsequence = '';
  DB<1> n
main::(example6-4:18):if (@ARGV) {
  DB<1> n
main::(example6-4:19):    my $subsequence = $ARGV[0];
  DB<1> n
main::(example6-4:24):my $base1 = substr($subsequence, 0, 1);
  DB<1> n
main::(example6-4:25):my $base2 = substr($subsequence, 1, 1);
  DB<1> n
main::(example6-4:28):@dna = split ( '', $dna );
  DB<1> p $subsequence
```

```
DB<2> p $base1

DB<3> p $base2

DB<4>
```

Okay, for some reason the $subsequence, and therefore the $base1 and $base2 variables, are not getting set right. How come?

Check out line 19 where you declared a new my variable in the block of the if statement with the same name, $subsequence. That's the variable you're setting, but it's disappearing as soon as the if statement is over, because it's scoped in the block since it's a my variable.

So again, you fix that problem by removing the my declaration on line 19 and instead inserting an assignment $subsequence = $ARGV[0]; and run the program again:

```
$ perl example6-4
TAAGGCGA
$ perl example6-4 AA
AAGGCGA
```

Here, finally, is success.

use warnings; and use strict; redux

Example 6-4 was somewhat artificial. It turns out that these problems would have been reported easily if warnings had been used. So let's see an actual example of the benefits of use strict; and use warnings;, as discussed earlier in this chapter.

If you go back to the original Example 6-4 and add the use warnings; directive near the top of the program, you get the following output:

```
$ perl example6-4
Name "main::recievingcommitment" used only once: possible typo at example6-4 line 47.
TA
```

As you see, the warnings found the first bug immediately. They noticed there was a variable that was used only once, usually a sign of a misspelled variable. (I can never spell "receiving" or "commitment" properly.) So fix the misspelling at line 66, and run it again:

```
$ perl example6-4
TAAGGCGA
$ perl example6-4 AA
substr outside of string at example6-4 line 26.
Use of uninitialized value in regexp compilation at example6-4 line 45.
Use of uninitialized value in print at example6-4 line 46.
GACGTCTTCTAAGGCGA
```

So, the first bug is fixed. The second bug remains with a few warnings that are, per-haps, hard to understand. But focus on the first error message, and see that it com-plains about line 26:

```
my $base2 = substr($subsequence, 1, 1);
```

So, there's something wrong with $subsequence. Often, error messages will be off by one line, so it may well be that the error starts on the line before, the first time $subsequence is operated on by the substr. But that's not the case here.

Nonetheless, the warnings have pointed directly to the problem. In this case, you still have to take a little initiative; look back at the $subsequence variable and notice the extra my declaration within the if block on line 20 that is preventing the variable from being initialized properly. Now this is not necessarily always a bug—declaring a variable scoped within a block and that overrides another variable of the same name that is outside the block. In fact, it's perfectly legal, so the programmers who wrote the warnings did not flag it as an obvious error. However, it seems to have caused a real problem here!

One final point: if you go back to the original, buggy program, notice there's no use strict; in the program. If you add that and run the program without arguments, you get the following:

```
$ perl example6-4
Global symbol "$recievingcommitment" requires explicit package name at example6-4
line 47.
Execution of example6-4 aborted due to compilation errors.
```

Fixing the misspelled variable, and running the program with the argument, you get:

```
$ perl example6-4 AA
GACGTCTTCTAAGGCGA
```

You can see that use strict; didn't help for the other bug. Remember, it's best to employ both use strict; and use warnings;.

Exercises

Exercise 6.1

Write a subroutine to concatenate two strings of DNA.

Exercise 6.2

Write a subroutine to report the percentage of each nucleotide in DNA. You've seen the plus operator +. You will also want to use the divide operator / and the multiply operator *. Count the number of each nucleotide, divide by the total length of the DNA, then multiply by 100 to get the percentage. Your arguments should be the DNA and the nucleotide you want to report on. The int function can be used to discard digits after the decimal point, if needed.

Exercise 6.3

Write a subroutine to prompt a user with any message, and collect the user's answer. The subroutine's argument should be the message, and the return value should be the (one-line) answer.

Exercise 6.4

Write a subroutine to look for command-line arguments such as -help, -h, and --help. Recall that command-line arguments appear in the @ARGV array. Call your subroutine from a main program. If you give the program any of the named command-line arguments, when you pass them into the subroutine it should return a true value. If this is the case, have the program print out a help message in a $USAGE variable and exit.

Exercise 6.5

Write a subroutine to check if a file exists, is a regular file, and is nonzero in size. Use the file test operators (See Appendix B).

Exercise 6.6

Use Exercise 6.3 in a subroutine that keeps prompting until a valid file is entered by the user or until five attempts have failed.

Exercise 6.7

Write a module that contains subroutines that report various statistics on DNA sequences, for instance length, GC content, presence or absence of poly-T sequences (long stretches of mostly T's at the 5' (left) end of many $DNA sequences), or other measures of interest.

Exercise 6.8

Write a subroutine to do something a biologist normally does. (Here's an opportunity to look around the lab and write a useful program!)

Exercise 6.9

Read the documentation about the debugger and become familiar with its use by applying it during your programming.

Exercise 6.10

Write a subroutine that alters an array of lines in a file. Use pass by reference for the array. Pass the subroutine a reference to the array, a regular expression, and a string to replace the regular expression. All the lines of the array should be altered by substituting the matches found for the regular expression by the replacement string.

CHAPTER 7
Mutations and Randomization

As every biologist knows, mutation is a fundamental topic in biology. Mutations in DNA occur all the time in cells. Most of them don't affect the actions of proteins and are benign. Some of them do affect the proteins and may result in diseases such as cancer. Mutations can also lead to nonviable offspring that dies during development; occasionally they can lead to evolutionary change. Many cells have very complex mechanisms to repair mutations.

Mutations in DNA can arise from radiation, chemical agents, replication errors, and other causes. We're going to model mutations as random events, using Perl's random number generator.

Randomization is a computer technique that crops up regularly in everyday programs, most commonly in cryptography, such as when you want to generate a hard-to-guess password. But it's also an important branch of algorithms: many of the fastest algorithms employ randomization.

Using randomization, it's possible to simulate and investigate the mechanisms of mutations in DNA and their effect upon the biological activity of their associated proteins. Simulation is a powerful tool for studying systems and predicting what they will do; randomization allows you to better simulate the "ordered chaos" of a biological system. The ability to simulate mutations with computer programs can aid in the study of evolution, disease, and basic cellular processes such as division and DNA repair mechanisms. Computer models of cell development and function, now in their early stages, will become much more accurate and useful in coming years, and mutation is a basic biological mechanism these models will incorporate.

From the standpoint of programming technique, as well as from the standpoint of modeling evolution, mutation, and disease, randomization is a powerful—and, luckily for us, easy-to-use—programming skill.

Here's a breakdown of what we will accomplish in this chapter:

- Randomly select an index into an array and a position in a string: these are the basic tools for picking random locations in DNA (or other data)

- Model mutation with random numbers by learning how to randomly select a nucleotide in DNA and then mutate it to some other (random) nucleotide

- Use random numbers to generate DNA sequence data sets, which can be used to study the extent of randomness in actual genomes

- Repeatedly mutate DNA to study the effect of mutations accumulating over time during evolution

Random Number Generators

A *random number generator* is a subroutine you can call. For most practical purposes, you needn't worry about what's inside it. The values you get for random numbers on the computer differ somewhat from the values of real-world random events as measured, for example, by detecting nuclear decay events. Some computers actually have devices such as geiger counters attached so as to have a source of truly random events. But I'd be willing to bet your computer doesn't. What you have in place of a geiger counter, is an algorithm called a random number generator.

The numbers that are output by random number generators are not really random; they are thus called *pseudo-random numbers*. A random number generator, being an algorithm, is predictable. A random number generator needs a *seed*, an input you can change to get a different series of (pseudo-)random numbers.

The numbers from a random number generator give an even distribution of values. This is one of the most important characteristics of randomness and largely justifies the use of these algorithms where some amount of random behavior is desired.

The other "take-home message" about random number generators is that the seed you start them up with should itself be selected randomly. If you seed with the same number every time, you'll get the same sequence of "random numbers" every time as well. (Not very random!) Try to pick a seed that has some randomness in it, such as a number calculated from some computer event that changes haphazardly over time.*

In the examples that follow, I use a simple method for seed picking that's okay for most purposes. If you use random numbers for data encryption with critical privacy issues (such as patient records), you should read further into the Perl documentation about the several advanced options Perl provides for random number generation. In this book, I use a Perl method that is good enough for most purposes.

---

* Even here, for critical applications, you're not out of the woods. Unless you pick your seeds carefully, hackers will figure out how you're picking them and crack your random numbers and therefore your passwords. The method used to generate seeds in this chapter, time|$$, is crackable by dedicated hackers. A better choice is time() ^ ($$+($$<<15)). If program security is important, you should consult the Perl documentation, and the *Math::Random* and *Math::TrulyRandom* modules from CPAN

A Program Using Randomization

Example 7-1 introduces randomization in the context of a simple program. It randomly combines parts of sentences to construct a story. This isn't a bioinformatics program, but I've found that it's an effective way to learn the basics of randomization. You will learn how to randomly select elements from arrays, which you'll apply in the future examples that mutate DNA.

The example declares a few arrays filled with parts of sentences, then randomizes their assembly into complete sentences. It's a trivial children's game; yet it teaches several programming points.

Example 7-1. Children's game with random numbers

```perl
#!/usr/bin/perl
# Children's game, demonstrating primitive artificial intelligence,
#  using a random number generator to randomly select parts of sentences.

use strict;
use warnings;

# Declare the variables
my $count;
my $input;
my $number;
my $sentence;
my $story;

# Here are the arrays of parts of sentences:
my @nouns = (
'Dad',
'TV',
'Mom',
'Groucho',
'Rebecca',
'Harpo',
'Robin Hood',
'Joe and Moe',
);

my @verbs = (
'ran to',
'giggled with',
'put hot sauce into the orange juice of',
'exploded',
'dissolved',
'sang stupid songs with',
'jumped with',
);

my @prepositions = (
'at the store',
```

Example 7-1. Children's game with random numbers (continued)

```perl
'over the rainbow',
'just for the fun of it',
'at the beach',
'before dinner',
'in New York City',
'in a dream',
'around the world',
);

# Seed the random number generator.
# time|$$ combines the current time with the current process id
# in a somewhat weak attempt to come up with a random seed.
srand(time|$$);

# This do-until loop composes six-sentence "stories".
#   until the user types "quit".
do {
    # (Re)set $story to the empty string each time through the loop
    $story = '';

    # Make 6 sentences per story.
    for ($count = 0; $count < 6; $count++) {

        #   Notes on the following statements:
        #   1) scalar @array gives the number of elements in the array.
        #   2) rand returns a random number greater than 0 and
        #        less than scalar(@array).
        #   3) int removes the fractional part of a number.
        #   4) . joins two strings together.
        $sentence   = $nouns[int(rand(scalar @nouns))]
                    . " "
                    . $verbs[int(rand(scalar @verbs))]
                    . " "
                    . $nouns[int(rand(scalar @nouns))]
                    . " "
                    . $prepositions[int(rand(scalar @prepositions))]
                    . '. ';

        $story .= $sentence;
    }

    # Print the story.
    print "\n",$story,"\n";

    # Get user input.
    print "\nType \"quit\" to quit, or press Enter to continue: ";

    $input = <STDIN>;
```

Example 7-1. Children's game with random numbers (continued)

```
    # Exit loop at user's request
} until($input =~ /^\s*q/i);

exit;
```

Here is some typical output from Example 7-1:

```
Joe and Moe jumped with Rebecca in New York City. Rebecca exploded Groucho
in a dream. Mom ran to Harpo over the rainbow. TV giggled with Joe and Moe
over the rainbow. Harpo exploded Joe and Moe at the beach. Robin Hood giggled
with Harpo at the beach.

Type "quit" to quit, or press Enter to continue:

Harpo put hot sauce into the orange juice of TV before dinner. Dad ran to
Groucho in a dream. Joe and Moe put hot sauce into the orange juice of TV
in New York City. Joe and Moe giggled with Joe and Moe over the rainbow. TV
put hot sauce into the orange juice of Mom just for the fun of it. Robin Hood
ran to Robin Hood at the beach.

Type "quit" to quit, or press Enter to continue: quit
```

The structure of the example is quite simple. After enforcing the declarations of variables, and turning on warnings, with:

```
use strict;
use warnings;
```

the variables are declared, and the arrays are initialized with values.

Seeding the Random Number Generator

Next, the random number generator is seeded by a call to the built-in function srand. It takes one argument, the seed for the random number generator discussed earlier. As mentioned, you have to give a different seed at this step to get a different series of random numbers. Try changing this statement to something like:

```
srand(100);
```

and then run the program more than once. You'll get the same results each time.[*] The seed you're using:

```
time|$$
```

is a calculation that returns a different seed each time.

time returns a number representing the time, $$ returns a number representing the ID of the Perl program that's running (this typically changes each time you run the

---

[*] The latest random number generators automatically change the series, so if this experiment doesn't work, you're probably using a very new random number generator. However, sometimes you want to repeat a series. Note that newer versions of Perl automatically give you a good seed if you call srand like so: srand;.

program), and | means bitwise OR and combines the bits of the two numbers (for details see the Perl documentation). There are other ways to pick a seed, but let's stick with this popular one.

Control Flow

The main loop of the program is a do-until loop. These loops are handy when you want to do something (like print a little story) before taking any actions (like asking the user if he wants to continue) each time through the loop. The do-until loop first executes the statements in the block and then performs a test to determine if it should repeat the statements in the block. Note that this is the reverse of the other types of loops you've seen that do the test first and then the block.

Since the $story variable is always being appended to, it needs to be emptied at the top of each loop. It's common to forget that variables that are increased in some way need to be reset at the correct spot, so watch for that in your programming. The clue is increasingly long strings or big numbers.

The for loop contains the main work of the program. As you've seen before, this loop initializes a counter, performs a test, and then increments the counter at the end of the block.

Making a Sentence

In Example 7-1, note that the statement that makes a sentence stretches out over a few lines of code. It's a bit complicated, and it's the real work of the whole program, so there are comments attached to help read it. Notice that the statement has been carefully formatted so that it's neatly laid out over its eight lines. The variable names have been well chosen, so it's clear that you're making a sentence out of a noun, a verb, a noun, and a prepositional phrase.

However, even with all that, there are rather deeply nested expressions within the square brackets that specify the array positions, and it requires a bit of scrutiny to read this code. You will see that you're building a string out of sentence parts separated by spaces and ending with a period and a space. The string is built by several applications of the dot string concatenation operator. These have been placed at the beginning of each line to clarify the overall structure of the statement.

Randomly Selecting an Element of an Array

Let's look closely at one of the sentence part selectors:

```
$verbs[int(rand(scalar @verbs))]
```

These kinds of nested braces need to be read and evaluated from the inside out. So the expression that's most deeply surrounded by braces is:

```
scalar @verbs
```

You see from the comments before the statement that the built-in function `scalar` returns the number of elements in an array. The array in question, `@verbs`, has seven elements, so this expression returns 7.

So now you have:

```
$verbs[int(rand(7))]
```

and the most deeply nested expression is now:

```
rand(7)
```

The helpful comments in the code before the statement remind you that this statement returns a (pseudo)random number greater than or equal to 0 and less than 7. This number is a *floating-point number* (decimal number with a fraction). Recall that an array with seven elements will number them from 0 to 6.

So now you have something like this:

```
$verbs[int(3.47429)]
```

and you want to evaluate the expression:

```
int(3.47429)
```

The `int` function discards the fractional part of a floating-point number and returns just the integer part, in this case 3.

So you've come to the final step:

```
$verbs[3]
```

which gives you the fourth element of the `@verbs` array, as the comments have been kind enough to remind you.

Formatting

To randomly select a verb, you call a few functions:

`scalar`
Determines the size of the array

`rand`
Picks a random number in the range determined by the size of the array

`int`
Transforms the floating-point number `rand` returns into the integer value you need for an array element

Several of these function calls are combined in one line using nested braces. Sometimes this produces hard-to-read code, and the gentle reader may be nodding his or her head vigorously at this unflattering characterization of the author's painstaking handiwork. You could try rewriting these lines, using additional temporary variables. For instance, you can say:

```
$verb_array_size = scalar @verbs;
$random_floating_point = rand ( $verb_array_size );
$random_integer = int $random_floating_point;
$verb = $verbs[$random_integer];
```

and repeat for the other parts of speech, finally building your sentence with a statement such as:

```
$sentence = "$subject $verb $object $prepositional_phrase. ";
```

It's a matter of style. You will make these kinds of choices all the time as you program. The choice of layout in Example 7-1 was based on a tradeoff between a desire to express the overall task clearly (which won) balanced against the difficulty of reading highly nested function calls (which lost). Another reason for this layout choice is that, in the programs that follow, you'll select random elements in arrays with some regularity, so you'll get used to seeing this particular nesting of calls. In fact, perhaps you should make a little subroutine out of this kind of call if you will do the same thing many times?

Readability is the most important thing here, as it is in most code. You have to be able to read and understand code, your own as well as the code of others, and that is usually more important than trying to achieve other laudable goals such as fastest speed, smallest amount of memory used, or shortest program. It's not always important, but usually it's best to write for readability first, then go back and try to goose up the speed (or whatever) if necessary. You can even leave the more readable code in there as comments, so whoever has to read the code can still get a clear idea of the program and how you went about improving the speed (or whatever).

Another Way to Calculate the Random Position

Perl often has several ways to accomplish a task. the following is an alternate way to write this random number selection; it uses the same function calls but without the parentheses:

```
$verbs[int rand scalar @verbs]
```

This chaining of functions, each of which takes one argument, is common in Perl. To evaluate the expression, Perl first takes @verbs as an argument to scalar, which returns the size of the array. Then it takes that value as an argument to rand, which returns a floating-point number from 0 to less than the size of the array. It then uses that floating-point number as an argument to int, which returns the greatest integer less than the floating-point number. In other words, it calculates the same number to be used as the subscript for the array @verbs.

Why does Perl allow this? Because such calculations are very frequent, and, in the spirit of "Let the computer do the work," Perl designer Larry Wall decided to save you (and himself) the bother of typing and matching all those parentheses.

Having gone that far, Larry decided it'd be easy to add even more. You can eliminate the scalar and the int function calls and use:

```
$verbs[rand @verbs]
```

What's going on here? Since rand already expects a scalar value, it evaluates @verbs in a scalar context, which simply returns the size of the array. Larry cleverly designed array subscripts (which, of course, are always integer values) to automatically take just the integer part of a floating-point value if it was given as a subscript; so, out with the int.

A Program to Simulate DNA Mutation

Example 7-1 gave you the tools you'll need to mutate DNA. In the following examples, you'll represent DNA, as usual, by a string made out of the alphabet A, C, G, and T. You'll randomly select positions in the string and then use the substr function to alter the DNA.

This time, let's go about things a little differently and first compose some of the useful subroutines you'll need before showing the whole program.

Pseudocode Design

Starting with simple pseudocode, here's a design for a subroutine that mutates a random position in DNA to a random nucleotide:

1. Select a random position in the string of DNA.
2. Choose a random nucleotide.
3. Substitute the random nucleotide into the random position in the DNA.

This seems short and to the point. So you decide to make each of the first two sentences into a subroutine.

Select a random position in a string

How can you randomly select a position in a string? Recall that the built-in function length returns the length of a string. Also recall that positions in strings are numbered from 0 to length-1, just like positions in arrays. So you can use the same general idea as in Example 7-1, and make a subroutine:

```
# randomposition
#
# A subroutine to randomly select a position in a string.
#
```

```
# WARNING: make sure you call srand to seed the
#   random number generator before you call this function.

sub randomposition {

    my($string) = @_;

    # This expression returns a random number between 0 and length-1,
    # which is how the positions in a string are numbered in Perl.

    return int(rand(length($string)));
}
```

randomposition is really a short function, if you don't count the comments. It's just like the idea in Example 7-1 to select a random array element.

Of course, if you were really writing this code, you'd make a little test to see if your subroutine worked:

```
#!/usr/bin/perl -w
# Test the randomposition subroutine

my $dna = 'AACCGTTAATGGGCATCGATGCTATGCGAGCT';

srand(time|$$);

for (my $i=0 ; $i < 20 ; ++$i ) {
    print randomposition($dna), " ";
}

print "\n";

exit;

sub randomposition {
    my($string) = @_;
    return int rand length $string;
}
```

Here's some representative output of the test (your results should vary):

```
28 26 20 1 29 7 1 27 2 24 8 1 23 7 13 14 2 12 13 27
```

Notice the new look of the for loop:

```
for (my $i=0 ; $i < 20 ; ++$i ) {
```

This shows how you can localize the counter variables (in this case, $i) to the loop by declaring them with my inside the for loop.

Choose a random nucleotide

Next, let's write a subroutine that randomly chooses one of the four nucleotides:

```
# randomnucleotide
#
# A subroutine to randomly select a nucleotide
#
# WARNING: make sure you call srand to seed the
#  random number generator before you call this function.

sub randomnucleotide {

    my(@nucs) = @_;

    # scalar returns the size of an array.
    # The elements of the array are numbered 0 to size-1
    return $nucs[rand @nucs];
}
```

Again, this subroutine is short and sweet. (Most useful subroutines are; although writing a short subroutine is no guarantee it will be useful. In fact, you'll see in a bit how you can improve this one.)

Let's test this one too:

```
#!/usr/bin/perl -w
# Test the randomnucleotide subroutine

my @nucleotides = ('A', 'C', 'G', 'T');

srand(time|$$);

for (my $i=0 ; $i < 20 ; ++$i ) {
    print randomnucleotide(@nucleotides), " ";
}

print "\n";

exit;

sub randomnucleotide {
    my(@nucs) = @_;

    return $nucs[rand @nucs];
}
```

Here's some typical output (it's random, of course, so there's a high probability your output will differ):

```
C A A A A T T T T A C A C T A A G G G
```

Place a random nucleotide into a random position

Now for the third and final subroutine, that actually does the mutation. Here's the code:

```
# mutate
#
# A subroutine to perform a mutation in a string of DNA
#

sub mutate {

    my($dna) = @_;
    my(@nucleotides) = ('A', 'C', 'G', 'T');

    # Pick a random position in the DNA
    my($position) = randomposition($dna);

    # Pick a random nucleotide
    my($newbase) = randomnucleotide(@nucleotides);

    # Insert the random nucleotide into the random position in the DNA.
    # The substr arguments mean the following:
    #   In the string $dna at position $position change 1 character to
    #   the string in $newbase
    substr($dna,$position,1,$newbase);

    return $dna;
}
```

Here, again, is a short program. As you look it over, notice that it's relatively easy to read and understand. You mutate by picking a random position then selecting a nucleotide at random and substituting that nucleotide at that position in the string. (If you've forgotten how substr works, refer to Appendix B or other Perl documentation. If you're like me, you probably have to do that a lot, especially to get the order of the arguments right.)

There's a slightly different style used here for declaring variables. Whereas you've been declaring them at the beginning of a program, here you're declaring each variable the first time it's used. There are pros and cons for each programming style. Having all the variables at the top of the program gives good organization and can help in reading; declaring them on-the-fly can seem like a more natural way to write. The choice is yours.

Also, notice how this subroutine is mostly built from other subroutines, with a little bit added. That has a lot to do with its readability. At this point, you may be thinking that you've actually decomposed the problem pretty well, and the pieces are fairly easy to build and, in the end, they fit together well. But do they?

Improving the Design

You're about to pat yourself on the back for writing the program so quickly, but you notice something. You keep having to declare that pesky @nucleotides array and then pass it in to the randomnucleotide subroutine. But the only place you use the array is inside the randomnucleotide subroutine. So why not change your design a little? Here's a new try:

```
# randomnucleotide
#
# A subroutine to randomly select a nucleotide
#
# WARNING: make sure you call srand to seed the
#  random number generator before you call this function.

sub randomnucleotide {
    my(@nucs) = ('A', 'C', 'G', 'T');

    # scalar returns the size of an array.
    # The elements of the array are numbered 0 to size-1
    return $nucs[rand @nucs];
}
```

Notice that this function now has no arguments. It's called like so:

```
$randomnucleotide = randomnucleotide( );
```

It's asking for a random element from a very specific set. Of course, you're always thinking, and you say, "It'd be handy to have a subroutine that randomly selects an element from any array. I might not need it right now, but I bet I'll need it soon!" So you define two subroutines instead of one:

```
# randomnucleotide
#
# A subroutine to randomly select a nucleotide
#
# WARNING: make sure you call srand to seed the
#  random number generator before you call this function.

sub randomnucleotide {
    my(@nucleotides) = ('A', 'C', 'G', 'T');

    # scalar returns the size of an array.
    # The elements of the array are numbered 0 to size-1
    return randomelement(@nucleotides);
}

# randomelement
#
# A subroutine to randomly select an element from an array
#
# WARNING: make sure you call srand to seed the
#  random number generator before you call this function.
```

```
    sub randomelement {

        my(@array) = @_;

        return $array[rand @array];
    }
```

Look back and notice that you didn't have to change your subroutine mutate; just the internal workings of randomnucleotide changed, not its behavior.

Combining the Subroutines to Simulate Mutation

Now you've got all your ducks in place, so you write your main program as in Example 7-2 and see if your new subroutine works.

Example 7-2. Mutate DNA

```perl
#!/usr/bin/perl
# Mutate DNA
#   using a random number generator to randomly select bases to mutate

use strict;
use warnings;

# Declare the variables

# The DNA is chosen to make it easy to see mutations:
my $DNA = 'AAAAAAAAAAAAAAAAAAAAAAAAAAAAAAAA';

# $i is a common name for a counter variable, short for "integer"
my $i;

my $mutant;

# Seed the random number generator.
# time|$$ combines the current time with the current process id
srand(time|$$);

# Let's test it, shall we?
$mutant = mutate($DNA);

print "\nMutate DNA\n\n";

print "\nHere is the original DNA:\n\n";
print "$DNA\n";

print "\nHere is the mutant DNA:\n\n";
print "$mutant\n";

# Let's put it in a loop and watch that bad boy accumulate mutations:
print "\nHere are 10 more successive mutations:\n\n";

for ($i=0 ; $i < 10 ; ++$i) {
```

Example 7-2. Mutate DNA (continued)

```perl
    $mutant = mutate($mutant);
    print "$mutant\n";
}

exit;
###############################################################################
# Subroutines for Example 7-2
###############################################################################

#  Notice, now that we have a fair number of subroutines, we
#  list them alphabetically

# A subroutine to perform a mutation in a string of DNA
#
# WARNING: make sure you call srand to seed the
#  random number generator before you call this function.

sub mutate {

    my($dna) = @_;

    my(@nucleotides) = ('A', 'C', 'G', 'T');

    # Pick a random position in the DNA
    my($position) = randomposition($dna);

    # Pick a random nucleotide
    my($newbase) = randomnucleotide(@nucleotides);

    # Insert the random nucleotide into the random position in the DNA
    # The substr arguments mean the following:
    #  In the string $dna at position $position change 1 character to
    #  the string in $newbase
    substr($dna,$position,1,$newbase);

    return $dna;
}

# A subroutine to randomly select an element from an array
#
# WARNING: make sure you call srand to seed the
#  random number generator before you call this function.

sub randomelement {

    my(@array) = @_;

    return $array[rand @array];
}

# randomnucleotide
#
```

Example 7-2. Mutate DNA (continued)

```
# A subroutine to select at random one of the four nucleotides
#
# WARNING: make sure you call srand to seed the
#   random number generator before you call this function.

sub randomnucleotide {

    my(@nucleotides) = ('A', 'C', 'G', 'T');

    # scalar returns the size of an array.
    # The elements of the array are numbered 0 to size-1
    return randomelement(@nucleotides);
}


# randomposition
#
# A subroutine to randomly select a position in a string.
#
# WARNING: make sure you call srand to seed the
#   random number generator before you call this function.

sub randomposition {

    my($string) = @_;

    # Notice the "nested" arguments:
    #
    # $string is the argument to length
    # length($string) is the argument to rand
    # rand(length($string))) is the argument to int
    # int(rand(length($string))) is the argument to return
    # But we write it without parentheses, as permitted.
    #
    # rand returns a decimal number between 0 and its argument.
    # int returns the integer portion of a decimal number.
    #
    # The whole expression returns a random number between 0 and length-1,
    #   which is how the positions in a string are numbered in Perl.
    #

    return int rand length $string;
}
```

Here's some typical output from Example 7-2:

```
Mutate DNA

Here is the original DNA:

AAAAAAAAAAAAAAAAAAAAAAAAAAAAAA
```

```
Here is the mutant DNA:

AAAAAAAAAAAAAAAAAAAAAGAAAAAAAA

Here are 10 more successive mutations:

AAAAAAAAAAAAAAAAAAAAAGACAAAAAA
AAAAAAAAAAAAAAAAAAAAAGACAAAAAA
AAAAAAAAAAAAAAAAAAAAAGACAAAAAA
AAAAAAAAAAAAAACAAAAAGACAAAAAA
AAAAAAAAAAAAAACAACAAGACAAAAAA
AAAAAAAAAAAAAACAACAAGACAAAAAA
AAAAAAAAAGAAAACAACAAGACAAAAAA
AAAAAATAAGAAAACAACAAGACAAAAAA
AAAAAATAAGAAAACAACAAGACAAAAAA
AAAAAATTAGAAAACAACAAGACAAAAAA
```

Example 7-2 was something of a programming challenge, but you end up with the satisfaction of seeing your (simulated) DNA mutate. How about writing a graphical display for this, so that every time a base gets mutated, it makes a little explosion and the color gets highlighted, so you can watch it happening in real-time?

Before you scoff, you should know how important good graphical displays are for the success of most programs. This may be a trivial-sounding graphic, but if you can demonstrate the most common mutations in, for instance, the BRCA breast cancer genes in this way, it might be useful.

A Bug in Your Program?

To return to the business at hand, you may have noticed something when you looked over the output from Example 7-2. Look at the first two lines of the "10 more successive mutations." They are exactly the same! Could it be that after patting yourself on the back and telling yourself what a good bit of work you'd done, you've discovered a bug?

How can you track it down? You may want to step through the running of the program with the Perl debugger, which you saw in Chapter 6. However, this time, you stop and think about your design instead. You're replacing the bases at random positions with randomly chosen bases. Aha! Sometimes the base at the position you randomly choose is exactly the same as the base you randomly choose to plug into its place! You're replacing a base with itself on occasion![*]

Let's say you decide that behavior is not useful. At each successive mutation, you need to see one base change. How can you alter your code to ensure that? Let's start with some pseudocode for the mutate subroutine:

---

[*] How often? In DNA that's all one base, it's happening 1/4 of the time. In DNA that's equally populated with the four bases, it's happening...1/4 of the time!

```
Select a random position in the string of DNA

Repeat:

    Choose a random nucleotide

Until: random nucleotide differs from the nucleotide in the random position

Substitute the random nucleotide into the random position in the DNA
```

This seems like something that should work, so you alter the mutate subroutine, calling it the mutate_better subroutine:

```perl
# mutate_better
#
# Subroutine to perform a mutation in a string of DNA—version 2, in which
#  it is guaranteed that one base will change on each call
#
# WARNING: make sure you call srand to seed the
#  random number generator before you call this function.

sub mutate_better {

    my($dna) = @_;
    my(@nucleotides) = ('A', 'C', 'G', 'T');

    # Pick a random position in the DNA
    my($position) = randomposition($dna);

    # Pick a random nucleotide
    my($newbase);

    do {
        $newbase = randomnucleotide(@nucleotides);

    # Make sure it's different than the nucleotide we're mutating
    }until ( $newbase ne substr($dna, $position,1) );

    # Insert the random nucleotide into the random position in the DNA
    # The substr arguments mean the following:
    #  In the string $dna at position $position change 1 character to
    #  the string in $newbase
    substr($dna,$position,1,$newbase);

    return $dna;
}
```

When you plug this subroutine in place of mutate and run the code, you get the following output:

```
Mutate DNA
```

```
Here is the original DNA:

AAAAAAAAAAAAAAAAAAAAAAAAAAAAAAAA

Here is the mutant DNA:

AAAAAAAAAAAAATAAAAAAAAAAAAAAAAAA

Here are 10 more successive mutations:

AAAAAAAAAAAAATAAAAAAAACAAAAAAA
AAAAATAAAAAAATAAAAAAAACAAAAAAA
AAATATAAAAAAATAAAAAAAACAAAAAAA
AAATATAAAAAAATAAAAAAAACAACAAAA
AATTATAAAAAAATAAAAAAAACAACAAAA
AATTATTAAAAAATAAAAAAAACAACAAAA
AATTATTAAAAAATAAAAAAAACAACACAA
AATTATTAAAAAGTAAAAAAAACAACACAA
AATTATTAAAAAGTGAAAAAACAACACAA
AATTATTAAAAAGTGATAAAAACAACACAA
```

which seems to indeed make a real change on every iteration.

Notice one more thing about declaring variables. In this code for `mutate_better`, if you'd declared `$newbase` within the loop, since the loop is enclosed in a block, the variable `$newbase` would not then be visible outside of that loop. In particular, it wouldn't be available in the `substr` call that does the actual base change for the mutation. So, in `mutate_better`, you had to declare the variable outside of the loop.

This is a frequent source of confusion for programmers who like to declare variables on the fly and a powerful argument for getting into the habit of collecting variable definitions together at the top of the program.

Even so, there are often times when you want to hide a variable within a block, because that's the only place where you will use it. Then you may want to do the declaration in the block. (Perhaps at the top of the block, if it's a long one?)

Generating Random DNA

It's often useful to generate random data for test purposes. Random DNA can also be used to study the organization of actual DNA from an organism. In this section, we'll write some programs to generate random DNA sequences.

Such random DNA sequences have proved useful in several ways. For instance, the popular BLAST program (see Chapter 12) depends on the properties of random DNA for the analytic and empirical results that underpin the sequence similarity scores, statistics that are used to rank the "hits" that BLAST returns to the user.

Let's assume what's needed is a set of random DNA fragments of varying length. Your program will have to specify a maximum and a minimum length, as well as how many fragments to generate.

Bottom-up Versus Top-down

In Example 7-2, you wrote the basic subroutines, then a subroutine that called the basic subroutines, and finally the main program. If you ignore the pseudocode, this is an example of *bottom-up design*; start with the building blocks, then assemble them into a larger structure.

Now let's see what it's like to start with the main program, with its subroutine calls, and write the subroutines after you find a need for them. This is called *top-down design*.

Subroutines for Generating a Set of Random DNA

Given our goal of generating random DNA, perhaps what you want is a data-generating subroutine:

```
@random_DNA = make_random_DNA_set( $minimum_length, $maximum_length, $size_of_set );
```

This looks okay, but of course, it begs the question of how to actually accomplish the overall task. (That's top-down design for you!) So you need to move down and write pseudocode for the make_random_DNA_set subroutine:

```
repeat $size_of_set times:

    $length = random number between minimum and maximum length

    $dna = make_random_DNA ( $length );

    add $dna to @set
}

return @set
```

Now, continuing the top-down design, you need some pseudocode for the make_random_DNA subroutine:

```
from 1 to $size

    $base = randomnucleotide

    $dna .= $base
}

return $dna
```

Don't go any further: you've already got a *randomnucleotide* subroutine from Example 7-2.

(Are you bothered by the absence of balanced curly braces in the pseudocode? Here, you're relying on indentation and lining up the right braces to indicate the blocks. Since it's pseudocode, anything is allowed as long as it works.)

Turning the Design into Code

Now that we've got a top-down design, how to proceed with the coding? Let's follow the top-down design, just to see how it works.

Example 7-3 starts with the main program and proceeds, following the order of the top-down design you did in pseudocode, then followed by the subroutines.

Example 7-3. Generate random DNA

```perl
#!/usr/bin/perl
# Generate random DNA
#   using a random number generator to randomly select bases

use strict;
use warnings;

# Declare and initialize the variables
my $size_of_set = 12;
my $maximum_length = 30;
my $minimum_length = 15;

# An array, initialized to the empty list, to store the DNA in
my @random_DNA = ( );

# Seed the random number generator.
# time|$$ combines the current time with the current process id
srand(time|$$);

# And here's the subroutine call to do the real work
@random_DNA = make_random_DNA_set( $minimum_length, $maximum_length, $size_of_set );

# Print the results, one per line
print "Here is an array of $size_of_set randomly generated DNA sequences\n";
print "  with lengths between $minimum_length and $maximum_length:\n\n";

foreach my $dna (@random_DNA) {

    print "$dna\n";
}

print "\n";

exit;

##############################################################################
# Subroutines
##############################################################################
```

Example 7-3. Generate random DNA (continued)

```perl
# make_random_DNA_set
#
# Make a set of random DNA
#
#   Accept parameters setting the maximum and minimum length of
#      each string of DNA, and the number of DNA strings to make
#
# WARNING: make sure you call srand to seed the
#   random number generator before you call this function.

sub make_random_DNA_set {

    # Collect arguments, declare variables
    my($minimum_length, $maximum_length, $size_of_set) = @_;

    # length of each DNA fragment
    my $length;

    # DNA fragment
    my $dna;

    # set of DNA fragments
    my @set;

    # Create set of random DNA
    for (my $i = 0; $i < $size_of_set ; ++$i) {

        # find a random length between min and max
        $length = randomlength ($minimum_length, $maximum_length);

        # make a random DNA fragment
        $dna = make_random_DNA ( $length );

        # add $dna fragment to @set
        push( @set, $dna );
    }

    return @set;
}

# Notice that we've just discovered a new subroutine that's
# needed: randomlength, which will return a random
# number between (or including) the min and max values.
# Let's write that first, then do make_random_DNA

# randomlength
#
# A subroutine that will pick a random number from
# $minlength to $maxlength, inclusive.
#
# WARNING: make sure you call srand to seed the
#   random number generator before you call this function.
```

Example 7-3. Generate random DNA (continued)

```perl
sub randomlength {

    # Collect arguments, declare variables
    my($minlength, $maxlength) = @_;

    # Calculate and return a random number within the
    #  desired interval.
    # Notice how we need to add one to make the endpoints inclusive,
    #  and how we first subtract, then add back, $minlength to
    #  get the random number in the correct interval.
    return ( int(rand($maxlength - $minlength + 1)) + $minlength );
}

# make_random_DNA
#
# Make a string of random DNA of specified length.
#
# WARNING: make sure you call srand to seed the
#  random number generator before you call this function.

sub make_random_DNA {

    # Collect arguments, declare variables
    my($length) = @_;

    my $dna;

    for (my $i=0 ; $i < $length ; ++$i) {

        $dna .= randomnucleotide( );
    }

    return $dna;
}

# We also need to include the previous subroutine
# randomnucleotide.
# Here it is again for completeness.

# randomnucleotide
#
# Select at random one of the four nucleotides
#
# WARNING: make sure you call srand to seed the
#  random number generator before you call this function.

sub randomnucleotide {

    my(@nucleotides) = ('A', 'C', 'G', 'T');

    # scalar returns the size of an array.
    # The elements of the array are numbered 0 to size-1
```

Example 7-3. Generate random DNA (continued)

```
    return randomelement(@nucleotides);
}

# randomelement
#
# randomly select an element from an array
#
# WARNING: make sure you call srand to seed the
#   random number generator before you call this function.

sub randomelement {

    my(@array) = @_;

    return $array[rand @array];
}
```

Here's the output from Example 7-3:

```
Here is an array of 12 randomly generated DNA sequences
   with lengths between 15 and 30:

TACGCTTGTGTTTTCGGGGGAC
GGGGTGTGGTAAGGCTGTCTCAGATGTGC
TGAACGACAACCTCCTGGACTTTACT
ATCTATGCTTTGCCATGCTAGT
CCGCTCATTCCTCTTCCTCGGC
TGTACCCCTAATACACTTTAGCCGAATTTA
ATAGGTCGGGGCGACAGCGCCGG
GATTGACCTCTGTAA
AAAATCTCTAGGATCGAGC
GTATGTGCTTGGGTAAAT
ATGGAGTTGCGAGGAAGTAGCTGAGT
GGCCCATGACCAGCATCCAGACAGCA
```

Analyzing DNA

In this final example dealing with randomization, you'll collect some statistics on DNA in order to answer the question: on average, what percentage of bases are the same between two random DNA sequences? Although some simple mathematics can answer the question for you, the point of the program is to show that you now have the necessary programming ability to ask and answer questions about your DNA sequences. (If you were using real DNA, say a collection of some particular gene as it appears in several organisms in slightly different forms, the answer would be somewhat more interesting. You may want to try that later.)

So let's generate a set of random DNA, all the same length, then ask the following question about the set. What's the average percentage of positions that are the same between pairs of DNA sequences in this set?

As usual, let's try to sketch an idea of the program in pseudocode:

```
Generate a set of random DNA sequences, all the same length

For each pair of DNA sequences

    How many positions in the two sequences are identical as a fraction?

}

Report the mean of the preceding calculations as a percentage
```

Clearly, to write this code, you can reuse at least some of the work you've already done. You certainly know how to generate a set of random DNA sequences. Also, although you don't have a subroutine that compares, position by position, the bases in two sequences, you know how to look at the positions in DNA strings. So that subroutine shouldn't be hard to write. In fact, let's write some pseudocode that compares each nucleotide in one sequence with the nucleotide in the same position in another sequence:

```
assuming DNA1 is the same length as DNA2,

for each position from 1 to length(DNA)

    if the character at that position is the same in DNA_1 and DNA_2

        ++$count
    }
}

return count/length
```

The whole problem now seems eminently do-able. You also have to write the code that picks each pair of sequences, collects the results, and finally takes the mean of the results and report it as a percentage. That can all go into the main program. Example 7-4 gives it a try, all in one shot.

Example 7-4. Calculate average % identity between pairs of random DNA sequences

```
#!/usr/bin/perl
# Calculate the average percentage of positions that are the same
# between two random DNA sequences, in a set of 10 sequences.

use strict;
use warnings;

# Declare and initialize the variables
my $percent;
my @percentages;
my $result;

# An array, initialized to the empty list, to store the DNA in
my @random_DNA = ( );
```

Example 7-4. Calculate average % identity between pairs of random DNA sequences (continued)

```perl
# Seed the random number generator.
# time|$$ combines the current time with the current process id
srand(time|$$);

#  Generate the data set of 10 DNA sequences.
@random_DNA = make_random_DNA_set( 10, 10, 10 );

# Iterate through all pairs of sequences
for (my $k = 0 ; $k < scalar @random_DNA - 1 ; ++$k) {
    for (my $i = ($k + 1) ; $i < scalar @random_DNA ; ++$i) {

        # Calculate and save the matching percentage
        $percent = matching_percentage($random_DNA[$k], $random_DNA[$i]);
        push(@percentages, $percent);
    }
}

# Finally, the average result:
$result = 0;

foreach $percent (@percentages) {
  $result += $percent;
}

$result = $result / scalar(@percentages);
#Turn result into a true percentage
$result = int ($result * 100);

print "In this run of the experiment, the average percentage of \n";
print "matching positions is $result%\n\n";

exit;

############################################################################
# Subroutines
############################################################################

# matching_percentage
#
# Subroutine to calculate the percentage of identical bases in two
# equal length DNA sequences

sub matching_percentage {

    my($string1, $string2) = @_;

    # we assume that the strings have the same length
    my($length) = length($string1);
    my($position);
    my($count) = 0;

    for ($position=0; $position < $length ; ++$position) {
```

Example 7-4. Calculate average % identity between pairs of random DNA sequences (continued)

```
        if(substr($string1,$position,1) eq substr($string2,$position,1)) {
            ++$count;
        }
    }

    return $count / $length;
}


# make_random_DNA_set
#
# Subroutine to make a set of random DNA
#
#   Accept parameters setting the maximum and minimum length of
#      each string of DNA, and the number of DNA strings to make
#
# WARNING: make sure you call srand to seed the
#   random number generator before you call this function.

sub make_random_DNA_set {

    # Collect arguments, declare variables
    my($minimum_length, $maximum_length, $size_of_set) = @_;

    # length of each DNA fragment
    my $length;

    # DNA fragment
    my $dna;

    # set of DNA fragments
    my @set;

    # Create set of random DNA
    for (my $i = 0; $i < $size_of_set ; ++$i) {

        # find a random length between min and max
        $length = randomlength ($minimum_length, $maximum_length);

        # make a random DNA fragment
        $dna = make_random_DNA ( $length );

        # add $dna fragment to @set
        push( @set, $dna );
    }

    return @set;
}

# randomlength
#
# A subroutine that will pick a random number from
# $minlength to $maxlength, inclusive.
#
```

Example 7-4. Calculate average % identity between pairs of random DNA sequences (continued)

```perl
# WARNING: make sure you call srand to seed the
#   random number generator before you call this function.

sub randomlength {

    # Collect arguments, declare variables
    my($minlength, $maxlength) = @_;

    # Calculate and return a random number within the
    #   desired interval.
    # Notice how we need to add one to make the endpoints inclusive,
    #   and how we first subtract, then add back, $minlength to
    #   get the random number in the correct interval.
    return ( int(rand($maxlength - $minlength + 1)) + $minlength );
}

# make_random_DNA
#
# Make a string of random DNA of specified length.
#
# WARNING: make sure you call srand to seed the
#   random number generator before you call this function.

sub make_random_DNA {

    # Collect arguments, declare variables
    my($length) = @_;

    my $dna;

    for (my $i=0 ; $i < $length ; ++$i) {
        $dna .= randomnucleotide();
    }

    return $dna;
}

# randomnucleotide
#
# Select at random one of the four nucleotides
#
# WARNING: make sure you call srand to seed the
#   random number generator before you call this function.

sub randomnucleotide {

    my(@nucleotides) = ('A', 'C', 'G', 'T');

    # scalar returns the size of an array.
    # The elements of the array are numbered 0 to size-1
    return randomelement(@nucleotides);
}
```

Example 7-4. Calculate average % identity between pairs of random DNA sequences (continued)

```
# randomelement
#
# randomly select an element from an array
#
# WARNING: make sure you call srand to seed the
#   random number generator before you call this function.

sub randomelement {

    my(@array) = @_;

    return $array[rand @array];
}
```

If the code in Example 7-4 seems somewhat repetitive of code from previous examples, it is. In the interest of presentation, I included the subroutine code in the program. (You'll start using modules in Chapter 8 as a way to avoid this repetition.)

Here's the output of Example 7-4:

```
In this run of the experiment, the average number of
matching positions is 0.24%
```

Well, that seems reasonable. You might say, it's obvious: a quarter of the positions match, and there are four bases. But the point isn't to verify elementary probability, it's to show you have enough programming under your belt to write some programs that ask and answer questions about DNA sequences.

Some Notes About the Code

Notice in the main program that when it calls:

```
@random_DNA = make_random_DNA_set( 10, 10, 10 );
```

you don't need to declare and initialize variables such as `$minimum_length`. You can just fill in the actual numbers when you call the subroutine. (However it's often a good idea to put such things in variables declared at the top of the program, where it's easy to find and change them.) Here, you set the maximum and minimum lengths to 10 and ask for 10 sequences.

Let's restate the problem we just solved. You have to compare all pairs of DNA, and for each pair, calculate the percentage of positions that have the same nucleotides. Then, you have to take the mean of these percentages.

Here's the code that accomplishes this in the main program of Example 7-4:

```
# Iterate through all pairs of sequences
for (my $k = 0 ; $k < scalar @random_DNA - 1 ; ++$k) {
    for (my $i = ($k + 1) ; $i < scalar @random_DNA ; ++$i) {
```

```
        # Calculate and save the matching percentage
        $percent = matching_percentage($random_DNA[$k], $random_DNA[$i]);
        push(@percentages, $percent);
    }
}
```

To look at each pair, you use a nested loop. A *nested loop* is simply a loop within another loop. These are fairly common in programming but must be handled with care. They may seem a little complex; take some time to see how the nested loop works, because it's common to have to select all combinations of two (or more) elements from a set.

The nested loop involves looking at (n * (n-1)) / 2 pairs of sequences, which is a square function of the size of the data set. This can get very big! Try gradually increasing the size of the data set and rerunning the program, and you'll see your compute time increase, and more than gradually.

See how the looping works? First sequence 0 (indexed by $K) is paired with sequences 1,2,3,...,9, in turn (indexed by $i). Then sequence 1 is paired with 2,3,... ,9, etc. Finally, 8 is paired with 9. (Recall that array elements are numbered starting at 0, so the last element of an array with 10 elements is numbered 9. Also recall that scalar @random_DNA returns the number of elements in the array.)

You might find it a worthwhile exercise to let the number of sequences be some small value, say 3 or 4, and think through (paper and pencil in hand) how the nested loops and the variables $k and $i evolve during the running of the program. Or you can use the Perl debugger to watch how it happens.

Exercises

Exercise 7.1

Write a program that asks you to pick an amino acid and then keeps (randomly) guessing which amino acid you picked.

Exercise 7.2

Write a program that picks one of the four nucleotides and then keeps prompting until you correctly guess the nucleotide it picked.

Exercise 7.3

Write a subroutine to randomly shuffle the elements of an array. The subroutine should take an array as an argument and return an array with the same elements but shuffled in a random order. Each element of the original array should appear exactly once in the output array, just like shuffling a deck of cards.

Exercise 7.4

Write a program to mutate protein sequence, similar to the code in Example 7-2 that mutates DNA.

Exercise 7.5

Write a subroutine that, given a *codon* (a fragment of DNA of length 3), returns a random mutation in the codon.

Exercise 7.6

Some versions of Perl automatically seed the random number generator, making it superfluous to call srand for that purpose before using rand to generate random numbers. Experiment to see if your implementation of rand calls srand automatically, or if you have to explicitly call srand yourself, as you have seen done in the code in this chapter.

Exercise 7.7

Sometimes not all choices are will be picked in a random selection. Write a subroutine that randomly returns a nucleotide, in which the probability of each nucleotide can be specified. Pass the subroutine four numbers as arguments, representing the probabilities of each nucleotide; if each probability is 0.25, the subroutine is equally likely to pick each nucleotide. As error checking, have the subroutine ensure that the sum of the four probabilities is 1.

Hint: one way to accomplish this is to divide the range between 0 and 1 into four intervals with lengths corresponding to the probability of the respective nucleotides. Then, simply pick a random number between 0 and 1, see in which interval it falls, and return the corresponding nucleotide.

Exercise 7.8

This is a more difficult exercise. The study function in Perl may speed up searches for motifs in DNA or protein. Read the Perl documentation on this function. Its use is simple: given some sequence data in a variable $sequence, type:

```
study $sequence;
```

before doing the searches. Do you think study will speed up searches in DNA or protein, based on what you've read about it in the documentation?

For lots of extra credit! Now read the Perl documentation on the standard module Benchmark. (Type perldoc Benchmark, or visit the Perl home page at *http://www.perl.com.*) See if your guess is right by writing a program that benchmarks motif searches of DNA and of protein, with and without study.

## CHAPTER 8

The Genetic Code

Up to this point we've used Perl to search for motifs, simulate DNA mutations, generate random sequences, and transcribe DNA to RNA. These are all important activities, and they serve as a good introduction to the computational techniques you can use to study biological systems.

In this chapter, we'll write Perl programs to simulate how the genetic code directs the translation of DNA into protein. I will start by introducing the hash datatype. Then, after a brief discussion of how different data structures (like hashes and arrays) and database systems can store and access experimental information, we will write a program to translate DNA to protein. We'll also continue exploring regular expressions and write code to handle FASTA files.

Hashes

There are three main datatypes in Perl. You've already seen two: scalar variables and arrays. Now we'll start to use the third: *hashes* (also called associative arrays).

A hash provides very fast lookup of the value associated with a key. As an example, say you have a hash called %english_dictionary. (Yes, hashes start with the percent sign.) If you want to look up the definition of the word "recreant," you say:

```
$definition = $english_dictionary{'recreant'};
```

The scalar 'recreant' is the key, and the scalar definition that's returned is the value. As you see from this example, hashes (like arrays) change their leading character to a dollar sign when you access a single element, because the value returned from a hash lookup is a scalar value. You can tell a hash lookup from an array element by the type of braces they use: arrays use square brackets []; hashes use curly braces {}.

If you want to assign a value to a key, it's similarly an easy, single statement:

```
$english_dictionary{'recreant'} = "One who calls out in surrender.";
```

Also, if you want to initialize a hash with some key-value pairs, it's done much like initializing arrays, but every pair becomes a key-value:

```
%classification = (
    'dog',      'mammal',
    'robin',    'bird',
    'asp',      'reptile',
);
```

which initializes the key 'dog' with the value 'mammal', and so on. There's another way of writing this, which shows what's happening a little more clearly. The following does exactly the same thing as the preceding code, while showing the key-value relationship more clearly:

```
%classification = (
    'dog'   => 'mammal',
    'robin' => 'bird',
    'asp',  => 'reptile',
);
```

You can get an array of all the keys of a hash:

```
@keys  = keys %my_hash;
```

You can get an array of all the values of a hash:

```
@values  = values %my_hash;
```

You use hashes in lots of different situations, especially when your data is in the form of key-value or you need to look up the value of a key fast. For instance, later in this chapter, we'll develop programs that use hashes to retrieve information about a gene. The gene name is the key; the information about the gene is the value of that key. Mathematically, a Perl hash always represents a finite function.

The name "hash" comes from something called a hash function, which practically any book on algorithms will define, if you've a mind to look it up. Let's skip the details of how they work under the hood and just talk about their behavior.

Data Structures and Algorithms for Biology

Biologists explore biological data and try to figure out how to do things with it based on its existing structure in living systems. Bioinformatics is often used to model that existing structure as closely as possible. (Bear with me; I'm speaking in generalities!)

Bioinformatics also can take a slightly different approach. It thinks about what it wants to do with the data and then tries to figure out how to organize it to accomplish that goal. In other words, it tries to produce an algorithm by representing the data in a convenient data structure.

Now that you've got the three datatypes of Perl in hand—namely scalars, arrays, and hashes—it's time to take a look at these interrelated topics of algorithms and data structures. We've already talked about algorithms in Chapter 3. The present discussion highlights the importance of the organization of the data for algorithms, in other words, the data structures for the algorithm.

The most important point here is that different algorithms often require different data structures.

A Gene Expression Database

Let's consider a typical problem. Say you're studying an organism that has a total of about 30,000 genes. (Yep, you're right, it's human.) Say you're looking at a type of cell that's never been well characterized under certain interesting environmental conditions, and you are determining, for each gene, whether it's being expressed.* You have a nice microarray facility that has given you the expression information for that cell. Now, for each gene, you need to look up whether it's expressed in the cell. You have to put this look-up capability on your web site, so visitors who read your results in your upcoming paper can find the expression data for the genes.

There are several ways to proceed. Let's look at a few alternatives as a short and gentle introduction to the art and science of algorithms and data structures.

What is your data? For simplicity, let's say you have the names for all the genes in the organism and a number for the expressed genes indicating the level of the expression in your experiment; the unexpressed genes have the number 0.

Gene Expression Data Using Unsorted Arrays

Now let's suppose you want to know if the genes were expressed, but not the expression levels, and you want to solve this programming problem using arrays. After all, you are somewhat familiar with arrays by this point. How do you proceed?

You might store in the array only the names of the genes that are being expressed and discard the other gene names. Say there were 8,000 expressed genes. Then, for any query, the answer requires looking through the array and comparing the query with each gene in the array until either you find it or get to the end of the array without finding it.

That works, but there are problems. Mainly, it's kind of slow. This isn't bad if you just do it now and then, but if you've got a lot of people hitting your web site asking questions about this new expression data, it can be a problem. On average, a lookup for an expressed gene requires looking through 4,000 gene names. A lookup for an unexpressed gene takes 8,000 comparisons.

---

* For the nonbiologists: a gene is expressed when it is transcribed into RNA, so that a protein can be made from it.

Also, if someone asked about a gene missing from your study, you couldn't respond, since you discarded the unexpressed gene names. The query gives a negative response, not an error message saying the gene being searched for isn't part of your experiment. This might even be a false negative if the query gene that wasn't part of your study actually is expressed in the cell type (but you just missed it). You'd prefer it if your program would report to the user that no gene by that name was studied.

So you decide to keep all 30,000 genes in the array. (Of course, now a search will be slower.) But how to distinguish the expressed from the unexpressed genes? You can load each gene's name into the array and then append the expression measurement after the name of each gene. Then you will definitely know if a gene is missing from your experiment.

However, the program is still a bit slow. You still have to search through the entire array until you find the gene or determine that it wasn't studied. You may find it right away if it's the first element in the array, or you may have to wait until the last element. On average, you have to search through half of the array. Plus, you have to compare the name of the searched-for gene with the names of the genes in the array one by one. It will average 15,000 comparisons per query: slow. (Actually, on a modern computer, not too horribly slow, really, but I'm making a point. These sorts of things do add up with a program that runs too slowly.)

Another problem is that you're now keeping two values in one scalar: the gene name and the expression measurement. To do anything with this data, you have to also separate the gene name from the measurement of the expression of the gene.

Despite these drawbacks, this method will work. Now, let's think about alternatives.

Gene Expression Data Using Sorted Arrays and Binary Search

You might try storing all the gene names in alphabetical order in the array and then use the following search technique. First, look at the middle element. (You can tell the size of the array, as we've seen, with the expression scalar @array). If your gene name is before that middle element alphabetically, you ignore the second half of the array and pick the middle element of the remaining half of the array. You continue, at each step narrowing the search to half the previous number of elements, until you find a match or discover there is none. Here it is in pseudocode:

```
Given a sorted array, and an element:

Until you find the element or discover it's not there,

    Pick the midpoint of the array, $array[scalar(@array)/2]

    Compare your element with the element at the midpoint
```

```
    If that matches your element, you're done.

    Else, ignore the half of the array that your element is not in
}
```

To compare two strings alphabetically in Perl, you use the cmp operator, which returns 0 if the two strings are the same, -1 if they are in alphabetical order, and 1 if they are in reverse alphabetical order. For example, the following returns 0:

```
'ZZZ' cmp 'ZZZ';
```

This returns -1:

```
'AAA' cmp 'ZZZ';
```

Finally, this returns 1:

```
'ZZZ' cmp 'AAA';
```

This algorithm is called a *binary search*, and it considerably speeds up the process of searching in an array, for example, to search 30,000 genes takes only about 15 times through the loop, maximum. (As compared to 15,000 comparisons, average, for the unsorted array.) Of course, you also have to sort the list, which might take awhile. If you need to keep adding elements, you have to either insert them in the right place or add them to the end and sort the array again. All that inserting or sorting might slow things down considerably. But if you're just sorting it once and then doing lots of lookups, a binary search might be worth doing.

While we're at it, let's look at how to sort an array. Here's how to sort an array of strings alphabetically:

```
@array = sort @array;
```

Here's how to sort an array of numbers in ascending order:

```
@array = sort { $a <=> $b } @array;
```

Many other kinds of sorting can be done, but these are the most common. For more details, see the Perl documentation for the sort function.

Gene Expression Data Using Hashes

You can also use hashes to find a gene in your data. To do so, you can load the hash so that the keys are the gene names and the values are the expression measurement. Then a single call on the hash, with the name of the desired gene as a key, returns the results of the experiment for that gene, and you've got your answer. This process is also cleaner than storing the gene name and the expression result in one scalar string; here the key is a scalar, and the value is a separate scalar.

Furthermore, due to how hashes are made, you get an answer back very quickly, because decent hashes don't have to search hard to find the value of a key. Using hashes is typically faster than binary searches. Plus, you'd know if the gene being searched for was in the data, because you can explicitly ask if a hash value is defined by saying something like:

```
if( defined $myhash{'mykey'} ) { ... }
```

Also, you'll get an error message if you have warnings turned on, and you refer to an undefined value.

Another advantage of hashes over binary searching is that you can add or subtract elements to hashes without resorting the entire array.

Finally, because hashes are built into Perl as a basic datatype, they are easy to use, and you won't have to do much programming to accomplish your goal. It is usually the case that it's more important to save time writing a program then it is to save time running it. I mention this in Chapter 3, but it's worth emphasizing. To a programmer, the lazy way is often the most efficient way: let the machine do the work!

Don't get the idea that hashes are always the right way to go, however. For instance, they don't store their elements in a sorted order, so if you need to look at the data that way, you have to explicitly sort it, like so:

```
@sorted_keys = sort keys %my_hash;
```

This is do-able, but it can be a bit slow on a large array. (You could also sort the values, of course.)

To conclude the discussion of data structures for our expression data example, here's an informal survey of the properties of some different data structures in Perl for searching, adding and deleting, and maintaining sorted order in a set of gene names:

- Use a hash if you just need to see if something is in a set and don't need to list the set in order.

- A sorted array combined with a binary search algorithm will do if you need an ordered set and pretty fast lookup and don't need to add or subtract elements very often.

- An array, in conjunction with the Perl functions push and pop, works well if you don't need to sort the elements but do need to quickly get at the most recently added element.

- A Perl array with the functions push and shift will serve if you don't need the elements sorted but need to add elements. It's especially useful to always remove the "oldest" element (the element that has been in the array the longest).

For more information, see Appendix A and especially *Mastering Algorithms with Perl* (published by O'Reilly).

Relational Databases

Databases are programs that store and retrieve large amounts of data. They provide the most common forms of datatypes to use in algorithms. There are several popular databases. Some good ones that are free of charge (the best ones are very expensive), and Perl provides access to all the most popular ones. The Perl/DBI modules, for instance, provide convenient access to relational databases from Perl programs.

Most databases are called *relational*, which describes how they store data. Another common name for these types of databases is *relational database management systems*, or RDMS.

Relational databases store data organized in tables. The data is usually entered and extracted with a query language called *Structured Query Language*, or SQL, which is a fairly simple language for accessing the data in the tables and following links between the tables.

Relational databases are the most popular way to store and retrieve large amounts of data, but they do require a fair bit of learning. Programming with relational databases is beyond the scope of this book, but if you end up doing a lot of programming with Perl, you'll find that knowing the basics of using a database is a valuable skill. See the discussion in Chapter 13.

In particular, it's perfectly reasonable to store your gene expression data in a relational database and use that in your program to respond to queries made on your web site.

DBM

Perl has a simple, built-in way to store hash data, called *database management* (DBM). It's simple to use: after starting up, it "ties" a hash to a file on your computer disk, so you can save a hash to reuse at a later date. This is, in effect, a simple (and very useful) database. Apart from the initialization, you use it as you would any other hash. You can store your genes and expression data in a DBM file and then use it as a hash. There's more on DBM in Chapter 10

The Genetic Code

The genetic code is how a cell translates the information contained in its DNA into amino acids and then proteins, which do the real work in the cell.

Background

Herein is a short introduction for the nonbiologists.

As stated earlier, DNA encodes the primary structure (i.e., the amino acid sequence) of proteins. DNA has four nucleotides, and proteins have 20 amino acids. The encoding works by taking each group of three nucleotides from the DNA and "translating" them to an amino acid or a stop signal. Each group of three nucleotides is called a *codon*. We'll see in detail how this coding and translation works.

Actually, *transcription* first uses DNA to make RNA, and then *translation* uses RNA to make proteins. This is called the *central dogma* of molecular biology. But in this course, I'll abbreviate the process and somewhat inaccurately call the entire process from DNA to protein "translation."

The reason for this cavalier distinction is that the whole business is much easier to simulate on computer using strings to represent the DNA, RNA, and proteins. In fact, as shown in Chapter 4, transcribing DNA to RNA is very easy indeed. In your computer simulations, you can simply skip that step, since it's just a matter of changing one letter to another. (The actual process in the cell, of course, is much more complex.)

Note that with four kinds of bases, each group of three bases of DNA can represent as many as $4 \times 4 \times 4 = 64$ possible amino acids. Since there are only 20 amino acids plus a stop signal, the genetic code has evolved some redundancy, so that some amino acids are represented by more than one codon. Every possible three bases of DNA—each codon—represents some amino acid (apart from the three codons that represent a stop signal).

Figure 8-1 shows each codon and its associated amino acid: the genetic code. There are many interesting things to note about the genetic code. For our purposes, the most important is redundancy—the way more than one codon translates to the same amino acid. We'll program this using character classes and regular expressions, as you'll soon see.*

The machinery of the cell actually starts at some point along the RNA and "reads" the sequences codon after codon, attaching the encoded amino acid to the end of the growing protein sequence. Example 8-1 simulates this, reading the string of DNA three bases at a time and concatenating the symbol for the encoded amino acid to the end of the growing protein string. In the cell, the process stops when one of the three codons is encountered.

Translating Codons to Amino Acids

The first task is to enable the following programs to do the translation from the three-nucleotide codons to the amino acids. This is the most important step in implementing the genetic code, which is the encoding of amino acids by three-nucleotide codons.

---

* Also note that the genetic code in Figure 8-1 is properly based on RNA, where uracil appears instead of thymine. In our programs, we're going to go directly from DNA to amino acids, so our codons will use thymine instead of uracil.

		Second Position								
		U		**C**		**A**		**G**		
First Position	**U**	UUU	Phe	UCU	Ser	UAU	Tyr	UGU	Cys	U
		UUC		UCC		UAC		UGC		C
		UUA	Leu	UCA		UAA	Stop	UGA	Stop	A
		UUG		UCG		UAG	Stop	UGG	Trp	G
	C	CUU	Leu	CCU	Pro	CAU	His	CGU	Arg	U
		CUC		CCC		CAC		CGC		C
		CUA		CCA		CAA	Gln	CGA		A
		CUG		CCG		CAG		CGG		G
	A	AUU	Ile	ACU	Thr	AAU	Asn	AGU	Ser	U
		AUC		ACC		AAC		AGC		C
		AUA		ACA		AAA	Lys	AGA	Arg	A
		AUG	Met (start)	ACG		AAG		AGG		G
	G	GUU	Val	GCU	Ala	GAU	Asp	GGU	Gly	U
		GUC		GCC		GAC		GGC		C
		GUA		GCA		GAA	Glu	GGA		A
		GUG		GCG		GAG		GGG		G

Figure 8-1. The genetic code

Here's a subroutine that returns an amino acid (represented by a one-letter abbreviation) given a three-letter DNA codon:

```
# codon2aa
#
# A subroutine to translate a DNA 3-character codon to an amino acid

sub codon2aa {
    my($codon) = @_;

        if ( $codon =~ /TCA/i )    { return 'S' }    # Serine
    elsif ( $codon =~ /TCC/i )    { return 'S' }    # Serine
    elsif ( $codon =~ /TCG/i )    { return 'S' }    # Serine
    elsif ( $codon =~ /TCT/i )    { return 'S' }    # Serine
    elsif ( $codon =~ /TTC/i )    { return 'F' }    # Phenylalanine
    elsif ( $codon =~ /TTT/i )    { return 'F' }    # Phenylalanine
    elsif ( $codon =~ /TTA/i )    { return 'L' }    # Leucine
    elsif ( $codon =~ /TTG/i )    { return 'L' }    # Leucine
    elsif ( $codon =~ /TAC/i )    { return 'Y' }    # Tyrosine
    elsif ( $codon =~ /TAT/i )    { return 'Y' }    # Tyrosine
    elsif ( $codon =~ /TAA/i )    { return '_' }    # Stop
    elsif ( $codon =~ /TAG/i )    { return '_' }    # Stop
    elsif ( $codon =~ /TGC/i )    { return 'C' }    # Cysteine
```

```
elsif ( $codon =~ /TGT/i )   { return 'C' }   # Cysteine
elsif ( $codon =~ /TGA/i )   { return '_' }   # Stop
elsif ( $codon =~ /TGG/i )   { return 'W' }   # Tryptophan
elsif ( $codon =~ /CTA/i )   { return 'L' }   # Leucine
elsif ( $codon =~ /CTC/i )   { return 'L' }   # Leucine
elsif ( $codon =~ /CTG/i )   { return 'L' }   # Leucine
elsif ( $codon =~ /CTT/i )   { return 'L' }   # Leucine
elsif ( $codon =~ /CCA/i )   { return 'P' }   # Proline
elsif ( $codon =~ /CCC/i )   { return 'P' }   # Proline
elsif ( $codon =~ /CCG/i )   { return 'P' }   # Proline
elsif ( $codon =~ /CCT/i )   { return 'P' }   # Proline
elsif ( $codon =~ /CAC/i )   { return 'H' }   # Histidine
elsif ( $codon =~ /CAT/i )   { return 'H' }   # Histidine
elsif ( $codon =~ /CAA/i )   { return 'Q' }   # Glutamine
elsif ( $codon =~ /CAG/i )   { return 'Q' }   # Glutamine
elsif ( $codon =~ /CGA/i )   { return 'R' }   # Arginine
elsif ( $codon =~ /CGC/i )   { return 'R' }   # Arginine
elsif ( $codon =~ /CGG/i )   { return 'R' }   # Arginine
elsif ( $codon =~ /CGT/i )   { return 'R' }   # Arginine
elsif ( $codon =~ /ATA/i )   { return 'I' }   # Isoleucine
elsif ( $codon =~ /ATC/i )   { return 'I' }   # Isoleucine
elsif ( $codon =~ /ATT/i )   { return 'I' }   # Isoleucine
elsif ( $codon =~ /ATG/i )   { return 'M' }   # Methionine
elsif ( $codon =~ /ACA/i )   { return 'T' }   # Threonine
elsif ( $codon =~ /ACC/i )   { return 'T' }   # Threonine
elsif ( $codon =~ /ACG/i )   { return 'T' }   # Threonine
elsif ( $codon =~ /ACT/i )   { return 'T' }   # Threonine
elsif ( $codon =~ /AAC/i )   { return 'N' }   # Asparagine
elsif ( $codon =~ /AAT/i )   { return 'N' }   # Asparagine
elsif ( $codon =~ /AAA/i )   { return 'K' }   # Lysine
elsif ( $codon =~ /AAG/i )   { return 'K' }   # Lysine
elsif ( $codon =~ /AGC/i )   { return 'S' }   # Serine
elsif ( $codon =~ /AGT/i )   { return 'S' }   # Serine
elsif ( $codon =~ /AGA/i )   { return 'R' }   # Arginine
elsif ( $codon =~ /AGG/i )   { return 'R' }   # Arginine
elsif ( $codon =~ /GTA/i )   { return 'V' }   # Valine
elsif ( $codon =~ /GTC/i )   { return 'V' }   # Valine
elsif ( $codon =~ /GTG/i )   { return 'V' }   # Valine
elsif ( $codon =~ /GTT/i )   { return 'V' }   # Valine
elsif ( $codon =~ /GCA/i )   { return 'A' }   # Alanine
elsif ( $codon =~ /GCC/i )   { return 'A' }   # Alanine
elsif ( $codon =~ /GCG/i )   { return 'A' }   # Alanine
elsif ( $codon =~ /GCT/i )   { return 'A' }   # Alanine
elsif ( $codon =~ /GAC/i )   { return 'D' }   # Aspartic Acid
elsif ( $codon =~ /GAT/i )   { return 'D' }   # Aspartic Acid
elsif ( $codon =~ /GAA/i )   { return 'E' }   # Glutamic Acid
elsif ( $codon =~ /GAG/i )   { return 'E' }   # Glutamic Acid
elsif ( $codon =~ /GGA/i )   { return 'G' }   # Glycine
elsif ( $codon =~ /GGC/i )   { return 'G' }   # Glycine
elsif ( $codon =~ /GGG/i )   { return 'G' }   # Glycine
elsif ( $codon =~ /GGT/i )   { return 'G' }   # Glycine
else {
```

```
        print STDERR "Bad codon \"$codon\"!!\n";
        exit;
    }
}
```

This code is clear and simple, and the layout makes it obvious what's happening. However, it can take a while to run. For instance, given the codon GGT for glycine, it has to check each test until it finally succeeds on the last one, and that's a lot of string comparisons. Still, the code achieves its purpose.

There's something new happening in the code's error message. Recall filehandles from Chapter 4 and how they access data in files. From Chapter 5, remember the special filehandle STDIN that reads user input from the keyboard. STDOUT and STDERR are also special filehandles that are always available to Perl programs. STDOUT directs output to the screen (usually) or another standard place. When a filehandle is missing from a print statement, STDOUT is assumed. The print statement accepts a filehandle as an optional argument, but so far, we've been printing to the default STDOUT. Here, error messages are directed to STDERR, which usually prints to the screen, but on many computer systems they can be directed to a special error file or other location. Alternatively, you sometimes want to direct STDOUT to a file or elsewhere but want STDERR error messages to appear on your screen. I mention these options because you are likely to come across them in Perl code; we don't use them much in this book (see Appendix B for more information).

The Redundancy of the Genetic Code

I've remarked on the redundancy of the genetic code, and the last subroutine clearly displays this redundancy. It might be interesting to express that in your subroutine. Notice that groups of redundant codons almost always have the same first and second bases and vary in the third. You've used character classes in regular expressions to match any of a set of characters. Now, let's try to redo the subroutine to make one test for each redundant group of codons:

```
# codon2aa
#
# A subroutine to translate a DNA 3-character codon to an amino acid
#    Version 2

sub codon2aa {
    my($codon) = @_;

        if ( $codon =~ /GC./i)      { return 'A' }    # Alanine
     elsif ( $codon =~ /TG[TC]/i)   { return 'C' }    # Cysteine
     elsif ( $codon =~ /GA[TC]/i)   { return 'D' }    # Aspartic Acid
     elsif ( $codon =~ /GA[AG]/i)   { return 'E' }    # Glutamic Acid
     elsif ( $codon =~ /TT[TC]/i)   { return 'F' }    # Phenylalanine
     elsif ( $codon =~ /GG./i)      { return 'G' }    # Glycine
     elsif ( $codon =~ /CA[TC]/i)   { return 'H' }    # Histidine
     elsif ( $codon =~ /AT[TCA]/i)  { return 'I' }    # Isoleucine
```

```
    elsif ( $codon =~ /AA[AG]/i)      { return 'K' }    # Lysine
    elsif ( $codon =~ /TT[AG]|CT./i) { return 'L' }    # Leucine
    elsif ( $codon =~ /ATG/i)         { return 'M' }    # Methionine
    elsif ( $codon =~ /AA[TC]/i)      { return 'N' }    # Asparagine
    elsif ( $codon =~ /CC./i)         { return 'P' }    # Proline
    elsif ( $codon =~ /CA[AG]/i)      { return 'Q' }    # Glutamine
    elsif ( $codon =~ /CG.|AG[AG]/i) { return 'R' }    # Arginine
    elsif ( $codon =~ /TC.|AG[TC]/i) { return 'S' }    # Serine
    elsif ( $codon =~ /AC./i)         { return 'T' }    # Threonine
    elsif ( $codon =~ /GT./i)         { return 'V' }    # Valine
    elsif ( $codon =~ /TGG/i)         { return 'W' }    # Tryptophan
    elsif ( $codon =~ /TA[TC]/i)      { return 'Y' }    # Tyrosine
    elsif ( $codon =~ /TA[AG]|TGA/i) { return '_' }    # Stop
    else {
        print STDERR "Bad codon \"$codon\"!!\n";
        exit;
    }
}
```

Using character classes and regular expressions, this code clearly shows the redundancy of the genetic code. Also notice that the one-character codes for the amino acids are now in alphabetical order.

A character class such as [TC] matches a single character, either T or C. The . is the regular expression that matches any character except a newline. The /GT./i expression for valine matches GTA, GTC, GTG, and GTT, all of which are codons for valine. (Of course, the period matches any other character, but the $codon is assumed to have only A,C,G, or T characters.) The i after the regular expression means match uppercase or lowercase, for instance /T/i matches T or t.

The new feature in these regular expressions is the use of the vertical bar or pipe (|) to separate two choices. Thus for serine, /TC.|AG[TC]/ matches /TC./ or /AG[TC]/. In this program, you need only two choices per regular expression, but you can use as many vertical bars as you like.

You can also group parts of a regular expression in parentheses, and use vertical bars in them. For example, /give me a (break|meal)/ matches "give me a break" or "give me a meal."

Using Hashes for the Genetic Code

If you think about using a hash for this translation, you'll see it's a natural way to proceed. For each codon key the amino acid value is returned. Here's the code:

```
#
# codon2aa
#
# A subroutine to translate a DNA 3-character codon to an amino acid
#   Version 3, using hash lookup

sub codon2aa {
```

```
my($codon) = @_;

$codon = uc $codon;

my(%genetic_code) = (

'TCA' => 'S',      # Serine
'TCC' => 'S',      # Serine
'TCG' => 'S',      # Serine
'TCT' => 'S',      # Serine
'TTC' => 'F',      # Phenylalanine
'TTT' => 'F',      # Phenylalanine
'TTA' => 'L',      # Leucine
'TTG' => 'L',      # Leucine
'TAC' => 'Y',      # Tyrosine
'TAT' => 'Y',      # Tyrosine
'TAA' => '_',      # Stop
'TAG' => '_',      # Stop
'TGC' => 'C',      # Cysteine
'TGT' => 'C',      # Cysteine
'TGA' => '_',      # Stop
'TGG' => 'W',      # Tryptophan
'CTA' => 'L',      # Leucine
'CTC' => 'L',      # Leucine
'CTG' => 'L',      # Leucine
'CTT' => 'L',      # Leucine
'CCA' => 'P',      # Proline
'CCC' => 'P',      # Proline
'CCG' => 'P',      # Proline
'CCT' => 'P',      # Proline
'CAC' => 'H',      # Histidine
'CAT' => 'H',      # Histidine
'CAA' => 'Q',      # Glutamine
'CAG' => 'Q',      # Glutamine
'CGA' => 'R',      # Arginine
'CGC' => 'R',      # Arginine
'CGG' => 'R',      # Arginine
'CGT' => 'R',      # Arginine
'ATA' => 'I',      # Isoleucine
'ATC' => 'I',      # Isoleucine
'ATT' => 'I',      # Isoleucine
'ATG' => 'M',      # Methionine
'ACA' => 'T',      # Threonine
'ACC' => 'T',      # Threonine
'ACG' => 'T',      # Threonine
'ACT' => 'T',      # Threonine
'AAC' => 'N',      # Asparagine
'AAT' => 'N',      # Asparagine
'AAA' => 'K',      # Lysine
'AAG' => 'K',      # Lysine
'AGC' => 'S',      # Serine
'AGT' => 'S',      # Serine
'AGA' => 'R',      # Arginine
'AGG' => 'R',      # Arginine
```

```
   'GTA' => 'V',     # Valine
   'GTC' => 'V',     # Valine
   'GTG' => 'V',     # Valine
   'GTT' => 'V',     # Valine
   'GCA' => 'A',     # Alanine
   'GCC' => 'A',     # Alanine
   'GCG' => 'A',     # Alanine
   'GCT' => 'A',     # Alanine
   'GAC' => 'D',     # Aspartic Acid
   'GAT' => 'D',     # Aspartic Acid
   'GAA' => 'E',     # Glutamic Acid
   'GAG' => 'E',     # Glutamic Acid
   'GGA' => 'G',     # Glycine
   'GGC' => 'G',     # Glycine
   'GGG' => 'G',     # Glycine
   'GGT' => 'G',     # Glycine
   );

   if(exists $genetic_code{$codon}) {
       return $genetic_code{$codon};
   }else{

           print STDERR "Bad codon \"$codon\"!!\n";
           exit;
   }
}
```

This subroutine is simple: it initializes a hash and then performs a single lookup of its single argument in the hash. The hash has 64 keys, one for each codon.

Notice there's a function exists that returns true if the key $codon exists in the hash. It's equivalent to the else statement in the two previous versions of the codon2aa subroutine.[*]

Also notice that to make this subroutine work on lowercase DNA as well as uppercase, you translate the incoming argument into uppercase to match the data in the %genetic_code hash. You can't give a regular expression to a hash as a key; it must be a simple scalar value, such as a string or a number, so the case translation must be done first. (Alternatively, you can make the hash twice as big.) Similarly, character classes don't work in the keys for hashes, so you have to specify each one of the 64 codons individually.

You may wonder why bother wrapping this last bit of code in a subroutine at all. Why not just declare and initialize the hash and do the lookups directly in the hash instead of going through the subroutine? Well, the subroutine does do a little bit of

---

[*] A key might exist in a hash, but its value can be undefined. The defined function checks for defined values. Also, of course, the value might be 0 or the empty string, in which case, it fails a test such as if ($hash{$key}) because, even though the key exists and the value is defined, the value evaluates to false in a conditional test.

error checking for nonexistent keys, so having a subroutine saves doing that error checking yourself each time you use the hash.

Additionally, wrapping the code in a subroutine gives a little insurance for the future. If all the code you write does codon translation by means of our subroutine, it would be simplicity itself to switch over to a new way of doing the translation. Perhaps a new kind of datatype will be added to Perl in the future, or perhaps you want to do lookups from a database or a DBM file. Then all you have to do is change the internals of this one subroutine. As long as the interface to the subroutine remains the same—that is to say, as long as it still takes one codon as an argument and returns a one-character amino acid—you don't need to worry about how it accomplishes the translation from the standpoint of the rest of the programs. Our subroutine has become a *black box*. This is one significant benefit of modularization and organization of programs with subroutines.

There's another good, and biological, reason why you should use a subroutine for the genetic code. There is actually more than one genetic code, because there are differences as to how DNA encodes amino acids among mammals, plants, insects, and yeast—especially in the mitochondria. So if you have modularized the genetic code, you can easily modify your program to work with a range of organisms.

One of the benefits of hashes is that they are fast. Unfortunately, our subroutine declares the whole hash each time the subroutine is called, even for one lookup. This isn't so efficient; in fact, it's kind of slow. There are other, much faster ways that involve declaring the genetic code hash only once as a global variable, but they would take us a little far afield at this point. Our current version has the advantage of being easy to read. So, let's be officially happy with the hash version of codon2aa and put it into our module in the file *BeginPerlBioinfo.pm* (see Chapter 6).

Now that we've got a satisfactory way to translate codons to amino acids, we'll start to use it in the next section and in the examples.

Translating DNA into Proteins

Example 8-1 shows how the new codon2aa subroutine translates a whole DNA sequence into protein.

Example 8-1. Translate DNA into protein

```
#!/usr/bin/perl
# Translate DNA into protein

use strict;
use warnings;
use BeginPerlBioinfo;      # see Chapter 6 about this module

# Initialize variables
my $dna = 'CGACGTCTTCGTACGGGACTAGCTCGTGTCGGTCGC';
```

Example 8-1. Translate DNA into protein (continued)

```perl
my $protein = '';
my $codon;

# Translate each three-base codon into an amino acid, and append to a protein
for(my $i=0; $i < (length($dna) - 2) ; $i += 3) {
    $codon = substr($dna,$i,3);
    $protein .= codon2aa($codon);
}

print "I translated the DNA\n\n$dna\n\n  into the protein\n\n$protein\n\n";

exit;
```

To make this work, you'll need the *BeginPerlBioinfo.pm* module for your subroutines in a separate file the program can find, as discussed in Chapter 6. You also have to add the codon2aa subroutine to it. Alternatively, you can add the code for the subroutine condon2aa directly to the program in Example 8-1 and remove the reference to the *BeginPerlBioinfo.pm* module.

Here's the output from Example 8-1:

```
I translated the DNA

CGACGTCTTCGTACGGGACTAGCTCGTGTCGGTCGC

  into the protein

RRLRTGLARVGR
```

You've seen all the elements in Example 8-1 before, except for the way it loops through the DNA with this statement:

```perl
for(my $i=0; $i < (length($dna) - 2) ; $i += 3) {
```

Recall that a for loop has three parts, delimited by the two semicolons. The first part initializes a counter: my $i=0 statically scopes the $i variable so it's visible only inside this block, and any other $i elsewhere in the code (well, in this case, there aren't any, but it can happen) is now invisible inside the block. The third part of the for loop increments the counter after all the statements in the block are executed and before returning to the beginning of the loop:

```perl
$i += 3
```

Since you're trying to march through the DNA three bases at a shot, you increment by three.

The second, middle part of the for loop tests whether the loop should continue:

```perl
$i < (length($dna) - 2)
```

The point is that if there are none, one, or two bases left, you should quit, because there's not enough to make a codon. Now, the positions in a string of DNA of a certain length are numbered from 0 to length-1. So if the position counter $i has reached length-2, there's only two more bases (at positions length-2 and length-1), and you should quit. Only if the position counter $i is less than length-2 will you still have at least three bases left, enough for a codon. So the test succeeds only if:

```
$i < (length($dna) -2)
```

(Notice also how the whole expression to the right of the less-than sign is enclosed in parentheses; we'll discuss this in Chapter 9 in the section "Precedence of Operations and Parentheses.")

The line of code:

```
$codon = substr ($dna, $i 3);
```

actually extracts the 3-base codon from the DNA. The call to the substr function specifies a substring of $dna at position $i of length 3, and saves it in the variable $codon.

If you know you'll need to do this DNA-to-protein translation a lot, you can turn Example 8-1 into a subroutine. Whenever you write a subroutine, you have to think about which arguments you may want to give the subroutine. So you realize, there may come a time when you'll have some large DNA sequence but only want to translate a given part of it. Should you add two arguments to the subroutine as beginning and end points? You could, but decide not to. It's a judgment call—part of the art of decomposing a collection of code into useful fragments. But it might be better to have a subroutine that just translates; then you can make it part of a larger subroutine that picks endpoints in the sequence, if needed. The thinking is that you'll usually just translate the whole thing and always typing in 0 for the start and length($dna)-1 at the end, would be an annoyance. Of course, this depends on what you're doing, so this particular choice just illustrates your thinking when you write the code.

You should also remove the informative print statement at the end, because it's more suited to a main program than a subroutine.

Anyway, you've now thought through the design and just want a subroutine that takes one argument containing DNA and returns a peptide translation:

```
# dna2peptide
#
# A subroutine to translate DNA sequence into a peptide

sub dna2peptide {

    my($dna) = @_;

    use strict;
    use warnings;
    use BeginPerlBioinfo;     # see Chapter 6 about this module
```

```
# Initialize variables
my $protein = '';

# Translate each three-base codon to an amino acid, and append to a protein
for(my $i=0; $i < (length($dna) - 2) ; $i += 3) {
    $protein .= codon2aa( substr($dna,$i,3) );
}

return $protein;
}
```

Now add subroutine dna2peptide to the *BeginPerlBioinfo.pm* module.

Notice that you've eliminated one of the variables in making the subroutine out of Example 8-1: the variable $codon. Why?

Well, one reason is because you can. In Example 8-1, you were using substr to extract the codon from $dna, saving it in variable $codon and then passing it into the subroutine codon2aa. This new way eliminates the middleman. Put the call to substr that extracts the codon as the argument to the subroutine codon2aa so that the value is passed in just as before, but without having to copy it to the variable $codon first.

This has somewhat improved efficiency and speed. Since copying strings is one of the slower things computer programs do, eliminating a bunch of string copies is an easy and effective way to speed up a program.

But has it made the program less readable? You be the judge. I think it has, a little, but the comment right before the loop seems to make everything clear enough, for me, anyway. It's important to have readable code, so if you really need to boost the speed of a subroutine, but find it makes the code harder to read, be sure to include enough comments for the reader to be able to understand what's going on.

For the first time use function calls are being included in a subroutine instead of the main program:

```
use strict;
use warnings;
use BeginPerlBioinfo;
```

This may be redundant with the calls in the main program, but it doesn't do any harm (Perl checks and loads a module only once). If this subroutine should be called from a module that doesn't already load the modules, it's done some good after all.

Now let's improve how we deal with DNA in files.

Reading DNA from Files in FASTA Format

Over the fairly short history of bioinformatics, several different biologists and programmers invented several ways to format sequence data in computer files, and so bioinformaticians must deal with these different formats. We need to extract the sequence data and the annotations from these files, which requires writing code to deal with each different format.

There are many such formats, perhaps as many as 20 in regular use for DNA alone. The very multiplicity of these formats can be an annoyance when you're analyzing a sequence in the lab: it becomes necessary to translate from one format to another for the various programs you use to examine the sequence. Here are some of the most popular:

FASTA

> The FASTA and Basic Local Alignment Search Technique (BLAST) programs are popular; they both use the FASTA format. Because of its simplicity, the FASTA format is perhaps the most widely used of all formats, aside from GenBank.

Genetic Sequence Data Bank (GenBank)

> GenBank is a collection of all publicly released genetic data. It includes lots of information in addition to the DNA sequence. It's very important, and we'll be looking closely at GenBank files in Chapter 10.

European Molecular Biology Laboratory (EMBL)

> The EMBL database has substantially the same data as the GenBank and the DDBJ (DNA Data Bank of Japan), but the format is somewhat different.

Simple data, or Applied Biosystems (ABI) sequencer output

> This is DNA sequence data that has no formatting whatsoever, just the characters that represent the bases; it is output into files by the sequencing machines from ABI and from other machines and programs.

Protein Identification Resource (PIR)

> PIR is a well-curated collection of protein sequence data.

Genetics Computer Group (GCG)

> The GCG program (a.k.a. the GCG Wisconsin package) from Accelrys is used at many large research institutions. Data must be in GCG format to be usable by their programs.

Of these six sequence formats, GenBank and FASTA are by far the most common. The next few sections take you through the process of reading and manipulating data in FASTA.

FASTA Format

Let's write a subroutine that can handle FASTA-style data. This is useful in its own right and as a warm-up for the upcoming chapters on GenBank, PDB, and BLAST.

FASTA format is basically just lines of sequence data with newlines at the end so it can be printed on a page or displayed on a computer screen. The length of the lines isn't specified, but for compatibility, it's best to limit them to 80 characters in length. There is also *header information*, a line or lines at the beginning of the file that start with the greater-than > character, that can contain any text whatsoever (or no text). Typically, a header line contains the name of the DNA or the gene it comes from, often separated by a vertical bar from additional information about the sequence, the experiment that produced it, or other, nonsequence information of that nature.

Much FASTA-aware software insists that there must be only one header line; others permit several lines. Our subroutine will accept either one or several header lines plus comments beginning with #.

The following is a FASTA file. We'll call it *sample.dna* and use it in several programs. You should copy it, download it from this book's web site, or make up your own file with your own data.

```
> sample dna | (This is a typical fasta header.)
agatggcggcgctgaggggtcttgggggctctaggccggccacctactgg
tttgcagcggagacgacgcatggggcctgcgcaataggagtacgctgcct
gggaggcgtgactagaagcggaagtagttgtgggcgcctttgcaaccgcc
tgggacgccgccgagtggtctgtgcaggttcgcgggtcgctggcgggggt
cgtgagggagtgcgccgggagcggagatatggagggagatggttcagacc
cagagcctccagatgccggggaggacagcaagtccgagaatggggagaat
gcgcccatctactgcatctgccgcaaaccggacatcaactgcttcatgat
cgggtgtgacaactgcaatgagtggttccatggggactgcatccggatca
ctgagaagatggccaaggccatccgggagtggtactgtcgggagtgcaga
gagaaagaccccaagctagagattcgctatcggcacaagaagtcacggga
gcgggatggcaatgagcgggacagcagtgagccccgggatgagggtggag
ggcgcaagaggcctgtccctgatccagacctgcagcgccgggcagggtca
gggacaggggttggggccatgcttgctcggggctctgcttcgccccacaa
atcctctccgcagcccttggtggccacacccagccagcatcaccagcagc
agcagcagcagatcaaacggtcagcccgcatgtgtggtgagtgtgaggca
tgtcggcgcactgaggactgtggtcactgtgatttctgtcgggacatgaa
gaagttcggggggcccaacaagatccggcagaagtgccggctgcgccagt
gccagctgcgggcccgggaatcgtacaagtacttccctcctcgctctca
ccagtgacgccctcagagtccctgccaaggccccgccggccactgcccac
ccaacagcagccacagccatcacagaagttagggcgcatccgtgaagatg
aggggggcagtggcgtcatcaacagtcaaggagcctcctgaggctacagcc
acacctgagccactctcagatgaggaccta
```

A Design to Read FASTA Files

In Chapter 4, you learned how to read in sequence data; here, you just have to extend that method to deal with the header lines. You'll also learn how to discard empty lines and lines that begin with the pound sign #, i.e., comments in Perl and other languages and file formats. (These don't appear in the FASTA file *sample.dna* just shown.)

There are two choices when reading in the data. You can read from the open file one line at a time, making decisions as you go. Or, you can slurp the whole file into an array and then operate on the array. For very big files, it's sometimes best to read them one line at a time, especially if you're looking for some small bit of information.

(This is because reading a large file into an array uses a large amount of memory. If your system isn't robust enough, it may crash.)

For smaller, normal-sized files, the advantage to reading all the data into an array is that you can then easily look through at the data and do operations on it. That's what we'll do with our subroutine, but remember, this approach can cause memory space problems with larger files, and there are other ways of proceeding.

Let's write a subroutine that, given as an argument a filename containing FASTA-formatted data, returns the sequence data.

Before doing so you should think about whether you should have just one subroutine, or perhaps one subroutine that opens and reads a file, called by another subroutine that extracts the sequence data. Let's use two subroutines, keeping in mind that you can reuse the subroutine that deals with arbitrary files every time you need to write such a program for other formats.

Let's start with some pseudocode:

```
subroutine get data from a file

    argument = filename

    open file
        if can't open, print error message and exit

    read in data and

    return @data
}

Subroutine extract sequence data from fasta file

    argument = array of file data in fasta format

        Discard all header lines
        (and blank and comment lines for good measure)
        If first character of first line is >, discard it

    Read in the rest of the file, join in a scalar,
        edit out nonsequence data

    return sequence
}
```

In the first subroutine that gets data from a file, there's a question as to what's the best thing to do when the file can't be read. Here, we're taking the drastic approach: yelling "Fire!" and exiting. But you wouldn't necessarily want your program to just stop whenever it can't open a file. Maybe you're asking for filenames from the user at the keyboard or on a web page, and you'd like to give them three chances to type in the filename correctly. Or maybe, if the file can't be opened, you want a default file instead.

Maybe you can return a false value, such as an empty array, if you can't open the file. Then a program that calls this subroutine can exit, try again, or whatever it wants. But what if you successfully open the file, but it was absolutely empty? Then you'd have succeeded and returned an empty array, and the program calling this subroutine would think incorrectly, that the file couldn't be opened. So, that wouldn't work.

There are other options, such as returning the special "undefined" value. Let's keep what we've got, but it's important to remember that handling errors can be an important, and sometimes tricky, part of writing *robust code*, code that responds well in unusual circumstances.

The second subroutine takes the array of FASTA-formatted sequence and returns just the unformatted sequence in a string.

A Subroutine to Read FASTA Files

Now that you've thought about the problem, written some pseudocode, considered alternate ways of designing the subroutines and the costs and benefits of the choices, you're ready to code:

```
# get_file_data
#
# A subroutine to get data from a file given its filename

sub get_file_data {

    my($filename) = @_;

    use strict;
    use warnings;

    # Initialize variables
    my @filedata = ( );

    unless( open(GET_FILE_DATA, $filename) ) {
        print STDERR "Cannot open file \"$filename\"\n\n";
        exit;
    }

    @filedata = <GET_FILE_DATA>;

    close GET_FILE_DATA;

    return @filedata;
}
```

```
# extract_sequence_from_fasta_data
#
# A subroutine to extract FASTA sequence data from an array

sub extract_sequence_from_fasta_data {

    my(@fasta_file_data) = @_;

    use strict;
    use warnings;

    # Declare and initialize variables
    my $sequence = '';

    foreach my $line (@fasta_file_data) {

        # discard blank line
        if ($line =~ /^\s*$/) {
            next;

        # discard comment line
        } elsif($line =~ /^\s*#/) {
            next;

        # discard fasta header line
        } elsif($line =~ /^>/) {
            next;

        # keep line, add to sequence string
        } else {
            $sequence .= $line;
        }
    }

    # remove non-sequence data (in this case, whitespace) from $sequence string
    $sequence =~ s/\s//g;

    return $sequence;
}
```

Notice that nowhere in the code for extract_sequence_from_fasta_data do you check to see what's in the file: is it really DNA or protein sequence data in FASTA format? Of course, you can write a subroutine—call it is_fasta—that checks the data to see if it's what we expect. But I'll leave that for the exercises.

A few comments about the extract_sequence_from_fasta_data subroutine should be made. The following line includes a variable declaration as it is used in a loop:

```
foreach my $line (@fasta_file_data) {
```

You've seen this in for loops as well. It's often convenient to declare a loop's "index variable" (like $line) as a my variable, right on the spot in the loop, as they tend to have common names and aren't used outside the loop.

Some of the regular expressions deserve brief comment. In this line:

```
if ($line =~ /^\s*$/) {
```

the \s matches whitespace, that is, space, tab, formfeed, carriage return, or newline. \s* matches any amount of whitespace (even none). The ^ matches the beginning of the line, and the $ matches the end of the line. So altogether, this regular expression matches blank lines with nothing or only whitespace in them.

This regular expression also has nothing or only whitespace at the beginning of the line, up to a pound sign:

```
} elsif($line =~ /^\s*#/) {
```

This expression matches a greater-than sign at the beginning of the line:

```
} elsif($line =~ /^>/) {
```

Finally, the following statement removes whitespace, including newlines:

```
$sequence =~ s/\s//g;
```

We've placed these two new subroutines into our *BeginPerlBioinfo.pm* module. Now let's write a main program for these subroutines and look at the output. First, there's one more subroutine to write that handles the printing of long sequences.

Writing Formatted Sequence Data

When you try to print the "raw" sequence data, it can be a problem if the data is much longer than the width of the page. For most practical purposes, 80 characters is about the maximum length you should try to fit across a page. Let's write a print_sequence subroutine that takes as its arguments some sequence and a line length and prints out the sequence, breaking it up into lines of that length. It will have a strong similarity to the dna2peptide subroutine. Here it is:

```
# print_sequence
#
# A subroutine to format and print sequence data

sub print_sequence {

    my($sequence, $length) = @_;

    use strict;
    use warnings;

    # Print sequence in lines of $length
    for ( my $pos = 0 ; $pos < length($sequence) ; $pos += $length ) {
        print substr($sequence, $pos, $length), "\n";
    }
}
```

The code depends on the behavior of substr, which gives the partial substring at the end of the string, even if it's less than the requested length. You can see there's a new print_sequence subroutine in the *BeginPerlBioinfo.pm* module (see Chapter 6). We remembered to keep the statement 1; as the last line of the module. Example 8-2 shows the main program.

Example 8-2. Read a FASTA file and extract the sequence data

```perl
#!/usr/bin/perl
# Read a fasta file and extract the sequence data

use strict;
use warnings;
use BeginPerlBioinfo;      # see Chapter 6 about this module

# Declare and initialize variables
my @file_data = ();
my $dna = '';

# Read in the contents of the file "sample.dna"
@file_data = get_file_data("sample.dna");

# Extract the sequence data from the contents of the file "sample.dna"
$dna = extract_sequence_from_fasta_data(@file_data);

# Print the sequence in lines 25 characters long
print_sequence($dna, 25);

exit;
```

Here's the output of Example 8-2:

```
agatggcggcgctgaggggtcttgg
gggctctaggccggccacctactgg
tttgcagcggagacgacgcatgggg
cctgcgcaataggagtacgctgcct
gggaggcgtgactagaagcggaagt
agttgtgggcgcctttgcaaccgcc
tgggacgccgccgagtggtctgtgc
aggttcgcgggtcgctggcgggggt
cgtgagggagtgcgccgggagcgga
gatatggagggagatggttcagacc
cagagcctccagatgccggggagga
cagcaagtccgagaatggggagaat
gcgcccatctactgcatctgccgca
aaccggacatcaactgcttcatgat
cgggtgtgacaactgcaatgagtgg
ttccatggggactgcatccggatca
ctgagaagatggccaaggccatccg
ggagtggtactgtcgggagtgcaga
gagaaagaccccaagctagagattc
gctatcggcacaagaagtcacggga
gcgggatggcaatgagcgggacagc
agtgagccccgggatgagggtggag
ggcgcaagaggcctgtccctgatcc
agacctgcagcgccgggcagggtca
```

```
gggacaggggttggggccatgcttg
ctcggggctctgcttcgccccacaa
atcctctccgcagcccttggtggcc
acacccagccagcatcaccagcagc
agcagcagcagatcaaacggtcagc
ccgcatgtgtggtgagtgtgaggca
tgtcggcgcactgaggactgtggtc
actgtgatttctgtcgggacatgaa
gaagttcgggggcccaacaagatc
cggcagaagtgccggctgcgccagt
gccagctgcgggcccgggaatcgta
caagtacttcccttcctcgctctca
ccagtgacgccctcagagtccctgc
caaggccccgccggccactgcccac
ccaacagcagccacagccatcacag
aagttagggcgcatccgtgaagatg
aggggcagtggcgtcatcaacagt
caaggagcctcctgaggctacagcc
acacctgagccactctcagatgagg
accta
```

A Main Program for Reading DNA and Writing Protein

Now, one final program for this section. Let's add to the preceding program a translation from DNA to protein and print out the protein instead. Notice how short Example 8-3 is! As you accumulate useful subroutines in our modules, programs get easier and easier to write.

Example 8-3. Read a DNA FASTA file, translate to protein, and format output

```perl
#!/usr/bin/perl
# Read a fasta file and extract the DNA sequence data
# Translate it to protein and print it out in 25-character-long lines

use strict;
use warnings;
use BeginPerlBioinfo;     # see Chapter 6 about this module

# Initialize variables
my @file_data = ( );
my $dna = '';
my $protein = '';

# Read in the contents of the file "sample.dna"
@file_data = get_file_data("sample.dna");

# Extract the sequence data from the contents of the file "sample.dna"
$dna = extract_sequence_from_fasta_data(@file_data);

# Translate the DNA to protein
$protein = dna2peptide($dna);
```

Example 8-3. Read a DNA FASTA file, translate to protein, and format output (continued)

```
# Print the sequence in lines 25 characters long
print_sequence($protein, 25);

exit;
```

Here's the output of Example 8-3:

```
RWRR_GVLGALGRPPTGLQRRRRMG
PAQ_EYAAWEA_LEAEVVVGAFATA
WDAAEWSVQVRGSLAGVVRECAGSG
DMEGDGSDPEPPDAGEDSKSENGEN
APIYCICRKPDINCFMIGCDNCNEW
FHGDCIRITEKMAKAIREWYCRECR
EKDPKLEIRYRHKKSRERDGNERDS
SEPRDEGGGRKRPVPDPDLQRRAGS
GTGVGAMLARGSASPHKSSPQPLVA
TPSQHHQQQQQQIKRSARMCGECEA
CRRTEDCGHCDFCRDMKKFGGPNKI
RQKCRLRQCQLRARESYKYFPSSLS
PVTPSESLPRPRRPLPTQQQPQPSQ
KLGRIREDEGAVASSTVKEPPEATA
TPEPLSDEDL
```

Reading Frames

The biologist knows that, given a sequence of DNA, it is necessary to examine all six *reading frames* of the DNA to find the coding regions the cell uses to make proteins.

What Are Reading Frames?

Very often you won't know where in the DNA you're studying the cell actually begins translating the DNA into protein. Only about 1–1.5% of human DNA is in genes, which are the parts of DNA used for the translation into proteins. Furthermore, genes very often occur in pieces that are spliced together during the transcription/translation process.

If you don't know where the translation starts, you have to consider the six possible reading frames. Since the codons are three bases long, the translation happens in three "frames," for instance starting at the first base, or the second, or perhaps the third. (The fourth would be the same as starting from the first.) Each starting place gives a different series of codons, and, as a result, a different series of amino acids.

Also, transcription and translation can happen on either strand of the DNA; that is, either the DNA sequence, or its reverse complement, might contain DNA code that is actually translated. The reverse complement can also be read in any one of three frames. So a total of six reading frames have to be considered when looking for *coding regions*, that part of the DNA that encodes proteins.

It is therefore quite common to examine all six reading frames of a DNA sequence and to look at the resulting protein translations for long stretches of amino acids that lack stop codons.

The *stop codons* are definite breaks in the DNA→protein translation process. During translation (actually of RNA to protein, but I'm being deliberately informal and vague about the biochemistry), if a stop codon is reached, the translation stops, and the growing peptide chain grows no more.

Long stretches of DNA that don't contain any stop codons are called *open reading frames* (ORFs) and are important clues to the presence of a gene in the DNA under study. So gene finder programs need to perform the type of reading frame analysis we'll do in this chapter.

Translating Reading Frames

Based on the facts just presented, let's write some code that translates the DNA in all six reading frames.

In the real world, you'd look around for some subroutines that are already written to do that task. Given the basic nature of the task—something anyone who studies DNA has to do—you'd likely find something. But this is a tutorial, not the real world, so let's soldier on.

This problem doesn't sound too daunting. So, take stock of the subroutines at your disposal, think of where you are and how you can get to your destination.

Looking through the subroutines we've already written, recall dna2peptide. You may recall considering adding some arguments to specify starting and end points. Let's do this now.

Remember that although we calculated reverse complements back in Chapter 4, we never made a subroutine out of it. So let's start there:

```
# revcom
#
# A subroutine to compute the reverse complement of DNA sequence

sub revcom {

    my($dna) = @_;

    # First reverse the sequence
    my $revcom = reverse $dna;

    # Next, complement the sequence, dealing with upper and lower case
    # A->T, T->A, C->G, G->C
    $revcom =~ tr/ACGTacgt/TGCAtgca/;

    return $revcom;
}
```

Now, a little pseudocode to sketch an idea for the subroutine that will translate specific ranges of DNA:

```
Given DNA sequence

subroutine translate_frame ( DNA, start, end)

    return dna2peptide( substr( DNA, start, end - start + 1 ) )

}
```

That went well! Luckily, the substr built-in Perl function made it easy to apply the desired start and end points, while passing the DNA into the already written dna2peptide subroutine.

Note that the length of the sequence is end-start+1. To give a small example: if you start at position 3 and end at position 5, you've got the bases at positions 3, 4, and 5, three bases in all, which is exactly what $5 - 3 + 1$ equals.

Dealing with indices like this has to be done carefully, or the code won't work. For many programs, this is the worst the mathematics gets.

 Pay attention to the indices!

You have to decide if you wish to keep the numbering of positions from 0, which is Perl's way to do it, or the first character of the sequence is in position 1, which is the biologist's way to do it. Let's do it the biologist's way. The positions will be decreased by one when passed to the Perl function substr, which, of course, does it Perl's way.

The corrected pseudocode looks like this:

```
Given DNA sequence

subroutine translate_frame ( DNA, start, end)

    # start and end are numbering the sequence from 1 to length

    return dna2peptide( substr( DNA, start - 1, end - start + 1 ) )
}
```

The length of the desired sequence doesn't change with the change in indices, since:

```
(end - 1) - (start - 1) + 1 = end - start + 1
```

So let's write this subroutine:

```
# translate_frame
#
# A subroutine to translate a frame of DNA
```

```perl
sub translate_frame {

    my($seq, $start, $end) = @_;

    my $protein;

    # To make the subroutine easier to use, you won't need to specify
    #  the end point—it will just go to the end of the sequence
    #  by default.
    unless($end) {
        $end = length($seq);
    }

    # Finally, calculate and return the translation
        return dna2peptide ( substr ( $seq, $start - 1, $end -$start + 1) );
}
```

Example 8-4 translates the DNA in all six reading frames.

Example 8-4. Translate a DNA sequence in all six reading frames

```perl
#!/usr/bin/perl
# Translate a DNA sequence in all six reading frames

use strict;
use warnings;
use BeginPerlBioinfo;      # see Chapter 6 about this module

# Initialize variables
my @file_data = ( );
my $dna = '';
my $revcom = '';
my $protein = '';

# Read in the contents of the file "sample.dna"
@file_data = get_file_data("sample.dna");

# Extract the sequence data from the contents of the file "sample.dna"
$dna = extract_sequence_from_fasta_data(@file_data);

# Translate the DNA to protein in six reading frames
#    and print the protein in lines 70 characters long
print "\n -------Reading Frame 1--------\n\n";
$protein = translate_frame($dna, 1);
print_sequence($protein, 70);

print "\n -------Reading Frame 2--------\n\n";
$protein = translate_frame($dna, 2);
print_sequence($protein, 70);

print "\n -------Reading Frame 3--------\n\n";
$protein = translate_frame($dna, 3);
print_sequence($protein, 70);
```

Example 8-4. Translate a DNA sequence in all six reading frames (continued)

```
# Calculate reverse complement
$revcom = revcom($dna);

print "\n -------Reading Frame 4--------\n\n";
$protein = translate_frame($revcom, 1);
print_sequence($protein, 70);

print "\n -------Reading Frame 5--------\n\n";
$protein = translate_frame($revcom, 2);
print_sequence($protein, 70);

print "\n -------Reading Frame 6--------\n\n";
$protein = translate_frame($revcom, 3);
print_sequence($protein, 70);

exit;
```

Here's the output of Example 8-4:

```
    -------Reading Frame 1--------

RWRR_GVLGALGRPPTGLQRRRRMGPAQ_EYAAWEA_LEAEVVVGAFATAWDAAEWSVQVRGSLAGVVRE
CAGSGDMEGDGSDPEPPDAGEDSKSENGENAPIYCICRKPDINCFMIGCDNCNEWFHGDCIRITEKMAKA
IREWYCRECREKDPKLEIRYRHKKSRERDGNERDSSEPRDEGGGRKRPVPDPDLQRRAGSGTGVGAMLAR
GSASPHKSSPQPLVATPSQHHQQQQQQIKRSARMCGCEEACRRTEDCGHCDFCRDMKKFGGPNKIRQKCR
LRQCQLRARESYKYFPSSLSPVTPSESLPRPRRPLPTQQQPQPSQKLGRIREDEGAVASSTVKEPPEATA
TPEPLSDEDL


    -------Reading Frame 2--------

DGGAEGSWGL_AGHLLVCSGDDAWGLRNRSTLPGRRD_KRK_LWAPLQPPGTPPSGLCRFAGRWRGS_GS
APGAEIWREMVQTQSLQMPGRTASPRMGRMRPSTASAANRTSTAS_SGVTTAMSGSMGTASGSLRRWPRP
SGSGTVGSAERKTPS_RFAIGTRSHGSGMAMSGTAVSPGMRVEGARGLSLIQTCSAGQGQGQGLGPCLLG
ALLRPTNPLRSPWWPHPASITSSSSSRSNGQPACVVSVRHVGALRTVVTVISVGT_RSSGAPTRSGRSAG
CASASCGPGNRTSTSLPRSHQ_RPQSPCQGPAGHCPPNSSHSHHRS_GASVKMRGQWRHQQSRSLLRLQP
HLSHSQMRT


    -------Reading Frame 3--------

MAALRGLGGSRPATYWFAAETTHGACAIGVRCLGGVTRSGSSCGRLCNRLGRRRVVCAGSRVAGGGREGV
RRERRYGGRWFRPRASRCRGGQQVREWGECAHLLHLPQTGHQLLHDRV_QLQ_VVPWGLHPDH_EDGQGH
PGVVLSGVQRERPQARDSLSAQEVTGAGWQ_AGQQ_APG_GWRAQEACP_SRPAAPGRVRDRGWGHACSG
LCFAPQILSAALGGHTQPASPAAAAADQTVSPHVW_V_GMSAH_GLWSL_FLSGHEEVRGPQQDPAEVPA
APVPAAGPGIVQVLPFLALTSDALRVPAKAPPATAHPTAATAITEVRAHP_R_GGSGVINSQGAS_GYSH
T_ATLR_GP


    -------Reading Frame 4--------

_VLI_EWLRCGCSLRRLLDC__RHCPLIFTDAP_LL_WLWLLLGGQWPAGPWQGL_GRHW_ERGREVLVR
FPGPQLALAQPALLPDLVGAPELLHVPTEITVTTVLSAPTCLTLTTHAG_PFDLLLLLLVMLAGCGHQGL
RRGFVGRSRAPSKHGPNPCP_PCPALQVWIRDRPLAPSTLIPGLTAVPLIAIPLP_LLVPIANL_LGVFL
```

```
SALPTVPLPDGLGHLLSDPDAVPMEPLIAVVTPDHEAVDVRFAADAVDGRILPILGLAVLPGIWRLWV_T
ISLHISAPGALPHDPRQRPANLHRPLGGVPGGCKGAHNYFRF_SRLPGSVLLLRRPHASSPLQTSRWPA_
SPQDPSAPPS


-------Reading Frame 5--------


RSSSESGSGVAVASGGSLTVDDATAPSSSRMRPNFCDGCGCCWVGSGRRGLGRDSEGVTGESEEGKYLYD
SRARSWHWRSRHFCRILLGPPNFFMSRQKSQ_PQSSVRRHASHSPHMRADRLICCCCCW_CWLGVATKGC
GEDLWGEAEPRASMAPTPVPDPARRCRSGSGTGLLRPPPSSRGSLLSRSLPSRSRDFLCR_RISSLGSFS
LHSRQYHSRMALAIFSVIRMQSPWNHSLQLSHPIMKQLMSGLRQMQ_MGAFSPFSDLLSSPASGGSGSEP
SPSISPLPAHSLTTPASDPRTCTDHSAASQAVAKAPTTTSASSHASQAAYSYCAGPMRRLRCKPVGGRPR
APKTPQRRH


-------Reading Frame 6--------


GPHLRVAQVWL_PQEAP_LLMTPLPPHLHGCALTSVMAVAAVGWAVAGGALAGTLRASLVRARKGSTCTI
PGPAAGTGAAGTSAGSCWGPRTSSCPDRNHSDHSPQCADMPHTHHTCGLTV_SAAAAAGDAGWVWPPRAA
ERICGAKQSPEQAWPQPLSLTLPGAAGLDQGQASCALHPHPGAHCCPAHCHPAPVTSCADSESLAWGLSL
CTPDSTTPGWPWPSSQ_SGCSPHGTTHCSCHTRS_SS_CPVCGRCSRWAHSPHSRTCCPPRHLEALGLNH
LPPYLRSRRTPSRPPPATREPAQTTRRRPRRLQRRPQLLPLLVTPPRQRTPIAQAPCVVSAANQ_VAGLE
PPRPLSAAI
```

Exercises

Exercise 8.1
> Write a subroutine that checks a string and returns true if it's a DNA sequence. Write another that checks for protein sequence data.

Exercise 8.2
> Write a program that can search by name for a gene in an unsorted array.

Exercise 8.3
> Write a program that can search by name for a gene in a sorted array; use the Perl sort function to sort an array. For extra credit: write a binary search subroutine to do the searching.

Exercise 8.4
> Write a subroutine that inserts an element into a sorted array. Hint: use the splice Perl function to insert the element, as shown in Chapter 4.

Exercise 8.5
> Write a program that searches by name for a gene in a hash. Get the genes from your own work or try downloading a list of all genes for a given organism from *www.ncbi.nlm.nih.gov* or one of the web sites given in Appendix A. Make a hash of all the genes (key=name, value=gene ID or sequence). Hint: you may have to write a short Perl program to reformat the list of genes you start with to make it easy to populate the Perl hash.

Exercise 8.6
> Write a subroutine that checks an array of data and returns true if it's in FASTA format. Note that FASTA expects the standard IUB/IUPAC amino acid and

nucleic acid codes, plus the dash (–) that represents a gap of unknown length. Also, the asterisk (*) represents a stop codon for amino acids. Be careful using an asterisk in regular expressions; use a * to escape it to match an actual asterisk.

The remaining problems deal with the effect of mutations in DNA on the proteins they encode. They combine the subject of randomization and mutations from Chapter 7 plus the subject of the genetic code from this chapter.

Exercise 8.7

For each codon, make note of what effect single nucleotide mutations have on the codon: does the same amino acid result, or does the codon now encode a different amino acid? Which one? Write a subroutine that, given a codon, returns a list of all the amino acids that may result from any single mutation in the codon.

Exercise 8.8

Write a subroutine that, given an amino acid, randomly changes it to one of the amino acids calculated in Exercise 8.7.

Exercise 8.9

Write a program that randomly mutates the amino acids in a protein but restricts the possibilities to those that can occur due to a single mutation in the original codons, as in Exercises 8.7 and 8.8.

Exercise 8.10

Some codons are more likely than others to occur in random DNA. For instance, there are 6 of the 64 possible codons that code for the amino acid serine, but only 2 of the 64 codes for phenylalanine. Write a subroutine that, given an amino acid, returns the probability that it's coded by a randomly generated codon (see Chapter 7).

Exercise 8.11

Write a subroutine that takes as arguments an amino acid; a position 1, 2, or 3; and a nucleotide. It then takes each codon that encodes the specified amino acid (there may be from one to six such codons), and mutates it at the specified position to the specified nucleotide. Finally, it returns the set of amino acids that are encoded by the mutated codons.

Exercise 8.12

Write a program that, given two amino acids, returns the probability that a single mutation in their underlying (but unspecified) codons results in the codon of one amino acid mutating to the codon of the other amino acid.

## CHAPTER 9

Restriction Maps and Regular Expressions

In this chapter, I'll give an overview of Perl regular expressions and Perl operators, two essential features of the language we've been using all along. We'll also investigate the programming of a standard, fundamental molecular-biology technique: the discovery of a restriction map for a sequence. Restriction digests were one of the original ways to "fingerprint" DNA; this can now be simulated on the computer.

Restriction maps and their associated restriction digests are common calculations in the laboratory and are provided by several software packages. They are essential tools in the planning of cloning experiments; they can be used to insert a desired stretch of DNA into a cloning vector, for instance. Restriction maps also find application in sequencing projects, for instance in shotgun or directed sequencing.

Regular Expressions

We've been dealing with regular expressions for a while now. This section fills in some background an.d ties together the somewhat scattered discussions of regular expressions from earlier parts of the book.

Regular expressions are interesting, important, and rich in capabilities. Jeffrey Friedl's book *Mastering Regular Expressions* (O'Reilly) is entirely devoted to them. Perl makes particularly good use of regular expressions, and the Perl documentation explains them well. Regular expressions are useful when programming with biological data such as sequence, or with GenBank, PDB, and BLAST files.

Regular expressions are ways of representing—and searching for—many strings with one string. Although they are not strictly the same thing, it's useful to think of regular expressions as a kind of highly developed set of wildcards. The special characters in regular expressions are more properly known as metacharacters.

Most people are familiar with wildcards, which are found in search engines or in the game of poker. You might find the reference to every word that starts with biolog by typing biolog*, for instance. Or you may find yourself holding five aces. (Different situations may use different wildcards. Perl regular expressions use * to mean "0 or more of the preceding item," not "followed by anything" as in the wildcard example just given.)

In computer science, these kinds of wildcards or metacharacters have an important history, both practically and theoretically. The asterisk character in particular is called the Kleene closure after the eminent logician who invented it. As a nod to the theory, I'll mention there is a simple model of a computer, less powerful than a Turing machine, that can deal with exactly the same kinds of languages that can be described by regular expressions. This machine model is called a *finite state automaton*. But enough theory for now.

We've already seen many examples that use regular expressions to find things in a DNA or protein sequence. Here I'll talk briefly about the fundamental ideas behind regular expressions as an introduction to some terminology. There is a useful summary of regular-expression features in Appendix B. Finally, we'll see how to learn more about them in the Perl documentation.

So let's start with a practical example that should be familiar by now to those who have been reading this text sequentially: using character classes to search DNA. Let's say there is a small motif you'd like to find in your library of DNA that is six basepairs long: CT followed by C or G or T followed by ACG. The third nucleotide in this motif is never A, but it can be C, G, or T. You can make a regular expression by letting the character class [CGT] stand for the variable position. The motif can then be represented by a regular expression that looks like this: CT[CGT]ACG. This is a motif that is six base pairs long with a C,G, or T in the third position. If your DNA was in a scalar variable $dna, you can test for the presence of the motif by using the regular expression as a conditional test in a pattern-matching statement, like so:

```
if( $dna =~ /CT[CGT]ACG/ ) {
    print "I found the motif!!\n";
}
```

Regular expressions are based on three fundamental ideas:

Repetition (or closure)
> The asterisk (*), also called Kleene closure or star, indicates 0 or more repetitions of the character just before it. For example, abc* matches any of these strings: ab, abc, abcc, abccc, abcccc, and so on. The regular expression matches an infinite number of strings.

Alternation
> In Perl, the pattern (a|b) (read: a or b) matches the string a or the string b.

Concatenation
> This is a real obvious one. In Perl, the string ab means the character a followed by (concatenated with) the character b.

The use of parentheses for grouping is important: they are also metacharacters. So, for instance, the string (abc|def)z*x matches such strings as abcx, abczx, abczzx, defx, defzx, defzzzzzx, and so on. In English, it matches either abc or def followed by zero or more z's, and ending with an x. This example combines the ideas of grouping, alternation, closure, and concatenation. The real power of regular expressions is seen in this combining of the three fundamental ideas.

Perl has many regular-expression features. They are basically shortcuts for the three fundamental ideas we've just seen—repetition, alternation, and concatenation. For instance, the character class shown earlier can be written using alternation as (C|G|T). Another common feature is the period, which can stand for any character, except a newline. So ACG.*GCA stands for any DNA that starts with ACG and ends with GCA. In English, this reads as: ACG followed by 0 or more characters followed by GCA.

In Perl, regular expressions are usually enclosed within forward slashes and are used as pattern-matching specifiers. Check the documentation (or Appendix B), for m//, which includes some options that affect the behavior of the regular expressions. Regular expressions are also used in many of Perl's built-in commands, as you will see.

The Perl documentation is essential: start with the *perlre* section of the Perl manual at *http://www.perl.com/pub/doc/manual/html/pod/perlre.html#Regular_Expressions*.

Restriction Maps and Restriction Enzymes

One of the great discoveries in molecular biology, which paved the way for the current golden age in biological research, was the discovery of restriction enzymes. For the nonbiologist, and to help set up the programming material that follows, here's a short overview.

Background

Restriction enzymes are proteins that cut DNA at short, specific sequences; for example, the popular restriction enzymes EcoRI and HindIII are widely used in the lab. EcoRI cuts where it finds GAATTC, between the G and A. Actually, it cuts both complementary strands, leaving an overhang on each end. These "sticky ends" of a few bases in single strands make it possible for the fragments to re-form, making possible the insertion of DNA into vectors for cloning and sequencing, for instance. HindIII cuts at AAGCTT and cuts between the As. Some restriction enzymes cut in the middle and result in "blunt ends" with no overhang. About 1,000 restriction enzymes are known.

If you look at the reverse complement of the restriction enzyme EcoRI, you see it's GAATTC, the same sequence. This is a biological version of a palindrome, a word that reads the same in reverse. Many restriction sites are palindromes.

Computing restriction maps is a common and practical bioinformatics calculation in the laboratory. Restriction maps are computed to plan experiments, to find the best way to cut DNA to insert a gene, to make a site-specific mutation, or for several other applications of recombinant DNA techniques. By computing first, the laboratory scientist saves considerably on the necessary trial-and-error at the laboratory bench. Look for more about restriction enzymes at *http://www.neb.com/rebase/rebase.html*.

We'll now write a program that does something useful in the lab: it will look for restriction enzymes in a sequence of DNA and report back with a restriction map of exactly where in the DNA the restriction enzymes appear.

Planning the Program

Back in Chapter 5, you saw how to look for regular expressions in text. So you've an idea of how to find motifs in sequences with Perl. Now let's think about how to use those techniques to create restriction maps. Here are some questions to ask:

Where do I find restriction enzyme data?
  Restriction enzyme data can be found at the Restriction Enzyme Database, (REBASE), which is on the Web at *http://www.neb.com/rebase/rebase.html*.

How do I represent restriction enzymes in regular expressions?
  Exploring that site, you'll see that restriction enzymes are represented in their own language. We'll try to translate that language into the language of regular expressions.

How do I store restriction enzyme data?
  There are about 1,000 restriction enzymes with names and definitions. This makes them candidates for the fast key-value type of lookup hashes provide. When you write a real application, say for the Web, it's a good idea to create a DBM file to store the information, ready to use when a program needs a lookup. I will cover DBM files in Chapter 10; here, I'll just demonstrate the principle. We'll keep only a few restriction enzyme definitions in the program.

How do I accept queries from the user?
  You can ask for a restriction enzyme name, or you can allow the user to type in a regular expression directly. We'll do the first. Also, you want to let the user specify which sequence to use. Again, to simplify matters, you'll just read in the data from a sample DNA file.

How do I report back the restriction map to the user?
  This is an important question. The simplest way is to generate a list of positions with the names of the restriction enzymes found there. This is useful for further processing, as it presents the information very simply.

  But what if you don't want to do further processing; you just want to communicate the restriction map to the user? Then, perhaps it'd be more useful to present a graphical display, perhaps print out the sequence with a line above it that flags the presence of the enzymes.

There are lots of fancy bells and whistles you can use, but let's do it the simple way for now and output a list.

So, the plan is to write a program that includes restriction enzyme data translated into regular expressions, stored as the values of the keys of the restriction enzyme names. DNA sequence data will be used from the file, and the user will be prompted for names of restriction enzymes. The appropriate regular expression will be retrieved from the hash, and we'll search for all instances of that regular expression, plus their locations. Finally, the list of locations found will be returned.

Restriction Enzyme Data

The restriction enzyme data is available in a variety of formats, as a visit to the REBASE web site will show you. After looking around, you decide to get the information from the *bionet* file, which has a fairly simple layout. Here's the header and a few restriction enzymes from that file:

```
REBASE version 104                                          bionet.104


    =-=-=-=-=-=-=-=-=-=-=-=-=-=-=-=-=-=-=-=-=-=-=-=-=-=-=-=-=-=-=-=-=
    REBASE, The Restriction Enzyme Database   http://rebase.neb.com
    Copyright (c) Dr. Richard J. Roberts, 2001.   All rights reserved.
    =-=-=-=-=-=-=-=-=-=-=-=-=-=-=-=-=-=-=-=-=-=-=-=-=-=-=-=-=-=-=-=-=


Rich Roberts                                                Mar 30 2001

Aaal (XmaIII)                    C^GGCCG
AacI (BamHI)                     GGATCC
AaeI (BamHI)                     GGATCC
AagI (ClaI)                      AT^CGAT
AaqI (ApaLI)                     GTGCAC
AarI                             CACCTGCNNNN^
AarI                             ^NNNNNNNNGCAGGTG
AatI (StuI)                      AGG^CCT
AatII                            GACGT^C
AauI (Bsp1407I)                  T^GTACA
AbaI (BclI)                      T^GATCA
AbeI (BbvCI)                     CC^TCAGC
AbeI (BbvCI)                     GC^TGAGG
AbrI (XhoI)                      C^TCGAG
AcaI (AsuII)                     TTCGAA
AcaII (BamHI)                    GGATCC
AcaIII (MstI)                    TGCGCA
AcaIV (HaeIII)                   GGCC
AccI                             GT^MKAC
AccII (FnuDII)                   CG^CG
AccIII (BspMII)                  T^CCGGA
Acc16I (MstI)                    TGC^GCA
```

```
Acc36I  (BspMI)          ACCTGCNNNN^
Acc36I  (BspMI)          ^NNNNNNNNGCAGGT
Acc38I  (EcoRII)         CCWGG
Acc65I  (KpnI)           G^GTACC
Acc113I (ScaI)           AGT^ACT
AccB1I  (HgiCI)          G^GYRCC
AccB2I  (HaeII)          RGCGC^Y
AccB7I  (PflMI)          CCANNNN^NTGG
AccBSI  (BsrBI)          CCG^CTC
AccBSI  (BsrBI)          GAG^CGG
AccEBI  (BamHI)          G^GATCC
AceI    (TseI)           G^CWGC
AceII   (NheI)           GCTAG^C
AceIII                   CAGCTCNNNNNNN^
AceIII                   ^NNNNNNNNNNNGAGCTG
AciI                     C^CGC
AciI                     G^CGG
AclI                     AA^CGTT
AclNI   (SpeI)           A^CTAGT
AclWI   (BinI)           GGATCNNNN^
```

Your first task is to read this file and get the names and the recognition site (or restriction site) for each enzyme. To simplify matters for now, simply discard the parenthesized enzyme names.

How can this data be read?

```
Discard header lines

For each data line:

    remove parenthesized names, for simplicity's sake

    get and store the name and the recognition site

    Translate the recognition sites to regular expressions
        --but keep the recognition site, for printing out results
}

return the names, recognition sites, and the regular expressions
```

This is high-level undetailed pseudocode, so let's refine and expand it. (Notice that the curly brace isn't properly matched. That's okay, because there are no syntax rules for pseudocode; do whatever works for you!) Here's some pseudocode that discards the header lines:

```
foreach line

    if /Rich Roberts/

        break out of the foreach loop

}
```

This is based on the format of the file, in which the string you're looking for is the last text before the data lines start. (Of course, if the format of the file should change, this might no longer work.)

Now let's further expand the pseudocode, thinking how to do the tasks involved:

```
# Discard header lines
# This keeps reading lines, up to a line containing "Rich Roberts"
foreach line
    if /Rich Roberts/
        break out of the foreach loop
}

For each data line:

    # Split the two or three (if there's a parenthesized name) fields
    @fields = split( " ", $_);

    # Get and store the name and the recognition site
    $name = shift @fields;

    $site = pop @fields;

    # Translate the recognition sites to regular expressions
        --but keep the recognition site, for printing out results
}

    return the names, recognition sites, and the regular expressions
```

This isn't the translation, but let's look at what you've done.

First, you want to extract the name and recognition site data from a string. The most common way to separate words in a line of Perl, especially if the string is nicely formatted, is with the Perl built-in function split.

If you have two or three per line that have whitespace and are separated from each other by whitespace, you can get them into an array with the following simple call to split (which acts on the line as stored in the special variable @_.:

```
($name, $site) = split(" ")
```

The @fields array may have two or three elements depending on whether there was a parenthesized alternate enzyme named. But you always want the first and the last elements:

```
$name = shift@fields;
$site = pop@fields;
```

You now have the problem of translating the recognition site to a regular expression.

Looking over the recognition sites and having read the documentation on REBASE you found on its web site, you know that the cut site is represented by the caret (^). This doesn't help make a regular expression that finds the site in sequence, so you should remove it (see Exercise 9.6).

Also notice that the bases given in the recognition sites are not just the bases A, C, G, and T, but they also use the more extended alphabet presented in Table 4-1. These additional letters include a letter for every possible group of two, three, or four bases. They're really like abbreviations for character classes in that respect. Aha! Let's write a subroutine that substitutes character classes for these codes, and then we'll have our regular expression.

Of course, REBASE uses them, because a given restriction enzyme might well match a few different recognition sites.

Example 9-1 is a subroutine that, given a string, translates these codes into character classes.

Example 9-1. Translate IUB ambiguity codes to regular expressions

```
# IUB_to_regexp
#
# A subroutine that, given a sequence with IUB ambiguity codes,
# outputs a translation with IUB codes changed to regular expressions
#
# These are the IUB ambiguity codes
# (Eur. J. Biochem. 150: 1-5, 1985):
# R = G or A
# Y = C or T
# M = A or C
# K = G or T
# S = G or C
# W = A or T
# B = not A (C or G or T)
# D = not C (A or G or T)
# H = not G (A or C or T)
# V = not T (A or C or G)
# N = A or C or G or T

sub IUB_to_regexp {

    my($iub) = @_;

    my $regular_expression = '';

    my %iub2character_class = (

        A => 'A',
        C => 'C',
        G => 'G',
        T => 'T',
        R => '[GA]',
        Y => '[CT]',
        M => '[AC]',
        K => '[GT]',
        S => '[GC]',
        W => '[AT]',
```

```
        B => '[CGT]',
        D => '[AGT]',
        H => '[ACT]',
        V => '[ACG]',
        N => '[ACGT]',
    );

    # Remove the ^ signs from the recognition sites
    $iub =~ s/\^//g;

    # Translate each character in the iub sequence
    for ( my $i = 0 ; $i < length($iub) ; ++$i ) {
        $regular_expression
            .= $iub2character_class{substr($iub, $i, 1)};
    }

    return $regular_expression;
}
```

It seems you're almost ready to write a subroutine to get the data from the REBASE datafile. But there's one important item you haven't addressed: what exactly is the data you want to return?

You plan to return three data items per line of the original REBASE file: the enzyme name, the recognition site, and the regular expression. This doesn't fit easily into a hash. You can return an array that stores these three data items in three consecutive slots. This can work: to read the data, you'd have to read groups of three items from the array. It's doable but might make lookup a little difficult. As you get into more advanced Perl, you'll find that you can create your own complex data structures.

Since you've learned about split, maybe you can have a hash in which the key is the enzyme name, and the value is a string with the recognition site and the regular expression separated by whitespace. Then you can look up the data fast and just extract the desired values using split. Example 9-2 shows this method.

Example 9-2. Subroutine to parse a REBASE datafile

```
# parseREBASE—Parse REBASE bionet file
#
# A subroutine to return a hash where
#    key   = restriction enzyme name
#    value = whitespace-separated recognition site and regular expression

sub parseREBASE {

    my($rebasefile) = @_;

    use strict;
    use warnings;
    use BeginPerlBioinfo;      # see Chapter 6 about this module
```

Example 9-2. Subroutine to parse a REBASE datafile (continued)

```perl
# Declare variables
my @rebasefile = ( );
my %rebase_hash = ( );
my $name;
my $site;
my $regexp;

# Read in the REBASE file
@rebasefile = get_file_data($rebasefile);

foreach ( @rebasefile ) {

    # Discard header lines
    ( 1 .. /Rich Roberts/ ) and next;

    # Discard blank lines
    /^\s*$/ and next;

    # Split the two (or three if includes parenthesized name) fields
    my @fields = split( " ", $_ );

    # Get and store the name and the recognition site

    # Remove parenthesized names, for simplicity's sake,
    # by not saving the middle field, if any,
    # just the first and last
    $name = shift @fields;

    $site = pop @fields;

    # Translate the recognition sites to regular expressions
    $regexp = IUB_to_regexp($site);

    # Store the data into the hash
    $rebase_hash{$name} = "$site $regexp";
}

# Return the hash containing the reformatted REBASE data
return %rebase_hash;
}
```

This parseREBASE subroutine does quite a lot. Is there, however, too much in one subroutine; should it be rewritten? It's a good question to ask yourself as you're writing code. In this case, let's leave it as it is. However, in addition to doing a lot, it also does it in a few new ways, which we'll look at now.

Logical Operators and the Range Operator

You're using a foreach loop to process the lines of the *bionet* file stored in the @rebasefile array.

Within that loop you use a new feature of Perl to skip the header lines, called the *range operator* (..), which is used in this line:

```
( 1 .. /Rich Roberts/ ) and next;
```

This has the effect of skipping everything from the first line up to and including the line with "Rich Roberts," in other words, the header lines. (Range operators must have at least one of their endpoints given as a number to work like this.)

The and function is a *logical operator*. Logical operators are available in most programming languages. In Perl they've become very popular, so although we haven't used them a great deal in this book, you'll often come across code that does. In fact, you'll start to see them a bit more as the book continues.

Logical operators can test if two conditions are both true, for instance:

```
if( $string eq 'kinase'  and   $num == 3) {
  ...
}
```

Only if both the conditions are true is the entire statement true.

Similarly, with logical operators you can test if at least one of the conditions is true using the or operator, for instance:

```
if( $string eq 'kinase'  or   $num == 3) {
  ...
}
```

Here, the if statement is true if either or both of the conditionals are true.

There is also the not logical operator, a negation operator with which you can test if something is false:

```
if( not  6 == 9 ) {
  ...
}
```

6 == 9 returns false, which is negated by the not operator, so the entire conditional returns true.

There are also the closely related operators, && for and, || for or, and ! for not. These have slightly different behavior (actually, different precedence); most Perl code uses the versions I've shown, but both are common.

When in doubt about precedence, you can always parenthesize expressions to ensure your statement means what you intend it to mean. (See the section "Precedence of Operations and Parentheses" later in this chapter.)

Logical operators also have an order of evaluation, which makes them useful for controlling the flow of programs. Let's take a look at how the and operator evaluates its two arguments. It first evaluates the left argument, and if it's true, evaluates and returns the right. If the left argument evaluates to false, the right argument is never touched. So the and operator can act like a mini if statement. For instance, the following two examples are equivalent:

```
if( $verbose ) {
    print $helpful_but_verbose_message;
}

$verbose and print $helpful_but_verbose_message;
```

Of course, the if statement is more flexible, because it allows you to easily add more statements to the block, and elsif and else conditions to their own blocks. But for simple situations, the and operator works well.*

The logical operator or evaluates and returns the left argument if it's true; if the left argument doesn't evaluate to true, the or operator then evaluates and returns the right argument. So here's another way to write a one-line statement that you'll often see in Perl programs:

```
open(MYFILE, $file) or die "I cannot open file $file: $!";
```

This is basically equivalent to our frequent:

```
unless(open(MYFILE, $file)) {
    print "I cannot open file $file\n";
    exit;
}
```

Let's go back and take a look at the parseREBASE subroutine with the line:

```
( 1 .. /Rich Roberts/ ) and next;
```

The left argument is the range 1 .. /Rich Roberts/. When you're in that range of lines, the range operator returns a true value. Because it's true, the and boolean operator goes on to see if the value on the other side is true and finds the next function, which evaluates to true, even as it takes you back to the "next" iteration of the enclosing foreach loop. So if you're between the first line and the Rich Roberts line, you skip the rest of the loop.

Similarly, the line:

```
/^\s*$/ and next;
```

takes you back to the next iteration of the foreach if the left argument, which matches a blank line, is true.

The other parts of this parseREBASE subroutine have already been discussed, during the design phase.

---

* You can even chain logical operators one after the other to build up more complicated expressions and use parentheses to group them. Personally, I don't like that style much, but in Perl, there's more than one way to do it!

Finding the Restriction Sites

So now it's time to write a main program and see our code in action. Let's start with a little pseudocode to see what still needs to be done:

```
#
# Get DNA
#
get_file_data

extract_sequence_from_fasta_data

#
# Get the REBASE data into a hash, from file "bionet"
#
parseREBASE('bionet');

for each user query

    If query is defined in the hash
        Get positions of query in DNA

    Report on positions, if any

}
```

You now need to write a subroutine that finds the positions of the query in the DNA. Remember that trick of putting a global search in a while loop from Example 5-7 and take heart. No sooner said than:

```
Given arguments $query and $dna

while ( $dna =~ /$query/ig ) {
    save the position of the match
}

    return @positions
```

When you used this trick before, you just counted how many matches there were, not what the positions were. Let's check the documentation for clues, specifically the list of built-in functions in the documentation. It looks like the pos function will solve the problem. It gives the location of the last match of a variable in an m//g search. Example 9-3 shows the main program followed by the required subroutine. It's a simple subroutine, given the Perl functions like pos that make it easy.

Example 9-3. Make restriction map from user queries

```
#!/usr/bin/perl
# Make restriction map from user queries on names of restriction enzymes

use strict;
use warnings;
use BeginPerlBioinfo;      # see Chapter 6 about this module
```

Example 9-3. Make restriction map from user queries (continued)

```perl
# Declare and initialize variables
my %rebase_hash = ();
my @file_data = ();
my $query = '';
my $dna = '';
my $recognition_site = '';
my $regexp = '';
my @locations = ();

# Read in the file "sample.dna"
@file_data = get_file_data("sample.dna");

# Extract the DNA sequence data from the contents of the file "sample.dna"
$dna = extract_sequence_from_fasta_data(@file_data);

# Get the REBASE data into a hash, from file "bionet"
%rebase_hash = parseREBASE('bionet');

# Prompt user for restriction enzyme names, create restriction map
do {
    print "Search for what restriction site for (or quit)?: ";

    $query = <STDIN>;

    chomp $query;

    # Exit if empty query
    if ($query =~ /^\s*$/ ) {

        exit;
    }

    # Perform the search in the DNA sequence
    if ( exists $rebase_hash{$query} ) {

        ($recognition_site, $regexp) = split ( " ", $rebase_hash{$query});

        # Create the restriction map
        @locations = match_positions($regexp, $dna);

        # Report the restriction map to the user
        if (@locations) {
            print "Searching for $query $recognition_site $regexp\n";
            print "A restriction site for $query at locations:\n";
            print join(" ", @locations), "\n";
        } else {
            print "A restriction site for $query is not in the DNA:\n";
        }
    }
    print "\n";
} until ( $query =~ /quit/ );
```

Example 9-3. Make restriction map from user queries (continued)

```
exit;

###############################################################################
#
# Subroutine
#
# Find locations of a match of a regular expression in a string
#
#
# return an array of positions where the regular expression
#   appears in the string
#

sub match_positions {

    my($regexp, $sequence) = @_;

    use strict;

    use BeginPerlBioinfo;      # see Chapter 6 about this module

    #
    # Declare variables
    #

    my @positions = ( );

    #
    # Determine positions of regular expression matches
    #

    while ( $sequence =~ /$regexp/ig ) {

        push ( @positions, pos($sequence) - length($&) + 1);
    }

    return @positions;
}
```

Here is some sample output from Example 9-3:

```
Search for what restriction enzyme (or quit)?: AceI
Searching for AceI G^CWGC GC[AT]GC
A restriction site for AceI at locations:
54 94 582 660 696 702 840 855 957

Search for what restriction enzyme (or quit)?: AccII
Searching for AccII CG^CG CGCG
A restriction site for AccII at locations:
181
```

```
Search for what restriction enzyme (or quit)?: AaeI
A restriction site for AaeI is not in the DNA:

Search for what restriction enzyme (or quit)?: quit
```

Notice the length($&) in the subroutine match_positions. That $& is a special variable that's set after a successful regular-expression match. It stands for the sequence that matched the regular expression. Since pos gives the position of the first base *following* the match, you have to subtract the length of the matching sequences, plus one (to make the bases start at position 1 instead of position 0) to report the starting position of the match. Other special variables include $` which contains everything in the string before the successful match; and $´, which contains everything in the string after the successful match. So, for example: '123456' =~ /34/ succeeds at setting these special variables like so: $` = '12', $& = '34', and $´ = '56'.

What we have here is admittedly bare bones, but it does work. See the exercises at the end of the chapter for ways to extend this code.

Perl Operations

We've made it pretty far in this introductory programming book without talking about basic arithmetic operations, because you haven't really needed much more than addition to increment counters.

However, an important part of any programming language, Perl included, is the ability to do mathematical calculations. Look at Appendix B, which shows the basic operations available in Perl.

Precedence of Operations and Parentheses

Operations have rules of precedence. These enable the language to decide which operations should be done first when there are a few of them in a row. The order of operations can change the result, as the following example demonstrates.

Say you have the code 8 + 4 / 2. If you did the division first, you'd get 8 + 2, or 10. However, if you did the addition first, you'd get 12 / 2, or 6.

Now programming languages assign precedences to operations. If you know these, you can write expressions such as 8 + 4 / 2, and you'd know what to expect. But this is a slippery slope.

For one thing, what if you get it wrong? Or, what if someone else has to read the code who doesn't have the memorization powers you do? Or, what if you memorize it for one language and Perl does it differently? (Different languages do indeed have different precedence rules.)

There is a solution, and it's called *using parentheses*. For Example 9-3, if you simply add parentheses: (8 + (4 / 2)), it's clear to you, other readers, and the Perl program, that you want to do the division first. Note that "inner" parentheses, contained within another pair of parentheses, are evaluated first.

Remember to use parentheses in complicated expressions to specify the order of operations. Among other things, it will save you some long debugging sessions!

Exercises

Exercise 9.1
  Modify Example 9-3 to accept DNA from the command line; if it's not specified there, prompt the user for a FASTA filename and read in the DNA sequence data.

Exercise 9.2
  Modify Exercise 9.1 to read in, and make a hash of, the entire REBASE restriction site data from the *bionet* file.

Exercise 9.3
  Modify Exercise 9.2 to store the REBASE hash created in a DBM file if it doesn't exist or to use the DBM file if it does exist. (Look ahead to Chapter 10 for more information about DBM.)

Exercise 9.4
  Modify Example 5-3 to report on the locations of the motifs that it finds, even if motif appears multiple times in the sequence data.

Exercise 9.5
  Include a graphic display of the cut sites in the restriction map by printing the sequence and labeling the recognition sites with the enzyme name. Can you make a map that handles multiple restriction enzymes? How can you handle overlapping restriction sites?

Exercise 9.6
  Write a subroutine that returns a restriction digest, the fragments of DNA left after performing a restriction reaction. Remember to take into account the location of the cut site. (This requires you to parse the REBASE *bionet* in a different manner. You may, if you wish, ignore restriction enzymes that are not given with a ^ indicating a cut site.)

Exercise 9.7
  Extend the restriction map software to take into account the opposite strand for nonpalindromic recognition sites.

Exercise 9.8
  Given an arithmetic expression without parentheses, write a subroutine that adds the appropriate parentheses to conform to Perl's precedence rules. (Warning: this is a pretty hard exercise and should be skipped by all but the true believers who have extra time on their hands. See the Perl documentation for the precedence rules.)

## CHAPTER 10

GenBank

GenBank (Genetic Sequence Data Bank) is a rapidly growing international repository of known genetic sequences from a variety of organisms. Its use is central to modern biology and to bioinformatics.

This chapter shows you how to write Perl programs to extract information from GenBank files and libraries. Exercises include looking for patterns; creating special libraries; and parsing the flat-file format to extract the DNA, annotation, and features. You will learn how to make a DBM database to create your own rapid-access lookups on selected data in a GenBank library.

Perl is a great tool for dealing with GenBank files. It enables you to extract and use any of the detailed data in the sequence and in the annotation, such as in the FEATURES table and elsewhere. When I first started using Perl, I wrote a program that searched GenBank for all sequence records annotated as being located on human chromosome 22. I found many genes where that information was so deeply buried within the annotation, that the major gene mapping database, Genome Database (GDB), hadn't included them in their chromosome map. I think you'll discover the same feeling of power over the information when you start applying Perl to GenBank files.

Most biologists are familiar with GenBank. Researchers can perform a search, e.g., a BLAST search on some query sequence, and collect a set of GenBank files of related sequences as a result. Because the GenBank records are maintained by the individual scientists who discovered the sequences, if you find some new sequence of interest, you can publish it in GenBank.

GenBank files have a great deal of information in them in addition to sequence data, including identifiers such as accession numbers and gene names, phylogenetic classification, and references to published literature. A GenBank file may also include a detailed FEATURES table that summarizes facts about the sequence, such as the location of the regulatory regions, the protein translation, and exons and introns.

GenBank is sometimes referred to as a *databank* or *data store*, which is different from a *database*. Databases typically have a relational structure imposed upon the data, including associated indices and links and a query language. GenBank in comparison is a *flat file*, that is, an ASCII text file that is easily readable by humans.*

From its humble beginnings GenBank has rapidly grown, and the flat-file format has seen signs of strain during the growth. With a quickly advancing body of knowledge, especially one that's growing as quickly as genetic data, it's difficult for the design of a databank to keep up. Several reworkings of GenBank have been done, but the flat-file format—in all its frustrating glory—still remains.

Due to a certain flexibility in the content of some sections of a GenBank record, extracting the information you're looking for can be tricky. This flexibility is good, in that it allows you to put what you think is most important into the data's annotation. It's bad, because that same flexibility makes it harder to write programs that to find and extract the desired annotations. As a result, the trend has been towards more structure in the annotations.

Since Perl's data structures and its use of regular expressions make it a good tool for manipulating flat files, Perl is especially well-suited to deal with GenBank data. Using these features in Perl and building on the skills you've developed from previous chapters, you can write programs to access the accumulated genetic knowledge of the scientific community in GenBank.

Since this is a beginning book that requires no programming experience, you should not expect to find the most finished, multipurpose software here. Instead you'll find a solid introduction to parsing and building fast lookup tables for GenBank files. If you've never done so, I strongly recommend you explore the National Center for Biotechnology Information (NCBI) at the National Institutes of Health (NIH) (*http://www.ncbi.nlm.nih.gov*). While you're at it, stop by the European Bioinformatics Institute (EBI) at *http://www.ebi.ac.uk* and the bioinformatics arm of the European Molecular Biology Laboratory (EMBL) at *http://www.embl-heidelberg.de/*. These are large, heavily funded governmental bioinformatics powerhouses, and they have (and distribute) a great deal of state-of-the-art bioinformatics software.

GenBank Files

The primary repositories for genetic information are the NCBI GenBank, EMBL in Europe, and the DNA Data Bank of Japan (DDBJ). All have almost identical information due to international cooperative agreements. Each entry or record in Gen-Bank or its mirror sites may contain identifying, descriptive, and genetic information in ASCII-format files. Each record is written in a specific standard format, organized

---

* GenBank is also distributed in ASN.1 format, for which you need specialized tools, provided by NCBI.

so that both humans and computer programs can extract the desired information with reasonable ease.

Let's look at a relatively short GenBank record and at how the fields are defined, before writing any code. I'll save this information in a file called *record.gb*, for use in later programs.

```
LOCUS       AB031069    2487 bp    mRNA          PRI       27-MAY-2000
DEFINITION  Homo sapiens PCCX1 mRNA for protein containing CXXC domain 1,
            complete cds.
ACCESSION   AB031069
VERSION     AB031069.1  GI:8100074
KEYWORDS    .
SOURCE      Homo sapiens embryo male lung fibroblast cell_line:HuS-L12 cDNA to
            mRNA.
  ORGANISM  Homo sapiens
            Eukaryota; Metazoa; Chordata; Craniata; Vertebrata; Euteleostomi;
            Mammalia; Eutheria; Primates; Catarrhini; Hominidae; Homo.
REFERENCE   1  (sites)
  AUTHORS   Fujino,T., Hasegawa,M., Shibata,S., Kishimoto,T., Imai,Si. and
            Takano,T.
  TITLE     PCCX1, a novel DNA-binding protein with PHD finger and CXXC domain,
            is regulated by proteolysis
  JOURNAL   Biochem. Biophys. Res. Commun. 271 (2), 305-310 (2000)
  MEDLINE   20261256
REFERENCE   2  (bases 1 to 2487)
  AUTHORS   Fujino,T., Hasegawa,M., Shibata,S., Kishimoto,T., Imai,S. and
            Takano,T.
  TITLE     Direct Submission
  JOURNAL   Submitted (15-AUG-1999) to the DDBJ/EMBL/GenBank databases.
            Tadahiro Fujino, Keio University School of Medicine, Department of
            Microbiology; Shinanomachi 35, Shinjuku-ku, Tokyo 160-8582, Japan
            (E-mail:fujino@microb.med.keio.ac.jp,
            Tel:+81-3-3353-1211(ex.62692), Fax:+81-3-5360-1508)
FEATURES             Location/Qualifiers
     source          1..2487
                     /organism="Homo sapiens"
                     /db_xref="taxon:9606"
                     /sex="male"
                     /cell_line="HuS-L12"
                     /cell_type="lung fibroblast"
                     /dev_stage="embryo"
     gene            229..2199
                     /gene="PCCX1"
     CDS             229..2199
                     /gene="PCCX1"
                     /note="a nuclear protein carrying a PHD finger and a CXXC
                     domain"
                     /codon_start=1
                     /product="protein containing CXXC domain 1"
                     /protein_id="BAA96307.1"
                     /db_xref="GI:8100075"
                     /translation="MEGDGSDPEPPDAGEDSKSENGENAPIYCICRKPDINCFMIGCD
```

```
NCNEWFHGDCIRITEKMAKAIREWYCRECREKDPKLEIRYRHKKSRERDGNERDSSEP
RDEGGGRKRPVPDPDLQRRAGSGTGVGAMLARGSASPHKSSPQPLVATPSQHHQQQQQ
QIKRSARMCGECEACRRTEDCGHCDFCRDMKKFGGPNKIRQKCRLRQCQLRARESYKY
FPSSLSPVTPSESLPRPRRPLPTQQQPQPSQKLGRIREDEGAVASSTVKEPPEATATP
EPLSDEDLPLDPDLYQDFCAGAFDDHGLPWMSDTEESPFLDPALRKRAVKVKHVKRRE
KKSEKKKEERYKRHRQKQKHKDKWKHPERADAKDPASLPQCLGPGCVRPAQPSSKYCS
DDCGMKLAANRIYEILPQRIQQWQQSPCIAEEHGKKLLERIRREQQSARTRLQEMERR
FHELEAIILRAKQQAVREDEESNEGDSDDTDLQIFCVSCGHPINPRVALRHMERCYAK
YESQTSFGSMYPTRIEGATRLFCDVYNPQSKTYCKRLQVLCPEHSRDPKVPADEVCGC
PLVRDVFELTGDFCRLPKRQCNRHYCWEKLRRAEVDLERVRVWYKLDELFEQERNVRT
AMTNRAGLLALMLHQTIQHDPLTTDLRSSADR"
BASE COUNT     564 a    715 c    768 g    440 t
ORIGIN
        1 agatggcggc gctgaggggt cttgggggct ctaggccggc cacctactgg tttgcagcgg
       61 agacgacgca tggggcctgc gcaataggag tacgctgcct gggaggcgtg actagaagcg
      121 gaagtagttg tgggcgcctt tgcaaccgcc tgggacgccg ccgagtggtc tgtgcaggtt
      181 cgcgggtcgc tggcggggt cgtgagggag tgcgccggga gcggagatat ggagggagat
      241 ggttcagacc cagagcctcc agatgccggg gaggacagca agtccgagaa tggggagaat
      301 gcgcccatct actgcatctg ccgcaaaccg gacatcaact gcttcatgat cgggtgtgac
      361 aactgcaatg agtggttcca tggggactgc atccggatca ctgagaagat ggccaaggcc
      421 atccgggagt ggtactgtcg ggagtgcaga gagaaagacc ccaagctaga gattcgctat
      481 cggcacaaga agtcacggga gcgggatggc aatgagcggg acagcagtga gccccgggat
      541 gagggtggag ggcgcaagag gcctgtccct gatccagacc tgcagcgccg ggcagggtca
      601 gggacagggg ttggggccat gcttgctcgg ggctctgctt cgccccacaa atcctctccg
      661 cagcccttgg tggccacacc cagccagcat caccagcagc agcagcagca gatcaaacgg
      721 tcagcccgca tgtgtggtga gtgtgaggca tgtcggcgca ctgaggactg tggtcactgt
      781 gatttctgtc gggacatgaa gaagttcggg ggccccaaca agatccggca gaagtgccgg
      841 ctgcgccagt gccagctgcg ggcccgggaa tcgtacaagt acttcccttc ctcgctctca
      901 ccagtgacgc cctcagagtc cctgccaagg ccccgccggc cactgcccac ccaacagcag
      961 ccacagccat cacagaagtt agggcgcatc cgtgaagatg aggggggcagt ggcgtcatca
     1021 acagtcaagg agcctcctga ggctacagcc acacctgagc cactctcaga tgaggaccta
     1081 cctctggatc ctgacctgta tcaggacttc tgtgcagggg cctttgatga ccatggcctg
     1141 ccctggatga gcgacacaga agagtcccca ttcctggacc ccgcgctgcg gaagagggca
     1201 gtgaaagtga agcatgtgaa gcgtcgggag aagaagtctg agaagaagaa ggaggagcga
     1261 tacaagcggc atcggcagaa gcagaagcac aaggatataa ggaaacaccc agagagggct
     1321 gatgccaagg accctgcgtc actgccccag tgcctggggc ccggctgtgt gcgccccgcc
     1381 cagcccagct ccaagtattg ctcagatgac tgtggcatga agctggcagc caaccgcatc
     1441 tacgagatcc tcccccagcg catccagcag tggcagcaga gcccttgcat tgctgaagag
     1501 cacggcaaga agctgctcga acgcattcgc cgagagcagc agagtgcccg cactcgcctt
     1561 caggaaatgg aacgccgatt ccatgagctt gaggccatca ttctacgtgc caagcagcag
     1621 gctgtgcgcg aggatgagga gagcaacgag ggtgacagtg atgacacaga cctgcagatc
     1681 ttctgtgttt cctgtgggca ccccatcaac ccacgtgttg ccttgcgcca catggagcgc
     1741 tgctacgcca agtatgagag ccagacgtcc tttgggtcca tgtaccccac acgcattgaa
     1801 ggggccacac gactcttctg tgatgtgtat aatcctcaga gcaaaacata ctgtaagcgg
     1861 ctccaggtgc tgtgccccga gcactcacgg gaccccaaag tgccagctga cgaggtatgc
     1921 gggtgccccc ttgtacgtga tgtctttgag ctcacgggtg acttctgccg cctgcccaag
     1981 cgccagtgca atcgccatta ctgctgggag aagctgcggc gtgcggaagt ggacttggag
     2041 cgcgtgcgtg tgtggtacaa gctggacagg ctgtttgagc aggagcgcaa tgtgcgcaca
     2101 gccatgacaa accgcgcggg attgctggcc ctgatgctgc accagacgat ccagcacgat
     2161 cccctcacta ccgacctgcg ctccagtgcc gaccgctgag cctcctggcc cggacccctt
     2221 acaccctgca ttccagatgg gggagccgcc cggtgcccgt gtgtccgttc ctccactcat
     2281 ctgtttctcc ggttctccct gtgcccatcc accggttgac cgcccatctg cctttatcag
```

```
2341 agggactgtc cccgtcgaca tgttcagtgc ctggtggggc tgcggagtcc actcatcctt
2401 gcctcctctc cctgggtttt gttaataaaa ttttgaagaa accaaaaaaa aaaaaaaaa
2461 aaaaaaaaaa aaaaaaaaaa aaaaaaa
//
```

Even if you're used to seeing GenBank files, it's worth taking the time to look one over, while considering how you would write a program to extract various parts of the data. For instance, how would you extract the sequence data? What's the format of the FEATURES table and its various subfields?

There's a lot of information packed into a typical GenBank entry, and it's important to be able to separate the different parts. For instance, if you can extract the sequence, you can search for motifs, calculate statistics on the sequence, look for similarity with other sequences, and so forth. Similarly, you'll want to separate out—or parse—the various parts of the data annotation. In GenBank, this includes ID numbers, gene names, genus and species, publications, etc. The FEATURES table part of the annotation can include specific information about the DNA, such as the locations of exons, regulatory regions, important mutations, and so on.

The format specification of GenBank files and a great deal of other information about GenBank can be found in the GenBank release notes, *gbrel.txt*, on the Gen-Bank web site at *ftp://ncbi.nlm.nih.gov/genbank/gbrel.txt*.

gbrel.txt gives complete detail about the structure of GenBank files to help programmers, so you may want to refer to it as your searches become more complex. As a Perl programmer, you won't need all of the detail because you can parse data using regular expressions or the split function. You need to get the data out and make it available to your programs. The code that accomplishes this task can be fairly simple, as you will see in this chapter.

GenBank Libraries

GenBank is distributed as a set of libraries—flat files containing many records in succession.[*] As of GenBank release 125.0, August 2001, there are 243 files, most of which are over 200 MB in size. Altogether, GenBank contains 12,813516 loci and 13,543,364,296 bases from 12,813,516 reported sequences. The libraries are usually distributed compressed, which means you can download somewhat smaller files, but you need to uncompress them after you received them. Uncompressed, this amounts to about 50 GB of data. Since 1982, the number of sequences in GenBank has doubled about every 14 months.

---

[*] The data is also distributed in the ASN.1 format.

GenBank libraries are further organized into divisions by the classification of the sequences they contain, either phylogenetically or by sequencing technology. Here are the divisions:

- PRI: primate sequences
- ROD: rodent sequences
- MAM: other mammalian sequences
- VRT: other vertebrate sequences
- INV: invertebrate sequences
- PLN: plant, fungal, and algal sequences
- BCT: bacterial sequences
- VRL: viral sequences
- PHG: bacteriophage sequences
- SYN: synthetic and chimeric sequences
- UNA: unannotated sequences
- EST: EST sequences (expressed sequence tags)
- PAT: patent sequences
- STS: STS sequences (sequence tagged sites)
- GSS: GSS sequences (genome survey sequences)
- HTG: HTGS sequences (high throughput genomic sequencing data)
- HTC: HTC sequences (high throughput cDNA sequencing data)

Some divisions are very large: the largest, the EST, or expressed sequence tag division, is comprised of 123 library files! A portion of human DNA is stored in the PRI division, which contains (as of this writing) 13 library files, for a total of almost 3.5 GB of data. Human data is also stored in the STS, GSS, HTGS, and HTC divisions. Human data alone in GenBank makes up almost 5 million record entries with over 8 trillion bases of sequence.

The public database servers such as Entrez or BLAST at *http://www.ncbi.nlm.nih.gov/* give you access to well-maintained and updated sequence data and programs, but many researchers find that they need to write their own programs to manipulate and analyze the data. The problem is, there's so much data. For many purposes, you can download a selected set of records from NCBI or other locations, but sometimes you need the whole dataset.

It's possible to set up a desktop workstation (Windows, Mac, Unix, or Linux) that contains all of GenBank; just be sure to buy a very large hard disk! Getting all that data onto your hard drive, however, is more difficult. A Perl program called *mirror.pl* helps to address this need. Downloading it, even with a university-standard, high-speed Internet connection can be time-consuming; downloading an entire dataset with a modem can be an exercise in frustration. The best solution is to download only the files you need, in compressed form. The EST data, for example, is about half the entire database; don't download it unless you really need to. If you need to download GenBank, I recommend contacting the help desk at NCBI. They'll help you get the most up-to-date information.

Since you're learning to program, it makes more sense to practice on a tiny, five-record library file, but the programs you'll write will work just fine on the real files.

Separating Sequence and Annotation

In previous chapters you saw how to examine the lines of a file using Perl's array operations. Usually, you do this by saving the data in an array with each appearing as an element of the array.

Let's look at two methods to extract the annotation and the DNA from a GenBank file. In the first method, you'll slurp the file into an array and look through the lines, as in previous programs. In the second, you'll put the whole GenBank record into a scalar variable and use regular expressions to parse the information. Is one approach better than the other? Not necessarily: it depends on the data. There are advantages and disadvantages to each, but both get the job done.

I've put five GenBank records in a file called *library.gb*. As before, you can download the file from this book's web site. You'll use this datafile and the file *record.gb* in the next few examples.

Using Arrays

Example 10-1 shows the first method, which operates on an array containing the lines of the GenBank record. The main program is followed by a subroutine that does the real work.

Example 10-1. Extract annotation and sequence from GenBank file

```
#!/usr/bin/perl
# Extract annotation and sequence from GenBank file

use strict;
use warnings;
use BeginPerlBioinfo;     # see Chapter 6 about this module

# declare and initialize variables
my @annotation = ();
my $sequence = '';
my $filename = 'record.gb';

parse1(\@annotation, \$sequence, $filename);
```

Example 10-1. Extract annotation and sequence from GenBank file (continued)

```
# Print the annotation, and then
#    print the DNA in new format just to check if we got it okay.
print @annotation;

print_sequence($sequence, 50);

exit;

#################################################################
# Subroutine
#################################################################

# parse1
#
# -parse annotation and sequence from GenBank record

sub parse1 {

    my($annotation, $dna, $filename) = @_;

    # $annotation-reference to array
    # $dna        -reference to scalar
    # $filename  -scalar

    # declare and initialize variables
    my $in_sequence = 0;
    my @GenBankFile = ( );

    # Get the GenBank data into an array from a file
    @GenBankFile = get_file_data($filename);

    # Extract all the sequence lines
    foreach my $line (@GenBankFile) {

        if( $line =~ /^\/\/\n/ ) { # If $line is end-of-record line //\n,
            last; #break out of the foreach loop.
        } elsif( $in_sequence) { # If we know we're in a sequence,
            $$dna .= $line; # add the current line to $$dna.
        } elsif ( $line =~ /^ORIGIN/ ) { # If $line begins a sequence,
            $in_sequence = 1; # set the $in_sequence flag.
        } else{ # Otherwise
            push( @$annotation, $line); # add the current line to @annotation.
        }
    }

    # remove whitespace and line numbers from DNA sequence
    $$dna =~ s/[\s0-9]//g;
}
```

Here's the beginning and end of Example 10-1's output of the sequence data:

```
agatggcggcgctgaggggtcttgggggctctaggccggccacctactgg
tttgcagcggagacgacgcatggggcctgcgcaataggagtacgctgcct
```

```
gggaggcgtgactagaagcggaagtagttgtgggcgcctttgcaaccgcc
tgggacgccgccgagtggtctgtgcaggttcgcgggtcgctggcgggggt
cgtgagggagtgcgccgggagcggagatatggagggagatggttcagacc
...
cggtgcccgtgtgtccgttcctccactcatctgtttctccggttctccct
gtgcccatccaccggttgaccgcccatctgcctttatcagagggactgtc
cccgtcgacatgttcagtgcctggtggggctgcggagtccactcatcctt
gcctcctctccctgggttttgttaataaaattttgaagaaaccaaaaaaa
aaaaaaaaaaaaaaaaaaaaaaaaaaaaaaaaaaaaaaaaa
```

The foreach loop in subroutine parse1 in Example 10-1 moves one by one through the lines from the GenBank file stored in the array @GenBankFile. It takes advantage of the structure of a GenBank file, which begins with annotation and runs until the line:

```
ORIGIN
```

is found, after which sequence appears until the end-of-record line // is reached. The loop uses a flag variable $in_sequence to remember that it has found the ORIGIN line and is now reading sequence lines.

The foreach loop has a new feature: the Perl built-in function last, which breaks out of the nearest enclosing loop. It's triggered by the end-of-record line //, which is reached when the entire record has been seen.

A regular expression is used to find the end-of-record line. To correctly match the end-of-record (forward) slashes, you must escape them by putting a backslash in front of each one, so that Perl doesn't interpret them as prematurely ending the pattern. The regular expression also ends with a newline \/\/\n, which is then placed inside the usual delimiters: /\/\/\n/. (When you have a lot of forward slashes in a regular expression, you can use another delimiter around the regular expression and precede it with an m, thus avoiding having to backslash the forward slashes. It's done like so: m!//\n!).

An interesting point about subroutine parse1 is the order of the tests in the foreach loop that goes through the lines of the GenBank record. As you read through the lines of the record, you want to first gather the annotation lines, set a flag when the ORIGIN start-of-sequence line is found, and then collect the lines until the end-of-record // line is found.

Notice that the order of the tests is exactly the opposite. First, you test for the end-of-record line, collect the sequence if the $in_sequence flag is set, and then test for the start-of-sequence ORIGIN line. Finally, you collect the annotation.

The technique of reading lines one by one and using flag variables to mark what section of the file you're in, is a common programming technique. So, take a moment to think about how the loop would behave if you changed the order of the tests. If you collected sequence lines before testing for the end-of-record, you'd never get to the end-of-record test!

Other methods of collecting annotation and sequence lines are possible, especially if you go through the lines of the array more than once. You can scan through the array, keeping track of the start-of-sequence and end-of-record line numbers, and then go back and extract the annotation and sequence using an array splice (which was described in the parseREBASE subroutine in Example 9-2). Here's an example:

```
# find line numbers of ORIGIN and // in the GenBank record

$linenumber = 0;
foreach my $line (@GenBankFile) {
    if ( $line =~ /^\/\/\n/ ) {   # end-of-record // line
        $end = $linenumber;
        last;
    } elsif ( $line =~ /^ORIGIN/ ) { # end annotation, begin sequence
        $origin = $linenumber;
    }
    $linenumber++;
}

# extract annotation and sequence with "array splice"

@annotation = @GenBankFile[0..($origin-1)];
@sequence   = @GenBankFile[($origin+1)..($end-1)];
</programlisting>
```

Using Scalars

A second way to separate annotations from sequences in GenBank records is to read the entire record into a scalar variable and operate on it with regular expressions. For some kinds of data, this can be a more convenient way to parse the input (compared to scanning through an array, as in Example 10-1).

Usually string data is stored one line per scalar variable with its newlines, if any, at the end of the string. Sometimes, however, you store several lines concatenated together in one string that is, in turn, stored in a single scalar variable. These multiline strings aren't uncommon; you used them to gather the sequence from a FASTA file in Examples 6-2 and 6-3. Regular expressions have pattern modifiers that can be used to make multiline strings with their embedded newlines easy to use.

Pattern modifiers

The pattern modifiers we've used so far are /g, for global matching, and /i, for case-insensitive matching. Let's take a look at two more that affect the way regular expressions interact with the newlines in scalars.

Recall that previous regular expressions have used the caret (^), dot (.), and dollar sign ($) metacharacters. The ^ anchors a regular expression to the beginning of a string, by default, so that /^THE BEGUINE/ matches a string that begins with "THE

BEGUINE". Similarly, $ anchors an expression to the end of the string, and the dot (.) matches any character except a newline.

The following pattern modifiers affect these three metacharacters:

- The /s modifier assumes you want to treat the whole string as a single line, even with embedded newlines, so it makes the dot metacharacter match any character *including* newlines.

- The /m modifier assumes you want to treat the whole string as a multiline, with embedded newlines, so it extends the ^ and the $ to match after, or before, a newline, embedded in the string.

Examples of pattern modifiers

Here's an example of the default behavior of caret (^), dot (.), and dollar sign ($):

```
use warnings;
"AAC\nGTT" =~ /^.*$/;
print $&, "\n";
```

This demonstrates the default behavior without the /m or /s modifiers and prints the warning:

```
Use of uninitialized value in print statement at line 3.
```

The print statement tries to print $&, a special variable that is always set to the last successful pattern match. This time, since the pattern doesn't match, the variable $& isn't set, and you get a warning message for attempting to print an uninitialized value.

Why doesn't the match succeed? First, let's examine the ^.*$ pattern. It begins with a ^, which means it must match from the beginning of the string. It ends with a $, which means it must also match at the end of the string (the end of the string may contain a single newline, but no other newlines are allowed). The .* means it must match zero or more (*) of any characters (.) except the newline. So, in other words, the pattern ^.*$ matches any string that doesn't contain a newline except for a possible single newline as the last character. But since the string in question, "ACC\nGTT" does contain an embedded newline \n that isn't the last character, the pattern match fails.

In the next examples, the pattern modifiers /m and /s change the default behaviors for the metacharacters ^, and $, and the dot:

```
"AAC\nGTT" =~ /^.*$/m;
print $&, "\n";
```

This snippet prints out AAC and demonstrates the /m modifier. The /m extends the meaning of the ^ and the $ so they also match around embedded newlines. Here, the pattern matches from the beginning of the string up to the first embedded newline.

The next snippet of code demonstrates the /s modifier:

```
"AAC\nGTT" =~ /^.*$/s;
print $&, "\n";
```

which produces the output:

```
AAC
GTT
```

The /s modifier changes the meaning of the dot metacharacter so that it matches any character including newlines. With the /s modifier, the pattern matches everything from the beginning of the string to the end of the string, including the newline. Notice when it prints, it prints the embedded newline.

Separating annotations from sequence

Now that you've met the pattern-matching modifiers and regular expressions that will be your main tools for parsing a GenBank file as a scalar, let's try separating the annotations from the sequence.

The first step is to get the GenBank record stored as a scalar variable. Recall that a GenBank record starts with a line beginning with the word "LOCUS" and ends with the end-of-record separator: a line containing two forward slashes.

First you want to read a GenBank record and store it in a scalar variable. There's a device called an *input record separator* denoted by the special variable $/ that lets you do exactly that. The input record separator is usually set to a newline, so each call to read a scalar from a filehandle gets one line. Set it to the GenBank end-of-record separator like so:

```
$/ = "//\n";
```

A call to read a scalar from a filehandle takes all the data up to the GenBank end-of-record separator. So the line $record = <GBFILE> in Example 10-2 stores the multiline GenBank record into the scalar variable $record. Later, you'll see that you can keep repeating this call in order to read in successive GenBank records from a GenBank library file.

After reading in the record, you'll parse it into the annotation and sequence parts making use of /s and /m pattern modifiers. Extracting the annotation and sequence is the easy part; parsing the annotation will occupy most of the remainder of the chapter.

Example 10-2. Extract annotation and sequence from Genbank record

```
#!/usr/bin/perl
# Extract the annotation and sequence sections from the first
#    record of a GenBank library

use strict;
use warnings;
```

Example 10-2. Extract annotation and sequence from Genbank record (continued)

```
use BeginPerlBioinfo;      # see Chapter 6 about this module

# Declare and initialize variables
my $annotation = '';
my $dna = '';
my $record = '';
my $filename = 'record.gb';
my $save_input_separator = $/;

# Open GenBank library file
unless (open(GBFILE, $filename)) {
    print "Cannot open GenBank file \"$filename\"\n\n";
    exit;
}

# Set input separator to "//\n" and read in a record to a scalar
$/ = "//\n";

$record = <GBFILE>;

# reset input separator
$/ = $save_input_separator;

# Now separate the annotation from the sequence data
($annotation, $dna) = ($record =~ /^(LOCUS.*ORIGIN\s*\n)(.*)\/\/\n/s);

# Print the two pieces, which should give us the same as the
#   original GenBank file, minus the // at the end
print $annotation, $dna;

exit;
```

The output from this program is the same as the GenBank file listed previously, minus the last line, which is the end-of-record separator //.

Let's focus on the regular expression that parses the annotation and sequence out of the $record variable. This is the most complicated regular expression so far:

```
$record = /^(LOCUS.*ORIGIN\s*\n)(.*)\/\/\n/s.
```

There are two pairs of parentheses in the regular expression: (LOCUS.*ORIGIN\s*\n) and (.*). The parentheses are metacharacters whose purpose is to remember the parts of the data that match the pattern within the parentheses, namely, the annotation and the sequence. Also note that the pattern match returns an array whose elements are the matched parenthetical patterns. After you match the annotation and the sequence within the pairs of parentheses in the regular expression, you simply assign the matched patterns to the two variables $annotation and $dna, like so:

```
($annotation, $dna) = ($record =~ /^(LOCUS.*ORIGIN\s*\n)(.*)\/\/\n/s);
```

Notice that at the end of the pattern, we've added the /s pattern matching modifier, which, as you've seen earlier, allows a dot to match any character including an embedded newline. (Of course, since we've got a whole GenBank record in the $record scalar, there are a lot of embedded newlines.)

Next, look at the first pair of parentheses:

```
(LOCUS.*ORIGIN\s*\n)
```

This whole expression is anchored at the beginning of the string by preceding it with a ^ metacharacter. (/s doesn't change the meaning of the ^ character in a regular expression.)

Inside the parentheses, you match from where the string LOCUS appears at the beginning of the GenBank record, followed by any number of characters including newlines with .*, followed by the string ORIGIN, followed by possibly some whitespace with \s*, followed by a newline \n. This matches the annotation part of the GenBank record.

Now, look at the second parentheses and the remainder:

```
(.*)\/\/\n
```

This is easier. The .* matches any character, including newlines because of the /s pattern modifier at the end of the pattern match. The parentheses are followed by the end-of-record line, //, including the newline at the end, with the slashes preceded by backslashes to show that you want to match them exactly. They're not delimiters of the pattern matching operator. The end result is the GenBank record with the annotation and the sequence separated into the variables $annotation and $sequence. Although the regular expression I used requires a bit of explanation, the attractive thing about this approach is that it took only one line of Perl code to extract both annotation and sequence.

Parsing Annotations

Now that you've successfully extracted the sequence, let's look at parsing the annotations of a GenBank file.

Looking at a GenBank record, it's interesting to think about how to extract the useful information. The FEATURES table is certainly a key part of the story. It has considerable structure: what should be preserved, and what is unnecessary? For instance, sometimes you just want to see if a word such as "endonuclease" appears anywhere in the record. For this, you just need a subroutine that searches for any regular expression in the annotation. Sometimes this is enough, but when detailed surgery is necessary, Perl has the necessary tools to make the operation successful.

Using Arrays

Example 10-3 parses a few pieces of information from the annotations in a GenBank file. It does this using the data in the form of an array.

Example 10-3. Parsing GenBank annotations using arrays

```perl
#!/usr/bin/perl
# Parsing GenBank annotations using arrays

use strict;
use warnings;
use BeginPerlBioinfo;      # see Chapter 6 about this module

# Declare and initialize variables
my @genbank = ( );
my $locus = '';
my $accession = '';
my $organism = '';

# Get GenBank file data
@genbank = get_file_data('record.gb');

# Let's start with something simple.  Let's get some of the identifying
# information, let's say the locus and accession number (here the same
# thing) and the definition and the organism.

for my $line (@genbank) {
   if($line =~ /^LOCUS/) {
     $line =~ s/^LOCUS\s*//;
     $locus = $line;
   }elsif($line =~ /^ACCESSION/) {
     $line =~ s/^ACCESSION\s*//;
     $accession = $line;
   }elsif($line =~ /^  ORGANISM/) {
     $line =~ s/^\s*ORGANISM\s*//;
     $organism = $line;
   }
}

print "*** LOCUS ***\n";
print $locus;
print "*** ACCESSION ***\n";
print $accession;
print "*** ORGANISM ***\n";
print $organism;

exit;
```

Here's the output from Example 10-3:

```
*** LOCUS ***
AB031069     2487 bp     mRNA              PRI       27-MAY-2000
*** ACCESSION ***
AB031069
*** ORGANISM ***
Homo sapiens
```

Now let's slightly extend that program to handle the DEFINITION field. Notice that the DEFINITION field can extend over more than one line. To collect that field, use a trick you've already seen in Example 10-1: set a flag when you're in the "state" of collecting a definition. The flag variable is called, unsurprisingly, $flag.

Example 10-4. Parsing GenBank annotations using arrays, take 2

```perl
#!/usr/bin/perl
# Parsing GenBank annotations using arrays, take 2

use strict;
use warnings;
use BeginPerlBioinfo;      # see Chapter 6 about this module

# Declare and initialize variables
my @genbank = ();
my $locus = '';
my $accession = '';
my $organism = '';
my $definition = '';
my $flag = 0;

# Get GenBank file data
@genbank = get_file_data('record.gb');

# Let's start with something simple.  Let's get some of the identifying
# information, let's say the locus and accession number (here the same
# thing) and the definition and the organism.

for my $line (@genbank) {
  if($line =~ /^LOCUS/) {
    $line =~ s/^LOCUS\s*//;
    $locus = $line;
  }elsif($line =~ /^DEFINITION/) {
    $line =~ s/^DEFINITION\s*//;
    $definition = $line;
    $flag = 1;
  }elsif($line =~ /^ACCESSION/) {
    $line =~ s/^ACCESSION\s*//;
    $accession = $line;
    $flag = 0;
  }elsif($flag) {
    chomp($definition);
    $definition .= $line;
  }elsif($line =~ /^  ORGANISM/) {
    $line =~ s/^\s*ORGANISM\s*//;
    $organism = $line;
  }
}

print "*** LOCUS ***\n";
print $locus;
print "*** DEFINITION ***\n";
print $definition;
print "*** ACCESSION ***\n";
```

Example 10-4. Parsing GenBank annotations using arrays, take 2 (continued)

```
print $accession;
print "*** ORGANISM ***\n";
print $organism;

exit;
```

Example 10-4 outputs:

```
*** LOCUS ***
AB031069     2487 bp     mRNA              PRI       27-MAY-2000
*** DEFINITION ***
Homo sapiens PCCX1 mRNA for protein containing CXXC domain 1, complete cds.
*** ACCESSION ***
AB031069
*** ORGANISM ***
Homo sapiens
```

This use of flags to remember which part of the file you're in, from one iteration of a loop to the next, is a common technique when extracting information from files that have multiline sections. As the files and their fields get more complex, the code must keep track of many flags at a time to remember which part of the file it's in and what information needs to be extracted. It works, but as the files become more complex, so does the code. It becomes hard to read and hard to modify. So let's look at regular expressions as a vehicle for parsing annotations.

When to Use Regular Expressions

We've used two methods to parse GenBank files: regular expressions and looping through arrays of lines and setting flags. We used both methods to separate the annotation from the sequence in a previous section of this chapter. Both methods were equally well suited, since in GenBank files, the annotation is followed by the sequence, clearly delimited by an ORIGIN line: a simple structure. However, parsing the annotations seems a bit more complicated; therefore, let's try to use regular expressions to accomplish the task.

To begin, let's wrap the code we've been working on into some convenient subroutines to focus on parsing the annotations. You'll want to fetch GenBank records one at a time from a library (a file containing one or more GenBank records), extract the annotations and the sequence, and then if desired parse the annotations. This would be useful if, say, you were looking for some motif in a GenBank library. Then you can search for the motif, and, if found, you can parse the annotations to look for additional information about the sequence.

As mentioned previously, we'll use the file *library.gb*, which you can download from this book's web site.

Since dealing with annotation data is somewhat complex, let's take a minute to break our tasks into convenient subroutines. Here's the pseudocode:

```
sub open_file
    given the filename, return the filehandle

sub get_next_record
    given the filehandle, get the record
    (we can get the offset by first calling "tell")

sub get_annotation_and_dna
    given a record, split it into annotation and cleaned-up sequence

sub search_sequence
    given a sequence and a regular expression,
      return array of locations of hits

sub search_annotation
    given a GenBank annotation and a regular expression,
      return array of locations of hits

sub parse_annotation
    separate out the fields of the annotation in a convenient form

sub parse_features
    given the features field, separate out the components
```

The idea is to make a subroutine for each important task you want to accomplish and then combine them into useful programs. Some of these can be combined into other subroutines: for instance, perhaps you want to open a file and get the record from it, all in one subroutine call.

You're designing these subroutines to work with library files, that is, files with multiple GenBank records. You pass the filehandle into the subroutines as an argument, so that your subroutines can access open library files as represented by the filehandles. Doing so enables you to have a get_next_record function, which is handy in a loop. Using the Perl function tell also allows you to save the byte offset of any record of interest, and then return later and extract the record at that byte offset very quickly. (A *byte offset* is just the number of characters into the file where the information of interest lies.) The operating system supports Perl in letting you go immediately to any byte offset location in even huge files, thus bypassing the usual way of opening the file and reading from the beginning until you get where you want to be.

Using a byte offset is important when you're dealing with large files. Perl gives you built-in functions such as seek that allow you, on an open file, to go immediately to any location in the file. The idea is that when you find something in a file, you can save the byte offset using the Perl function tell. Then, when you want to return to that point in the file, you can just call the Perl function seek with the byte offset as an argument. You'll see this later in this chapter when you build a DBM file to look up records based on their accession numbers. But the main point is that with a 250-MB file, it takes too long to find something by searching from the beginning, and there are ways of getting around it.

The parsing of the data is done in three steps, according to the design:

1. You'll separate out the annotation and the sequence (which you'll clean up by removing whitespace, etc., and making it a simple string of sequence). Even at this step, you can search for motifs in the sequence, as well as look for text in the annotation.
2. Extract out the fields.
3. Parse the features table.

These steps seem natural, and, depending on what you want to do, allow you to parse to whatever depth is needed.

Here's a main program in pseudocode that shows how to use those subroutines:

```
open_file

while ( get_next_record )

    get_annotation_and_dna

    if ( search_sequence for a motif AND
         search_annotation for chromosome 22 )

        parse_annotation

        parse_features to get sizes of exons, look for small sizes
    }
}

    return accession numbers of records meeting the criteria
```

This example shows how to use subroutines to answer a question such as: what are the genes on chromosome 22 that contain a given motif and have small exons?

Main Program

Let's test these subroutines with Example 10-5, which has some subroutine definitions that will be added to the *BeginPerlBioinfo.pm* module:

Example 10-5. GenBank library subroutines

```perl
#!/usr/bin/perl
#  - test program of GenBank library subroutines

use strict;
use warnings;
# Don't use BeginPerlBioinfo
# Since all subroutines defined in this file
# use BeginPerlBioinfo;    # see Chapter 6 about this module
```

Example 10-5. GenBank library subroutines (continued)

```perl
# Declare and initialize variables
my $fh; # variable to store filehandle
my $record;
my $dna;
my $annotation;
my $offset;
my $library = 'library.gb';

# Perform some standard subroutines for test
$fh = open_file($library);

$offset = tell($fh);

while( $record = get_next_record($fh) ) {

    ($annotation, $dna) = get_annotation_and_dna($record);

    if( search_sequence($dna, 'AAA[CG].')) {
        print "Sequence found in record at offset $offset\n";
    }
    if( search_annotation($annotation, 'homo sapiens')) {
        print "Annotation found in record at offset $offset\n";
    }

    $offset = tell($fh);
}

exit;

##############################################################################
# Subroutines
##############################################################################

# open_file
#
#    - given filename, set filehandle

sub open_file {

    my($filename) = @_;
    my $fh;

    unless(open($fh, $filename)) {
        print "Cannot open file $filename\n";
        exit;
    }
    return $fh;
}

# get_next_record
#
```

Example 10-5. GenBank library subroutines (continued)

```perl
#    - given GenBank record, get annotation and DNA

sub get_next_record {

    my($fh) = @_;

    my($offset);
    my($record) = '';
    my($save_input_separator) = $/;

    $/ = "//\n";

    $record = <$fh>;

    $/ = $save_input_separator;

    return $record;
}

# get_annotation_and_dna
#
#    - given GenBank record, get annotation and DNA

sub get_annotation_and_dna {

    my($record) = @_;

    my($annotation) = '';
    my($dna) = '';

    # Now separate the annotation from the sequence data
    ($annotation, $dna) = ($record =~ /^(LOCUS.*ORIGIN\s*\n)(.*)\/\/\n/s);

    # clean the sequence of any whitespace or / characters
    #    (the / has to be written \/ in the character class, because
    #     / is a metacharacter, so it must be "escaped" with \)
    $dna =~ s/[\s\/]//g;

    return($annotation, $dna)
}

# search_sequence
#
#    - search sequence with regular expression

sub search_sequence {

    my($sequence, $regularexpression) = @_;

    my(@locations) = ();
```

Example 10-5. GenBank library subroutines (continued)

```
    while( $sequence =~ /$regularexpression/ig ) {
        push( @locations, pos );
    }

    return (@locations);
}

# search_annotation
#
#   - search annotation with regular expression

sub search_annotation {

    my($annotation, $regularexpression) = @_;

    my(@locations) = ();

    # note the /s modifier-. matches any character including newline
    while( $annotation =~ /$regularexpression/isg ) {
        push( @locations, pos );
    }

    return (@locations);
}
```

Example 10-5 generates the following output on our little GenBank library:

```
Sequence found in record at offset 0
Annotation found in record at offset 0
Sequence found in record at offset 6256
Annotation found in record at offset 6256
Sequence found in record at offset 12366
Annotation found in record at offset 12366
Sequence found in record at offset 17730
Annotation found in record at offset 17730
Sequence found in record at offset 22340
Annotation found in record at offset 22340
```

The tell function reports the byte offset of the file up to the point where it's been read; so you want to first call tell and then read the record to get the proper offset associated with the beginning of the record.

Parsing Annotations at the Top Level

Now let's parse the annotations.

There is a document from NCBI we mentioned earlier that gives the details of the structure of a GenBank record. This file is *gbrel.txt* and is part of the GenBank release, available at the NCBI web site and their FTP site. It's updated with every release (every two months at present), and it includes notices of changes to the format. If you program with GenBank records, you should read this document and keep a copy around for reference use, and check periodically for announced changes in the GenBank record format.

If you look back at the complete GenBank record earlier in this chapter, you'll see that the annotations have a certain structure. You have some fields, such as LOCUS, DEFINITION, ACCESSION, VERSION, KEYWORDS, SOURCE, REFERENCE, FEATURES, and BASE COUNT that start at the beginning of a line. Some of these fields have subfields, especially the FEATURES field, which has a fairly complex structure.

But for now, let's just extract the top-level fields. You will need a regular expression that matches everything from a word at the beginning of a line to a newline that just precedes another word at the beginning of a line.

Here's a regular expression that matches our definition of a field:

```
/^[A-Z].*\n(^\s.*\n)*/m
```

What does this regular expression say? First of all, it has the /m pattern matching modifier, which means the caret ^ and the dollar sign $ also match around embedded newlines (not just at the beginning and end of the entire string, which is the default behavior).

The first part of the regular expression:

```
^[A-Z].*\n
```

matches a capital letter at the beginning of a line, followed by any number of characters (except newlines), followed by a newline. That's a good description of the first lines of the fields you're trying to match.

The second part of the regular expression:

```
(^\s.*\n)*
```

matches a space or tab \s at the beginning of a line, followed by any number of characters (except newlines), followed by a newline. This is surrounded by parentheses and followed by a *, which means 0 or more such lines. This matches succeeding lines in a field, lines that start with whitespace. A field may have no extra lines of this sort or several such lines.

So, the two parts of the regular expression combined match the fields with their optional additional lines.

Example 10-6 shows a subroutine that, given the annotations section of a GenBank record stored in a scalar variable, returns a hash with keys equal to the names of the top-level fields and values equal to the contents of those fields.

Example 10-6. Parsing Genbank annotation

```
#!/usr/bin/perl
#  - test program for parse_annotation subroutine
```

Example 10-6. Parsing Genbank annotation (continued)

```perl
use strict;
use warnings;
use BeginPerlBioinfo;      # see Chapter 6 about this module

# Declare and initialize variables
my $fh;
my $record;
my $dna;
my $annotation;
my %fields;
my $library = 'library.gb';

# Open library and read a record
$fh = open_file($library);

$record = get_next_record($fh);

# Parse the sequence and annotation
($annotation, $dna) = get_annotation_and_dna($record);

# Extract the fields of the annotation
%fields = parse_annotation($annotation);

# Print the fields
foreach my $key (keys %fields) {
    print "******** $key ********\n";
    print $fields{$key};
}

exit;

##############################################################################
# Subroutine
##############################################################################

# parse_annotation
#
#  given a GenBank annotation, returns a hash  with
#    keys: the field names
#    values: the fields

sub parse_annotation {

    my($annotation) = @_;
    my(%results) = ();

    while( $annotation =~ /^[A-Z].*\n(^\s.*\n)*/gm ) {
        my $value = $&;
        (my $key = $value) =~ s/^([A-Z]+).*/$1/s;
```

Example 10-6. Parsing Genbank annotation (continued)

```
        $results{$key} = $value;
    }

    return %results;
}
```

In the subroutine parse_annotation, note how the variables $key and $value are scoped within the while block. One benefit of this is that you don't have to reinitialize the variables each time through the loop. Also note that the key is the name of the field, and the value is the whole field.

You should take the time to understand the regular expression that extracts the field name for the key:

```
    (my $key = $value) =~ s/^([A-Z]+).*/$1/s;
```

This first assigns $key the value $value. It then replaces everything in $key (note the /s modifier for embedded newlines) with $1, which is a special variable pattern between the first pair of parentheses ([A-Z]+). This pattern is one or more capital letters (anchored to the beginning of the string, i.e., the field name), so it sets $key to the value of the first word in the field name.

You get the following output from Example 10-6 (the test just fetches the first record in the GenBank library):

```
******** SOURCE *********
SOURCE      Homo sapiens embryo male lung fibroblast cell_line:HuS-L12 cDNA to
            mRNA.
  ORGANISM  Homo sapiens
            Eukaryota; Metazoa; Chordata; Craniata; Vertebrata; Euteleostomi;
            Mammalia; Eutheria; Primates; Catarrhini; Hominidae; Homo.
******** DEFINITION *********
DEFINITION  Homo sapiens PCCX1 mRNA for protein containing CXXC domain 1,
            complete cds.
******** KEYWORDS *********
KEYWORDS    .
******** VERSION *********
VERSION     AB031069.1  GI:8100074
******** FEATURES *********
FEATURES            Location/Qualifiers
    source          1..2487
                    /organism="Homo sapiens"
                    /db_xref="taxon:9606"
                    /sex="male"
                    /cell_line="HuS-L12"
                    /cell_type="lung fibroblast"
                    /dev_stage="embryo"
    gene            229..2199
                    /gene="PCCX1"
    CDS             229..2199
                    /gene="PCCX1"
                    /note="a nuclear protein carrying a PHD finger and a CXXC
```

```
                            domain"
                            /codon_start=1
                            /product="protein containing CXXC domain 1"
                            /protein_id="BAA96307.1"
                            /db_xref="GI:8100075"
                            /translation="MEGDGSDPEPPDAGEDSKSENGENAPIYCICRKPDINCFMIGCD
                            NCNEWFHGDCIRITEKMAKAIREWYCRECREKDPKLEIRYRHKKSRERDGNERDSSEP
                            RDEGGGRKRPVPDPDLQRRAGSGTGVGAMLARGSASPHKSSPQPLVATPSQHHQQQQQ
                            QIKRSARMCGECEACRRTEDCGHCDFCRDMKKFGGPNKIRQKCRLRQCQLRARESYKY
                            FPSSLSPVTPSESLPRPRRPLPTQQQPQPSQKLGRIREDEGAVASSTVKEPPEATATP
                            EPLSDEDLPLDPDLYQDFCAGAFDDHGLPWMSDTEESPFLDPALRKRAVKVKHVKRRE
                            KKSEKKKEERYKRHRQKQKHKDKWKHPERADAKDPASLPQCLGPGCVRPAQPSSKYCS
                            DDCGMKLAANRIYEILPQRIQQWQQSPCIAEEHGKKLLERIRREQQSARTRLQEMERR
                            FHELEAIILRAKQQAVREDEESNEGDSDDTDLQIFCVSCGHPINPRVALRHMERCYAK
                            YESQTSFGSMYPTRIEGATRLFCDVYNPQSKTYCKRLQVLCPEHSRDPKVPADEVCGC
                            PLVRDVFELTGDFCRLPKRQCNRHYCWEKLRRAEVDLERVRVWYKLDELFEQERNVRT
                            AMTNRAGLLALMLHQTIQHDPLTTDLRSSADR"
******** REFERENCE *********
REFERENCE   2  (bases 1 to 2487)
  AUTHORS   Fujino,T., Hasegawa,M., Shibata,S., Kishimoto,T., Imai,S. and
            Takano,T.
  TITLE     Direct Submission
  JOURNAL   Submitted (15-AUG-1999) to the DDBJ/EMBL/GenBank databases.
            Tadahiro Fujino, Keio University School of Medicine, Department of
            Microbiology; Shinanomachi 35, Shinjuku-ku, Tokyo 160-8582, Japan
            (E-mail:fujino@microb.med.keio.ac.jp,
            Tel:+81-3-3353-1211(ex.62692), Fax:+81-3-5360-1508)
******** ACCESSION *********
ACCESSION   AB031069
******** LOCUS *********
LOCUS       AB031069     2487 bp     mRNA            PRI       27-MAY-2000
******** ORIGIN *********
ORIGIN
******** BASE *********
BASE COUNT      564 a     715 c      768 g      440 t
```

As you see, the method is working, and apart from the difficulty of reading the regular expressions (which will become easier with practice), the code is very straightforward, just a few short subroutines.

Parsing the FEATURES Table

Let's take this one step further and parse the features table to its next level, composed of the source, gene, and CDS *features keys*. (See later in this section for a more complete list of these features keys.) In the exercises at the end of the chapter, you'll be challenged to descend further into the FEATURES table.

To study the FEATURES table, you should first look over the NCBI *gbrel.txt* document mentioned previously. Then you should study the most complete documentation for the FEATURES table, available at *http://www.ncbi.nlm.nih.gov/collab/FT/index.html*.

Features

Although our GenBank entry is fairly simple and includes only three features, there are actually quite a few of them. Notice that the parsing code will find all of them, because it's just looking at the structure of the document, not for specific features.

The following is a list of the features defined for GenBank records. Although lengthy, I think it's important to read through it to get an idea of the range of information that may be present in a GenBank record.

allele
> Obsolete; see `variation` feature key

attenuator
> Sequence related to transcription termination

C_region
> Span of the C immunological feature

CAAT_signal
> CAAT box in eukaryotic promoters

CDS
> Sequence coding for amino acids in protein (includes stop codon)

conflict
> Independent sequence determinations differ

D-loop
> Displacement loop

D_segment
> Span of the D immunological feature

enhancer
> Cis-acting enhancer of promoter function

exon
> Region that codes for part of spliced mRNA

gene
> Region that defines a functional gene, possibly including upstream (promoter, enhancer, etc.) and downstream control elements, and for which a name has been assigned

GC_signal
> GC box in eukaryotic promoters

iDNA
> Intervening DNA eliminated by recombination

intron
> Transcribed region excised by mRNA splicing

J_region
    Span of the J immunological feature

LTR
    Long terminal repeat

mat_peptide
    Mature peptide coding region (doesn't include stop codon)

misc_binding
    Miscellaneous binding site

misc_difference
    Miscellaneous difference feature

misc_feature
    Region of biological significance that can't be described by any other feature

misc_recomb
    Miscellaneous recombination feature

misc_RNA
    Miscellaneous transcript feature not defined by other RNA keys

misc_signal
    Miscellaneous signal

misc_structure
    Miscellaneous DNA or RNA structure

modified_base
    The indicated base is a modified nucleotide

mRNA
    Messenger RNA

mutation
    Obsolete: see `variation` feature key

N_region
    Span of the N immunological feature

old_sequence
    Presented sequence revises a previous version

polyA_signal
    Signal for cleavage and polyadenylation

polyA_site
    Site at which polyadenine is added to mRNA

precursor_RNA
    Any RNA species that isn't yet the mature RNA product

prim_transcript
    Primary (unprocessed) transcript

primer

Primer binding region used with PCR

primer_bind

Noncovalent primer binding site

promoter

A region involved in transcription initiation

protein_bind

Noncovalent protein binding site on DNA or RNA

RBS

Ribosome binding site

rep_origin

Replication origin for duplex DNA

repeat_region

Sequence containing repeated subsequences

repeat_unit

One repeated unit of a repeat_region

rRNA

Ribosomal RNA

S_region

Span of the S immunological feature

satellite

Satellite repeated sequence

scRNA

Small cytoplasmic RNA

sig_peptide

Signal peptide coding region

snRNA

Small nuclear RNA

source

Biological source of the sequence data represented by a GenBank record; mandatory feature, one or more per record; for organisms that have been incorporated within the NCBI taxonomy database, an associated /db_xref="taxon:NNNN" qualifier will be present (where NNNNN is the numeric identifier assigned to the organism within the NCBI taxonomy database)

stem_loop

Hairpin loop structure in DNA or RNA

STS

Sequence Tagged Site: operationally unique sequence that identifies the combination of primer spans used in a PCR assay

TATA_signal
> TATA box in eukaryotic promoters

terminator
> Sequence causing transcription termination

transit_peptide
> Transit peptide coding region

transposon
> Transposable element (TN)

tRNA
> Transfer RNA

unsure
> Authors are unsure about the sequence in this region

V_region
> Span of the V immunological feature

variation
> A related population contains stable mutation

-
> Placeholder (hyphen)

-10_signal
> Pribnow box in prokaryotic promoters

-35_signal
> -35 box in prokaryotic promoters

3'clip
> 3'-most region of a precursor transcript removed in processing

3'UTR
> 3' untranslated region (trailer)

5'clip
> 5'-most region of a precursor transcript removed in processing

5'UTR
> 5' untranslated region (leader)

These feature keys can have their own additional features, which you'll see here and in the exercises.

Parsing

Example 10-8 finds whatever features are present and returns an array populated with them. It doesn't look for the complete list of features as presented in the last section; it finds just the features that are actually present in the GenBank record and returns them for further use.

It's often the case that there are multiple instances of the same feature in a record. For instance, there may be several exons specified in the FEATURES table of a Gen-Bank record. For this reason we'll store the features as elements in an array, rather than in a hash keyed on the feature name (as this allows you to store, for instance, only one instance of an exon).

Example 10-7. Testing subroutine parse_features

```perl
#!/usr/bin/perl
#  - main program to test parse_features

use strict;
use warnings;
use BeginPerlBioinfo;      # see Chapter 6 about this module

# Declare and initialize variables
my $fh;
my $record;
my $dna;
my $annotation;
my %fields;
my @features;
my $library = 'library.gb';

# Get the fields from the first GenBank record in a library
$fh = open_file($library);

$record = get_next_record($fh);

($annotation, $dna) = get_annotation_and_dna($record);

%fields = parse_annotation($annotation);

# Extract the features from the FEATURES table
@features = parse_features($fields{'FEATURES'});

# Print out the features
foreach my $feature (@features) {

    # extract the name of the feature (or "feature key")
    my($featurename) = ($feature =~ /^ {5}(\S+)/);

    print "******** $featurename ********\n";
    print $feature;
}

exit;


#############################################################################
# Subroutine
#############################################################################

# parse_features
#
```

Example 10-7. Testing subroutine parse_features (continued)

```
#  extract the features from the FEATURES field of a GenBank record

sub parse_features {

    my($features) = @_;    # entire FEATURES field in a scalar variable

    # Declare and initialize variables
    my(@features) = ();    # used to store the individual features

    # Extract the features
    while( $features =~ /^ {5}\S.*\n(^ {21}\S.*\n)*/gm ) {
        my $feature = $&;
    push(@features, $feature);
    }

    return @features;
}
```

Example 10-8 gives the output:

```
******** source *********
        source          1..2487
                        /organism="Homo sapiens"
                        /db_xref="taxon:9606"
                        /sex="male"
                        /cell_line="HuS-L12"
                        /cell_type="lung fibroblast"
                        /dev_stage="embryo"
******** gene *********
        gene            229..2199
                        /gene="PCCX1"
******** CDS *********
        CDS             229..2199
                        /gene="PCCX1"
                        /note="a nuclear protein carrying a PHD finger and a CXXC
                        domain"
                        /codon_start=1
                        /product="protein containing CXXC domain 1"
                        /protein_id="BAA96307.1"
                        /db_xref="GI:8100075"
                        /translation="MEGDGSDPEPPDAGEDSKSENGENAPIYCICRKPDINCFMIGCD
                        NCNEWFHGDCIRITEKMAKAIREWYCRECREKDPKLEIRYRHKKSRERDGNERDSSEP
                        RDEGGGRKRPVPDPDLQRRAGSGTGVGAMLARGSASPHKSSPQPLVATPSQHHQQQQQ
                        QIKRSARMCGECEACRRTEDCGHCDFCRDMKKFGGPNKIRQKCRLRQCQLRARESYKY
                        FPSSLSPVTPSESLPRPRRPLPTQQQPQPSQKLGRIREDEGAVASSTVKEPPEATATP
                        EPLSDEDLPLDPDLYQDFCAGAFDDHGLPWMSDTEESPFLDPALRKRAVKVKHVKRRE
                        KKSEKKKEERYKRHRQKQKHKDKWKHPERADAKDPASLPQCLGPGCVRPAQPSSKYCS
                        DDCGMKLAANRIYEILPQRIQQWQQSPCIAEEHGKKLLERIRREQQSARTRLQEMERR
                        FHELEAIILRAKQQAVREDEESNEGDSDDTDLQIFCVSCGHPINPRVALRHMERCYAK
                        YESQTSFGSMYPTRIEGATRLFCDVYNPQSKTYCKRLQVLCPEHSRDPKVPADEVCGC
                        PLVRDVFELTGDFCRLPKRQCNRHYCWEKLRRAEVDLERVRVWYKLDELFEQERNVRT
                        AMTNRAGLLALMLHQTIQHDPLTTDLRSSADR
```

In subroutine parse_features of Example 10-8, the regular expression that extracts the features is much like the regular expression used in Example 10-6 to parse the top level of the annotations. Let's look at the essential parsing code of Example 10-8:

```
while( $features =~ /^ {5}\S.*\n(^ {21}\S.*\n)*/gm ) {
```

On the whole, and in brief, this regular expression finds features formatted with the first lines beginning with 5 spaces, and optional continuation lines beginning with 21 spaces.

First, note that the pattern modifier /m enables the ^ metacharacter to match after embedded newlines. Also, the {5} and {21} are quantifiers that specify there should be exactly 5, or 21, of the preceding item, which in both cases is a space.

The regular expression is in two parts, corresponding to the first line and optional continuation lines of the feature. The first part ^ {5}\S.*\n means that the beginning of a line (^) has 5 spaces ({5}), followed by a non-whitespace character (\S) followed by any number of non-newlines (.*) followed by a newline (\n). The second part of the regular expression, (^ {21}\S.*\n)* means the beginning of a line (^) has 21 spaces ({21}) followed by a non-whitespace character (\S) followed by any number of non-newlines (.*) followed by a newline (\n); and there may be 0 or more such lines, indicated by the ()* around the whole expression.

The main program has a short regular expression along similar lines to extract the feature name (also called the feature key) from the feature.

So, again, success. The FEATURES table is now decomposed or "parsed" in some detail, down to the level of separating the individual features. The next stage in parsing the FEATURES table is to extract the detailed information for each feature. This includes the location (given on the same line as the feature name, and possibly on additional lines); and the qualifiers indicated by a slash, a qualifier name, and if applicable, an equals sign and additional information of various kinds, possibly continued on additional lines.

I'll leave this final step for the exercises. It's a fairly straightforward extension of the approach we've been using to parse the features. You will want to consult the documentation from the NCBI web site for complete details about the structure of the FEATURES table before trying to parse the location and qualifiers from a feature.

The method I've used to parse the FEATURES table maintains the structure of the information. However, sometimes you just want to see if some word such as "endonulease" appears anywhere in the record. For this, recall that you created a search_annotation subroutine in Example 10-5 that searches for any regular expression in the entire annotation; very often, this is all you really need. As you've now seen, however, when you really need to dig into the FEATURES table, Perl has its own features that make the job possible and even fairly easy.

Indexing GenBank with DBM

DBM stands for Database Management. Perl provides a set of built-in functions that give Perl programmers access to DBM files.

DBM Essentials

When you open a DBM file, you access it like a hash: you give it keys and it returns values, and you can add and delete key-value pairs. What's useful about DBM is that it saves the key-value data in a permanent disk file on your computer. It can thus save information between the times you run your program; it can also serve as a way to share information between different programs that need the same data. A DBM file can get very big without killing the main memory on your computer and making your program—and everything else—slow to a crawl.

There are two functions, dbmopen and dbmclose, that "tie" a hash to a DBM file; then you just use the hash. As you've seen, with a hash, lookups are easy, as are definitions. You can get a list of all the keys from a hash called %my_hash by typing keys %my_hash. You then can get a list of all values by typing values %my_hash. For large DBM files, you may not want to do this; the Perl function each allows you to read key-value pairs one at a time, thus saving the memory of your running program. There is also a delete function to remove the definitions of keys:

```
delete $my_hash{'DNA'}
```

entirely removes that key from the hash.

DBM files are a very simple database. They don't have the power of a relational database such as MySQL, Oracle, or PostgreSQL; however, it's remarkable how often a simple database is all that a problem really needs. When you have a set of key-value data (or several such sets), consider using DBM. It's certainly easy to use with Perl.

The main wrinkle to using DBM is that there are several, slightly different DBM implementations—NDBM, GDBM, SDBM, and Berkeley DB. The differences are small but real; but for most purposes, the implementations are interchangeable. Newer versions of Perl give you Berkeley DB by default, and it's easy to get it and install it for your Perl if you want. If you don't have really long keys or values, it's not a problem. Some older DBMs require you to add null bytes to keys and delete them from values:

```
$value = $my_hash{"$key\0"};
chop $value;
```

Chances are good that you won't have to do that. Berkeley DB handles long strings well (some of the other DBM implementations have limits), and because you have some potentially long strings in biology, I recommend installing Berkeley DB if you don't have it.

A DBM Database for GenBank

You've seen how to extract information from a GenBank record or from a library of GenBank records. You've just seen how DBM files can save your hash data on your hard disk between program runs. You've also seen the use of tell and seek to quickly access a location in a file.

Now let's combine the three ideas and use DBM to build a database of information about a GenBank library. It'll be something simple: you'll extract the accession numbers for the keys and store the byte offsets in the GenBank library of records for the values. You'll add some code that, given a library and an offset, returns the record at that offset, and write a main program that allows the user to interactively request GenBank records by accession number. When complete, your program should very quickly return a GenBank record if given its accession number.

This general idea is extended in the exercises at the end of the chapter to a considerable extent; you may want to glance ahead at them now to get an idea of the potential power of the technique I'm about to present.

With just the appropriate amount of further ado, here is a code fragment that opens (creating if necessary) a DBM file:

```
unless(dbmopen(%my_hash, 'DBNAME', 0644)) {

    print "Cannot open DBM file DBNAME with mode 0644\n";
    exit;
}
```

%my_hash is like any other hash in Perl, but it will be tied to the DBM file with this statement. DBNAME is the basename of the actual DBM files that will be created. Some DBM versions create one file of exactly that name; others create two files with file extensions *.dir* and *.pag*.

Another parameter is called the *mode*. Unix or Linux users will be familiar with file permissions in this form. Many possibilities exist; here are the most common ones:

0644
> You can read and write; others can just read.

0600
> Only you can read or write.

0666
> Anyone can read or write.

0444
> Anyone can read (nobody can write).

0400
> Only you can read (nobody else can do anything).

The dbmopen call fails if you try to open a file with a mode that assumes there are more permissions than were conferred on the DBM file when it was created. Usually, the mode 0644 is declared by the owner if only the owner should be allowed to write, and 0444 is declared by readers. Mode 0666 is declared by the owner and others if the file is meant to be read or written by anyone.

That's pretty much it; DBM files are that simple. Example 10-8 displays a DBM file that stores key-value pairs of accession numbers of GenBank records for keys, and byte offsets of the records as values.

Example 10-8. A DBM index of a GenBank library

```perl
#!/usr/bin/perl
#  - make a DBM index of a GenBank library,
#     and demonstrate its use interactively

use strict;
use warnings;
use BeginPerlBioinfo;     # see Chapter 6 about this module

# Declare and initialize variables
my $fh;
my $record;
my $dna;
my $annotation;
my %fields;
my %dbm;
my $answer;
my $offset;
my $library = 'library.gb';

# open DBM file, creating if necessary
unless(dbmopen(%dbm, 'GB', 0644)) {
    print "Cannot open DBM file GB with mode 0644\n";
    exit;
}

# Parse GenBank library, saving accession number and offset in DBM file
$fh = open_file($library);

$offset = tell($fh);

while ( $record = get_next_record($fh) ) {

    # Get accession field for this record.
    ($annotation, $dna) = get_annotation_and_dna($record);

    %fields = parse_annotation($annotation);

    my $accession = $fields{'ACCESSION'};

    # extract just the accession number from the accession field
```

Example 10-8. A DBM index of a GenBank library (continued)

```
    # -remove any trailing spaces
    $accession =~ s/^ACCESSION\s*//;

    $accession =~ s/\s*$//;

    # store the key/value of  accession/offset
    $dbm{$accession} = $offset;

    # get offset for next record
    $offset = tell($fh);
}

# Now interactively query the DBM database with accession numbers
#  to see associated records

print "Here are the available accession numbers:\n";

print join ( "\n", keys %dbm ), "\n";

print "Enter accession number (or quit): ";

while( $answer = <STDIN> ) {
    chomp $answer;
    if($answer =~ /^\s*q/) {
        last;
    }
    $offset = $dbm{$answer};

    if ($offset) {
        seek($fh, $offset, 0);
        $record = get_next_record($fh);
        print $record;
    }else{
        print "Do not have an entry for accession number $answer\n";
    }

    print "\nEnter accession number (or quit): ";
}

dbmclose(%dbm);

close($fh);

exit;
```

Here's the truncated output of Example 10-8:

```
Here are the available accession numbers:
XM_006271
NM_021964
XM_009873
AB031069
XM_006269
```

```
Enter accession number (or quit): NM_021964
LOCUS       NM_021964    3032 bp    mRNA              PRI       14-MAR-2001
DEFINITION  Homo sapiens zinc finger protein 148 (pHZ-52) (ZNF148), mRNA.
...
//

Enter accession number (or quit): q
```

Exercises

Exercise 10.1

Go to the NCBI, EMBL, and EBI web sites and become familiar with their use.

Exercise 10.2

Read the GenBank format documentation, *gbrel.txt*.

Exercise 10.3

Write a subroutine that passes a hash by value. Now rewrite it to pass the hash by reference.

Exercise 10.4

Design a module of subroutines to handle the following kinds of data: a flat file containing records consisting of gene names on a line and extra information of any sort on succeeding lines, followed by a blank line. Your subroutines should be able to read in the data and then do a fast lookup on the information associated with a gene name. You should also be able to add new records to the flat file. Now reuse this module to build an address book program.

Exercise 10.5

Descend further into the FEATURES table. Parse the features in the table into their next level by parsing the feature names, locations, and qualifiers. Check the document *gbrel.txt* for definitions of the structures of the fields.

Exercise 10.6

Write a program that takes a long DNA sequence as input and outputs the counts of all four-base subsequences (256 of them in all), sorted by frequency. A four-base subsequence starts at each location 1, 2, 3, and so on. (This kind of word-frequency analysis is common to many fields of study, including linguistics, computer science, and music.)

Exercise 10.7

Extend the program in Exercise 10.6 to count all the sequences in a GenBank library.

Exercise 10.8

Given an amino acid, find the frequency of occurrence of the adjacent amino acids coded in a DNA sequence; or in a GenBank library.

Exercise 10.10

Extract all the words (excluding words like "the" or other unnecessary words) from the annotation of a library of GenBank records. For each word found, add the offset of the GenBank record in the library to a DBM file that has keys equal to the words, and values that are strings with offsets separated by spaces. In other words, one key can have a space-separated list of offsets for a value. Then you can quickly find all records containing a word like "fibroblast" with a simple lookup, followed by extracting the offsets and seeking into the library with those offsets. How big is your DBM file compared to the GenBank library? What might be involved in constructing a search engine for the annotations in all of GenBank? For human DNA only?

Exercise 10.10

Write a program to make a custom library of oncogenes from the GBPRI division of GenBank.

CHAPTER 11

Protein Data Bank

The success of the Human Genome Project in decoding the DNA sequence of human genes has captured the public imagination, but another project has been quietly gaining momentum, and it promises equally revolutionary results. This project is an international effort to determine the 3D structure of a comprehensive range of proteins on a genome-wide level using high-throughput analytical technologies. This international effort is the foundation of the new field of structural genomics.

Recent and expected advances in technology promise an accelerating pace of protein structure determination. The storehouse for all of this data is the *Protein Data Bank* (PDB). The PDB may be found on the web at *http://www.rcsb.org/pdb/*.

Finding the amino acid or primary sequence is just the beginning of studying a protein. Proteins fold locally into secondary structures such as alpha helices, beta-strands, and turns. Two or three adjacent secondary structures might combine into common local folds called "motifs" or "supersecondary" structures such as beta sheets or alpha-alpha units. These building blocks then fold into the 3D or tertiary structure of a protein. Finally, one or more tertiary structures may be combined as subunits into a quaternary structure such as an enzyme or a virus.

Without knowing how a protein folds into a 3D structure, you are less likely to know what the protein does or how it does it. Even if you know that the protein is implicated in a disease, knowledge of its tertiary structure is usually needed to find a possible treatment. Knowing the tertiary conformation of the *active site* of a protein (which may involve amino acids that are far apart in terms of the primary sequence but which are brought together by the folding of the protein) is critical to guide the selection of targets for new drugs.

Now that the basic genetic information of a number of organisms, including humans, has been decoded, a primary challenge facing biologists is to learn as much as possible about the proteins those genes produce and how they interact.

In fact, one of the great questions of modern biology is how the primary amino acid sequence of a protein determines its ultimate 3D shape. If a computational method can be found to reliably predict the fold of a protein from its amino acid sequence, the effect on biology and medicine would be profound.

In this chapter, you'll learn the basics of PDB files and how to parse out selected information form them. You'll also explore interesting Perl techniques for finding and iterating over lots of files, as well as controlling other bioinformatics programs from a Perl program. The exercises at the end of the chapter challenge you to extend the introductory material presented here to gain access to more of the PDB data.

Overview of PDB

The main source for information about 3D structures of macromolecules (including proteins, peptides, viruses, protein/nucleic acid complexes, nucleic acids, and carbohydrates) is PDB, and its format is the de facto standard for the exchange of structural information. Most of these structures are determined experimentally by means of X-ray diffraction or nuclear magnetic resonance (NMR) studies.

PDB started in 1971 with seven proteins; it will soon grow to 20,000 structures. With the international effort in structural genomics increasing, the PDB is certain to continue its rapid growth. Within a few short years the number of known structures will approach 100,000.

PDB files are like GenBank records, in that they are human-readable ASCII flat files. The text conforms to a specific format, so computer programs may be written to extract the information. PDB is organized with one structure per file, unlike Genbank, which is distributed with many records in each "library" file.

Bioinformaticians who work extensively with PDB files report that there are serious problems with the consistency of the PDB format. For instance, as the field has advanced and the data format has evolved to meet new knowledge requirements, some of the older files have become out of date, and efforts are underway to address the uniformity of PDB data. Until these efforts are complete and a new data format is developed, inconsistencies in the current data format are a challenge programmers have to face. If you do a lot of programming with PDB files, you'll find many inconsistencies and errors in the data, especially in the older files. Plus, many parsing tools that work well on newer files perform poorly on older files.

As you become a more experienced programmer, these and other issues the PDB faces become more important. For instance, as PDB evolves, the code you write to interact with it must also evolve; you must always maintain your code with an eye on how the rest of the world is changing. As links between databases become better supported, your code will take advantage of the new opportunities the links provide. With new standards of data storage becoming established, your code will have to evolve to include them.

The PDB web site contains a wealth of information on how to download all the files. They are also conveniently distributed—and at no cost—on a set of CDs, which is a real advantage for those lacking high-throughput Internet connections.

Files and Folders

The PDB is distributed as files within directories. Each protein structure occupies its own file. PDB contains a huge amount of data, and it can be a challenge to deal with it. So in this section, you'll learn to deal with large numbers of files organized in directories and subdirectories.

You'll frequently find a need to write programs that manipulate large numbers of files. For example: perhaps you keep all your sequencing runs in a directory, organized into subdirectories labeled by the dates of the sequencing runs and containing whatever the sequencer produced on those days. After a few years, you could have quite a number of files.

Then, one day you discover a new sequence of DNA that seems to be implicated in cell division. You do a BLAST search (see Chapter 12) but find no significant hits for your new DNA. At that point you want to know whether you've seen this DNA before in any previous sequencing runs.* What you need to do is run a comparison subroutine on each of the hundreds or thousands of files in all your various sequencing run subdirectories. But that's going to take several days of repetitive, boring work sitting at the computer screen.

You can write a program in much less time than that! Then all you have to do is sit back and examine the results of any significant matches your program finds. To write the program, however, you have to know how to manipulate all the files and folders in Perl. The following sections show you how to do it.

Opening Directories

A filesystem is organized in a *tree* structure. The metaphor is apt. Starting from anyplace on the tree, you can proceed up the branches and get to any leaves that stem from your starting place. If you start from the root of the tree, you can reach all the leaves. Similarly, in a filesystem, if you start at a certain directory, you can reach all the files in all the subdirectories that stem from your starting place, and if you start at the root (which, strangely enough, is also called the "top") of the filesystem, you can reach all the files.

You've already had plenty of practice opening, reading from, writing to, and closing files. I will show a simple method with which you can open a folder (also called a

---

* You may do a comparison by keeping copies of all your sequencing runs in one large BLAST library; building such a BLAST library can be done using the techniques shown in this section.

directory) and get the filenames of all the files in that folder. Following that, you'll see how to get the names of all files from all directories and subdirectories from a certain starting point.

Let's look at the Perlish way to list all the files in a folder, beginning with some pseudocode:

```
open folder

read contents of folder (files and subfolders)

print their names
```

Example 11-1 shows the actual Perl code.

Example 11-1. Listing the contents of a folder (or directory)

```perl
#!/usr/bin/perl
#    Demonstrating how to open a folder and list its contents

use strict;
use warnings;
use BeginPerlBioinfo;      # see Chapter 6 about this module

my @files = ( );
my $folder = 'pdb';

# open the folder
unless(opendir(FOLDER, $folder)) {
    print "Cannot open folder $folder!\n";
    exit;
}

# read the contents of the folder (i.e. the files and subfolders)
@files = readdir(FOLDER);

# close the folder
closedir(FOLDER);

# print them out, one per line
print join( "\n", @files), "\n";

exit;
```

Since you're running this program on a folder that contains PDB files, this is what you'll see:

```
.
..
3c
44
pdb1a4o.ent
```

If you want to list the files in the current directory, you can give the directory name the special name "." for the current directory, like so:

```
my $folder = '.';
```

On Unix or Linux systems, the special files "." and ".." refer to the current directory and the parent directory, respectively. These aren't "really" files, at least not files you'd want to read; you can avoid listing them with the wonderful and amazing grep function. grep allows you to select elements from an array based on a test, such as a regular expression. Here's how to filter out the array entries "." and "..":

```
@files = grep( !/^\.\.?$/, @files);
```

grep selects all lines that don't match the regular expression, due to the negation operator written as the exclamation mark. The regular expression /^\.\.?$/ is looking for a line that begins with (the beginning of a line is indicated with the ^ metacharacter) a period \. (escaped with a backslash since a period is a metacharacter) followed by 0 or 1 periods \.? (the ? matches 0 or 1 of the preceding items), and nothing more (indicated by the $ end-of-string metacharacter).

In fact, this is so often used when reading a directory that it's usually combined into one step:

```
@files = grep (!/^\.\.?$/, readdir(FOLDER));
```

Okay, now all the files are listed. But wait: what if some of these files aren't files at all but are subfolders? You can use the handy file test operators to test each filename and then even open each subfolder and list the files in them. First, some pseudocode:

```
open folder

for each item in the folder

    if it's a file
        print its name

    else if it's a folder
        open the folder
        print the names of the contents of the folder
    }
}
```

Example 11-2 shows the program.

Example 11-2. List contents of a folder and its subfolders

```
#!/usr/bin/perl
#   Demonstrating how to open a folder and list its contents
#     -distinguishing between files and subfolders, which
#          are themselves listed

use strict;
use warnings;
use BeginPerlBioinfo;      # see Chapter 6 about this module
```

Example 11-2. List contents of a folder and its subfolders (continued)

```perl
my @files = ( );
my $folder = 'pdb';

# Open the folder
unless(opendir(FOLDER, $folder)) {
    print "Cannot open folder $folder!\n";
    exit;
}

# Read the folder, ignoring special entries "." and ".."
@files = grep (!/^\.\.?$/, readdir(FOLDER));

closedir(FOLDER);

# If file, print its name
# If folder, print its name and contents
#
# Notice that we need to prepend the folder name!
foreach my $file (@files) {

    # If the folder entry is a regular file
    if (-f "$folder/$file") {
        print "$folder/$file\n";

    # If the folder entry is a subfolder
    }elsif( -d "$folder/$file") {

        my $folder = "$folder/$file";

        # open the subfolder and list its contents
        unless(opendir(FOLDER, "$folder")) {
            print "Cannot open folder $folder!\n";
            exit;
        }

        my @files = grep (!/^\.\.?$/, readdir(FOLDER));

        closedir(FOLDER);

        foreach my $file (@files) {
            print "$folder/$file\n";
        }
    }
}

exit;
```

Here's the output of Example 11-2:

```
pdb/3c/pdb43c9.ent
pdb/3c/pdb43ca.ent
pdb/44/pdb144d.ent
pdb/44/pdb144l.ent
```

```
pdb/44/pdb244d.ent
pdb/44/pdb244l.ent
pdb/44/pdb344d.ent
pdb/44/pdb444d.ent
pdb/pdb1a4o.ent
```

Notice how variable names such as $file and @files have been reused in this code, using lexical scoping in the inner blocks with my. If the overall structure of the program wasn't so short and simple, this could get really hard to read. When the program says $file, does it mean this $file or that $file? This code is an example of how to get into trouble. It works, but it's hard to read, despite its brevity.

In fact, there's a deeper problem with Example 11-2. It's not well designed. By extending Example 11-1, it can now list subdirectories. But what if there are further levels of subdirectories?

Recursion

If you have a subroutine that lists the contents of directories and recursively calls itself to list the contents of any subdirectories it finds, you can call it on the top-level directory, and it eventually lists all the files.

Let's write another program that does just that. A *recursive* subroutine is defined simply as a subroutine that calls itself. Here is the pseudocode and the code (Example 11-3) followed by a discussion of how recursion works:

```
subroutine list_recursively

    open folder

    for each item in the folder

        if it's a file
            print its name

        else if it's a folder
            list_recursively
    }
}
```

Example 11-3. A recursive subroutine to list a filesystem

```perl
#!/usr/bin/perl
# Demonstrate a recursive subroutine to list a subtree of a filesystem

use strict;
use warnings;
use BeginPerlBioinfo;      # see Chapter 6 about this module

list_recursively('pdb');
```

Example 11-3. A recursive subroutine to list a filesystem (continued)

```perl
exit;

#################################################################################
# Subroutine
#################################################################################

# list_recursively
#
#    list the contents of a directory,
#                    recursively listing the contents of any subdirectories

sub list_recursively {

    my($directory) = @_;

    my @files = ( );

    # Open the directory
    unless(opendir(DIRECTORY, $directory)) {
        print "Cannot open directory $directory!\n";
        exit;
    }

    # Read the directory, ignoring special entries "." and ".."
    @files = grep (!/^\.\.?$/, readdir(DIRECTORY));

    closedir(DIRECTORY);

    # If file, print its name
    # If directory, recursively print its contents

    # Notice that we need to prepend the directory name!
    foreach my $file (@files) {

        # If the directory entry is a regular file
        if (-f "$directory/$file") {

            print "$directory/$file\n";

        # If the directory entry is a subdirectory
        }elsif( -d "$directory/$file") {

            # Here is the recursive call to this subroutine
            list_recursively("$directory/$file");
        }
    }
}
```

Here's the output of Example 11-3 (notice that it's the same as the output of Example 11-2):

```
pdb/3c/pdb43c9.ent
pdb/3c/pdb43ca.ent
pdb/44/pdb144d.ent
pdb/44/pdb144l.ent
pdb/44/pdb244d.ent
pdb/44/pdb244l.ent
pdb/44/pdb344d.ent
pdb/44/pdb444d.ent
pdb/pdb1a4o.ent
```

Look over the code for Example 11-3 and compare it to Example 11-2. As you can see, the programs are largely identical. Example 11-2 is all one main program; Example 11-3 has almost identical code but has packaged it up as a subroutine that is called by a short main program. The main program of Example 11-3 simply calls a recursive function, giving it a directory name (for a directory that exists on my computer; you may need to change the directory name when you attempt to run this program on your own computer). Here is the call:

```
list_recursively('pdb');
```

I don't know if you feel let down, but I do. This looks just like any other subroutine call. Clearly, the recursion must be defined within the subroutine. It's not until the very end of the list_recursively subroutine, where the program finds (using the -d file test operator) that one of the contents of the directory that it's listing is itself a directory, that there's a significant difference in the code as compared with Example 11-2. At that point, Example 11-2 has code to once again look for regular files or for directories. But this subroutine in Example 11-3 simply calls a subroutine, which happens to be itself, namely, list_recursively:

```
list_recursively("$directory/$file");
```

That's recursion.

As you've seen here, there are times when the data—for instance, the hierarchical structure of a filesystem—is well matched by the capabilities of recursive programs. The fact that the recursive call happens at the end of the subroutine means that it's a special type of recursion called *tail recursion*. Although recursion can be slow, due to all the subroutine calls it can create, the good news about tail recursion is that many compilers can optimize the code to make it run much faster. Using recursion can result in clean, short, easy-to-understand programs. (Although Perl doesn't yet optimize it, current plans for Perl 6 include support for optimizing tail recursion.)

Processing Many Files

Perl has modules for a variety of tasks. Some come standard with Perl; more can be installed after obtaining them from CPAN or elsewhere: *http://www.CPAN.org/*.

Example 11-3 in the previous section showed how to locate all files and directories under a given directory. There's a module that is standard in any recent version of Perl called *File::Find*. You can find it in your manual pages: on Unix or Linux, for instance, you issue the command `perldoc File::Find`. This module makes it easy— and efficient—to process all files under a given directory, performing whatever operations you specify.

Example 11-4 uses *File::Find*. Consult the documentation for more examples of this useful module. The example shows the same functionality as Example 11-3 but now uses *File::Find*. It simply lists the files and directories. Notice how much less code you have to write if you find a good module, ready to use!

Example 11-4. Demonstrate File::Find

```perl
#!/usr/bin/perl
# Demonstrate File::Find

use strict;
use warnings;
use BeginPerlBioinfo;      # see Chapter 6 about this module

use File::Find;

find ( \&my_sub, ('pdb') );

sub my_sub {
    -f and (print $File::Find::name, "\n");
}

exit;
```

Notice that a reference is passed to the my_sub subroutine by prefacing it with the backslash character. You also need to preface the name with the ampersand character, as mentioned in Chapter 6.

The call to find can also be done like this:

```perl
find sub { -f and (print $File::Find::name, "\n") }, ('pdb');
```

This puts an anonymous subroutine in place of the reference to the my_sub subroutine, and it's a convenience for these types of short subroutines.

Here's the output:

```
pdb/pdb1a4o.ent
pdb/44/pdb144d.ent
pdb/44/pdb144l.ent
pdb/44/pdb244d.ent
pdb/44/pdb244l.ent
pdb/44/pdb344d.ent
pdb/44/pdb444d.ent
pdb/3c/pdb43c9.ent
pdb/3c/pdb43ca.ent
```

As a final example of processing files with Perl, here's the same functionality as the preceding programs, with a one-line program, issued at the command line:

```
perl -e 'use File::Find;find sub{-f and (print $File::Find::name,"\n")},("pdb")'
```

Pretty cool, for those who admire terseness, although it doesn't really eschew obfuscation. Also note that for those on Unix systems, `ls -R pdb` and `find pdb -print` do the same thing with even less typing.

The reason for using a subroutine that you define is that it enables you to perform any arbitrary tests on the files you find and then take any actions with those files. It's another case of *modularization*: the *File::Find* module makes it easy to recurse over all the files and directories in a file structure and lets you do as you wish with the files and directories you find.

PDB Files

Here's a section of an actual PDB file:

```
HEADER    SUGAR BINDING PROTEIN                    03-MAR-99   1C1F
TITLE     LIGAND-FREE CONGERIN I
COMPND    MOL_ID: 1;
COMPND   2 MOLECULE: CONGERIN I;
COMPND   3 CHAIN: A;
COMPND   4 FRAGMENT: CARBOHYDRATE-RECOGNITION-DOMAIN;
COMPND   5 BIOLOGICAL_UNIT: HOMODIMER
SOURCE    MOL_ID: 1;
SOURCE   2 ORGANISM_SCIENTIFIC: CONGER MYRIASTER;
SOURCE   3 ORGANISM_COMMON: CONGER EEL;
SOURCE   4 TISSUE: SKIN MUCUS;
SOURCE   5 SECRETION: NON-CLASSICAL
KEYWDS    GALECTIN, LECTIN, BETA-GALACTOSE-BINDING, SUGAR BINDING
KEYWDS   2 PROTEIN
EXPDTA    X-RAY DIFFRACTION
AUTHOR    T.SHIRAI,C.MITSUYAMA,Y.NIWA,Y.MATSUI,H.HOTTA,T.YAMANE,
AUTHOR   2 H.KAMIYA,C.ISHII,T.OGAWA,K.MURAMOTO
REVDAT   2   14-OCT-99 1C1F    1       SEQADV HEADER
REVDAT   1   08-OCT-99 1C1F    0
JRNL        AUTH   T.SHIRAI,C.MITSUYAMA,Y.NIWA,Y.MATSUI,H.HOTTA,
JRNL        AUTH 2 T.YAMANE,H.KAMIYA,C.ISHII,T.OGAWA,K.MURAMOTO
JRNL        TITL   HIGH-RESOLUTION STRUCTURE OF CONGER EEL GALECTIN,
JRNL        TITL 2 CONGERIN I, IN LACTOSE- LIGANDED AND LIGAND-FREE
JRNL        TITL 3 FORMS: EMERGENCE OF A NEW STRUCTURE CLASS BY
JRNL        TITL 4 ACCELERATED EVOLUTION
JRNL        REF    STRUCTURE (LONDON)            V.   7 1223 1999
JRNL        REFN   ASTM STRUE6  UK ISSN 0969-2126                2005
REMARK   1
REMARK   2
REMARK   2 RESOLUTION. 1.6 ANGSTROMS.
REMARK   3
REMARK   3 REFINEMENT.
REMARK   3   PROGRAM     : X-PLOR 3.1
```

```
REMARK   3    AUTHORS      : BRUNGER
REMARK   3
REMARK   3  DATA USED IN REFINEMENT.
REMARK   3   RESOLUTION RANGE HIGH (ANGSTROMS) : 1.60
REMARK   3   RESOLUTION RANGE LOW  (ANGSTROMS) : 8.00
REMARK   3   DATA CUTOFF            (SIGMA(F)) : 3.000
REMARK   3   DATA CUTOFF HIGH        (ABS(F)) : NULL
REMARK   3   DATA CUTOFF LOW         (ABS(F)) : NULL
REMARK   3   COMPLETENESS (WORKING+TEST)   (%) : 85.0
REMARK   3   NUMBER OF REFLECTIONS           : 17099
REMARK   3
REMARK   3
REMARK   3  FIT TO DATA USED IN REFINEMENT.
REMARK   3   CROSS-VALIDATION METHOD        : THROUGHOUT
REMARK   3   FREE R VALUE TEST SET SELECTION  : RANDOM
REMARK   3   R VALUE            (WORKING SET) : 0.201
REMARK   3   FREE R VALUE                  : 0.247
REMARK   3   FREE R VALUE TEST SET SIZE   (%) : 5.000
REMARK   3   FREE R VALUE TEST SET COUNT   : 855
REMARK   3   ESTIMATED ERROR OF FREE R VALUE  : NULL
REMARK   3
...  (file truncated here)
REMARK   4
REMARK   4 1C1F COMPLIES WITH FORMAT V. 2.3, 09-JULY-1998
REMARK   7
REMARK   7 >>> WARNING: CHECK REMARK 999 CAREFULLY
REMARK   8
REMARK   8 SIDE-CHAINS OF SER123 AND LEU124 ARE MODELED AS ALTERNATIVE
REMARK   8 CONFORMERS.
REMARK   9
REMARK   9 SER1 IS ACETYLATED.
REMARK  10
REMARK  10 TER
REMARK  10  SER: THE N-TERMINAL RESIDUE WAS NOT OBSERVED
REMARK 100
REMARK 100 THIS ENTRY HAS BEEN PROCESSED BY RCSB ON 07-MAR-1999.
REMARK 100 THE RCSB ID CODE IS RCSB000566.
REMARK 200
REMARK 200 EXPERIMENTAL DETAILS
REMARK 200  EXPERIMENT TYPE          : X-RAY DIFFRACTION
REMARK 200  DATE OF DATA COLLECTION      : NULL
REMARK 200  TEMPERATURE          (KELVIN) : 291.0
REMARK 200  PH                    : 9.00
REMARK 200  NUMBER OF CRYSTALS USED    : 1
REMARK 200
REMARK 200  SYNCHROTRON          (Y/N) : Y
REMARK 200  RADIATION SOURCE          : PHOTON FACTORY
REMARK 200  BEAMLINE              : BL6A
REMARK 200  X-RAY GENERATOR MODEL       : NULL
REMARK 200  MONOCHROMATIC OR LAUE   (M/L) : M
REMARK 200  WAVELENGTH OR RANGE      (A) : 1.00
REMARK 200  MONOCHROMATOR             : NULL
REMARK 200  OPTICS                : NULL
REMARK 200
```

```
...  (file truncated here)
REMARK 500
REMARK 500 GEOMETRY AND STEREOCHEMISTRY
REMARK 500 SUBTOPIC: COVALENT BOND ANGLES
REMARK 500
REMARK 500 THE STEREOCHEMICAL PARAMETERS OF THE FOLLOWING RESIDUES
REMARK 500 HAVE VALUES WHICH DEVIATE FROM EXPECTED VALUES BY MORE
REMARK 500 THAN 4*RMSD (M=MODEL NUMBER; RES=RESIDUE NAME; C=CHAIN
REMARK 500 IDENTIFIER; SSEQ=SEQUENCE NUMBER; I=INSERTION CODE).
REMARK 500
REMARK 500 STANDARD TABLE:
REMARK 500 FORMAT: (10X,I3,1X,A3,1X,A1,I4,A1,3(1X,A4,2X),12X,F5.1)
REMARK 500
REMARK 500 EXPECTED VALUES: ENGH AND HUBER, 1991
REMARK 500
REMARK 500 M RES CSSEQI ATM1   ATM2   ATM3
REMARK 500    HIS A  44   N  - CA  - C   ANGL. DEV. =-10.3 DEGREES
REMARK 500    LEU A 132   CA - CB  - CG  ANGL. DEV. = 12.5 DEGREES
REMARK 700
REMARK 700 SHEET
REMARK 700 DETERMINATION METHOD: AUTHOR-DETERMINED
REMARK 999
REMARK 999 SEQUENCE
REMARK 999 LEU A 135 IS NOT PRESENT IN SEQUENCE DATABASE
REMARK 999
DBREF  1C1F A    1   136  SWS    P26788   LEG_CONMY        1    135
SEQADV 1C1F LEU A  135  SWS  P26788             SEE REMARK 999
SEQRES   1 A  136  SER GLY GLY LEU GLN VAL LYS ASN PHE ASP PHE THR VAL
SEQRES   2 A  136  GLY LYS PHE LEU THR VAL GLY GLY PHE ILE ASN ASN SER
SEQRES   3 A  136  PRO GLN ARG PHE SER VAL ASN VAL GLY GLU SER MET ASN
SEQRES   4 A  136  SER LEU SER LEU HIS LEU ASP HIS ARG PHE ASN TYR GLY
SEQRES   5 A  136  ALA ASP GLN ASN THR ILE VAL MET ASN SER THR LEU LYS
SEQRES   6 A  136  GLY ASP ASN GLY TRP GLU THR GLU GLN ARG SER THR ASN
SEQRES   7 A  136  PHE THR LEU SER ALA GLY GLN TYR PHE GLU ILE THR LEU
SEQRES   8 A  136  SER TYR ASP ILE ASN LYS PHE TYR ILE ASP ILE LEU ASP
SEQRES   9 A  136  GLY PRO ASN LEU GLU PHE PRO ASN ARG TYR SER LYS GLU
SEQRES  10 A  136  PHE LEU PRO PHE LEU SER LEU ALA GLY ASP ALA ARG LEU
SEQRES  11 A  136  THR LEU VAL LYS LEU GLU
FORMUL   2  HOH   *81(H2 O1)
HELIX    1   1 GLY A   66  ASN A   68  5                              3
SHEET    1  S1 1 GLY A   3   VAL A   6  0
SHEET    1  S2 1 PHE A 121   GLY A 126  0
SHEET    1  S3 1 ARG A  29   GLY A  35  0
SHEET    1  S4 1 LEU A  41   ASN A  50  0
SHEET    1  S5 1 GLN A  55   THR A  63  0
SHEET    1  S6 1 GLN A  74   SER A  76  0
SHEET    1  F1 1 ALA A 128   GLU A 136  0
SHEET    1  F2 1 PHE A  16   ILE A  23  0
SHEET    1  F3 1 TYR A  86   TYR A  93  0
SHEET    1  F4 1 LYS A  97   ILE A 102  0
SHEET    1  F5 1 ASN A 107   PRO A 111  0
CRYST1   94.340   36.920   40.540  90.00  90.00  90.00 P 21 21 2    4
ORIGX1      1.000000  0.000000  0.000000        0.00000
ORIGX2      0.000000  1.000000  0.000000        0.00000
```

```
ORIGX3        0.000000  0.000000  1.000000        0.00000
SCALE1        0.010600  0.000000  0.000000        0.00000
SCALE2        0.000000  0.027085  0.000000        0.00000
SCALE3        0.000000  0.000000  0.024667        0.00000
ATOM     1  N   GLY A   2      1.888  -8.251  -2.511  1.00 36.63           N
ATOM     2  CA  GLY A   2      2.571  -8.428  -1.248  1.00 33.02           C
ATOM     3  C   GLY A   2      2.586  -7.069  -0.589  1.00 30.43           C
ATOM     4  O   GLY A   2      2.833  -6.107  -1.311  1.00 33.27           O
ATOM     5  N   GLY A   3      2.302  -6.984   0.693  1.00 24.67           N
ATOM     6  CA  GLY A   3      2.176  -5.723   1.348  1.00 18.88           C
ATOM     7  C   GLY A   3      0.700  -5.426   1.526  1.00 16.58           C
ATOM     8  O   GLY A   3     -0.187  -6.142   1.010  1.00 12.47           O
ATOM     9  N   LEU A   4      0.494  -4.400   2.328  1.00 15.00           N
... (file truncated here)
ATOM  1078  CG  GLU A 136     -0.873   9.368  16.046  1.00 38.96           C
ATOM  1079  CD  GLU A 136     -0.399   9.054  17.456  1.00 44.66           C
ATOM  1080  OE1 GLU A 136      0.789   8.749  17.641  1.00 47.97           O
ATOM  1081  OE2 GLU A 136     -1.236   9.099  18.361  1.00 47.75           O
ATOM  1082  OXT GLU A 136      0.764  12.146  12.712  1.00 26.22           O
TER   1083      GLU A 136
HETATM 1084  O   HOH   200    -1.905  -7.624   2.822  1.00 14.50           O
HETATM 1085  O   HOH   201    -8.374   7.981   9.202  1.00 20.77           O
HETATM 1086  O   HOH   202    -4.047   9.199  11.632  1.00 38.24           O
HETATM 1087  O   HOH   203     6.172  14.210   8.483  1.00 14.50           O
HETATM 1088  O   HOH   204     2.903   7.804  15.329  1.00 24.51           O
HETATM 1089  O   HOH   205    16.654   0.676  11.968  1.00 10.49           O
... (file truncated here)
HETATM 1157  O   HOH   286     6.960  14.840  -3.025  1.00 35.59           O
HETATM 1158  O   HOH   287    -3.222  10.410   7.061  1.00 38.91           O
HETATM 1159  O   HOH   288    28.306   0.551   4.876  1.00 52.13           O
HETATM 1160  O   HOH   290    21.506 -12.424   9.751  1.00 31.68           O
HETATM 1161  O   HOH   291    12.951  10.424  -7.324  1.00 46.10           O
HETATM 1162  O   HOH   292    18.119 -15.184  14.793  1.00 56.82           O
HETATM 1163  O   HOH   293    13.501  22.220   8.216  1.00 43.30           O
HETATM 1164  O   HOH   294    13.916 -11.387   9.695  1.00 47.13           O
MASTER      240    0    0    1   11    0    0    6 1163    1    0   11
END
```

PDB files are long, mostly due to the need for information about each atom in the molecule; this relatively short one, when complete, is extensive—28 formatted pages. I cut it here to a little over three pages, showing just enough of the principal sections to give you the overall idea.

The PDB web site has the basic documents you need to read and program with PDB files. The Protein Data Bank Contents Guide (*http://www.rcsb.org/pdb/docs/format/ pdbguide2.2/guide2.2_frame.html*) is the best reference, and there are also FAQs and additional documents available.

In the following sections, you'll extract information from these files. Since the information in these files describes the 3D structure of macromolecules, the files are frequently used by graphical programs that display a spatial representation of the molecules. The scope of this book does not include graphics; however, you will see how to get spatial coordinates out of the files. The largest part of PDB files are the ATOM record type lines containing the coordinates of the atoms. Because of this level of detail, PDB files are typically longer than GenBank records. (Note the inconsistent terminology—a unit of PDB is the file, which contains one structure; a unit of GenBank is the record, which contains one entry.)

PDB File Format

Let's take a look at a PDB file and the documentation that tells how the information is formatted in a PDB file. Based on that information, you'll parse the file to extract information of interest.

PDB files are composed of lines of 80 columns that begin with one of several predefined record names and end with a newline. ("Column" means position on a line: the first character is in the first column, and so forth.) Blank columns are padded with spaces. A *record type* is one or more lines with the same record name. Different record types have different types of fields defined within the lines. They are also grouped according to function.

The SEQRES record type is one of four record types in the Primary Structure Section, which presents the primary structure of the peptide or nucleotide sequence:

DBREF
Reference to the entry in the sequence database(s)

SEQADV
Identification of conflicts between PDB and the named sequence database

SEQRES
Primary sequence of backbone residues

MODRES
Identification of modifications to standard residues

The DBREF and SEQADV record types in the example PDB entry from the previous section give reference information and details on conflicts between the PDB and the original database. (The example doesn't include a MODRES record type.) Here are those record types from the entry:

```
DBREF  1C1F A    1   136  SWS    P26788   LEG_CONMY        1    135
SEQADV 1C1F LEU A  135  SWS  P26788               SEE REMARK 999
```

Briefly, the DBREF line states there's a PDB file called *1C1F* (from a file named *pdb1c1f.ent*), the residues in chain A are numbered from 1 to 136 in the original Swiss-Prot (SWS) database, the ID number P26788 and the name LEG_CONMY are assigned in that database (in many databases these are identical), and the residues are numbered 1 to 135 in PDB. The discrepancy in the numbering between the original database and PDB is explained in the SEQADV record type, which refers you to a REMARK 999 line (not shown here) where you discover that the PDB entry disagrees with the Swiss-Prot sequence concerning a leucine at position 135 (perhaps two different groups determined the structure, and they disagree at this point).*

You can see that to parse the information in those two lines by a program requires several steps, such as following links to other lines in the PDB entry that further explain discrepancies and identifying other databases.

Links between databases are important in bioinformatics. Table 11-1 displays the databases that are referred to in PDB files. As you already know, there are many biological databases; those shown here have a good deal of protein or structural data.

Table 11-1. Databases referenced in PDB files

Database	PDB code
BioMagResBank	BMRB
BLOCKS	BLOCKS
European Molecular Biology Laboratory	EMBL
GenBank	GB
Genome Data Base	GDB
Nucleic Acid Database	NDB
PROSITE	PROSIT
Protein Data Bank	PDB
Protein Identification Resource	PIR
SWISS-PROT	SWS
TREMBL	TREMBL

SEQRES

For starters, let's try a fairly easy task in Perl: extracting the amino acid sequence data. To extract the amino acid primary sequence information, you need to parse the record type SEQRES. Here is a SEQRES line from the PDB file listed earlier:

```
SEQRES    1 A  136   SER GLY GLY LEU GLN VAL LYS ASN PHE ASP PHE THR VAL
```

The following code shows the SEQRES record type as defined in the Protein Data Bank Contents Guide. This section on SEQRES, which is a fairly simple record type, is shown in its entirely to help familiarize you with this kind of documentation.

---

* The cross-referencing to different databases is problematic in older PDB files: it may be missing, or buried somewhere in a REMARK 999 line.

SEQRES

Overview

SEQRES records contain the amino acid or nucleic acid sequence of residues in each chain of the macromolecule that was studied.

Record Format

COLUMNS	DATA TYPE	FIELD	DEFINITION
1 - 6	Record name	"SEQRES"	
9 - 10	Integer	serNum	Serial number of the SEQRES record for the current chain. Starts at 1 and increments by one each line. Reset to 1 for each chain.
12	Character	chainID	Chain identifier. This may be any single legal character, including a blank which is used if there is only one chain.
14 - 17	Integer	numRes	Number of residues in the chain. This value is repeated on every record.
20 - 22	Residue name	resName	Residue name.
24 - 26	Residue name	resName	Residue name.
28 - 30	Residue name	resName	Residue name.
32 - 34	Residue name	resName	Residue name.
36 - 38	Residue name	resName	Residue name.
40 - 42	Residue name	resName	Residue name.
44 - 46	Residue name	resName	Residue name.
48 - 50	Residue name	resName	Residue name.
52 - 54	Residue name	resName	Residue name.
56 - 58	Residue name	resName	Residue name.
60 - 62	Residue name	resName	Residue name.
64 - 66	Residue name	resName	Residue name.
68 - 70	Residue name	resName	Residue name.

Details

* PDB entries use the three-letter abbreviation for amino acid names and the one-letter code for nucleic acids.

* In the case of non-standard groups, a hetID of up to three (3) alphanumeric characters is used. Common HET names appear in the HET dictionary.

* Each covalently contiguous sequence of residues (connected via the "backbone" atoms) is represented as an individual chain.

* Heterogens which are integrated into the backbone of the chain are listed as being part of the chain and are included in the SEQRES records for that chain.

* Each set of SEQRES records and each HET group is assigned a component number. The component number is assigned serially beginning with 1 for the first set of SEQRES records. This number is given explicitly in the FORMUL record, but only implicitly in the SEQRES record.

* The SEQRES records must list residues present in the molecule studied, even if the coordinates are not present.

* C- and N-terminus residues for which no coordinates are provided due to disorder must be listed on SEQRES.

* All occurrences of standard amino or nucleic acid residues (ATOM records) must be listed on a SEQRES record. This implies that a numRes of 1 is valid.

* No distinction is made between ribo- and deoxyribonucleotides in the SEQRES records. These residues are identified with the same residue name (i.e., A, C, G, T, U, I).

* If the entire residue sequence is unknown, the serNum in column 10 is "0", the number of residues thought to comprise the molecule is entered as numRes in columns 14 - 17, and resName in columns 20 - 22 is "UNK".

* In case of microheterogeneity, only one of the sequences is presented. A REMARK is generated to explain this and a SEQADV is also generated.

Verification/Validation/Value Authority Control

The residues presented on the SEQRES records must agree with those found in the ATOM records.

The SEQRES records are checked by PDB using the sequence databases and information provided by the depositor.

SEQRES is compared to the ATOM records during processing, and both are checked against the sequence database. All discrepancies are either resolved or annotated in the entry.

```
Relationships to Other Record Types

The residues presented on the SEQRES records must agree with those found in
the ATOM records. DBREF refers to the corresponding entry in the sequence
databases. SEQADV lists all discrepancies between the entry's sequence for
which there are coordinates and that referenced in the sequence database.
MODRES describes modifications to a standard residue.

Example

            1         2         3         4         5         6         7
   12345678901234567890123456789012345678901234567890123456789012345678901234567890
   SEQRES   1 A   21  GLY ILE VAL GLU GLN CYS CYS THR SER ILE CYS SER LEU
   SEQRES   2 A   21  TYR GLN LEU GLU ASN TYR CYS ASN
   SEQRES   1 B   30  PHE VAL ASN GLN HIS LEU CYS GLY SER HIS LEU VAL GLU
   SEQRES   2 B   30  ALA LEU TYR LEU VAL CYS GLY GLU ARG GLY PHE PHE TYR
   SEQRES   3 B   30  THR PRO LYS ALA
   SEQRES   1 C   21  GLY ILE VAL GLU GLN CYS CYS THR SER ILE CYS SER LEU
   SEQRES   2 C   21  TYR GLN LEU GLU ASN TYR CYS ASN
   SEQRES   1 D   30  PHE VAL ASN GLN HIS LEU CYS GLY SER HIS LEU VAL GLU
   SEQRES   2 D   30  ALA LEU TYR LEU VAL CYS GLY GLU ARG GLY PHE PHE TYR
   SEQRES   3 D   30  THR PRO LYS ALA

Known Problems

Polysaccharides do not lend themselves to being represented in SEQRES.

There is no mechanism provided to describe sequence runs when the exact
ordering of the sequence is not known.

For cyclic peptides, PDB arbitrarily assigns a residue as the N-terminus.

For microheterogeneity only one of the possible residues in a given position
is provided in SEQRES.

No distinction is made between ribo- and deoxyribonucleotides in the SEQRES
records. These residues are identified with the same residue name (i.e., A,
C, G, T, U).
```

The structure of the line containing the SEQRES record type is fairly straightforward, with fields assigned to specific locations or columns in the line. You'll see later how to use these locations to parse the information. Note that the documentation includes many details that arise when handling such complex experimental data.

Apart from the fairly standard problem of accumulating the sequence, there is the added complication of multiple strands. By reading the documentation just shown, you'll see that the SEQRES identifier is followed by a number representing the line number for that chain, and the chain is given in the next field (although in older records it was optional and may be blank). Following those fields comes a number that gives the total number of residues in the chain. Finally, after that, come residues represented as three-letter codes. What is needed, and what can be ignored to meet our programming goals?

Parsing PDB Files

First, Example 11-5 shows the main program and three subroutines that will be discussed in this section.

Example 11-5. Extract sequence chains from PDB file

```perl
#!/usr/bin/perl
#  Extract sequence chains from PDB file

use strict;
use warnings;
use BeginPerlBioinfo;      # see Chapter 6 about this module

# Read in PDB file:  Warning - some files are very large!
my @file = get_file_data('pdb/c1/pdb1c1f.ent');

# Parse the record types of the PDB file
my %recordtypes = parsePDBrecordtypes(@file);

# Extract the amino acid sequences of all chains in the protein
my @chains = extractSEQRES( $recordtypes{'SEQRES'} );

# Translate the 3-character codes to 1-character codes, and print
foreach my $chain (@chains) {
    print "****chain $chain **** \n";
    print "$chain\n";
    print iub3to1($chain), "\n";
}

exit;

##############################################################################
# Subroutines for Example 11-5
##############################################################################

# parsePDBrecordtypes
#
#-given an array of a PDB file, return a hash with
#    keys   = record type names
#    values = scalar containing lines for that record type

sub parsePDBrecordtypes {

    my @file = @_;

    use strict;
    use warnings;

    my %recordtypes = ();

    foreach my $line (@file) {
```

Example 11-5. Extract sequence chains from PDB file (continued)

```
            # Get the record type name which begins at the
            # start of the line and ends at the first space
            # The pattern (\S+) is returned and saved in $recordtype
            my($recordtype) = ($line =~ /^(\S+)/);

            # .= fails if a key is undefined, so we have to
            # test for definition and use either .= or = depending
            if(defined $recordtypes{$recordtype} ) {
                $recordtypes{$recordtype} .= $line;
            }else{
                $recordtypes{$recordtype} = $line;
            }
        }
    }

    return %recordtypes;
}

# extractSEQRES
#
#-given an scalar containing SEQRES lines,
#    return an array containing the chains of the sequence

sub extractSEQRES {

    use strict;
    use warnings;

    my($seqres) = @_;

    my $lastchain = '';
    my $sequence = '';
    my @results = ();

    # make array of lines
    my @record = split ( /\n/, $seqres);

    foreach my $line (@record) {
        # Chain is in column 12, residues start in column 20
        my ($thischain) = substr($line, 11, 1);
        my($residues)  = substr($line, 19, 52); # add space at end

        # Check if a new chain, or continuation of previous chain
        if("$lastchain" eq "") {
            $sequence = $residues;
        }elsif("$thischain" eq "$lastchain") {
            $sequence .= $residues;

        # Finish gathering previous chain (unless first record)
        }elsif ( $sequence ) {
            push(@results, $sequence);
            $sequence = $residues;
        }
```

Example 11-5. Extract sequence chains from PDB file (continued)

```perl
        $lastchain = $thischain;
    }

    # save last chain
    push(@results, $sequence);

    return @results;
}

# iub3to1
#
#-change string of 3-character IUB amino acid codes (whitespace separated)
#    into a string of 1-character amino acid codes

sub iub3to1 {

    my($input) = @_;

    my %three2one = (
        'ALA' => 'A',
        'VAL' => 'V',
        'LEU' => 'L',
        'ILE' => 'I',
        'PRO' => 'P',
        'TRP' => 'W',
        'PHE' => 'F',
        'MET' => 'M',
        'GLY' => 'G',
        'SER' => 'S',
        'THR' => 'T',
        'TYR' => 'Y',
        'CYS' => 'C',
        'ASN' => 'N',
        'GLN' => 'Q',
        'LYS' => 'K',
        'ARG' => 'R',
        'HIS' => 'H',
        'ASP' => 'D',
        'GLU' => 'E',
    );

    # clean up the input
    $input =~ s/\n/ /g;

    my $seq = '';

    # This use of split separates on any contiguous whitespace
    my @code3 = split(' ', $input);

    foreach my $code (@code3) {
        # A little error checking
        if(not defined $three2one{$code}) {
```

Example 11-5. Extract sequence chains from PDB file (continued)

```
            print "Code $code not defined\n";
            next;
        }
        $seq .= $three2one{$code};
    }
    return $seq;
}
```

It's important to note that the main program, which calls the subroutine get_file_ data to read in the PDB file, has included a warning about the potentially large size of any given PDB file. (For instance, the PDB file *1gav* weighs in at 3.45 MB.) Plus, the main program follows the reading in of the entire file, with the subroutine parsePDBrecordtypes that makes copies of all lines in the input file, separated by record type. At this point, the running program is using twice the amount of memory as the size of the file. This design has the advantage of clarity and modularity, but it can cause problems if main memory is in short supply. The use of memory can be lessened by not saving the results of reading in the file, but instead passing the file data directly to the parsePDBrecordtypes subroutine, like so:

```
# Get the file data and parse the record types of the PDB file
%recordtypes = parsePDBrecordtypes(get_file_data('pdb/c1/pdb1c1f.ent'));
```

Further savings of memory are possible. For instance, you can rewrite the program to just read the file one line at a time while parsing the data into the record types. I point out these considerations to give you an idea of the kinds of choices that are practically important in processing large files. However, let's stick with this design for now. It may be expensive in terms of memory, but it's very clear in terms of overall program structure.

In Chapter 10, I demonstrated two ways to parse GenBank files into sequence and annotation and then how to parse the annotation into finer and finer levels of detail.

The first method involved iterating through an array of the lines of the record. Recall that due to the structure of multiline fields, it was necessary to set flags while iterating to keep track of which field the input line was in.[*]

The other method, which worked better for GenBank files, involved regular expressions. Which method will work best for PDB files? (Or should you settle on a third approach?)

There are several ways to extract this information. PDB makes it easy to collect record types, since they all start with the same keyword at the beginning of the line.

---

[*] In GenBank, the multiline information sets were called fields; in PDB, they're called record types. Just as in biology different researchers may use their own terminology for some structures or concepts, so too in computer science there can be a certain creativity in terminology. This is one of the interesting difficulties in integrating biological data sources.

The technique in the last chapter that used regular expressions parsed the top-level fields of the file; this would be somewhat unwieldy for PDB files. (See the exercises at the end of the chapter.) For instance, a regular expression such as the following matches all adjacent SEQRES lines into a scalar string:

```
$record =~ /SEQRES.*\n(SEQRES.*\n)*/;
$seqres = $&;
```

The regular expression matches a single SEQRES line with SEQRES.*\n and then matches zero or more additional lines with (SEQRES.*\n)*. Notice how the final * indicates zero or more of the preceding item, namely, the parenthesized expression (SEQRES.*\n). Also note that the .* matches zero or more nonnewline characters. Finally, the second line captures the pattern matched, denoted by $&, into the variable $seqres.

To extend this to capture all record types, see the exercises at the end of the chapter.

For PDB files, each line starts with a keyword that explicitly states to which record type that line belongs. You will find in the documentation that each record type has all its lines adjacent to each other in a group. In this case, it seems that simply iterating through the lines and collecting the record types would be the simplest programming approach.

Example 11-5 contains a subroutine parsePDBrecordtypes that parses the PDB record types from an array containing the lines of the PDB record. This is a short, clean subroutine that accomplishes what is needed. The comments describe what's happening pretty well, which, as you know, is a critical factor in writing good code. Basically, each line is examined for its record type and is then added to the value of a hash entry with the record type as the key. The hash is returned from the subroutine.

Extracting Primary Sequence

Let's examine the subroutine extractSEQRES, now that the record types have been parsed out, and extract the primary amino acid sequence.

You need to extract each chain separately and return an array of one or more strings of sequence corresponding to those chains, instead of just one sequence.

The previous parse, in Example 11-4, left the required SEQRES record type, which stretches over several lines, in a scalar string that is the value of the key 'SEQRES' in a hash. Our success with the previous parsePDBrecordtypes subroutine that used iteration over lines (as opposed to regular expressions over multiline strings) leads to the same approach here. The split Perl function enables you to turn a multiline string into an array.

As you iterate through the lines of the SEQRES record type, notice when a new chain is starting, save the previous chain in @results, reset the $sequence array, and reset the $lastchain flag to the new chain. Also, when done with all the lines, make sure to save the last sequence chain in the @results array.

Also notice (and verify by exploring the Perl documentation for the function) that split, with the arguments you gave it, does what you want.

The third and final subroutine of Example 11-5 is called iub3to1. Since in PDB the sequence information is in three-character codes, you need this subroutine to change those sequences into one-character codes. It uses a straightforward hash lookup to perform the translation.

We've now decomposed the problem into a few complementary subroutines. It's always interesting as to how to best divide a problem into cooperating subroutines. You can put the call to iub3to1 inside the extractSEQRES subroutine; that might be a cleaner way to package these subroutines together, since, outside the PDB file format, you won't have use for the strings of amino acids in three-character codes.

The important observation at this juncture is to point out that a few short subroutines, tied together with a very short main program, were sufficient to do a great deal of parsing of PDB files.

Finding Atomic Coordinates

So far, I've tried not to give more than a very brief overview of protein structure. However, in parsing PDB files, you will be faced with a great deal of detailed information about the structures and the experimental conditions under which they were determined. I will now present a short program that extracts the coordinates of atoms in a PDB file. I don't cover the whole story: for that, you will want to read the PDB documentation in detail and consult texts on protein structure, X-ray crystallography, and NMR techniques.

That said, let's extract the coordinates from the ATOM record type. ATOM record types are the most numerous of the several record types that deal with atomic-coordinate data: MODEL, ATOM, SIGATM, ANISOU, SIGUIJ, TER, HETATM, and ENDMDL. There are also several record types that handle coordinate transformation: ORIGXn, SCALEn, MTRIXn, and TVECT.

Here is part of the PDB documentation that shows the field definitions of each ATOM record:

```
ATOM

Overview

The ATOM records present the atomic coordinates for standard residues.
They also present the occupancy and temperature factor for each atom.
Heterogen coordinates use the HETATM record type. The element symbol
is always present on each ATOM record; segment identifier and charge
are optional.
```

```
Record Format

COLUMNS        DATA TYPE      FIELD       DEFINITION
--------------------------------------------------------------------------
 1 - 6         Record name    "ATOM  "

 7 - 11        Integer        serial      Atom serial number.

13 - 16        Atom           name        Atom name.

17             Character      altLoc      Alternate location indicator.

18 - 20        Residue name   resName     Residue name.

22             Character      chainID     Chain identifier.

23 - 26        Integer        resSeq      Residue sequence number.

27             AChar          iCode       Code for insertion of residues.

31 - 38        Real(8.3)      x           Orthogonal coordinates for X in
                                          Angstroms.

39 - 46        Real(8.3)      y           Orthogonal coordinates for Y in
                                          Angstroms.

47 - 54        Real(8.3)      z           Orthogonal coordinates for Z in
                                          Angstroms.

55 - 60        Real(6.2)      occupancy   Occupancy.

61 - 66        Real(6.2)      tempFactor  Temperature factor.

73 - 76        LString(4)     segID       Segment identifier, left-justified.

77 - 78        LString(2)     element     Element symbol, right-justified.

79 - 80        LString(2)     charge      Charge on the atom.
```

Here is a typical ATOM line:

```
ATOM      1  N   GLY A   2       1.888  -8.251  -2.511  1.00 36.63           N
```

Let's do something fairly simple: let's extract all x, y, and z coordinates for each atom, plus the serial number (a unique integer for each atom in the molecule) and the element symbol. Example 11-6 is a subroutine that accomplishes that, with a main program to exercise the subroutine.

Example 11-6. Extract atomic coordinates from PDB file

```
#!/usr/bin/perl
# Extract atomic coordinates from PDB file
```

Example 11-6. Extract atomic coordinates from PDB file (continued)

```perl
use strict;
use warnings;
use BeginPerlBioinfo;      # see Chapter 6 about this module

# Read in PDB file
my @file = get_file_data('pdb/c1/pdb1c1f.ent');

# Parse the record types of the PDB file
my %recordtypes = parsePDBrecordtypes(@file);

# Extract the atoms of all chains in the protein
my %atoms = parseATOM ( $recordtypes{'ATOM'} );

# Print out a couple of the atoms
print $atoms{'1'}, "\n";
print $atoms{'1078'}, "\n";

exit;

##############################################################################
# Subroutines of Example 11-6
##############################################################################

# parseATOM
#
# -extract x, y, and z coordinates, serial number and element symbol
#     from PDB ATOM record type
#     Return a hash with key=serial number, value=coordinates in a string

sub parseATOM {

    my($atomrecord) = @_;

    use strict;
    use warnings;

    my %results = ();

    # Turn the scalar into an array of ATOM lines
    my(@atomrecord) = split(/\n/, $atomrecord);

    foreach my $record (@atomrecord) {
        my $number  = substr($record,  6, 5);  # columns 7-11
        my $x       = substr($record, 30, 8);  # columns 31-38
        my $y       = substr($record, 38, 8);  # columns 39-46
        my $z       = substr($record, 46, 8);  # columns 47-54
        my $element = substr($record, 76, 2);  # columns 77-78

        # $number and $element may have leading spaces: strip them
        $number =~ s/^\s*//;
        $element =~ s/^\s*//;
```

Example 11-6. Extract atomic coordinates from PDB file (continued)

```
        # Store information in hash
        $results{$number} = "$x $y $z $element";
    }

    # Return the hash
    return %results;
}
```

The parseATOM subroutine is quite short: the strict format of these ATOM records makes parsing the information quite straightforward. You first split the scalar argument, which contains the ATOM lines, into an array of lines.

Then, for each line, use the substr function to extract the specific columns of the line that contains the needed data: the serial number of the atom; the x, y, and z coordinates; and the element symbol.

Finally, save the results by making a hash with keys equal to the serial numbers and values set to strings containing the other four relevant fields. Now, this may not always be the most convenient way to return the data. For one thing, hashes are not sorted on the keys, so that would need to be an additional step if you had to sort the atoms by serial number. In particular, an array is a logical choice to store information sorted by serial number. Or, it could be that what you really want is to find all the metals, in which case, another data structure would be suggested. Nevertheless, this short subroutine shows one way to find and report information.

It often happens that what you really need is a reformatting of the data for use by another program. Using the technique of this subroutine, you can see how to extract the needed data and add a print statement that formats the data into the desired form. Take a look at the printf and sprintf functions to get more specific control over the format. For real heavy-duty formatting, there's the format function, which merits its own chapter in O'Reilly's comprehensive *Programming Perl*. (See also Chapter 12 and Appendix B of this book.)

Here's the output from Example 11-6:

```
 1.888   -8.251   -2.511  N
18.955  -10.180   10.777  C
```

You can now extract at least the major portion of the atomic coordinates from a PDB file. Again, notice the good news: it doesn't take a long or particularly complex program to do what is needed.

This program has been designed so that its parts can be used in the future to work well for other purposes. You parse all record types, for instance, not only the ATOM record types. Let's take a look at a very short program that just parses the ATOM record type lines from an input file; by targeting only this one problem, you can write a much shorter program. Here's the program:

```
while(<>) {
        /^ATOM/ or next;

        my($n, $x, $y, $z, $element)
            = ($_ =~ /^.{6}(.{5}).{19}(.{8})(.{8})(.{8}).{22}(..)/);

        # $n and $element may have leading spaces: strip them
        $n       =~ s/^\s*//;
        $element =~ s/^\s*//;

        if (($n == 1) or ($n == 1078)) {
                printf "%8.3f%8.3f%8.3f %2s\n", $x, $y, $z, $element;
        }
}
```

For each line, a regular-expression match extracts just the needed information. Recall that a regular expression that contains parentheses metacharacters returns an array whose elements are the parts of the string that matched within the parentheses. You assign the five variables $number, $x, $y, $z, and $element to the substrings from these matched parentheses.

The actual regular expression is simply using dots and the quantifier operator .{num} to stand for *num* characters. In this way, you can, starting from the beginning of the string as represented by the caret ^ metacharacter, specify the columns with the information you want returned by surrounding them with parentheses.

For instance, you don't want the first six characters, so you specify them as ^.{6}, but you do want the next five characters because they contain the serial number of the atom; so, specify that field as (.{5}).

Frankly, I think that the use of substr is clearer for this purpose, but I wanted to show you an alternative way using regular expressions as well.

We've already seen the use of the printf function to format output with more options then with the print function.

This program has another important shortcut. It doesn't specify the file to open and read from. In Perl, you can give the input filename on the command line (or drag and drop it onto a Mac droplet), and the program takes its input from that file. Just use the angle brackets as shown in the first line of the program to read from the file. For short, fast programs, such as the one demonstrated here, this is a great convenience. You can leave out all the calls and tests for success of the open function and just use the angle brackets. You would call it from the command line like so, assuming you saved the program in a file called *get_two_atoms*:

```
%perl get_two_atoms pdb1a4o.ent
```

Alternatively, you can pipe data to the program with the commands:

```
% cat pdb1a40.cat | perl get_two_atoms
```

or:

```
% perl get_two__atoms < pdb1a40.ent
```

and use <STDIN> instead of <> in your program to read the data.

Controlling Other Programs

Perl makes it easy to start other programs and collect their output, all from within your Perl program. This is an extremely useful capability; for most programs, Perl makes it fairly simple to accomplish.

You may need to run some particular program many times, for instance over every file in PDB to extract secondary structure information. The program itself may not have a way to tell it "run yourself over all these files." Also, the output of the program may have all sorts of extraneous information. What you need is a much simpler report that just presents the information that interests you—perhaps in a format that could then be input to another program! With Perl you can write a program to do exactly this.

An important kind of program to automate is a web site that provides some useful program or data online. Using the appropriate Perl modules, you can connect to the web site, send it your input, collect the output, and then parse and reformat as you wish. It's actually not hard to do! O'Reilly's *Perl Cookbook*, a companion volume to *Programming Perl*, is an excellent source of short programs and helpful descriptions to get you started.

Perl is a great way to automate other programs. The next section shows an example of a Perl program that starts another program and collects, parses, reformats, and outputs the results. This program will control another program on the same computer. The example will be from a Unix or Linux environment; consult your Perl documentation on how to get the same functionality from your Windows or Macintosh platform.

The Stride Secondary Structure Predictor

We will use an external program to calculate the secondary structure from the 3D coordinates of a PDB file. As a secondary structure assignment engine, I use a program that outputs a secondary structure report, called *stride*. *stride* is available from EMBL (*http://www.embl.heidelberg.ole/stride/stride_info.html*) and runs on Unix, Linux, Windows, Macintosh, and VMS systems. The program works very simply; just give it a command-line argument of a PDB filename and collect the output in the subroutine call_stride that follows.

Example 11-7 is the entire program: two subroutines and a main program, followed by a discussion.

Example 11-7. Call another program for secondary structure prediction

```perl
#!/usr/bin/perl
#  Call another program to perform secondary structure prediction

use strict;
use warnings;

# Call "stride" on a file, collect the report
my(@stride_output)  = call_stride('pdb/c1/pdb1c1f.ent');

# Parse the stride report into primary sequence, and secondary
#   structure prediction
my($sequence, $structure)  = parse_stride(@stride_output);

# Print out the beginnings of the sequence and the secondary structure
print substr($sequence, 0, 80), "\n";
print substr($structure, 0, 80), "\n";

exit;

################################################################################
# Subroutine for Example 11-7
################################################################################

# call_stride
#
# -given a PDB filename, return the output from the "stride"
#      secondary structure prediction program

sub call_stride {

    use strict;
    use warnings;

    my($filename) = @_;

    # The stride program options
    my($stride) = '/usr/local/bin/stride';
    my($options) = '';
    my(@results) = ();

    # Check for presence of PDB file
    unless ( -e $filename ) {
        print "File \"$filename\" doesn\'t seem to exist!\n";
        exit;
    }

    # Start up the program, capture and return the output
    @results = `$stride $options $filename`;
```

Example 11-7. Call another program for secondary structure prediction (continued)

```
    return @results;
}

# parse_stride
#
#—given stride output, extract the primary sequence and the
#    secondary structure prediction, returning them in a
#    two-element array.

sub parse_stride {

    use strict;
    use warnings;

    my(@stridereport) = @_;
    my($seq) = '';
    my($str) = '';
    my $length;

    # Extract the lines of interest
    my(@seq) = grep(/^SEQ /, @stridereport);

    my(@str) = grep(/^STR /, @stridereport);

    # Process those lines to discard all but the sequence
    #   or structure information
    for (@seq) { $_ = substr($_, 10, 50) }
    for (@str) { $_ = substr($_, 10, 50) }

    # Return the information as an array of two strings
    $seq = join('', @seq);
    $str = join('', @str);

    # Delete unwanted spaces from the ends of the strings.
    # ($seq has no spaces that are wanted, but $str may)
    $seq =~ s/(\s+)$//;

    $length = length($1);

    $str =~ s/\s{$length}$//;

    return( ($seq, $str) );
}
```

As you can see in the subroutine call_stride, variables have been made for the program name ($stride) and for the options you may want to pass ($options). Since these are parts of the program you may want to change, put them as variables near the top of the code, to make them easy to find and alter. The argument to the subroutine is the PDB filename ($filename). (Of course, if you expect the options to change frequently, you can make them another argument to the subroutine.)

Since you're dealing with a program that takes a file, do a little error checking to see if a file by that name actually exists. Use the -e file test operator. Or you can omit this and let the *stride* program figure it out, and capture its error output. But that requires parsing the stride output for its error output, which involves figuring out how *stride* reports errors. This can get complicated, so I'd stick with using the -e file test operator.

The actual running of the program and collecting its output happens in just one line. The program to be run is enclosed in backticks, which run the program (first expanding variables) and return the output as an array of lines.

There are other ways to run a program. One common way is the system function call. It behaves differently from the backticks: it doesn't return the output of the command it calls (it just returns the exit status, an integer indicating success or failure of the command). Other methods include qx, the open system call, and the fork and exec functions.

Parsing Stride Output

I don't go into too much detail here about parsing the output of *stride*. Let's just exhibit some code that extracts the primary sequence and the secondary structure prediction. See the exercises at the end of the chapter for a challenge to extract the secondary structure information from a PDB file's HELIX, SHEET, and TURN record types and output the information in a similar format as *stride* does here.

Here is a typical section of a *stride* output (not the entire output):

```
SEQ  1    MDKNELVQKAKLAEQAERYDDMAACMKSVTEQGAELSNEERNLLSVAYKN    50      1A40
STR       HHHHHHHHHHHHH  HHHHHHHHHHHHHTTT   HHHHHHHHHHHHH             1A40
REM                                                                  1A40
REM                 .         .         .         .         .        1A40
SEQ  51   VVGARRSSWRVVSSIEQKEKKQQMAREYREKIETELRDICNDVLSLLEKF   100     1A40
STR       HHHHHHHHHHHHHHHHHHHHHHHHHHHHHHHHHHHHHHHHHHHHHHHHHHT         1A40
REM                                                                  1A40
REM                 .         .         .         .         .        1A40
SEQ  101  LIPNAAESKVFYLKMKGDYYRYLAEVAAGDDKKGIVDQSQQAYQEAFEIS   150     1A40
STR       TTTTT HHHHHHHHHHHHHHHHHHHH   HHHHHHHHHHHHHHHHHHHHHH         1A40
REM                                                                  1A40
REM                 .         .         .         .         .        1A40
SEQ  151  KKEMIRLGLALNFSVFYYACSLAKTAFDEAIAELLIMQLLRDNLTLW      197     1A40
STR       TTTTHHHHHHHHHHHHH  HHHHHHHHHHHH  HHHHHHHHH                  1A40
```

Notice that each line is prefaced by an identifier, which should make collecting the different record types easy. Without even consulting the documentation (a slightly dangerous but sometimes expedient approach), you can see that the primary sequence has keyword SEQ, the structure prediction has keyword STR, and the data of interest lies from position 11 up to position 60 on each line. (We'll ignore everything else for now.)

The following list shows the one-letter secondary structure codes used by *stride*:

H	Alpha helix
G	3-10 helix
I	PI helix
E	Extended conformation
B or b	Isolated bridge
T	Turn
C	Coil (none of the above)

Using the substr function, the two for loops alter each line of the two arrays by saving the 11th to the 60th positions of those strings. This is where the desired information lies.

Now let's examine the subroutine parse_stride in Example 11-7 that takes *stride* output and returns an array of two strings, the primary sequence and the structure prediction.

This is a very "Perlish" subroutine that uses some features that manipulate text. What's interesting is the brevity of the program, which some of Perl's built-in functions make possible.

First, you receive the output of the *stride* program in the subroutine argument @_. Next, use the grep function to extract those lines of interest, which are easy to identify in this output, as they begin with clear identifiers SEQ and STR.

Next, you want to save just those positions (or columns) of these lines that have the sequence or structure information; you don't need the keywords, position numbers, or the PDB entry name at the end of the lines.

Finally, join the arrays into single strings. Here, there's one detail to handle; you need to remove any unneeded spaces from the ends of the strings. Notice that *stride* sometimes leaves spaces in the structure prediction, and in this example, has left some at the end of the structure prediction. So you shouldn't throw away all the spaces at the ends of the strings. Instead, throw away all the spaces at the end of the sequence string, because they are just superfluous spaces on the line. Now, see how many spaces that was, and throw the equal amount away at the end of the structure prediction string, thus preserving spaces that correspond to undetermined secondary structure.

Example 11-7 contains a main program that calls two subroutines, which, since they are short, are all included (so there's no need here for the *BeginPerlBioinfo* module). Here's the output of Example 11-7:

```
GGLQVKNFDFTVGKFLTVGGFINNSPQRFSVNVGESMNSLSLHLDHRFNYGADQNTIVMNSTLKGDNGWETEQRSTNFTL
   TTTTTTBTTT EEEEEEETTTT EEEEEEEEETTEEEEEEEEEEEEETTEEEEEEEEEEETTGGG B   EEE
```

The first line shows the amino acids, and the second line shows the prediction of the secondary structure. Check the next section for a subroutine that will improve that output.

Exercises

Exercise 11.1

Use *File::Find* and the file test operators to find the oldest and largest files on the hard drive of your computer. (You can delete them or store them elsewhere if you're running short on disk space.)

Exercise 11.2

Find all the Perl programs on your computer.

Hint: Use *File::Find*. What do all Perl programs have in common?

Exercise 11.3

Parse the HEADER, TITLE, and KEYWORDS record types of all PDB files on your computer. Make a hash with *key* as a word from those record types and *value* as a list of filenames that contained that word. Save it as a DBM file and build a query program for it. In the end, you should be able to ask for, say, sugar, and get a list of all PDB files that contain that word in the HEADER, TITLE, or KEYWORDS records.

Exercise 11.4

Parse out the record types of a PDB file using regular expressions (as used in Chapter 10) instead of iterating through an array of input lines (as in this chapter.)

Exercise 11.5

Write a program that extracts the secondary structure information contained in the HELIX, SHEET, and TURN record types of PDB files. Print out the secondary structure and the primary sequence together, so that it's easy to see by what secondary structure a given residue is included. (Consider using a special alphabet for secondary structure, so that every residue in a helix is represented by H, for example.)

Exercise 11.6

Write a program that finds all PDB files under a given folder and runs a program (such as *stride*, or the program you wrote in Exercise 11.5) that reports on the secondary structure of each PDB file. Store the results in a DBM file keyed on the filename.

Exercise 11.7

Write a subroutine that, given two strings, prints them out one over the other, but with line breaks (similar to the *stride* program output). Use this subroutine to print out the strings from Example 11-7.

Exercise 11-8

Write a recursive subroutine to determine the size of an array. You may want to use the pop or unshift functions. (Ignore the fact that the scalar @ array returns the size of @array!)

Exercise 11.9

Write a recursive subroutine that extracts the primary amino acid sequence from the SEQRES record type of a PDB file.

Exercise 11.10

(*Extra credit*) Given an atom and a distance, find all other atoms in a PDB file that are within that distance of the atom.

Exercise 11.11

(*Extra credit*) Write a program to find some correlation between the primary amino acid sequence and the location of alpha helices.

CHAPTER 12
BLAST

In biological research, the search for sequence similarity is very important. For instance, a researcher who has discovered a potentially important DNA or protein sequence wants to know if it's already been identified and characterized by another researcher. If it hasn't, the researcher wants to know if it resembles any known sequence from any organism. This information can provide vital clues as to the role of the sequence in the organism.

The Basic Local Alignment Search Tool (BLAST) is one of the most popular software tools in biological research. It tests a query sequence against a library of known sequences in order to find similarity. BLAST is actually a collection of programs with versions for query-to-database pairs such as nucleotide-nucleotide, protein-nucleotide, protein-protein, nucleotide-protein, and more.

This chapter examines the output from the nucleotide-nucleotide version of the program, BLASTN. For simplicity's sake, I'll simply refer to it here as BLAST. The main goal of this chapter is to show how to write code to parse a BLAST output file using regular expressions. The code is simple and basic, but it does the job. Once you understand the basics, you can build more features into your parser or obtain one of the fancier BLAST output parsers that's available via the Web. In either case, you'll know enough about output parsers to use or extend them.

This chapter also gives you a brief introduction to Bioperl, which is a collection of Perl bioinformatics modules. The Bioperl project is an example of an open source project that you, the Perl bioinformatics programmer, can put to good use. The Perl programming language is itself an open source project. The program and its source code are available for use and modification with only very reasonable restrictions and at no cost.

Obtaining BLAST

There are a several implementations of BLAST. The most popular is probably the one offered free of charge by the National Center for Biotechnology Information (NCBI): *http://www.ncbi.nlm.nih.gov/BLAST/*. The NCBI web site features a publicly available BLAST server, a comprehensive set of databases, and a well-organized collection of documents and tutorials, in addition to the BLAST software available for downloading.

Also popular is the WU-BLAST implementation from Washington University. The main web site, including a list of other WU-BLAST servers, can be found at *http://blast.wustl.edu*. Older versions of WU-BLAST are available at no charge. Newer versions are free if you qualify as a research or nonprofit organization and agree to the licensing arrangements from Washington University where the program is developed and maintained. If you work at a major research organization, you may already have a site license for the WU-BLAST program. If you are a for-profit company, there is a rather hefty charge for the newer WU-BLAST program (older versions are freely available if you want to run BLAST on your own computer). Pennsylvania State University also develops some BLAST programs, available at *http://bio.cse.psu.edu/*. In addition to NCBI and WU-BLAST, many other BLAST server web sites are available. A Google search (*http://www.google.com*) on "BLAST server" will bring up many hits.

A big question that faces researchers when they use BLAST is whether to use a public BLAST server or to run it locally. There are significant advantages to using a public server, the largest being that the databases (such as GenBank) used by the BLAST server are always up to date. To keep your own up-to-date copy of these databases requires a significant amount of hard-disk space, a computer with a fairly high-end processor and a lot of memory (to run the BLAST engine), a high-capacity network link, and a lot of time setting up and overseeing the software that updates the databases. On the other hand, perhaps you have your own library of sequences that you want to use in BLAST searches, you do frequent or large searches, or you have other reasons to run your own in-house BLAST engine. If that's the case, it makes sense to invest in the hardware and run it locally.

The online documentation for BLAST is fairly extensive and includes details on the statistical methods the program uses to calculate similarity. In the next section, I touch briefly on some of those points, but you should refer to the BLAST home page and to the excellent material at the NCBI web site for the whole story and detailed references. Our interest here is not the theory, but rather to parse the output of the program.

String Matching and Homology

String matching is the computer-science term for algorithms that find one string embedded in another. It has a fairly long and fruitful history, and many string-matching algorithms have been developed using a variety of techniques and for different cases. (See the Gusfield book in Appendix A for an excellent treatment with a biological emphasis.) We've already done a fair amount of string matching, using the binding operator to search for motifs and other text with regular expressions.

BLAST is basically a string-matching program. Details of the string-matching algorithms, and of the algorithms used in BLAST in particular, are beyond the scope of this book. But first I want to define some terms that are frequently confused or used interchangeably. I also briefly introduce the BLAST statistics.

Biological string matching looks for similarity as an indication of homology. *Similarity* between the query and the sequences in the database may be measured by the *percent identity*, or the number of bases in the query that exactly match a corresponding region of a sequence from the database. It may also be measured by the degree of *conservation*, which finds matches between equivalent (redundant) codons or between amino acid residues with similar properties that don't alter the function of a protein (see Chapter 8). *Homology* between sequences means the sequences are related evolutionarily. Two sequences are or are not homologous; there's no degree of homology.

At the risk of oversimplifying a complex topic, I'll summarize a few facts about BLAST statistics. (See the BLAST documentation for a complete picture.) The output of a BLAST search reports a set of scores and statistics on the matches it has found based on the raw score S, various parameters of the scoring algorithm, and properties of the query and database. The *raw score S* is a measure of similarity and the size of the match. The BLAST output lists the hits ranked by their E value. The *E (expect) value* of a match measures, roughly, the chances that the string matching (allowing for gaps) occurs in a randomly generated database of the same size and composition. The closer to 0 the E value is, the less likely it occurred by chance. In other words, the lower the E value, the better the match. As a general rule of thumb for BLASTN, an E value less than 1 may be a solid hit, and an E value of less than 10 may be worth looking at, but this is not a hard and fast rule. (Of course, proteins can be homologous with even a very small percent identity; the percent similarity is typically higher for homologous DNA.)

Now that you have the basics, let's write code to parse BLAST output. First, you separate the hits, then extract the sequence, and finally, you find the annotation showing the E value statistic.

BLAST Output Files

The following is part of a BLAST output file. I created it by entering a few lines of the *sample.dna* file from Chapter 8 into the BLAST program at the NCBI web site, without changing any of the default parameters. I then saved the output as text in the file *blst.txt*, which is available from this book's web site. I've used it repeatedly in the parsing routines throughout this chapter. Because the output is several pages long, I've truncated it here to show the beginning, the middle, and the end of the file.

```
BLASTN 2.1.3 [Apr-11-2001]

Reference: Altschul, Stephen F., Thomas L. Madden, Alejandro A. Schaffer,
Jinghui Zhang, Zheng Zhang, Webb Miller, and David J. Lipman (1997),
"Gapped BLAST and PSI-BLAST: a new generation of protein database search
programs",  Nucleic Acids Res. 25:3389-3402.
RID: 991533563-27495-9092
Query=
        (400 letters)

Database: nt
          868,831 sequences; 3,298,558,333 total letters


                                                           Score     E
Sequences producing significant alignments:               (bits)  Value

dbj|AB031069.1|AB031069 Homo sapiens PCCX1 mRNA for protein cont...  793  0.0
ref|NM_014593.1| Homo sapiens CpG binding protein (CGBP), mRNA       779  0.0
gb|AF149758.1|AF149758 Homo sapiens CpG binding protein (CGBP) m...  779  0.0
ref|XM_008699.3| Homo sapiens CpG binding protein (CGBP), mRNA       765  0.0
emb|AL136862.1|HSM801830 Homo sapiens mRNA; cDNA DKFZp434F174 (f...  450  e-124
emb|AJ132339.1|HSA132339 Homo sapiens CpG island sequence, subcl... 446  e-123
emb|AJ236590.1|HSA236590 Homo sapiens chromosome 18 CpG island D... 406  e-111
dbj|AK010337.1|AK010337 Mus musculus ES cells cDNA, RIKEN full-l... 234  3e-59
dbj|AK017941.1|AK017941 Mus musculus adult male thymus cDNA, RIK... 210  5e-52
gb|AC009750.7|AC009750 Drosophila melanogaster, chromosome 2L, r...  46  0.017
gb|AE003580.2|AE003580 Drosophila melanogaster genomic scaffold ...  46  0.017
ref|NC_001905.1| Leishmania major chromosome 1, complete sequence   40  1.0
gb|AE001274.1|AE001274 Leishmania major chromosome 1, complete s...  40  1.0
gb|AC008299.5|AC008299 Drosophila melanogaster, chromosome 3R, r...  38  4.1
gb|AC018662.3|AC018662 Human Chromosome 7 clone RP11-339C9, comp...  38  4.1
gb|AE003774.2|AE003774 Drosophila melanogaster genomic scaffold ...  38  4.1
gb|AC008039.1|AC008039 Homo sapiens clone SCb-391H5 from 7q31, c...  38  4.1
gb|AC005315.2|AC005315 Arabidopsis thaliana chromosome II sectio...  38  4.1
emb|AL353748.13|AL353748 Human DNA sequence from clone RP11-317B... 38  4.1

ALIGNMENTS
>dbj|AB031069.1|AB031069 Homo sapiens PCCX1 mRNA for protein containing CXXC
domain 1,
            complete cds
            Length = 2487

 Score =  793 bits (400), Expect = 0.0
```

```
Identities = 400/400 (100%)
Strand = Plus / Plus


Query: 1    agatggcggcgctgaggggtcttgggggctctaggccggccacctactggtttgcagcgg 60
            ||||||||||||||||||||||||||||||||||||||||||||||||||||||||||||
Sbjct: 1    agatggcggcgctgaggggtcttgggggctctaggccggccacctactggtttgcagcgg 60

Query: 61   agacgacgcatggggcctgcgcaataggagtacgctgcctgggaggcgtgactagaagcg 120
            ||||||||||||||||||||||||||||||||||||||||||||||||||||||||||||
Sbjct: 61   agacgacgcatggggcctgcgcaataggagtacgctgcctgggaggcgtgactagaagcg 120

Query: 121  gaagtagttgtgggcgcctttgcaaccgcctgggacgccgccgagtggtctgtgcaggtt 180
            ||||||||||||||||||||||||||||||||||||||||||||||||||||||||||||
Sbjct: 121  gaagtagttgtgggcgcctttgcaaccgcctgggacgccgccgagtggtctgtgcaggtt 180

Query: 181  cgcgggtcgctggcggggggtcgtgagggagtgcgccgggagcggagatatggagggagat 240
            ||||||||||||||||||||||||||||||||||||||||||||||||||||||||||||
Sbjct: 181  cgcgggtcgctggcggggggtcgtgagggagtgcgccgggagcggagatatggagggagat 240

Query: 241  ggttcagacccagagcctccagatgccggggaggacagcaagtccgagaatggggagaat 300
            ||||||||||||||||||||||||||||||||||||||||||||||||||||||||||||
Sbjct: 241  ggttcagacccagagcctccagatgccggggaggacagcaagtccgagaatggggagaat 300

Query: 301  gcgcccatctactgcatctgccgcaaaccggacatcaactgcttcatgatcgggtgtgac 360
            ||||||||||||||||||||||||||||||||||||||||||||||||||||||||||||
Sbjct: 301  gcgcccatctactgcatctgccgcaaaccggacatcaactgcttcatgatcgggtgtgac 360

Query: 361  aactgcaatgagtggttccatggggactgcatccggatca 400
            ||||||||||||||||||||||||||||||||||||||||
Sbjct: 361  aactgcaatgagtggttccatggggactgcatccggatca 400


>ref|NM_014593.1| Homo sapiens CpG binding protein (CGBP), mRNA

... (file truncated here)

>dbj|AK010337.1|AK010337 Mus musculus ES cells cDNA, RIKEN full-length
enriched library,
          clone:2410002I16, full insert sequence
          Length = 2538

 Score =  234 bits (118), Expect = 3e-59
 Identities = 166/182 (91%)
 Strand = Plus / Plus


Query: 219  gagcggagatatggagggagatggttcagacccagagcctccagatgccggggaggacag 278
            |||||||||||||| |||||||| |||||||  || ||||| |||||||||| |||||
Sbjct: 260  gagcggagatatggaaggagatggctcagacctggaacctccggatgccggggacgacag 319

Query: 279  caagtccgagaatggggagaatgcgcccatctactgcatctgccgcaaaccggacatcaa 338
            ||||||  ||||||||||||| || ||||||||||||||||| |||||||||||||||||
Sbjct: 320  caagtctgagaatggggagaacgctcccatctactgcatctgtcgcaaaccggacatcaa 379

Query: 339  ctgcttcatgatcgggtgtgacaactgcaatgagtggttccatggggactgcatccggat 398
            |||||||||| || ||||||||||||| |||||||||||||| |||||||||||||||||
```

Sbjct: 380 ttgcttcatgattggatgtgacaactgcaacgagtggttccatggagactgcatccggat 439

Query: 399 ca 400
             ||
Sbjct: 440 ca 441
 Score = 44.1 bits (22), Expect = 0.066
 Identities = 25/26 (96%)
 Strand = Plus / Plus

Query: 118 gcggaagtagttgtgggcgcctttgc 143
            |||||||||||||| |||||||||||||
Sbjct: 147 gcggaagtagttgcgggcgcctttgc 172

>dbj|AK017941.1|AK017941 Mus musculus adult male thymus cDNA, RIKEN
full-length enriched library, clone:5830420C16, full insert sequence
             Length = 1461

 Score = 210 bits (106), Expect = 5e-52
 Identities = 151/166 (90%)
 Strand = Plus / Plus

Query: 235   ggagatggttcagacccagagcctccagatgccggggaggacagcaagtccgagaatggg 294
             |||||||| ||||||| || ||||| |||||||||||| |||||||||||| ||||||||
Sbjct: 1048 ggagatggctcagacctggaacctccggatgccggggacgacagcaagtctgagaatggg 1107

Query: 295   gagaatgcgcccatctactgcatctgccgcaaaccggacatcaactgcttcatgatcggg 354
             ||||| || |||||||||||||||||| |||||||||||||||||| |||||||||||| ||
Sbjct: 1108 gagaacgctcccatctactgcatctgtcgcaaaccggacatcaattgcttcatgattgga 1167

Query: 355   tgtgacaactgcaatgagtggttccatggggactgcatccggatca 400
             ||||||||||||||| |||||||||||||| ||||||||||||||||
Sbjct: 1168 tgtgacaactgcaacgagtggttccatggagactgcatccggatca 1213

 Score = 44.1 bits (22), Expect = 0.066
 Identities = 25/26 (96%)
 Strand = Plus / Plus

Query: 118 gcggaagtagttgtgggcgcctttgc 143
            |||||||||||||| |||||||||||||
Sbjct: 235 gcggaagtagttgcgggcgcctttgc 260

>gb|AC009750.7|AC009750 Drosophila melanogaster, chromosome 2L, region 23F-24A,
BAC clone

 ... *(file truncated here)*

>emb|AL353748.13|AL353748 Human DNA sequence from clone RP11-317B17 on
chromosome 9, complete
             sequence [Homo sapiens]
          Length = 179155

 Score = 38.2 bits (19), Expect = 4.1
 Identities = 22/23 (95%)
 Strand = Plus / Plus

```
Query: 192    ggcgggggtcgtgagggagtgcg 214
              |||| |||||||||||||||||
Sbjct: 48258 ggcgtgggtcgtgagggagtgcg 48280

  Database: nt
    Posted date:  May 30, 2001  3:54 AM
  Number of letters in database: -996,408,959
  Number of sequences in database:  868,831

Lambda     K       H
   1.37    0.711    1.31

Gapped
Lambda     K       H
   1.37    0.711    1.31

Matrix: blastn matrix:1 -3
Gap Penalties: Existence: 5, Extension: 2
Number of Hits to DB: 436021
Number of Sequences: 868831
Number of extensions: 436021
Number of successful extensions: 7536
Number of sequences better than 10.0: 19
length of query: 400
length of database: 3,298,558,333
effective HSP length: 20
effective length of query: 380
effective length of database: 3,281,181,713
effective search space: 1246849050940
effective search space used: 1246849050940
T: 0
A: 30
X1: 6 (11.9 bits)
X2: 15 (29.7 bits)
S1: 12 (24.3 bits)
S2: 19 (38.2 bits)
```

As you can see, the file consists of three parts: some header information at the beginning followed by a summary of the alignments, the alignments, and then some additional summary parameters and statistics at the end.

Parsing BLAST Output

So why parse BLAST output? One reason is to see if your DNA has any new matches
against the DNA stored in the constantly growing databases. You can write a program to automatically perform a daily BLAST search and compare its results with
those of the previous day by parsing the summary list of hits and comparing it with
the previous day's summary list. You can then have the program email you if something new has turned up.

Extracting Annotation and Alignments

Example 12-1 consists of a main program and two new subroutines. The subroutines—parse_blast and parse_blast_alignment—use regular expressions to extract the various bits of data from a scalar string. I chose this method because the data, although structured, does not clearly identify each line with its function. (See the discussion in Chapters 10 and 11.)

Example 12-1. Extract annotation and alignments from BLAST output file

```
#!/usr/bin/perl
# Extract annotation and alignments from BLAST output file

use strict;
use warnings;
use BeginPerlBioinfo;     # see Chapter 6 about this module

# declare and initialize variables
my $beginning_annotation = '';
my $ending_annotation = '';
my %alignments = ( );
my $filename = 'blast.txt';

parse_blast(\$beginning_annotation, \$ending_annotation, \%alignments, $filename);

# Print the annotation, and then
#    print the DNA in new format just to check if we got it okay.
print $beginning_annotation;

foreach my $key (keys %alignments) {
    print "$key\nXXXXXXXXXXXX\n", $alignments{$key}, "\nXXXXXXXXXXXX\n";
}

print $ending_annotation;

exit;

########################################################################
# Subroutines for Example 12-1
########################################################################

# parse_blast
#
# -parse beginning and ending annotation, and alignments,
#     from BLAST output file

sub parse_blast {

    my($beginning_annotation, $ending_annotation, $alignments, $filename) = @_;

    # $beginning_annotation-reference to scalar
    # $ending_annotation    -reference to scalar
    # $alignments           -reference to hash
```

Example 12-1. Extract annotation and alignments from BLAST output file (continued)

```
    # $filename            —scalar

    # declare and initialize variables
    my $blast_output_file = '';
    my $alignment_section = '';

    # Get the BLAST program output into an array from a file
    $blast_output_file = join( '', get_file_data($filename));

    # Extract the beginning annotation, alignments, and ending annotation
    ($$beginning_annotation, $alignment_section, $$ending_annotation)
    = ($blast_output_file =~ /(.*^ALIGNMENTS\n)(.*)(^  Database:.*)/ms);

    # Populate %alignments hash
    # key = ID of hit
    # value = alignment section
    %$alignments = parse_blast_alignment($alignment_section);
}

# parse_blast_alignment
#
# —parse the alignments from a BLAST output file,
#        return hash with
#        key = ID
#        value = text of alignment

sub parse_blast_alignment {

    my($alignment_section) = @_;

    # declare and initialize variables
    my(%alignment_hash) = ();

    # loop through the scalar containing the BLAST alignments,
    # extracting the ID and the alignment and storing in a hash
    #
    # The regular expression matches a line beginning with >,
    # and containing the ID between the first pair of | characters;
    # followed by any number of lines that don't begin with >

    while($alignment_section =~ /^>.*\n(^(?!>).*\n)+/gm) {
        my($value) = $&;
        my($key) = (split(/\|/, $value)) [1];
        $alignment_hash{$key} = $value;
    }

    return %alignment_hash;
}
```

The main program does little more than call the parsing subroutine and print the results. The arguments, initialized as empty, are passed by reference (see Chapter 6).

The subroutine parse_blast does the top-level parsing job of separating the three sections of a BLAST output file: the annotation at the beginning, the alignments in the middle, and the annotation at the end. It then calls the parse_blast_alignment subroutine to extract the individual alignments from that middle alignment section. The data is first read in from the named file with our old friend the get_file_data subroutine from Chapter 8. Use the join function to store the array of file data into a scalar string.

The three sections of the BLAST output file are separated by the following statement:

```
($$beginning_annotation, $alignment_section, $$ending_annotation)

    = ($blast_output_file =~ /(.*^ALIGNMENTS\n)(.*)(^  Database:.*)/ms);
```

The pattern match contains three parenthesized expressions:

```
(.*^ALIGNMENTS\n)
```

which is returned into $$beginning_annotation;

```
(.*)
```

which is saved in $alignment_section; and:

```
(^  Database:.*)
```

which is saved in $$ending_annotation.

The use of $$ instead of $ at the beginning of two of these variables indicates that they are references to scalar variables. Recall that they were passed in as arguments to the subroutine, where they were preceded by a backslash, like so:

```
parse_blast(\$beginning_annotation, \$ending_annotation, \%alignments, $filename);
```

You've seen references to variables before, starting in Chapter 6. Let's review them briefly. Within the parse_blast subroutine, those variables with only one $ are references to the scalar variables. They need an additional $ to represent actual scalar variables. This is how references work; they need an additional special character to indicate what kinds of variables they are references to. So a reference to a scalar variable needs to start with $$, a reference to an array variable needs to start with @$, and a reference to a hash variable needs to start with %$.

The regular expression in the previous code snippet matches everything up to the word ALIGNMENTS at the end of a line (.*^ALIGNMENTS\n); then everything for a while (.*); then a line that begins with two spaces and the word Database: followed by the rest of the file (^ Database:.*). These three expressions in parentheses correspond to the three desired parts of the BLAST output file; the beginning annotation, the alignment section, and the ending annotation.

The alignments saved in $alignment_section are separated out by the subroutine parse_blast_alignment. This subroutine has one important loop:

```
while($alignment_section =~ /^>.*\n(^(?!>).*\n)+/gm) {
    my($value) = $&;
```

```
        my($key) = (split(/\|/, $value)) [1];
        $alignment_hash{$key} = $value;
    }
```

You're probably thinking that this regular expression looks downright evil. At first glance, regular expressions do sometimes seem incomprehensible, so let's take a closer look. There are a few new things to examine.

The five lines comprise a while loop, which (due to the global /g modifier on the pattern match in the while loop) keeps matching the pattern as many times as it appears in the string. Each time the program cycles through the loop, the pattern match finds the value (the entire alignment), then determines the key. The key and values are saved in the hash %alignment_hash.

Here's an example of one of the matches that's found by this while loop when parsing the BLAST output shown in the previous section "BLAST Output Files":

```
>emb|AL353748.13|AL353748 Human DNA sequence from clone RP11-317B17 on
chromosome 9, complete
              sequence [Homo sapiens]
          Length = 179155

 Score = 38.2 bits (19), Expect = 4.1
 Identities = 22/23 (95%)
 Strand = Plus / Plus

Query: 192   ggcgggggtcgtgagggagtgcg 214
             |||| |||||||||||||||||||
Sbjct: 48258 ggcgtgggtcgtgagggagtgcg 48280
```

This text starts with a line beginning with a > character. In the complete BLAST output, sections like these follow one another. What you want to do is start matching from a line beginning with > and include all following adjacent lines that don't start with a > character. You also want to extract the identifier, which appears between the first and second vertical bar | characters on the first line (e.g., AL353748.13 in this alignment).

Let's dissect the regular expression:

```
$alignment_section =~ /^>.*\n(^(?!>).*\n)+/gm
```

This pattern match, which appears in a while loop within the code, has the modifier m for multiline. The m modifier allows ^ to match any beginning-of-line inside the multiline string, and $ to match any end-of-line.

The regular expression breaks down as follows. The first part is:

```
^>.*\n
```

It looks for > at the beginning of the BLAST output line, followed by .*, which matches any quantity of anything (except newlines), up to the first newline. In other words, it matches the first line of the alignment.

Here's the rest of the regular expression:

```
(^(?!>).*\n)+
```

After the ^ which matches the beginning of the line, you'll see a *negative lookahead assertion*, (?!>), which ensures that a > doesn't follow. Next, the .* matches all non-newline characters, up to the final \n at the end of the line. All of that is wrapped in parentheses with a surrounding +, so that you match all the available lines.

Now that you've matched the entire alignment, you want to extract the key and populate the hash with your key and value. Within the while loop, the alignment that you just matched is automatically set by Perl as the value of the special variable $& and saved in the variable $value. Now you need to extract your key from the alignment. It can be found on the first line of the alignment stored in $value, between the first and second | symbols.

Extracting this identifying key is done using the split function, which breaks the string into an array. The call to split:

```
split(/\|/, $value)
```

splits $value into pieces delimited by | characters. That is, the | symbol is used to determine where one list element ends and the next one begins. (Remember that the vertical bar | is a metacharacter and must be escaped as \|.) By surrounding the call to split with parentheses and adding an array offset ([1]), you can isolate the key and save it into $key.

Let's step back now and look at Example 12-1 in its entirety. Notice that it's very short—barely more than two pages, including comments. Although it's not an easy program, due to the complexity of the regular expressions involved, you can make sense of it if you put a little effort into examining the BLAST output files and the regular expressions that parse it.

Regular expressions have lots of complex features, but as a result, they can do lots of useful things. As a Perl programmer, the effort you put into learning them is well worth it and can have significant payoffs down the road.

Parsing BLAST Alignments

Let's take the parsing of the BLAST output file a little further. Notice that some of the alignments include more than one aligned string—for instance, the alignment for ID AK017941.1, shown again here:

```
>dbj|AK017941.1|AK017941 Mus musculus adult male thymus cDNA, RIKEN
full-length enriched
            library, clone:5830420C16, full insert sequence
```

```
              Length = 1461

  Score =   210 bits (106), Expect = 5e-52
  Identities = 151/166 (90%)
  Strand = Plus / Plus

Query: 235  ggagatggttcagacccagagcctccagatgccgggggaggacagcaagtccgagaatggg 294
            |||||||| |||||||  || ||||| |||||||||||| |||||||||| ||||||||||
Sbjct: 1048 ggagatggctcagacctggaacctccggatgccggggacgacagcaagtctgagaatggg 1107

Query: 295  gagaatgcgcccatctactgcatctgccgcaaaccggacatcaactgcttcatgatcggg 354
            ||||| || |||||||||||||||| |||||||||||||||||| ||||||||||||| ||
Sbjct: 1108 gagaacgctcccatctactgcatctgtcgcaaaccggacatcaattgcttcatgattgga 1167

Query: 355  tgtgacaactgcaatgagtggttccatggggactgcatccggatca 400
            ||||||||||||| |||||||||||||| |||||||||||||||||
Sbjct: 1168 tgtgacaactgcaacgagtggttccatggagactgcatccggatca 1213

  Score = 44.1 bits (22), Expect = 0.066
  Identities = 25/26 (96%)
  Strand = Plus / Plus

Query: 118  gcggaagtagttgtgggcgcctttgc 143
            ||||||||||||| ||||||||||||
Sbjct: 235  gcggaagtagttgcgggcgcctttgc 260
```

To parse these alignments, we have to parse out each of the matched strings, which in BLAST terminology are called *high-scoring pairs* (HSPs).

Each HSP also contains some annotation, and then the HSP itself. Let's parse each HSP into annotation, query string, and subject string, together with the starting and ending positions of the strings. More parsing is possible; you can extract specific features of the annotation, as well as the locations of identical and nonidentical bases in the HSP, for instance.

Example 12-2 includes a pair of subroutines; one to parse the alignments into their HSPs, and the second to extract the sequences and their end positions. The main program extends Example 12-1 using these new subroutines.

Example 12-2. Parse alignments from BLAST output file

```perl
#!/usr/bin/perl
# Parse alignments from BLAST output file

use strict;
use warnings;
use BeginPerlBioinfo;     # see Chapter 6 about this module

# declare and initialize variables
my $beginning_annotation = '';
my $ending_annotation = '';
my %alignments = ();
my $alignment = '';
```

Example 12-2. Parse alignments from BLAST output file (continued)

```perl
my $filename = 'blast.txt';
my @HSPs = ( );
my($expect, $query, $query_range, $subject, $subject_range) = ('','','','','');

parse_blast(\$beginning_annotation, \$ending_annotation, \%alignments, $filename);

$alignment = $alignments{'AK017941.1'};

@HSPs = parse_blast_alignment_HSP($alignment);

($expect, $query, $query_range, $subject, $subject_range)
 = extract_HSP_information($HSPs[1]);

# Print the results
print "\n-> Expect value:    $expect\n";
print "\n-> Query string:    $query\n";
print "\n-> Query range:     $query_range\n";
print "\n-> Subject String:  $subject\n";
print "\n-> Subject range:   $subject_range\n";

exit;

##############################################################################
# Subroutines for Example 12-2
##############################################################################

# parse_blast_alignment_HSP
#
# -parse beginning annotation, and HSPs,
#     from BLAST alignment
#     Return an array with first element set to the beginning annotation,
#     and each successive element set to an HSP

sub parse_blast_alignment_HSP {

    my($alignment ) = @_;

    # declare and initialize variables
    my $beginning_annotation  = '';
    my $HSP_section  = '';
    my @HSPs = ( );

    # Extract the beginning annotation and HSPs
    ($beginning_annotation, $HSP_section )
        = ($alignment =~ /(.*?)(^ Score =.*)/ms);

    # Store the $beginning_annotation as the first entry in @HSPs
    push(@HSPs, $beginning_annotation);

    # Parse the HSPs, store each HSP as an element in @HSPs
    while($HSP_section =~ /(^ Score =.*\n)(^(?! Score =).*\n)+/gm) {
```

Example 12-2. Parse alignments from BLAST output file (continued)

```
        push(@HSPs, $&);
    }

    # Return an array with first element = the beginning annotation,
    # and each successive element = an HSP
    return(@HSPs);
}

# extract_HSP_information
#
# -parse a HSP from a BLAST output alignment section
#        - return array with elements:
#     Expect value
#     Query string
#     Query range
#     Subject string
#     Subject range

sub extract_HSP_information {

    my($HSP) = @_;

    # declare and initialize variables
    my($expect) = '';
    my($query) = '';
    my($query_range) = '';
    my($subject) = '';
    my($subject_range) = '';

    ($expect) = ($HSP =~ /Expect = (\S+)/);

    $query = join ( '' , ($HSP =~ /^Query.*\n/gm) );

    $subject = join ( '' , ($HSP =~ /^Sbjct.*\n/gm) );

    $query_range = join('..', ($query =~ /(\d+).*\D(\d+)/s));

    $subject_range = join('..', ($subject =~ /(\d+).*\D(\d+)/s));

    $query =~ s/[^acgt]//g;

    $subject =~ s/[^acgt]//g;

    return ($expect, $query, $query_range, $subject, $subject_range);
}
```

Example 12-2 gives the following output:

```
-> Expect value:    5e-52

-> Query string:    ggagatggttcagacccagagcctccagatgccggggaggacagcaagtccgagaatggg
gagaatgcgcccatctactgcatctgccgcaaaccggacatcaactgcttcatgatcgggtgtgacaactgcaatgagt
ggttccatggggactgcatccggatca

-> Query range:    235..400

-> Subject String: ctggagatggctcagacctggaacctccggatgccggggacgacagcaagtctgagaatg
ggctgagaacgctcccatctactgcatctgtcgcaaaccggacatcaattgcttcatgattggacttgtgacaactgca
acgagtggttccatggagactgcatccggatca

-> Subject range:  1048..1213
```

Let's discuss the new features of Example 12-2 and its subroutines. First notice that the two new subroutines from Example 12-1 have been placed into the *BeginPerlBioinfo.pm* module, so they aren't printed again here.

The main program, Example 12-2, starts the same as Example 12-1; it calls the parse_blast subroutine to separate the annotation from the alignments in the BLAST output file.

The next line fetches one of the alignments from the %alignments hash, which is then used as the argument to the parse_blast_alignment_HSP subroutine, which then returns an array of annotation (as the first element) and HSPs in @HSPs. Here you see that not only can a subroutine return an array on a scalar value; it can also return a hash.

Finally, Example 12-2 does the lower-level parsing of an individual HSP by calling the extract_HSP_information subroutine, and the extracted parts of one of the HSPs are printed.

Example 12-2 shows a certain inconsistency in our design. Some subroutines call their arguments by reference; others call them by value (see Chapter 6). You may ask: is this a bad thing?

The answer is: not necessarily. The subroutine parse_blast mixes several arguments, and one of them is not a scalar type. Recall that this is a potentially good place to use call-by-reference in Perl. The other subroutines don't mix argument types this way. However, they can be designed to call their arguments by reference.

Continuing with the code, let's examine the subroutine parse_blast_alignment_HSP. This takes one of the alignments from the BLAST output and separates out the individual HSP string matches. The technique used is, once again, regular expressions operating on a single string that contains all the lines of the alignment given as the input argument.

The first regular expression parses out the annotation and the section containing the HSPs:

```
($beginning_annotation, $HSP_section )

= ($alignment =~ /(.*?)(^ Score =.*)/ms);
```

The first parentheses in the regular expression is (.*?) This is the nongreedy or minimal matching mentioned in Chapter 9. Here it gobbles up everything before the first line that begins Score = (without the ? after the *, it would gobble everything until the final line that begins Score =). This is the exact dividing line between the beginning annotation and the HSP string matches.

The next loop and regular expression separates the individual HSP string matches:

```
while($HSP_section =~ /(^ Score =.*\n)(^(?! Score =).*\n)+/gm) {

    push(@HSPs, $&);
}
```

This is the same kind of global string match in a while loop you've seen before; it keeps iterating as long as the match can be found. The other modifier /m is the multiline modifier, which enables the metacharacters $ and ^ to match before and after embedded newlines.

The expression within the first pair of parentheses—(^ Score =.*\n)—matches a line that begins Score =, which is the kind of line that begins an HSP string match section.

The code within the second pair of parentheses—(^(?! Score =).*\n)+—matches one or more (the + following the other parentheses) lines that do not begin with Score =. The ?! at the beginning of the embedded parentheses is the negative lookahead assertion you encountered in Example 12-1. So, in total, the regular expression captures a line beginning with Score = and all succeeding adjacent lines that don't begin with Score =.

Presenting Data

Up to now, we've relied on the print statement to format output. In this section, I introduce three additional Perl features for writing output:

- printf function
- here documents
- format and write functions

The entire story about these Perl output features is beyond the scope of this book, but I'll tell you just enough to give you an idea of how they can be used.

The printf Function

The printf function is like the print function but with extra features that allow you to specify how certain data is printed out. Perl's printf function is taken from the C language function of the same name. Here's an example of a printf statement:

```
my $first  = '3.14159265';
my $second = 76;
my $third = "Hello world!";

printf STDOUT "A float: %6.4f An integer: %-5d and a string: %s\n",
     $first, $second,  $third;
```

This code snippet prints the following:

```
A float:  3.1416 An integer: 76    and a string: Hello world!
```

The arguments to the printf function consist of a format string, followed by a list of values that are printed as specified by the format string. The format string may also contain any text along with the directives to print the list of values. (You may also specify an optional filehandle in the same manner you would a print function.)

The directives consist of a percent sign followed by a required conversion specifier, which in the example includes f for floating point, d for integer, and s for string. The conversion specifier indicates what kind of data is in the variable to be printed. Between the % and the conversion specifier, there may be 0 or more flags, an optional minimum field width, an optional precision, and an optional length modifier. The list of values following the format string must contain data that matches the types of directives, in order.

There are many possible options for these flags and specifiers (some are listed in Appendix B). Here's what is in Example 12-3. First, the directive %6.4f specifies to print a floating point (that is, a decimal) number, with a minimum width of six characters overall (padded with spaces if necessary), and at most four positions for the decimal part. You see in the output that, although the $f floating-point number gives the value of pi to eight decimal places, the example specifies a precision of four decimal places, which are all that is printed out.

The %-5d directive specifies an integer to be printed in a field of width 5; the - flag causes the number to be left-justified in the field. Finally, the %s directive prints a string.

here Documents

Now we'll briefly examine here documents. These are convenient ways to specify multiline text for output with perhaps some variables to be interpolated, in a way that looks pretty much the same in your code as it will in the output—that is, without a lot of print statements or embedded newline \n characters. We'll follow Example 12-3 and its output with a discussion.

Example 12-3. Example of here document

```perl
#!/usr/bin/perl
# Example of here document

use strict;
use warnings;

my $DNA = 'AAACCCCCCGGGGGGGGTTTTTT';

for( my $i = 0 ; $i < 2 ; ++$i ) {
print <<HEREDOC;
    On iteration $i of the loop!
    $DNA

HEREDOC
}

exit;
```

Here's the output from Example 12-3:

```
On iteration 0 of the loop!
AAACCCCCCGGGGGGGGTTTTTT

On iteration 1 of the loop!
AAACCCCCCGGGGGGGGTTTTTT
```

In Example 12-3, a here document was put in a for loop, so that you can see the $i variable changing in the printout. The variables are interpolated into a here document in the same way they are interpolated into a double-quoted string. Every time they go through the loop, the contents of the here document are subject to variable interpolation and are printed out. The terminating string used in this example, HEREDOC, can be any string you specify. (There are several options for dealing with things like indentation and so forth; I won't discuss them here and refer you to the Perl documentation.) Here documents are handy for some tasks, such as when you have a long, multiline document with just a few changes applied each time you print it. A business form letter, with only the addressee changed, is a typical example. Using a here document preserves the look of the final output in the code, while allowing variable interpolation.

format and write

Finally, let's take a look at the format and write functions. format is designed to generate reports and can handle page numbers, headers, and various layout options such as centering and left and right justification. It's modelled on the FORTRAN programming-language conventions for formatting and so is particularly handy for producing reports based on that style, such as the PDB file format, in which fields are specified as occupying certain columns on the line.

Example 12-4 is a short example of a format that creates a FASTA-style output.

Example 12-4. Example of format function to produce FASTA output

```perl
#!/usr/bin/perl
# Create fasta format  DNA output with "format" function

use strict;
use warnings;

# Declare variables
my $id = 'A0000';
my $description = 'Highly weird DNA.  This DNA is so unlikely!';
my $DNA = 'AAAAAACCCCCCCCCCCCCCGGGGGGGGGGGGGGGGGGGGGGGGGGTTTTTTTTTTTTTTTTTTTTTTT';

# Define the format
format STDOUT =
# The header line
>@<<<<<<<<< @<<<<<<<<<<<<<<<<<<<<<<<<<<<<<<<<<<<<...
$id,          $description
# The DNA lines
^<<<<<<<<<<<<<<<<<<<<<<<<<<<<<<<<<<<<<<<<<<<<<<<<<~~
$DNA
.

# Print the fasta-formatted DNA output
write;

exit;
```

Here's the output of Example 12-4:

```
>A0000      Highly unlikely DNA.  This DNA is so...
AAAAAACCCCCCCCCCCCCCGGGGGGGGGGGGGGGGGGGGGGGGGGGTTTTTTTTT
TTTTTTTTTTTT
```

After declaring and initializing the variables that fill in the form, the form is defined with:

```perl
format STDOUT =
```

and the format continues until it reaches the line with a period at the beginning.

The format is composed of three kinds of lines:

- A comment beginning with the pound sign #
- A picture line that specifies the layout of text
- An argument line that names the variables that fill in the preceding picture line

The picture line and the argument line must be adjacent; they can't be separated by a comment line, for instance.

The first picture line/argument line combo is for the header information:

```
>@<<<<<<<<< @<<<<<<<<<<<<<<<<<<<<<<<<<<<<<<<<<...
 $id,        $description
```

The picture line has two picture fields in it, associated with the variables `$id` and `$description`, respectively. The picture line begins with a greater-than sign, `>`, which is just text that begins each FASTA file header line, by definition. Then comes the first picture field, which is an `@` sign followed by nine `<` signs. The `@` sign declares a field that has the associated variable interpolated into it. The use of the nine less-than signs specifies that the value should be left-justified, for a total of 10 columns. If the value is bigger than 10 columns, it is truncated. A less-than sign left-justifies, a greater-than sign right-justifies, and a vertical bar | centers the data in the field.

The second picture field is almost identical. It is longer and ends with three dots (an ellipsis) which prints if the contents of the variable `$description` can't fit into the length of the picture field (which, in this case, is true.)

The next pair of picture/argument lines is:

```
^<<<<<<<<<<<<<<<<<<<<<<<<<<<<<<<<<<<<<<<<<<<<<<<<<<~~
 $DNA
```

The picture field starts with a caret, which declares a picture field that will handle variable-length records. The line also contains 49 less-than signs, for a total of 50 columns, left-justified. At the end are two tilde `~` signs, which indicate there should be additional lines for the data if it doesn't fit one on one line.

The `write` command simply prints the previously defined format. By default, the output goes to STDOUT, as is done in the example, but you can supply a filehandle to the `format` and `write` statements if you desire.

The upcoming release of Perl 6 will move formats out of the core of the language and make them into a module. Details are not available as of this writing, but this change will probably entail adding a statement such as `use Formats;` near the top of your code in order to load the module for using formats.

Bioperl

The *Bioperl* project is an important collection of Perl code for bioinformatics that has been in development since 1998. Although Bioperl uses the more advanced object-oriented style of Perl program design, it's possible to take an introductory look here at how it's organized and used.

The main focus of Bioperl modules is to perform sequence manipulation, provide access to various biology databases (both local and web-based), and parse the output of various programs.

Bioperl is available at *http://www.bioperl.org/*. Some of its features rely on having additional Perl modules—available from CPAN (*http://www.cpan.org/*)—installed. This situation is quite common, and as you do more Perl programming, you'll become familiar with installing modules from CPAN. The Bioperl tutorials include information on installing Bioperl and additional modules for the three major operating systems: Unix or Linux, Mac, and Windows.

Bioperl doesn't provide complete programs. Rather, it provides a fairly large—and growing—set of modules for accomplishing common tasks, including some tasks you've seen in this book. You're responsible for writing the code that holds the modules together. By providing these ready and (usually) easy-to-use modules, Bioperl makes developing bioinformatics applications in Perl faster and easier. There are example programs for most of the modules, which can be examined and modified to get started.

Like many open source projects, Bioperl has suffered from fragmentation and uneven documentation, due to the strictly volunteer and geographically dispersed group of contributors. But recent work on the project leading up to Release 0.7 in March 2001 has significantly improved the project. In particular, there is now enough tutorial information on using the modules to enable you to make good use of the code.

Some difficulties still remain. Most of the code has been developed on Unix or Linux systems. Not all of it works on Macs or Windows operating systems, but most will. There are some documents available at the Bioperl web site that discuss using Bioperl on non-Unix computers, but the bottom line is that you might find that some things don't work.

If you're going to give Bioperl a try (and I strongly recommend you do), you should make sure you have a fairly recent version of Perl installed. You'll need at least Version 5.004; it would be much better to install the latest stable release from the Perl web site *http://www.perl.com*.

Sample Modules

To give you an idea of what tasks Bioperl can make easier for you, Table 12-1 displays a representative sample of some of the most useful modules available.

Table 12-1 . Bioperl modules

Module	Description
Bio::Seq	Sequence object, with features
Bio::SimpleAlign	Multiple alignments held as a set of sequences
Bio::Species	Generic species object
Bio::DB::Ace	Database object interface to ACeDB servers
Bio::DB::GDB	Database object interface to GDB HTTP query

Table 12-1 . Bioperl modules (continued)

Module	Description
Bio::DB::GenBank	Database object interface to GenBank
Bio::DB::GenPept	Database object interface to GenPept
Bio::DB::NCBIHelper	A collection of routines useful for queries to NCBI databases
Bio::DB::SwissProt	Database object interface to SWISS-PROT retrieval
Bio::Index::Fasta	Interface for indexing FASTA files
Bio::Index::GenBank	Interface for indexing GenBank seq files, that is, flat files in GenBank format
Bio::Location::Simple	Implementation of a simple location on a sequence
Bio::Location::Split	Implementation of a location on a sequence that has multiple locations
Bio::SeqFeature::FeaturePair	Holds pair feature information, e.g., BLAST hits
Bio::SeqFeature::Generic	Generic SeqFeature
Bio::SeqFeature::Similarity	Sequence feature based on similarity
Bio::SeqFeature::SimilarityPair	Sequence feature based on the similarity of two sequences
Bio::SeqFeature::Gene::Exon	Feature representing an exon
Bio::SeqFeature::Gene::GeneStructure	Feature representing an arbitrarily complex structure of a gene
Bio::SeqFeature::Gene::Transcript	Feature representing a transcript
Bio::SeqFeature::Gene::TranscriptI	Interface for a feature representing a transcript of exons, promoter, UTR, and a poly-adenylation site
Bio::Tools::Blast	Bioperl BLAST sequence analysis object
Bio::Tools::BPbl2seq	Lightweight BLAST parser for pair-wise sequence alignment using the BLAST algorithm
Bio::Tools::BPlite	Lightweight BLAST parser
Bio::Tools::BPpsilite	Lightweight BLAST parser for PSIBLAST reports
Bio::Tools::CodonTable	Bioperl codon table object
Bio::Tools::Fasta	Bioperl FASTA utility object
Bio::Tools::IUPAC	Generates unique seq objects from an ambiguous seq object
Bio::Tools::RestrictionEnzyme	Bioperl object for a restriction endonuclease object
Bio::Tools::SeqPattern	Bioperl object for a sequence pattern or motif
Bio::Tools::SeqStats	Object holding statistics for one particular sequence
Bio::Tools::SeqWords	Object holding n-mer statistics for one sequence
Bio::Tools::Blast::HSP	Bioperl BLAST high-scoring segment pair object
Bio::Tools::Blast::HTML	Bioperl utility module for HTML-formatting BLAST reports
Bio::Tools::Blast::Sbjct	Bioperl BLAST "hit" object
Bio::Tools::Blast::Run::LocalBlast	Bioperl module for running BLAST analyses locally
Bio::Tools::Blast::Run::Webblast	Bioperl module for running BLAST analyses using an HTTP interface
Bio::Tools::Prediction::Exon	Predicted exon feature
Bio::Tools::Prediction::Gene	Predicted gene structure feature
Bio::Variation::AAChange	Sequence change class for polypeptides

Table 12-1 . Bioperl modules (continued)

Module	Description
Bio::Variation::AAReverseMutate	Point mutation and codon information from single amino acid changes
Bio::Variation::Allele	Sequence object with allele-specific attributes
Bio::Variation::DNAMutation	DNA-level mutation class
Bio::Variation::IO	Handler for sequence variation I/O formats

Bioperl Tutorial Script

Bioperl has a tutorial script to help you try out various parts of the package. In this section, I'll show how to start up and run some example computations.

I've mentioned already that you should learn how to download code from CPAN in order to add modules such as Bioperl. A great deal of the usefulness of the Perl programming environment now resides in these modules available on CPAN. This was a design decision: by concentrating on the core Perl language, the Perl designers can focus on making the language as good as they can. The Perl module developers can then concentrate on their many modules. By all means, take a look around the CPAN web site for an idea of the wealth of Perl modules available to you.

I won't give the details of how to install Bioperl here: as mentioned, they are available at the Bioperl web site, or you can visit the CPAN web site for information.

So, let's assume you've installed the Bioperl module and looked over the tutorial at the Bioperl web site. Now, let's see how to try out some Bioperl programs.

Go to the directory where the Bioperl software has been built on your system. For instance, on my Linux computer, I put the download file *bioperl-0.7.0.tar.gz* into the directory */usr/local/src*, and then unpacked it with the command:

```
tar xvzf bioperl-0.7.0.tar.gz
```

which creates the source directory */usr/local/src/bioperl-0.7.0*. After installing the module (check the documentation), you're ready to run the tutorial script.

Change to the source directory and type perl bptutorial.pl. Here's the result (I've shown the head of the tutorial to give the author and copyright information):

```
% head bptutorial.pl
# $Id: ch12,v 1.44 2001/10/10 20:37:42 troutman Exp mam $

=head1  BioPerl Tutorial

  Cared for by Peter Schattner <schattner@alum.mit.edu>

  Copyright Peter Schattner

    This tutorial includes "snippets" of code and text from various
    Bioperl documents including module documentation, example scripts
% perl bptutorial.pl
```

The following numeric arguments can be passed to run the corresponding demo-script.

```
1 => access_remote_db ,
2 => index_local_db ,
3 => fetch_local_db ,                    (# NOTE: needs to be run with demo 2)
4 => sequence_manipulations ,
5 => seqstats_and_seqwords ,
6 => restriction_and_sigcleave ,
7 => other_seq_utilities ,
8 => run_standaloneblast ,
9 => blast_parser ,
10 => bplite_parsing ,
11 => hmmer_parsing ,
12 => run_clustalw_tcoffee ,
13 => run_psw_bl2seq ,
14 => simplealign_univaln ,
15 => gene_prediction_parsing ,
16 => sequence_annotation ,
17 => largeseqs ,
18 => liveseqs ,
19 => demo_variations ,
20 => demo_xml ,
```

In addition the argument "100" followed by the name of a single
bioperl object will display a list of all the public methods
available from that object and from what object they are inherited.

Using the parameter "0" will run all tests.
Using any other argument (or no argument) will run this display.

So typical command lines might be:
To run all demo scripts:
```
 > perl -w  bptutorial.pl 0
```
or to just run the local indexing demos:
```
 > perl -w  bptutorial.pl 2 3
```
or to list all the methods available for object Bio::Tools::SeqStats -
```
 > perl -w  bptutorial.pl 100 Bio::Tools::SeqStats
```

%

Now let's try option 9, the BLAST parser, and option 1, access_remote_db. So here goes, starting with the BLAST parser:

```
% perl bptutorial.pl 9

Beginning blast.pm parser example...

QUERY NAME    : gi|1401126
QUERY DESC    : UNKNOWN
LENGTH        : 504
FILE          : t/blast.report
DATE          : Thu, 16 Apr 1998 18:56:18 -0400
PROGRAM       : TBLASTN
VERSION       : 2.0.4 [Feb-24-1998]</b>
DB-NAME       : Non-redundant GenBank+EMBL+DDBJ+PDB sequences
```

```
DB-RELEASE       : Apr 16, 1998   9:38 AM
DB-LETTERS       : 677679054
DB-SEQUENCES     : 336723
GAPPED           : YES
TOTAL HITS       : 100
CHECKED ALL      : YES
FILT FUNC        : NO
SIGNIF HITS      : 4
SIGNIF CUTOFF    : 1.0e-05 (EXPECT-VALUE)
LOWEST EXPECT    : 0.0
HIGHEST EXPECT   : 1e-05
HIGHEST EXPECT   : 7.6 (OVERALL)
MATRIX           : BLOSUM62
FILTER           : NONE
EXPECT           : 10
LAMBDA, K, H     : 0.270, 0.0470, 0.230 (SHARED STATS)
WORD SIZE        : 13
S                : 42, 74 (SHARED STATS)
GAP CREATION     : 11
GAP EXTENSION    : 1

Number of hits is 4
Fraction identical for hit 1 is 0.25
Sequence identities for hsp of hit 1 are 66-68 70 73 76 79 80 87-89 114 117
119 131 144 146 149 150 152 156 162 165 168 170 171 176 178-182 184 187 190
191 205-207 211 214 217 222 226 241 244 245 249 256 266-268 270 278 284 291
296 304 306 309 311 316 319 324
%
```

This is an interesting way to parse BLAST output! Now let's look at the access of the remote DB:

```
% perl bptutorial.pl 1
Beginning remote database access example...
seq1 display id is MUSIGHBA1
seq2 display id is AF303112
Display id of first sequence in stream is AF041456
%
```

Well, that was less informative as an output, but it seems you can infer that the remote DB access was successful. (By the way, if you're unsuccessful with this, it may be that you're behind a firewall which is denying access—a not uncommon occurrence in universities or large companies.)

The documentation suggests running the *bptutorial.pl* script under the Perl debugger to watch what happens step by step. I concur with that suggestion but won't include the output here. Try it yourself!

Since that last example wasn't much fun, let's try one more: here's the sequence manipulation tutorial:

```
% perl bptutorial.pl 4

Beginning sequence_manipulations and SeqIO example...
```

```
First sequence in fasta format...
>Test1
AGCTTTTCATTCTGACTGCAACGGGCAATATGTCTCTGTGTGGATTAAAAAAAGAGTGTC
TGATAGCAGCTTCTGAACTGGTTACCTGCCGTGAGTAAATTAAAATTTTATTGACTTAGG
TCACTAAATACTTTAACCAATATAGGCATAGCGCACAGACAGATAAAAATTACAGAGTAC
ACAACATCCATGAAACGCATTAGCACCACC
Seq object display id is Test1
Sequence is AGCTTTTCATTCTGACTGCAACGGGCAATATGTCTCTGTGTGGATTAAAAAAAGAGTGTCTGATAG
CAGCTTCTGAACTGGTTACCTGCCGTGAGTAAATTAAAATTTTATTGACTTAGGTCACTAAATACTTTAACCAATATA
GGCATAGCGCACAGACAGATAAAAATTACAGAGTACACAACATCCATGAAACGCATTAGCACCACC
Sequence from 5 to 10 is TTTCAT
Acc num is unknown
Moltype is dna
Primary id is Test1
Truncated Seq object sequence is TTTCAT
Reverse complemented sequence 5 to 10  is GTGCTA
Translated sequence 6 to 15 is LQRAICLCVD

Beginning 3-frame and alternate codon translation example...
ctgagaaaataa translated using method defaults   : LRK*
ctgagaaaataa translated as a coding region (CDS): MRK

Translating in all six frames:
 frame: 0 forward: LRK*
 frame: 0 reverse-complement: LFSQ
 frame: 1 forward: *ENX
 frame: 1 reverse-complement: YFLX
 frame: 2 forward: EKI
 frame: 2 reverse-complement: IFS
Translating with all codon tables using method defaults:
1 : LRK*
2 : L*K*
3 : TRK*
4 : LRK*
5 : LSK*
6 : LRKQ
9 : LSN*
10 : LRK*
11 : LRK*
12 : SRK*
13 : LGK*
14 : LSNY
15 : LRK*
16 : LRK*
21 : LSN*
%
```

That was more fun, because this part of Bioperl is doing several things we've done in this book.

I hope this brief look at Bioperl has whetted your appetite for more. It's a good idea to explore this set of modules. A Perl module for parsing BLAST output called *BPLite.pm* may also be of interest: it's now part of the Bioperl project.

Exercises

Exercise 12.1

> *Basic string matching.* Write a program that looks for a query string in a target string. For instance, if the query string is "gone", it finds a match at position 22 of the target string "goof through the way-gone-osphere." Don't use regular expressions or any of Perl's built-in string-matching abilities; instead, examine individual positions in the strings, compare characters, and invent your own algorithm.

Exercise 12.2

> Explore the NCBI BLAST web pages at *http://www.ncbi.nlm.nih/BLAST*. Familiarize yourself with the purpose and use of the various component programs and read the tutorial information on the meaning of the statistics.

Exercise 12.3

> Explore the Bioperl web pages at *http://www.bioperl.org*. Download the code and install it on your computer.

Exercise 12.4

> Perform BLAST searches at the NCBI web site. Search with DNA against DNA databases; then search with the same DNA against protein databases, and compare the output.

Exercise 12.5

> Perform two BLAST searches with related sequences. Parse the BLAST output of the searches and extract the top 10 hits in the header annotation of each search. Write a program that reports on the differences and similarities between the two searches.

Exercise 12.6

> Write a program that uses Bioperl to perform a BLAST search at the NCBI web site, then use Bioperl to parse the BLAST output.

Exercise 12.7

> Using Bioperl modules mixed with your own code, write a program that runs BLAST on a set of DNA sequences and saves the IDs of the list of hits of each BLAST run sorted in arrays. Allow the user to view each list, to view hits in common between multiple lists and hits unique to one of multiple lists. For each hit, enable the user to fetch its entire GenBank record.

Example 12.8

> Write an explanation of the code for the subroutine *extract_HSP_information*. Be sure to refer to the format of the data the code uses as input.

## CHAPTER 13

Further Topics

This book's goal has been to help you learn basic Perl programming. In this chapter, I will point the way to further learning in Perl.

The Art of Program Design

My emphasis on the art of *program design* has determined the way in which the programs were presented. They've generally progressed from a discussion of problems and ideas, to pseudocode, to small groups of small, cooperating subroutines, and finally to a close-up discussion of the code. At several points you've seen more than one way to do the same task. This is an important part of a programmer's mindset: the knowledge of, and willingness to try, alternatives.

The other recurrent theme has been to explain the *problem-solving strategies* programmers rely on. These include knowing how to use such sources of information as searchable newsgroup archives, books, and language documentation; having a good working knowledge of debugging tools; and understanding basic algorithm and data structure design and analysis.

As your skills improve, and your programs become more complex, you'll find that these strategies take on a much more important role. Designing and coding programs to solve complex problems or crunch lots of complex data requires advanced problem-solving strategies. So it's worth your while to learn to think like a computer scientist as well as a biologist.

Web Programming

The Internet is the most important source of bioinformatics data. From FTP sites to web-enabled programs, the Perl-literate bioinformatician needs to be able to access web resources. Just about every lab has to have its own web page these days, and many grants even require it. You'll need to learn the basics about the HTML and

XML markup languages that display web pages, about the difference between a web server and a web browser, and similar facts of life.

The popular *CGI.pm* module makes it fairly easy to create interactive web pages, and several other modules are available that make Internet programming tasks relatively painless. For instance, you can write code for your own web page that enables visitors to try out your latest sequence analyzer or search through your special-purpose database. You can also add code to your own programs to enable them to interact with other web sites, querying and retrieving data automatically. Collaborators who are geographically diverse can use such web programming to work cooperatively on a project.

Algorithms and Sequence Alignment

You will want to spend some time exploring the standard results in algorithms, as found in the texts recommended in Appendix A. A good place to start is the basic sequence alignment methods such as the Smith-Waterman algorithm. In terms of algorithms, the topics of parallelization, randomization, and approximation deserve at least a nodding acquaintance.

Sequence alignment is the subset of the family of algorithms called string matching algorithms that are used to find the extent of identity or similarity, or to find evidence of homology, between sequences. The Smith-Waterman algorithm, the treatment of gaps, the use of preprocessing, parallel techniques, the alignment of multiple sequences, and more are facets of this study.

Object-Oriented Programming

Object-oriented programming is a style of program design that provides a well-defined interface to data and subroutines (called methods in "OO-speak"). It's not hard to learn; it makes some things easy that would otherwise be hard (and vice versa, but you don't have to use it for everything!). A great deal of Perl code has been written in object-oriented style since the capability was added to the language a few years ago.

Perl Modules

I've frequently mentioned modules and CPAN—the large collection of Perl code—has a huge number of modules you can use. Most are free, but do make a point of checking for copyright restrictions and see the discussion in the Perl FAQs about copyright issues. These days, most modules, including the bulk of the code available on CPAN, are written in an object-oriented style. You'll need to extend your Perl knowledge to encompass this style, but you won't need an in-depth view of object-oriented techniques to use most modules in your programs.

Bioperl

An important and steadily developing suite of Perl modules for bioinformatics is the Bioperl project, which you can find at the web site *http://www.bioperl.org*. These modules give you lots of capabilities, all ready to use.

Complex Data Structures

Perl can handle complex data structures. This is useful in many programming situations; it's also necessary to learn in order to read a lot of existing Perl code that might come your way.

For example, in this book, you've parsed a lot of data. To do so, you developed groups of subroutines, each fairly short, and each parsing different levels of the structure of the data. By using complex data structures, you can store your parse in a form that reflects the structure of the data. This, combined with object-oriented methods for accessing the parsed data, is a useful way to accomplish a parse.

Complex data structures depend on references, which I've touched on in discussions of call by reference and of File::Find.

Relational Databases

Relational databases are another area Perl programmers and bioinformaticians need to explore. There comes a time when flat files or DBM just won't do for managing the data of a medium- or large-sized project, and you must turn to relational databases. Although they take a bit more effort to set up and program, they offer a standard and reliable way to store data and ask questions about it. In this book, we briefly discussed relational databases and actually used a simple DBM database. In the course of your work, however, you're likely to encounter Oracle, MySQL, PostgreSQL, Sybase, and others. The Perl module DBI, which stands for Database Independence, makes it possible to write code for manipulating relational databases that doesn't depend (too much) on which database you're actually using.

The fact is, writing code to handle databases isn't hard to do. The hardest part is making sure that the database is installed with the proper libraries, that the proper Perl modules are in place, and that you know how to connect to the database from your program. Once you have those things in place, using the database is generally easy.

That said, relational databases have their own lore, and there is a substantial body of knowledge about designing and managing good databases. Many programmers specialize in these issues, and that's true for plenty of bioinformaticians as well, since there are many interesting research questions related to designing better biological databases.

Microarrays and XML

Microarrays (miniaturized chip-based "laboratories" for studying gene expression) and XML (Extensible Markup Language) are two modern developments that are coming together. Now that whole genomes are available, microarray techniques enable you to measure the relative levels of thousands of gene transcripts at a time, and with their help, we hope to unravel the many pathways and interactions between the thousands of genes and gene products in the cell. XML is, to be painfully brief, a kind of new and improved HTML that is emerging as a standard for storing and interchanging data. (This book was written making extensive use of XML.) XML is becoming an important interface to many new kinds of experimental data.

Graphics Programming

Good graphical representation of data is critical for making your results useful to your colleagues. Graphics programming language present data and results and interact with software applications via attractive and easy-to-navigate interfaces. Many bioinformatics programs deal with large amounts of data, and a graphical user interface (GUI) can mean the difference between an application that helps you do your work and one that wastes your time. GUIs such as those commonly found on web pages are important not only for the display of output but also for the collection of user input.

The point-and-click method of interacting with software applications is a basic standard. A good GUI makes an application or program much easier to use. One difficulty of GUIs and graphic data displays, however, is that they tend to be less portable than programs with simpler graphics. You may want to explore the graphics capabilities of such Perl modules as Tk and GD, among others.

Modeling Networks

Networks of interacting biological systems, such as genes and gene products, can be modeled and investigated using graph algorithms. Despite the similarity to the term "graphics," graph algorithms are a different entity based on the discrete mathematical field of graph theory. Algorithms on graphs and their many variants (such as Petri nets) can store and investigate the properties of biochemical pathways and intra- and intercellular signalling pathways, for example.

DNA Computers

For the forward-thinking scientist, it is interesting and instructive to learn about new trends in computing such as DNA computers, optical computing, and quantum computing. DNA computers are especially fun. They use standard molecular biology laboratory techniques as a model of a general-purpose computer. They can implement algorithms, store data, and in general behave like a "real" computer. They are impractical as of this writing, but they are really fun to think about, and someday, who knows?

Resources

There is a wide array of resource material for Perl and for bioinformatics programming. This list is not at all exhaustive, but it includes those resources, both online and in print, that I think you may find interesting and useful as you expand your Perl programming repertoire.

Perl

The documentation for Perl is extensive. It includes lists of FAQs (Frequently Asked Questions, with answers), tutorials, precise definitions in the form of Unix-style manpages, and discussions of specific areas. There are various web sites, a well-organized storehouse of useful Perl programs called CPAN, newsgroups that have searchable archives, conferences, and many good books. It's also worth your while to find and cultivate your own local Perl community. Don't be afraid to engage your colleagues, though as your programming skills grow, they're liable to start asking you questions!

As I've mentioned before, Perl is free. It's part of the wider open source movement, which includes such developments as Linux, the Apache web server, and so on. Since Perl is free, it relies on a community of interested parties to develop code and to write documentation. Because of this, you may notice that a lot of the documentation is a bit fragmented (or, in some cases, very fragmented). Still, the level of support for all these projects equals that available for the best of the commercial software packages.

Web Site

http://www.perl.com

This is the starting point for all things Perl. By all means, explore it. From here, you'll find many more sites dedicated to various aspects of Perl programming. Among several, you might find *http://www.perl.org* especially useful.

CPAN: Comprehensive Perl Archive Network

http://www.cpan.org/

The Comprehensive Perl Archive Network is an important resource and is *the* place to look for Perl modules. It's also a repository for other software, documentation, and web links. Before taking the time to write a program yourself, look here first to see if it has already been written.

FAQs: Frequently Asked Questions

http://www.perl.com/pub/v/faqs

FAQs are a compendium of the most common questions newcomers ask, along with answers, that are usually quite helpful. As a beginning programmer, it is a good idea to take the time to read the Perl FAQs—skimming as necessary—in order to get the lay of the land.

You should spend at least enough time reading them to get an idea of what sorts of questions are archived in the FAQs. Be sure to check the FAQs before asking for help from a local expert or posting to a newsgroup. Repeatedly asking questions that have already been exhaustively answered in the FAQs, especially on the Perl newsgroups, might be considered irritating.

You'll find that the Perl FAQs are divided into several parts. When consulting FAQs, look for the date when they were last updated; this isn't a big problem with Perl, but in general, you can find lots of out-of-date information on the Web.

Beginners

There are several documents aimed at beginners in the FAQs and in the documentation. There are some other beginning books besides this one, mentioned elsewhere in this appendix. There are also some online tutorials and beginners' articles about Perl at *http://learn.perl.org* (this is new as I write but looks very promising). There are also a number of mailing lists you can subscribe to, including a mailing list called *beginners@perl.org*, which you can subscribe to by visiting *http://lists.perl.org*.

Online Manuals

http://www.perl.com/pub/v/documentation

The Perl manual is available online at the Perl web site mentioned earlier. It should also be installed on your computer. You can access it by typing `perldoc perl`. On Unix/Linux systems, you can also type `man perl` to get the beginning manpage. As that explains, the manual is split into several pages. For instance, to find the manual for Perl's built-in functions, type man perlfunc or perldoc. HTML versions of the manual exist, and they can be installed on your local computer. This is my preferred method of accessing the documentation: it gives you links that make navigating easier, and if it's installed locally, you can use it even when you're not connected to the Internet.

Books

There are lots of Perl books. Many of them are excellent; some are not. Here's a short list of the Perl books I've found most useful in my own work.

Programming Perl, Third Edition; by Larry Wall, Tom Christiansen, and Jon Orwant; O'Reilly & Associates. This is the standard book on Perl by the creator of the language. It explains pretty much everything, although it can lag behind the latest version of Perl. So the absolute authority for your installation should be the online manuals. *Programming Perl* covers a lot of ground; it's good as a reference, a tutorial, and as a ripping yarn if you're into that sort of thing. It presents some of the philosophy behind the language, so it's a good way to absorb some of the computer-science mindset. Earlier editions, if you happen to have them, will also serve; I'm particularly fond of the first edition.

Perl Cookbook, by Tom Christiansen and Nathan Torkington, O'Reilly & Associates. This is billed as the companion volume to *Programming Perl*, and so it is. Here, you will find examples that use Perl for different tasks. It's a great help in many situations, and if you will be doing much Perl programming, it's worth taking at least a few hours to peruse it.

Mastering Algorithms with Perl; by Jon Orwant, Jarkho Hietaniemi, and John Macdonald; O'Reilly & Associates. I've mentioned the importance of studying algorithms and this fine book presents many important algorithms in the context of Perl. It explains concepts and gives code; it doesn't, however, teach the mathematics of analyzing and measuring algorithms. Really serious algorithms students will find that information in texts such as *Introduction to Algorithms* by Corman, Leiserson, and Rivest. Even if you're a novice programmer, this is still a valuable book, and you'll find lots of code you'll be able to use.

Mastering Regular Expressions; by Jeffrey R. Friedl, O'Reilly & Associates. A good book on an important topic with excellent coverage of Perl.

Elements of Programming in Perl, by Andrew L. Johnson, Manning Publications. This is another book intended for beginners. It's very good, and I recommend it as a supplement to this text.

Learning Perl, Third Edition; by Randall L. Schwartz and Tom Christiansen; O'Reilly & Associates. This is the classic tutorial book on Perl. It's well-written and well-organized. If you've gotten through *Beginning Perl for Bioinformatics*, you should have no trouble with *Learning Perl*.

Object-Oriented Perl, by Damian Conway, Manning Publications. A superb book on the topic suitable for the beginning or advanced programmer.

Conference

O'Reilly Open Source Convention. This convention now includes the yearly Perl Conference. It's a chance to attend classes and lectures and meet Perl practitioners of all sorts. There are also regular YAPC (yet another Perl conference) meetings; you'll find the details at the main Perl web site.

Newsgroups

Perl newsgroups are an important resource for programmers. If you've never seen them, they're accessible over the Web (among other ways). They give you the ability to write a message to a large group of people with interests in any of hundreds of specific topics. If you have a question that you haven't been able to answer in the Perl documentation or the FAQs, searching the newsgroups for the topic of your question can often result in an answer. You can also post a question to a newsgroup if you can't find an answer already provided: but this is not often necessary.

I want to emphasize how useful this resource is. The drawback is that there tends to be a "low signal-to-noise ration": in other words, there's often a lot of uninformative material in newsgroups. But it can be worth wading through; even negative responses (no known solution to the problem) can save you time and effort.

There are a number of newsgroups related to Perl in the *comp.lang.perl* hierarchy. The search engine *deja.com* (recently sold to *google.com* but still available) lets you search the archives of these newsgroups. More information is available in the Perl FAQs about specific newsgroups; for instance, many specific Perl modules have their own newsgroups, mailing lists, or web sites. The CPAN web site is another place to find searchable newsgroup archives.

Computer Science

Even though you're programming for biological applications, you'll often find yourself venturing into the realm of traditional computer science. Here are some published resources to help you find your way.

Algorithms

Mastering Algorithms with Perl; by Jon Orwant, Jarkho Hietaniemi, and John Macdonald; O'Reilly & Associates. The best book for noncomputer scientists who program in Perl.

Introduction to Algorithms; by Thomas H. Cormen, Charles E. Leiserson, and Ronald L. Rivest; MIT Press and McGraw-Hill. This is a really good book on algorithms—in many ways, the best. It's one of the standard university texts (arguably *the* standard text) at both the graduate and undergraduate levels. It works well as a textbook and as a reference. Its target audience is computer-science students, so there is a fair amount of math included, but even nonmathematical programmers will find this book very helpful.

Fundamentals of Algorithmics, by Gilles Brassard and Paul Bratley, Prentice Hall. An easy overview of algorithmic techniques.

Algorithms on Strings, Trees, and Sequences: Computer Science and Computational Biology; by Dan Gusfield; Cambridge University Press. This book specializes in algorithms for strings, including such topics as sequence alignment. It's very detailed, but even so, not complete: this is a big field! The best single source on string algorithms, with lots of information about biological sequence similarity.

The following books are for advanced study.

The Design and Analysis of Computer Algorithms; by Alfred V. Aho, John E. Hopcroft, and Jeffrey D. Ullman; Addison-Wesley. This is the classic book on the science of algorithms.

Introduction to Parallel Algorithms and Architectures: Arrays, Trees, Hypercubes; by Frank Thomson Leighton; Morgan Kaufmann. A comprehensive and rigorous text and reference.

Randomized Algorithms, by Rajeev Motwani and Prabhakar Raghavan, Cambridge University Press. A clear, rigorous book.

Software Engineering

Software Engineering, Second Edition; by Ian Sommerville; Addison-Wesley. A good, general book that covers lots of important topics and generally avoids taking sides for or against competing styles.

Theory of Computer Science

Introduction to Automata Theory, Languages, and Computation, Second Edition; by John E. Hopcroft, Rajeev Motwani, and Jeffrey D. Ullman; Addison-Wesley. The classic text on computer-science theory.

Computers and Intractability: A Guide to the Theory of Np-Completeness, by Michael R. Garey and David S. Johnson, W.H. Freeman & Co. The classic, and superb, book on the topic.

General Programming

The Unix Programmers Manual, Steven V. Earhart, ed., Harcourt, Brace and Jovanovich School. This manual for Unix (whatever version of Unix) is a crash course in computer science with an emphasis on programming. The design of the interacting programs, and the concepts of pipes, redirection, processes, and so on, has been one of the great success stories of programming. This manual summarizes the system: Part I documents user programs; Parts II and III document the programming interface. The programmable shell, and the programs *grep*, *awk*, and *sed* were some of the primary inspirations for Perl.

The C Programming Language, by Brian W. Kernighan and Dennis M. Ritchie, Prentice Hall PTR. C and C++ are important languages in bioinformatics, and this classic book teaches C. If you work through the book, attempting all the programming exercises, you'll have some excellent programming training.

Structure and Interpretation of Computer Programs; by Harold Abelson, Gerald Jay Sussman, and Juke Sussman; MIT Press. A really interesting book that looks deeply at programming in the context of learning a dialect of Lisp.

The Unix Programming Environment, by Brian W. Kernighan and Robert Pike, Prentice Hall. This book is fun, and it talks about good software design.

Linux

If you have a Linux system, you have all the source code for the entire system available (this is also true for some Unix systems). (If it's not installed, you can get it from the distribution CDs, from the web site *http://www.linux.org*, or from the web site of the company that produced your version of Linux.) This is a great resource. You can take a look at how any program is actually written, even the operating system. Now you're really getting into programming!

Bioinformatics

Bioinformatics is a relatively new discipline that's attracting a lot of attention, so the available resources are multiplying fairly quickly. Here are a few books and other resources to help get you started.

Books

Developing Bioinformatics Computer Skills, by Cynthia Gibas and Per Jambeck, O'Reilly & Associates. This is a really good book for beginners. It covers setting up a Linux workstation and the installation and use of many of the best, and least expensive, bioinformatics programs. It teaches how to use bioinformatics programs, not how to program. It's the most practical bioinformatics book available.

Introduction to Computational Biology: Maps, Sequences and Genomes; by Michael S. Waterman; CRC Press. This is a classic book with a predominantly statistical outlook.

Bioinformatics: A Practical Guide to the Analysis of Genes and Proteins, Second Edition; edited by Andreas D. Baxecvanis and B.F. Francis Ouellette; John Wiley & Sons. Includes chapters on a wide range of topics by several authors.

Governmental Organizations

Absolutely essential. The following web sites are for the most important government-sponsored bioinformatics organizations:

http://www.ncbi.nlm.nih.gov/:
   the National Center for Biotechnology Information (NCBI). The U.S. government center.

http://www.embl.org/:
   the European Molecular Biology Laboratory (EMBL). The European Union laboratory.

http://www.ebi.ac.uk/:
   the European Bioinformatics Institute (EBI) of EMBL.

Conferences

Bioinformatics has long been a part of various biology conferences, for instance the Cold Spring Harbor conferences on sequencing. Now there are many conferences with such coverage, often under the heading of "genomics." Here are a few interesting conferences:

- *ISMB: Intelligent Systems for Molecular Biology*, now in its ninth year
- *Bioinformatics Open Source Conference, http://www.bioinformatics.org/*
- *RECOMB*: Conference on Computational Molecular Biology

Molecular Biology

Recombinant DNA, by James Watson, et al., W.H. Freeman & Co. This book, though getting old for such a fast-moving field, is a gem for programmers and computer scientists entering the bioinformatics field. Many standard techniques are clearly and briefly explained with excellent illustrations. Look for the second edition, if you can find it.

Molecular Biology of the Gene, Fourth Edition, by James Watson, et al., Addison-Wesley. The classic book in molecular biology. It's very detailed; at this level of coverage, it's definitely out of date, but it's—well—a classic. Makes a good reference for the basics.

Molecular Cell Biology, Fourth Edition, by Harvey Lodish, et al., W.H. Freeman & Co. An excellent and extensive introductory review of cell biology.

Perl Summary

This appendix summarizes those parts of the Perl programming language that will be most useful to you as you read this book. It is not a comprehensive summary of the Perl language. Remember that Perl is designed so that you don't need to know everything in order to use it. Source material for this appendix came from *Programming Perl*, *Third Edition* (O'Reilly & Associates).

Command Interpretation

The Perl programs in this book start with the line:

```
#!/usr/bin/perl -w
```

On Unix (or Linux) systems, the first line of a file can include the name of a program and some flags, which are optional. The line must start with #!, followed by the full pathname of the program (in our case, the Perl interpreter), followed optionally by a single group of one or more flags.

If the Perl program file was called *myprogram*, and had executable permissions, you can type myprogram (or possibly ./myprogram, or the full or relative pathname for the program) to start the program running.

The Unix operating system starts the program specified in the command interpretation line and gives it as input the rest of the file after the first line. So, in this case, it starts the Perl interpreter and gives it the program in the file to run.

This is just a shortcut for typing:

```
/usr/bin/perl -w myprogram
```

at the command line.

Comments

A comment begins with a # sign and continues from there to the end of the same line. It is ignored by the Perl interpreter and is only there for programmers to read. A comment can include any text.

Scalar Values and Scalar Variables

A scalar value is a single item of data, like a string or a number.

Strings

Strings are scalar values and are written as text enclosed within single quotes, like so:

```
'This is a string in single quotes.'
```

or double quotes, such as:

```
"This is a string in double quotes."
```

A single-quoted string prints out exactly as written. With double quotes, you can include a variable in the string, and its value will be inserted or "interpolated." You can also include commands such as \n to represent a newline (see Table B-3):

```
$aside = '(or so they say)';
$declaration = "Misery\n $aside \nloves company.";
print $declaration;
```

This snippet prints out:

```
Misery
 (or so they say)
loves company.
```

Numbers

Numbers are scalar values that can be:

- Integers:

  ```
  3
  -4
  0
  ```

- Floating-point (decimal):

  ```
  4.5326
  ```

- Scientific (exponential) notation (3.13×10^{23} or 313000000000000000000000):

  ```
  3.13E23
  ```

- Hexadecimal (base 16):

  ```
  0x12bc3
  ```

- Octal (base 8):

  ```
  05777
  ```

- Binary (base 2):

  ```
  0b10101011
  ```

Complex (or imaginary) numbers, such as 3 + i, and fractions (or ratios, or rational numbers), such as 1/3, can be a little tricky. Perl can handle fractions but converts them internally to floating-point numbers, which can make certain operations go wrong (Perl is not alone among computer languages in this regard.):

```
if ( 10/3  == ( (1/3) * 10 ) {
    print "Success!";
}else {
    print "Failure!";
}
```

This prints:

```
Failure!
```

To properly handle rational arithmetic with fractions, complex numbers, or many other mathematical constructs, there are mathematics modules available, which aren't covered here.

Scalar Variables

Scalar values can be stored in scalar variables. A scalar variable is indicated with a $ before the variable's name. The name begins with a letter or underscore and can have any number of letters, underscores, or digits. A digit, however, can't be the first character in a variable name. Here are some examples of legal names of scalar variables:

```
$Var
$var_1
```

Here are some improper names for scalar variables:

```
$1var
$var!iable
```

Names are case sensitive: $dna is different from $DNA.

These rules for making proper variable names (apart from the beginning $) also hold for the names of array and hash variables and for subroutine names.

A scalar variable may hold any type of scalar value mentioned previously, such as strings or the different types of numbers.

Assignment

Scalar variables are assigned scalar values with an assignment statement. For instance:

```
$thousand = 1000;
```

assigns the integer 1,000, a scalar value, to the scalar variable $thousand.

The assignment statement looks like an equal sign from elementary mathematics, but its meaning is different. The assignment statement is an instruction, not an assertion. It doesn't mean "$thousand equals 1,000." It means "store the scalar value 1,000 into the scalar variable $thousand". However, after the statement, the value of the scalar variable $thousand is, indeed, equal to 1000.

You can assign values to several scalar variables by surrounding variables and values in parentheses and separating them by commas, thus making lists:

```
($one, $two, $three) = ( 1, 2, 3);
```

There are several assignment operators besides = that are shorthand for longer expressions. For instance, $a += $b is equivalent to $a = $a + $b. Table B-1 is a complete list (it includes several operators that aren't covered in this book).

Table B-1. Assignment operator shorthands

Example of operator	Equivalent	
$a += $b	$a = $a + $b	(addition)
$a -= $b	$a = $a - $b	(subtraction)
$a *= $b	$a = $a * $b	(multiplication)
$a /= $b	$a = $a / $b	(division)
$a **= $b	$a = $a ** $b	(exponentiation)
$a %= $b	$a = $a % $b	(remainder of $a / $b)
$a x= $b	$a = $a x $b	(string $a repeated $b times)
$a &= $b	$a = $a & $b	(bitwise AND)
$a |= $b	$a = $a	$b	(bitwise OR)
$a ^= $b	$a = $a ^ $b	(bitwise XOR)
$a >>= $b	$a = $a >> $b	($a shift $b bits)
$a <<= $b	$a = $a >> $b	($a shift $b bits to left)
$a &&= $b	$a = $a && $b	(logical AND)
$a ||= $b	$a = $a || $b	(logical OR)
$a .= $b	$a = $a . $b	(append string $b to $a)

Statements and Blocks

Programs are composed of statements often grouped together into blocks.

A statement ends with a semicolon (;), which is optional for the last statement in a block.

A block is one or more statements usually surrounded by curly braces; here's an example:

```
{
    $thousand = 1000;
    print $thousand;
}
```

Blocks may stand by themselves but are often associated with such constructs as loops or if statements.

Arrays

Arrays are ordered collections of zero or more scalar values, indexed by position. An array variable begins with the at sign @ followed by a legal variable name. For instance, here are two possible array variable names:

```
@array1
@dna_fragments
```

You can assign scalar values to an array by placing the scalar values in a list, separated by commas and surrounded by a pair of parentheses. For instance, you can assign an array the empty list:

```
@array = ( );
```

or one or more scalar values:

```
@dna_fragments = ('ACGT', $fragment2, 'GGCGGA');
```

Notice that it's okay to specify a scalar variable such as $fragment2 in a list. Its current value, not the variable name, is placed into the array.

The individual scalar values of an array (the elements) are indexed by their position in the array. The index numbers begin at 0. You can specify the individual elements of an array by preceding the array name by a $ and following it with the index number of the element within square brackets [ ], like so:

```
$dna_fragments[2]
```

This equals the value of 'GGCGGA', given the values previously set for this array. Notice that the array has three scalar values, indexed by numbers 0, 1, and 2. The third and last element is indexed 2, one less than the total number of elements 3, because the first element is indexed number 0.

You can make a copy of an array using an assignment operator =, as in this example that makes a copy @output of an existing array @input:

```
@output = @input;
```

If you evaluate an array in scalar context, the value is the number of elements in the array. So if array @input has five elements, the following example assigns the value 5 to $count:

```
$count = @input;
```

Figure B-1 shows an array @myarray with three elements, which demonstrates the ordered nature of an array; by which each element appears, and can be found by its position in the array.

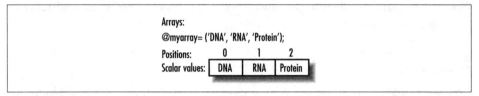

Figure B-1. Schematic of an array

Hashes

A hash (also called an associative array) is a collection of zero or more pairs of scalar values, called keys and values. The values are indexed by the keys. An array variable begins with the percent sign % followed by a legal variable name. For instance, possible hash variable names are:

```
%hash1
%genes_by_name
```

You can assign a value to a key with a simple assignment statement. For example, say you have a hash called %baseball_stadiums and a key Phillies to which you want to assign the value Veterans Stadium. This statement accomplishes the assignment:

```
$baseball_stadiums{'Phillies'} = 'Veterans Stadium';
```

Note that a single hash value is referenced by a $ instead of a % at the beginning of the hash name; this is similar to the way you reference individual array values by using a $ instead of a @.

You can assign several keys and values to a hash by placing their scalar values in a list, separated by commas and surrounded by a pair of parentheses. Each successive pair of scalars becomes a key and a value in the hash. For instance, you can assign a hash the empty list:

```
%hash = ( );
```

You can also assign one or more scalar key-value pairs:

```
%genes_by_name = ('gene1', 'AACCCGGTTGGTT', 'gene2', 'CCTTTCGGAAGGTC');
```

There is an another way to do the same thing, which makes the key-value pairs more readily apparent. This accomplishes the same thing as the preceding example:

```
%genes_by_name = (
    'gene1' => 'AACCCGGTTGGTT',
    'gene2' => 'CCTTTCGGAAGGTC'
);
```

To get the value associated with a particular key, precede the hash name with a $ and follow it with a pair of curly braces { } containing the scalar value of the key:

```
$genes_by_name{'gene1'}
```

This returns the value 'AACCCGGTTGGTT', given the value previously assigned to the key 'gene1' in the hash %genes_by_name. Figure B-2 shows a hash with three keys.

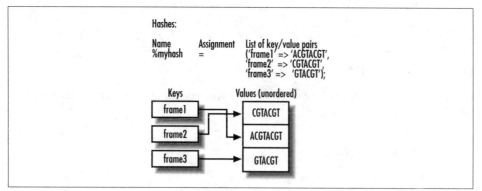

Figure B-2. Schematic of a hash

Operators

Operators are functions that represent basic operations on values: addition, subtraction, etc. They are frequently used and are core parts of the Perl programming language. They are really just functions that take arguments. For instance, + is the operator that adds two numbers, like so:

```
3 + 4;
```

Operators typically have one, two, or three operands; in the example just given, there are two operands 3 and 4.

Operators can appear before, between, or after their operands. For example, the plus operator + appears between its operands.

Operator Precedence

Operator precedence determines the order in which the operations are applied. For instance, in Perl, the expression:

    3 + 3 * 4

isn't evaluated left to right, which calculates 3 + 3 equals 6, and 6 times 4 results in a value of 24; the precedence rules cause the multiplication to be applied first, for a final result of 15. The precedence rules are available in the *perlop* manual page and in most Perl books. However, I recommend you use parentheses to make your code more readable and to avoid bugs. They make these expressions unambiguous; the first:

    (3 + 3) * 4

evaluates to 24, and the second:

    3 + (3 * 4)

evaluates to 15.

Basic Operators

For more information on how operators work, consult the *perlop* documentation bundled with Perl.

Arithmetic Operators

Perl has the basic five arithmetic operators:

+   Addition
−   Subtraction
*   Multiplication
/   Division
** Exponentiation

These operators work on both integers and floating-point values (and if you're not careful, strings as well).

Perl also has a modulus operator, which computes the remainder of two integers:

    % modulus

For example, 17 % 3 is 2, because 2 is left over when you divide 3 into 17.

Perl also has autoincrement and autodecrement operators:

    ++ add one
    -- subtract one

Unlike the previous six operators, these change a variable's value. $x++ adds one to $x, changing 4 to 5 (or a to b).

Bitwise Operators

All scalars, whether numbers or strings, are represented as sequences of individual bits "under the hood." Every once in a while, you need to manipulate those bits, and Perl provides five operators to help:

  &   Bitwise and

  | Bitwise or

  ^   Bitwise xor

  >>   Right shift

  <<   Left shift

String Operators

Two strings may be concatenated—joined together end to end—with the dot operator:

```
'This is a ' . 'joined string'
```

This results in the value 'This is a joined string'.

A string may be repeated with the x operator:

```
print "Hear ye! " x 3;
```

This prints out:

```
Hear ye! Hear ye! Hear ye!
```

File Test Operators

File test operators are unary operators that test files for certain characteristics, such as -e $file, which returns true if the file $file exists. Table B-2 lists some available file test operators.

Table B-2. File test operators

Operator	Meaning
−r	File is readable
−w	File is writable
−x	File is executable
−o	File is owned by "you"
−e	File exists
−z	File has zero size in bytes

Table B-2. File test operators (continued)

Operator	Meaning
−s	File has nonzero size (returns size in bytes)
−f	File is a plain file
−d	File is a directory (a.k.a. folder)
−l	File is a symbolic link
−t	Filehandle is opened to a terminal
−T	File is a text file
−B	File is a binary file
−M	Age of file (at startup of program) in days since modification
−A	Age of file (at startup of program) in days since last access
−C	Age of file (at startup of program) in days since last inode change

Conditionals and Logical Operators

This section covers conditional statements and logical operators.

true and false

In a conditional test, an expression evaluates to true or false, and based on the result, a statement or block may or may not be executed.

A scalar value can be true or false in a conditional. A string is false if it's the empty string (represented as "" or ''). A string is true if it's not the empty string.

Similarly, an array or a hash is false if empty, and true if nonempty.

A number is false if it's 0; a number is true if it's not 0.

Most things you evaluate in Perl return some value (such as a number from an arithmetic expression or an array returned from a subroutine), so you can use most things in Perl in conditional tests. Sometimes you may get an undefined value, for instance if you try to add a number to a variable that has not been assigned a value. Then things might fail to work as expected. For instance:

```
use strict;
use warnings;
my $a;
my $b;
$b = $a + 2;
```

produces the warning output:

```
Use of uninitialized value in addition (+) at - line 5.
```

You can test for defined and undefined values with the Perl function defined.

Logical Operators

There are four logical operators:

```
not
and
or
xor
```

not turns true values into `false` and `false` values into true. Its use is best illustrated in code:

```
if(not $done) {...}
```

This executes the code only if `$done` is `false`.

and is a binary operator that returns true if both its operands are true. If one or both of the operands are `false`, the operator returns `false`:

```
1    and  1     returns true
'a'  and  ''    returns false
''   and  0     returns false
```

or is a binary operator that returns true if one or both of the operands are true. If both operands are `false`, it returns `false`:

```
1    or  1     returns true
'a'  or  ''    returns true
''   or  0     returns false
```

xor, or exclusive-OR, returns true if one operand is true and the other operand is `false`; xor returns false if both operands are true or if both operands are `false`:

```
1 xor 0    returns true
0 xor 1    returns true
1 xor 1    returns false
0 xor 0    returns false
```

There are also variants on most of these:

```
! for not
&& for and
|| for or
```

These have different precedence but otherwise behave the same. Some older versions of Perl may only have:

```
!
||
&&
```

instead of not or and.

Using Logical Operators for Control Flow

A quick and popular way to take an action depending on the results of a previous action is to chain the statements together with logical operators. For instance, it's common in Perl programs to see the following statement to open a file:

```
open(FH, $filename) or die "Cannot open file $filename: $!";
```

The use of or in this statement shows another important thing about the binary logical operators: they evaluate their arguments left to right. In this case, if the open succeeds, the or operator never bothers to check the value of the second operand (die, which exits the program with the message in the string, plus additional messages if $! is included). The or never bothers, because if one operand is true, the or is true, so it doesn't need to check the second operand. However, if the open fails, the or needs to check that the second operand is true or false, so it goes ahead and executes the die statement.

You can use the and statement similarly to test the second operand only if the first operand succeeds.

xor doesn't work for control flow, since both its arguments have to be evaluated each time.

I haven't used this chaining of logical operators much; I've used if statements instead. This is because I often find that I want to add more statements following a test, and it's easier if the original is written as an if statement with a block, and harder if the original is written as a logical operator.

The if Statement

Conditional tests are commonly found in if statements and in their variants and loops. Here's an example of an if statement:

```
if (open (FH, $filename) {
    print "Hurray, I opened the file.";
}
```

The if statement is followed by a conditional expression enclosed in parentheses, which is followed by a block enclosed in curly braces {}. When the conditional expression evaluates as true, the statements in the block are executed.

The if statement may optionally be followed by an else, which is executed when the conditional evaluates to false:

```
if ( open(FH, $filename) {
    print "Hurray, I opened the file.";
} else {
    print "Rats. The file did not open.";
}
```

The if statement may also optionally include any number of elsif clauses, which check additional conditional statements if none of the preceding conditional statements are true:

```
if ( open(FH, $file1) {
    print "Hurray, I opened file 1.";
} elsif ( open(FH, $file2) {
    print "Hurray, I opened file 2.";
} elsif ( open(FH, $file3) {
    print "Hurray, I opened file 3.";
} else {
    print "None of the dadblasted files would open.";
}
```

In the preceding example, if file 1 opened successfully, the if statement doesn't try to open additional files.

There is also an unless statement, which is the same as an if statement with the conditional negated. So these two statements are equivalent:

```
unless ( open(FH, $filename) {
    print "Rats. The file did not open.";
}
```

```
if ( not open(FH, $filename) {
    print "Rats. The file did not open.";
}
```

Binding Operators

Binding operators are used for pattern matching, substitution, and transliteration on strings. They are used in conjunction with regular expressions that specify the patterns. Here's an example:

```
'ACGTACGTACGTACGT' =~ /CTA/
```

The pattern is the string CTA, enclosed by forward slashes //. The string binding operator is =~; it tells the program which string to search, returning true if the pattern appears in the string.

Another string binding operator is !~, which returns true if the pattern isn't in the string:

```
'ACGTACGTACGTACGT' !~ /CTA/
```

This is equivalent to:

```
not 'ACGTACGTACGTACGT' =~ /CTA/
```

You can substitute one pattern for another using the string binding operator. In the next example, s/thine/nine/ is the substitution command, which substitutes the first occurrence of thine with the string nine:

```
$poor_richard = 'A stitch in time saves thine.';
$poor_richard =~ s/thine/nine/;
print $poor_richard;
```

This produces the output:

```
A stitch in time saves nine.
```

Finally, the transliteration (or translate) operator tr substitutes characters in a string. It has several uses, but the two uses I've covered are first, to change bases to their complements A → T, C → G, G → C, and T → A:

```
$DNA = 'ACGTTTAA';
$DNA =~ tr/ACGT/TGCA/;
```

This produces the value:

```
TGCAAATT
```

Second, the tr operator counts the number of a particular character in a string, as in this example which counts the number of Gs in a string of DNA sequence data:

```
$DNA = 'ACGTTTAA';
$count = ($DNA =~ tr/A//);
print $count;
```

This produces the value 3. This shows that a pattern match can return a count of the number of translations made in a string, which is then assigned to the variable $count.

Loops

Loops repeatedly execute the statements in a block until a conditional test changes value. There are several forms of loops in Perl:

```
while(CONDITION) {BLOCK}
until(CONDITION) {BLOCK}
for(INITIALIZATION ; CONDITION ; RE-INITIALIZATION ) {BLOCK}
foreach VAR (LIST) {BLOCK}
for VAR (LIST) {BLOCK}
do {BLOCK} while (CONDITION)
do {BLOCK} until (CONDITION)
```

The while loop first tests if the conditional is true; if so, it executes the block and then returns to the conditional to repeat the process; if false, it does nothing, and the loop is over. For example:

```
$i = 3;
while ( $i ) {
    print "$i\n";
    $i--;
}
```

This produces the output:

```
3
2
1
```

Here's how the loop works. The scalar variable $i is first initialized to 3 (this isn't part of the loop). The loop is then entered, and $i is tested to see if it has a true (nonzero) value. It does, so the number 3 is printed, and the decrement operator is applied to $i, which reduces its value to 2. The block is now over, and the loop starts again with the conditional test. It succeeds with the true value 2, which is printed and decremented. The loop restarts with a test of $i, which is now the true value 1; 1 is printed and decremented to 0. The loop starts again; 0 is tested to see if it's true, and it's not, so the loop is now finished.

Loops often follow the same pattern, in which a variable is set, and a loop is called, which tests the variable's value and then executes a block, which includes changing the value of the variable.

The for loop makes this easy by including the variable initialization and the variable change in the loop statement. The following is exactly equivalent to the preceding example and produces the same output:

```
for ( $i = 3 ; $i ; $i-- ) {
    print "$i\n";
}
```

The foreach loop is a convenient way to iterate through the elements in an array. Here's an example:

```
@array = ('one', 'two', 'three');

foreach $element (@array) {
    print $element\n";
}
```

This prints the output:

```
one
two
three
```

The foreach loop specifies a scalar variable $element to be set to each element of the array. (You may use any variable name or none, in which case the special variable $_ is used automatically.) The array to be iterated over is then placed in parentheses, followed by the block. You can use for instead of foreach as the name of this loop, with identical behavior.

The first time through the loop, the value of the first element of the array is assigned to the foreach variable $element. On each succeeding pass through the loop, the value of the next element of the array is assigned to the foreach variable $element. The loop exits after it has reached the end of the array.

There is one important point to make, however. If in the block you change the value of the loop variable $element, the array is changed, and the change stays in effect after you've left the foreach loop. For example:

```
@array = ('one', 'two', 'three');

foreach $element (@array) {
    $element = 'four';
}

foreach $element (@array) {
    print $element,"\n";
}
```

produces the output:

```
four
four
four
```

In the do-until loop, the block is executed before the conditional test, and the test succeeds until the condition is true:

```
$i = 3;
do {
    print $i,"\n";
    $i--;
} until ( $i );
```

This prints:

```
3
```

In the do-while loop, the block is executed before the conditional test, and the test succeeds while the condition is true:

```
$i = 3;
do {
    print $i,"\n";
    $i--;
} while ( $i );
```

This prints:

```
3
2
1
```

Input/Output

This section covers getting information into programs and receiving data back from them.

Input from Files

Perl has several convenient ways to get information into a program. In this book, I've emphasized opening files and reading in the information contained in them, because it is frequently used, and because it behaves very much the same way on all different operating systems. You've observed the open and close system calls and how to associate a filehandle with a file when you open it, which then is used to read in the data. As an example:

```
open(FILEHANDLE, "informationfile");
@data_from_informationfile = <FILEHANDLE>;
close(FILEHANDLE);
```

This code opens the file *informationfile* and associates the filehandle FILEHANDLE with it. The filehandle is then used within angle brackets <> to actually read in the contents of the file and store the contents in the array @data_from_informationfile. Finally, the file is closed by referring once again to the opened filehandle.

Input from STDIN

Perl allows you to read in any input that is automatically sent to your program via standard input (STDIN). STDIN is a filehandle that by default is always open. Your program may be expecting some input that way. For instance, on a Mac, you can drag and drop a file icon onto the Perl applet for your program to make the file's contents appear in STDIN. On Unix systems, you can pipe the output of some other program into the STDIN of your program with shell commands such as:

```
someprog | my_perl_program
```

You can also pipe the contents of a file into your program with:

```
cat file | my_perl_program
```

or with:

```
my_perl_program < file.
```

Your program can then read in the data (from program or file) that comes as STDIN just as if it came from a file that you've opened:

```
@data_from_stdin = <STDIN>;
```

Input from Files Named on the Command Line

You can name your input files on the command line. <> is shorthand for <ARGV>. The ARGV filehandle treats the array @ARGV as a list of filenames and returns the contents of all those files, one line at a time. Perl places all command-line arguments into the array @ARGV. Some of these may be special flags, which should be read and removed from @ARGV if there will also be datafiles named. Perl assumes that anything in @ARGV refs to an input filename when it reaches a <> command. The contents of the file or files are then available to the program using the angle brackets <> without a filehandle, like so:

```
@data_from_files = <>;
```

For example, on Microsoft, Unix, or on the MacOS X, you specify input files at the command line, like so:

```
% my_program file1 file2 file3
```

Output Commands

The print statement is the most common way to output data from a Perl program. The print statement takes as arguments a list of scalars separated by commas. An array can be an argument, in which case, the elements of the array are all printed one after the other:

```
@array = ('DNA', 'RNA', 'Protein');
print @array;
```

This prints out:

```
DNARNAProtein
```

If you want to put spaces between the elements of an array, place it between double quotes in the print statement, like this:

```
@array = ('DNA', 'RNA', 'Protein');
print "@array";
```

This prints out:

```
DNA RNA Protein
```

The print statement can specify a filehandle as an optional indirect object between the print statement and the arguments, like so:

```
print FH "@array";
```

The printf function gives more control over the formatting of the output of numbers. For instance, you can specify field widths; the precision, or number of places after the decimal point; and whether the value is right- or left-justified in the field. I showed the most common options in Chapter 12 and refer you to the Perl documentation that comes with your copy of Perl for all the details.

The sprintf function is related to the printf function; it formats a string instead of printing it out.

The format and write commands are a way to format a multiline output, as when generating reports. format can be a useful command, but in practice it isn't used much. The full details are available in your Perl documentation, and O'Reilly's *Programming Perl* contains an entire chapter on format. You can also see format in Chapter 12 of this book.

Output to STDOUT, STDERR, and Files

Standard output, with the filehandle STDOUT, is the default destination for output from a Perl program, so it doesn't have to be named. The following two statements are equivalent unless you used select to change the default output filehandle:

```
print "Hello biology world!\n";
print STDOUT "Hello biology world!\n";
```

Note that the STDOUT isn't followed by a comma. STDOUT is usually directed to the computer screen, but it may be redirected at the command line to other programs or files. This Unix command pipes the STDOUT of my_program to the STDIN of your_program:

```
my_program | your_program
```

This Unix command directs the output of my_program to the file *outputfile*:

```
my_program > outputfile
```

It's also common to direct certain error messages to the predefined standard error filehandle STDERR or to a file you've opened for input and named with a particular filehandle. Here are examples of these two tasks:

```
print STDERR "If you reached this part of the program, something is terribly wrong!";

open(OUTPUTFD, ">output_file");
print OUTPUTFD "Here is the first line in the output file output_file\n";
```

STDERR is also usually directed to the computer screen by default, but it can be directed into a file from the command line. This is done differently for different systems, for example, as follows (on Unix with the *sh* or *bash* shells):

```
myprogram 2>myprogram.error
```

You can also direct STDERR to a file from within your Perl program by including code such as the following before the first output to STDERR. This is the most portable way to redirect STDERR:

```
open (STDERR, ">myprogram.error") or die "Cannot open error file
    myprogram.error:$!\n";
```

The problem with this is that the original STDERR is lost. This method, taken from *Programming Perl,* saves and restores the original STDERR:

```
open ERRORFILE, ">myprogram.error"
    or die "Can't open myprogram.error";
open SAVEERR, ">&STDERR";
open STDERR, ">&ERRORFILE;

print STDERR "This will appear in error file myprogram.error\n";

# now, restore STDERR
close STDERR;
```

```
open STDERR, ">&SAVEERR";

print STDERR "This will appear on the computer screen\n";
```

There are a lot of details concerning filehandles not covered in this book, and redirecting one of the predefined filehandles such as STDERR can cause problems, especially as your programs get bigger and rely more on modules and libraries of subroutines. One safe way is to define a new filehandle associated with an error file and to send all your error messages to it:

```
open (ERRORMESSAGES, ">myprogram.error")
    or die "Cannot open myprogram.error:$!\n";

print ERRORMESSAGES "This is an error message\n";
```

Note that the die function, and the closely related warn function, print their error messages to STDERR.

Regular Expressions

Regular expressions are, in effect, an extra language that lives inside the Perl language. In Perl, they have quite a lot of features. First, I'll summarize how regular expressions work in Perl; then, I'll present some of their many features.

Overview

Regular expressions describe patterns in strings. The pattern described by a single regular expression may match many different strings.

Regular expressions are used in pattern matching, that is, when you look to see if a certain pattern exists in a string. They can also change strings, as with the s/// operator that substitutes the pattern, if found, for a replacement. Additionally, they are used in the tr function that can transliterate several characters into replacement characters throughout a string. Regular expressions are case-sensitive, unless explicitly told otherwise.

The simplest pattern match is a string that matches itself. For instance, to see if the pattern 'abc' appears in the string 'abcdefghijklmnopqrstuvwxyz', write the following in Perl:

```
$alphabet = 'abcdefghijklmnopqrstuvwxyz';
if( $alphabet =~ /abc/ ) {
    print $&;
}
```

The =~ operator binds a pattern match to a string. /abc/ is the pattern abc, enclosed in forward slashes // to indicate that it's a regular-expression pattern. $& is set to the matched pattern, if any. In this case, the match succeeds, since 'abc' appears in the string $alphabet, and the code just given prints out abc.

Regular expressions are made from two kinds of characters. Many characters, such as 'a' or 'Z', match themselves. Metacharacters have a special meaning in the regular-expression language. For instance, parentheses ( ) are used to group other characters and don't match themselves. If you want to match a metacharacter such as (in a string, you have to precede it with the backslash metacharacter \(in the pattern.

There are three basic ideas behind regular expressions. The first is concatenation: two items next to each other in a regular-expression pattern (that's the string between the forward slashes // in the examples) must match two items next to each other in the string being matched (the $alphabet in the examples). So to match 'abc' followed by 'def', concatenate them in the regular expression:

```
$alphabet = 'abcdefghijklmnopqrstuvwxyz';
if( $alphabet =~ /abcdef/ ) {
        print $&;
}
```

This prints:

```
abcdef
```

The second major idea is alternation. Items separated by the | metacharacter match any one of the items. For example:

```
$alphabet = 'abcdefghijklmnopqrstuvwxyz';
if( $alphabet =~ /a(b|c|d)c/ ) {
        print $&;
}
```

prints as:

```
abc.
```

The example also shows how parentheses group things in a regular expression. The parentheses are metacharacters that aren't matched in the string; rather, they group the alternation, given as b|c|d, meaning any one of b, c, or d at that position in the pattern. Since b is actually in $alphabet at that position, the alternation, and indeed the entire pattern a(b|c|d)c, matches in the $alphabet. (One additional point: ab|cd means (ab)|(cd), not a(b|c)d.)

The third major idea of regular expressions is repetition (or closure). This is indicated in a pattern with the quantifier metacharacter *, sometimes called the Kleene star after one of the inventors of regular expressions. When * appears after an item, it means that the item may appear 0, 1, or any number of times at that place in the string. So, for example, all of the following pattern matches will succeed:

```
'AC' =~ /AB*C/;
'ABC' =~ /AB*C/;
'ABBBBBBBBBBBC' =~ /AB*C/;
```

Metacharacters

The following are metacharacters:

```
\ | ( ) [ { ^ $ * + ? .
```

Escaping with \

A backslash \ before a metacharacter causes it to match itself; for instance, \\ matches a single \ in the string.

Alternation with |

The pipe | indicates alternation, as described previously.

Grouping with ( )

The parentheses ( ) provide grouping, as described previously.

Character classes

Square brackets [ ] specify a character class. A character class matches one character, which can be any character specified. For instance, [abc] matches either a, or b, or c at that position (so it's the same as a|b|c). A-Z is a range that matches any uppercase letter, a-z matches any lowercase letter, and 0-9 matches any digit. For instance, [A-Za-z0-9] matches any single letter or digit at that position. If the first character in a character class is ^, any character except those specified match; for instance, [^0-9] matches any character that isn't a digit.

Matching any character with .

The period or dot . represents any character except a newline. (The pattern modifier /s makes it also match a newline.) So, . is like a character class that specifies every character.

Beginning and end of strings with ^ and $

The ^ metacharacter doesn't match a character; rather, it asserts that the item that follows must be at the beginning of the string. Similarly, the $ metacharacter doesn't match a character but asserts that the item that precedes it must be at the end of the string (or before the final newline). For example: /^Watson and Crick/ matches if the string starts with Watson and Crick; and /Watson and Crick$/ matches if the string ends with Watson and Crick or Watson and Crick\n.

Quantifiers: * + {MIN,} {MIN,MAX} ?

These metacharacters indicate the repetition of an item. The * metacharacter indicates zero, one, or more of the preceding item. The + metacharacter indicates one or more of the preceding item. The brace {} metacharacters let you specify exactly the number of previous items, or a range. For instance, {3} means exactly three of the preceding item; {3,7} means three, four, five, six, or seven of the preceding item; and {3,} means three or more of the preceding item. The ? matches none or one of the preceding item.

Making quantifiers match minimally with ?

The quantifiers just shown are greedy (or maximal) by default, meaning that they match as many items as possible. Sometimes, you want a minimal match that will match as few items as possible. You get that by following each of * + {} ? with a ?. So, for instance, *? tries to match as few as possible, perhaps even none, of the preceding item before it tries to match one or more of the preceding item. Here's a maximal match:

```
'hear ye hear ye hear ye' =~ /hear.*ye/;
print $&;
```

This matches 'hear' followed by .* (as many characters as possible), followed by 'ye', and prints:

```
hear ye hear ye hear ye
```

Here is a minimal match:

```
'hear ye hear ye hear ye' =~ /hear.*?ye/;
print $&;
```

This matches 'hear' followed by .*? (the fewest number of characters possible), followed by 'ye', and prints:

```
hear ye
```

Capturing Matched Patterns

You can place parentheses around parts of the pattern for which you want to know the matched string. For example:

```
$alphabet = 'abcdefghijklmnopqrstuvwxyz';
$alphabet =~ /k(lmnop)q/;
print $1;
```

prints:

```
lmnop
```

You can place as many pairs of parentheses in a regular expression as you like; Perl automatically stores their matched substrings in special variables named $1, $2, and so on. The matches are numbered in order of the left-to-right appearance of their opening parenthesis.

Here's a more intricate example of capturing parts of a matched pattern in a string:

```
$alphabet = 'abcdefghijklmnopqrstuvwxyz';
$alphabet =~ /(((a)b)c)/;
print "First pattern = ", $1,"\n";
print "Second pattern = ", $2,"\n";
print "Third pattern = ", $3,"\n";
```

This prints:

```
First pattern = abc
Second pattern = ab
Third pattern = a
```

Metasymbols

Metasymbols are sequences of two or more characters consisting of backslashes before normal characters. These metasymbols have special meanings in Perl regular expressions (and in double-quoted strings for most of them). There are quite a few of them, but that's because they're so useful. Table B-3 lists most of these metasymbols. The column "Atomic" indicates Yes if the metasymbol matches an item, No if the metasymbol just makes an assertion, and – if it takes some other action.

Table B-3. Alphanumeric metasymbols

Symbol	Atomic	Meaning
\0	Yes	Match the null character (ASCII NULL)
\NNN	Yes	Match the character given in octal, up to 377
\n	Yes	Match nth previously captured string (decimal)
\a	Yes	Match the alarm character (BEL)
\A	No	true at the beginning of a string
\b	Yes	Match the backspace character (BS)
\b	No	True at word boundary
\B	No	True when not at word boundary
\cX	Yes	Match the control character Control-X
\d	Yes	Match any digit character
\D	Yes	Match any nondigit character
\e	Yes	Match the escape character (ASCII ESC, not backslash)
\E	–	End case (\L, \U) or metaquote (\Q) translation
\f	Yes	Match the formfeed character (FF)
\G	No	true at end-of-match position of prior m//g
\l	–	Lowercase the next character only
\L	–	Lowercase till \E
\n	Yes	Match the newline character (usually NL, but CR on Macs)
\Q	–	Quote (do-meta) metacharacters till \E

Symbol	Atomic	Meaning
\r	Yes	Match the return character (usually CR, but NL on Macs)
\s	Yes	Match any whitespace character
\S	Yes	Match any nonwhitespace character
\t	Yes	Match the tab character (HT)
\u	–	Titlecase the next character only
\U	–	Uppercase (not titlecase) till \E
\w	Yes	Match any "word" character (alphanumerics plus _)
\W	Yes	Match any nonword character
\x{abcd}	Yes	Match the character given in hexadecimal
\z	No	true at end of string only
\Z	No	true at end of string or before optional newline

Extending Regular-Expression Sequences

Table B-4 includes several useful features that have been added to Perl's regular-expression capabilities.

Table B-4. Extended regular-expression sequences

Extension	Atomic	Meaning
(?#...)	No	Comment, discard
(?:...)	Yes	Cluster-only parentheses, no capturing
(?imsx-imsx)	No	Enable/disable pattern modifiers
(?imsx-imsx:...)	Yes	Cluster-only parentheses plus modifiers
(?=...)	No	True if lookahead assertion succeeds
(?!...)	No	True if lookahead assertion fails
(?<=...)	No	True if lookbehind assertion succeeds
(?<!...)	No	True if lookbehind assertion fails
(?>...)	Yes	Match nonbacktracking subpattern
(?{...})	No	Execute embedded Perl code
(??{...})	Yes	Match regex from embedded Perl code
(?(...)...|...)	Yes	Match with if-then-else pattern
(?(...)...)	Yes	Match with if-then pattern

Pattern Modifiers

Pattern modifiers are single-letter commands placed after the forward slashes. They are used to delimit a regular expression or a substitution and change the behavior of some regular-expression features. Table B-5 lists the most common pattern modifiers, followed by an example.

Table B-5. Pattern modifiers

Modifier	Meaning
/i	Ignore upper- or lowercase distinctions
/s	Let . match newline
/m	Let ^ and $ match next to embedded \n
/x	Ignore (most) whitespace and permit comments in patterns
/o	Compile pattern once only
/g	Find all matches, not just the first one

As an example, say you were looking for a name in text, but you didn't know if the name had an initial capital letter or was all capitalized. You can use the /i modifier, like so:

```
$text = "WATSON and CRICK won the Nobel Prize";
$text =~ /Watson/i;
print $&;
```

This matches (since /i causes upper- and lowercase distinctions to be ignored) and prints out the matched string WATSON.

Scalar and List Context

Every operation in Perl is evaluated in either scalar or list context. Many operators behave differently depending on the context they are in, returning a list in list context and a scalar in scalar context.

The simplest example of scalar and list contexts is the assignment statement. If the left side (the variable being assigned a value) is a scalar variable, the right side (the values being assigned) are evaluated in scalar context. In the following examples, the right side is an array @array of two elements. When the left side is a scalar variable, it causes @array to be evaluated in scalar context. In scalar context, an array returns the number of elements in an array:

```
@array = ('one', 'two');
$a = @array;
print $a;
```

This prints:

```
2
```

If you put parentheses around the $a, you make it a list with one element, which causes @array to be evaluated in list context:

```
@array = ('one', 'two');
($a) = @array;
print $a;
```

This prints:

```
one
```

Notice that when assigning to a list, if there are not enough variables for all the values, the extra values are simply discarded. To capture all the variables, you'd do this:

```
@array = ('one', 'two');
($a, $b) = @array;
print "$a $b";
```

This prints:

```
one two
```

Similarly, if you have too many variables on the left for the number of right variables, the extra variables are assigned the undefined value undef.

When reading about Perl functions and operations, notice what the documentation has to say about scalar and list context. Very often, if your program is behaving strangely, it's because it is evaluating in a different context than you had thought.

Here are some general guidelines on when to expect scalar or list context:

- You get list context from function calls (anything in the argument position is evaluated in list context) and from list assignments.

- You get scalar context from string and number operators (arguments to such operators as . and + are assumed to be scalars); from boolean tests such as the conditional of an if () statement or the arguments to the || logical operator; and from scalar assignment.

Subroutines and Modules

Subroutines are defined by the keyword sub, followed by the name of the subroutine, followed by a block enclosed by curly braces { } containing the body of the subroutine. Here's a simple example:

```
sub a_subroutine {
    print "I'm in a subroutine\n";
}
```

In general, you can call subroutines using the name of the subroutine followed by a parenthesized list of arguments:

```
a_subroutine();
```

Arguments can be passed into subroutines as a list of scalars. If any arrays are given as arguments, their elements are interpolated into the list of scalars. The subroutine receives all scalar values as a list in the special variable @_. This example illustrates a subroutine definition and the calling of the subroutine with some arguments:

```
sub concatenate_dna {
    my($dna1, $dna2) = @_;

    my($concatenation);

    $concatenation = "$dna1$dna2";

    return $concatenation;
}

print concatenate_dna('AAA', 'CGC');
```

This prints:

```
AAACGC
```

The arguments 'AAA' and 'CGC' are passed into the subroutine as a list of scalars. The first statement in the subroutine's block:

```
my($dna1, $dna2) = @_;
```

assigns this list, available in the special variable @_, to the variables $dna1 and $dna2.

The variables $dna1 and $dna2 are declared as my variables to keep them local to the subroutine's block. In general, you declare all variables as my variables; this can be enforced by adding the statement use strict; near the beginning of your program. However, it is possible to use global variables that are not declared with my, which can be used anywhere in a program, including within subroutines. In this book, I've not used global variables.

The statement:

```
my($concatenation);
```

declares another variable for use by the subroutine.

After the statement:

```
$concatenation = "$dna1$dna2";
```

performs the work of the subroutine, the subroutine defines its value with the return statement:

```
return $concatenation;
```

The value returned from a call to a subroutine can be used however you wish; in this example, it is given as the argument to the print function.

If any arrays are given as arguments, their elements are interpolated into the @_ list, as in the following example:

```
sub example_sub {
    my(@arguments) = @_;
```

```
    print "@arguments\n";
}

my @array = ('two', 'three', 'four');

example_sub('one', @array, 'five');
```

which prints:

```
one two three four five
```

Note that the following attempt to mix arrays and scalars in the arguments to a subroutine won't work:

```
# This won't work!!
sub bad_sub {
    my(@array, $scalar) = @_;

    print $scalar;
}

my @arr = ('DNA', 'RNA');
my $string = 'Protein';

bad_sub(@arr, $string);
```

In this example, the subroutine's variable @array on the left side in the assignment statement consumes the entire list on the right side in @_, namely ('DNA', 'RNA', 'Protein'). The subroutine's variable $scalar won't be set, so the subroutine won't print 'Protein' as intended. To pass separate arrays and hashes to a subroutine, you need to use references; see the section "Subroutines: Pass by Reference" in Chapter 6. Here's a brief example:

```
sub good_sub {
    my($arrayref, $hashref) = @_;

    print "@$arrayref", "\n";

    my @keys = keys %$hashref;

    print "@keys", "\n";
}

my @arr = ('DNA', 'RNA');
my %nums = ( 'one' => 1, 'two' => 2);

good_sub(\@arr, \%nums);
```

which prints:

```
DNA RNA
one two
```

Built-in Functions

Perl has a great many built-in functions. Table B-6 is a partial list with short descriptions.

Table B-6. Perl built-in functions

Function	Summary
abs VALUE	Return the absolute value of its numeric argument
atan2 Y, X	Return the principal value of the arc tangent of Y/X from $-\pi$ to π
chdir EXPR	Change the working directory to *EXPR* (or home directory by default)
chmod MODE LIST	Change the file permissions of the LIST of files to MODE
chomp (VARIABLE or LIST)	Remove ending newline from string(s), if present
chop (VARIABLE or LIST)	Remove ending character from string(s)
chown UID, GID, LIST	Change owner and group of LIST of files to numeric UID and GID
close FILEHANDLE	Close the file, socket, or pipe associated with FILEHANDLE
closedir DIRHANDLE	Close the directory associated with DIRHANDLE
cos EXPR	Return the cosine of the radian number EXPR
dbmclose HASH	Break the binding between a DBM file and a hash
dbmopen HASH, DBNAME, MODE	Bind a DBM file to a HASH with permissions given in MODE
defined EXPR	Return true or false if EXPR has a defined value or not
delete EXPR	Delete an element (or slice) from a hash or an array.
die LIST	Exit the program with an error message that includes LIST
each HASH	Step through a hash with one key, or key-value pair, at a time
exec PATHNAME LIST	Terminate the program and execute the program PATHNAME with arguments LIST
exists EXPR	Return true if hash key or array index exists
exit EXPR	Exit the program with the return value of EXPR
exp EXPR	Return the value of e raised to the exponent EXPR
format	Declare a format for use by the write function
grep EXPR, LIST	Return list of elements of LIST for which EXPR is true
gmtime	Get Greenwich mean time; Sunday is day 0, January is month 0, year is number of years since 1900—example: ($sec,$min,$hour,$mday,$mon,$year,$wday,$yday, $isdaylightsavingstime) = gmtime;
goto LABEL	Program control goes to statement marked with LABEL
hex EXPR	Return decimal value of hexadecimal EXPR
index STR, SUBSTR	Give the position of the first occurrence of SUBSTR in STR
int EXPR	Give the integer portion of the number in EXPR
join EXPR, LIST	Join the strings in LIST into a single string, separated by EXPR
keys HASH	Return a list of all the keys in HASH

Table B-6. Perl built-in functions (continued)

Function	Summary
last LABEL	Exit the immediately enclosing loop by default, or loop with LABEL
lc EXPR	Return a lowercased copy of string in EXPR
lcfirst EXPR	Return a copy of EXPR with first character lowercased
length EXPR	Return the length in characters of EXPR
localtime	Get local time in same format as in gmtime function
log EXPR	Return natural logarithm of number EXPR
m/PATTERN/	The match operator for the regular-expression PATTERN, often abbreviated as /PATTERN/
map BLOCK LIST (or map EXPR, LIST)	Evaluate BLOCK or EXPR for each element of LIST, return list of return values
mkdir FILENAME	Create the directory *FILENAME*
my EXPR	Localize the variables in EXPR to the enclosing block
next LABEL	Go to next iteration of enclosing loop by default or to loop marked with LABEL
oct EXPR	Return decimal value of octal value in EXPR
open FILEHANDLE, EXPR	Open a file by associating FILEHANDLE with the file and options given in EXPR
opendir DIRHANDLE, EXPR	Open the directory EXPR and assign handle DIRHANDLE
pop ARRAY	Remove and return the last element of ARRAY
pos SCALAR	Give location in string SCALAR where last m//g search left off
print FILEHANDLE LIST	Print LIST of strings to FILEHANDLE (default STDOUT)
printf FILEHANDLE FORMAT, LIST	Print string specified by FORMAT and variables LIST to FILEHANDLE
push ARRAY, LIST	Place the elements of LIST at the end of ARRAY
rand EXPR	Give pseudorandom decimal number from 0 to less than EXPR (default 1)
readdir DIRHANDLE	Return list of entries of directory DIRHANDLE
redo LABEL	Restart a loop block without reevaluating the conditional
ref EXPR	Return true or false if EXPR is a reference or not: if true, returned value indicates type of reference
rename OLDNAME, NEWNAME	Change the name of a file
return EXPR	Return from the current subroutine with value EXPR
reverse LIST	Give LIST in reverse order, or reverse strings in scalar context
rindex STR, SUBSTR	Like the index function but returns last occurrence of SUBSTR in STR
rmdir FILENAME	Delete the directory FILENAME
s/PATTERN/REPLACEMENT/	Replace the match of regular-expression PATTERN with string REPLACEMENT
scalar EXPR	Force EXPR to be evaluated in scalar context
seek FILEHANDLE, OFFSET, WHENCE	Position the file pointer for FILEHANDLE to OFFSET bytes (if WHENCE is 0, current position plus OFFSET if WHENCE is 1, or OFFSET bytes from the end if WHENCE is 2)
shift ARRAY	Remove and return the first element of ARRAY
sin EXPR	Return the sine of the radian number EXPR
sleep EXPR	Cause the program to sleep for EXPR seconds

Table B-6. Perl built-in functions (continued)

Function	Summary
sort USERSUB LIST (or sort BLOCK LIST)	Sort the LIST according to the order in USERSUB or BLOCK (default standard string order)
splice ARRAY, OFFSET, LENGTH, LIST	Remove LENGTH elements at OFFSET in ARRAY and replace with LIST, if present
split /PATTERN/, EXPR	Split the string EXPR at occurrences of /PATTERN/, return list
sprintf FORMAT, LIST	Return a string formatted as in the printf function
sqrt EXPR	Return the square root of the number EXPR.
srand EXPR	Set random number seed for rand operator; only needed in versions of Perl before 5.004
stat (FILEHANDLE or EXPR)	Return statistics on file *EXPR* or its FILEHANDLE—example: ($dev,$inode,$mode,$num_of_links,$uid,$gid,$rdev,$size,$accesstime, $modifiedtime,$changetime,$blksize,$blocks) = stat $filename;
study SCALAR	Try to optimize subsequent pattern matches on string SCALAR
sub NAME BLOCK	Define a subroutine named NAME with program code in BLOCK
substr EXPR, OFFSET, LENGTH,REPLACE-MENT	Return substring of string EXPR at position OFFSET and length LENGTH; the substring is replaced with REPLACEMENT if used
system PATHNAME LIST	Execute any program PATHNAME with arguments LIST; returns exit status of program, not its output; to capture ouput, use backticks—example: @output = `/bin/who`;
tell FILEHANDLE	Return current file position in bytes in FILEHANDLE
tr/ORIGINAL/REPLACEMENT/	Transliterates each character in ORIGINAL with corresponding character in REPLACEMENT
truncate (FILEHANDLE or EXPR), LENGTH	Shorten file EXPR or opened with FILEHANDLE to LENGTH bytes
uc EXPR	Return uppercased version of string EXPR
ucfirst EXPR	Return string EXPR with first character capitalized
undef EXPR	Return the undefined value; if a defined variable or subroutine EXPR is given, it's no longer defined; it can be assigned a value when you don't need to save the value
unlink LIST	Delete the LIST of files
unshift ARRAY, LIST	Add LIST elements to the beginning of ARRAY
use MODULE	Load the MODULE
values HASH	Return a list of all values of the HASH
wantarray	In a subroutine, return true if calling program expects a list return value
warn LIST	Print error message including LIST
write FILEHANDLE	Write formatted record to FILEHANDLE (default STDOUT) as defined by the format function

Index

We'd like to hear your suggestions for improving our indexes. Send email to *index@oreilly.com*.

autoincrement and autodecrement
        operators, 322
automating programs, 267–272
    secondary structure predictor, 267–270

B

backbone residues, primary sequence of, 252
backslash (\) (see \, under Symbols)
backups for programs, 19
base 16 (hexadecimal) numbers, 316
base 8 (octal) numbers, 317
bases, 2, 29
    complementary nature of, 3
    counting, 70
        directly from $DNA string, 78–81
        pseudocode for, 71
    restriction enzymes, recognition sites, 189
    reverse complements, changing to, 328
    (see also nucleotides)
Basic Local Alignment Search Tool (see
        BLAST)
beginners in Perl, resources for, 308
BeginPerlBioinfo module, downloading, 103
Berkeley DB, 232
beta sheets (protein supersecondary
        structure), 238
beta strands, 238
binary (base 2) numbers, 317
binary search algorithm, 152
    using with sorted arrays, 154
binary vs. source-code distributions of
        Perl, 12
binding operators, 327
    !~, 327
    (=~), 41, 69
        string matching with, 276
bioinformatics, ix
    BeginPerlBioinfo module,
        downloading, 103
    government-funded web sites, 200
    Internet as source of data, 302
    resources, 313
biology
    computer science and
        bioinformatics resources, 313
        data management, 4
        limits to solving biology problems, 5
        programming, 1
        simulating experiments, 4

conferences covering bioinformatics, 313
data structures and algorithms
    for, 150–155
molecular
    books about, 314
    central dogma, 156
bionet file, restriction enzymes, 186
Bioperl modules, 274, 294–301
    representative sample of, 295–297
    tutorial script, 297–301
    web site for, 304
    web site for downloading, 295
bitwise operators, 323
    & (bitwise and), 323
    | (OR operator), 123
blank line (user input), testing for, 69
BLAST (Basic Local Alignment Search
        Tool), 167, 274–301
    Bioperl, using with, 297–301
    documentation, 275
    output files, 277–280
        parsing, 280–290
        presenting data, 290–294
    public database servers, 204
    string matching and homology, 276
    versions of, 274
    WU-BLAST implementation, 275
blocks, 59, 90, 319
    code layout, making explicit in, 63
bottom-up program design, 137
BPLite.pm (Bioperl module for BLAST), 301
brackets [ ] (see [ ], under Symbols)
breakpoints, 112–114
    deleting, 113
built-in functions, Perl
    listing with descriptions, 344–346
    online manual, 309
by reference
    passing arguments into
        subroutines, 99–102
    subroutines, calling arguments by, 289
by value
    copying and passing data, 99
    subroutines, calling arguments by, 289
byte offsets, 216
    GenBank records, storing as values, 234
    reporting with tell function, 220

C

C compiler for Perl source code, 12
c (continue) command, 112
C (see cytosine)
calling
    Perl interpreter from command line, 104
    subroutine arguments by reference, 289
    subroutine arguments by value, 99
    subroutines, 87
        from other subroutines, 88
call_stride subroutine, 267, 269
capturing in patterns, 337
carboxyl group, 3
carriage returns
    matching with metasymbols, 68
    removing with chomp function, 66
case-insensitive matching, 208, 340
CDS feature key, 224
centering text, 294
central dogma of molecular biology, 156
CGI.pm module, creating interactive web
        pages, 303
chaining, logical operators, 193, 326
character classes, 336
    genetic code, redundancy of, 160
    hash keys and, 162
    IUB ambiguity codes, translating to, 189
    regular expressions and, 68
    searching DNA with, 183
characters
    in DNA sequence data, checking source
        documentation, 74
    letters representing nucleic acids, 31, 189
chemical bond between amino and carboxyl
        groups, 3
children's game with random numbers
        (example), 120–122
chip-based laboratories for studying gene
        expression, 305
chmod command, making Perl program
        executable, 14
chomp function, removing newlines with, 66
chop function, chomp vs., 66
close function, 61
close (system call), 331
cmp operator, 153
code
    breakpoints, 112–114
        deleting, 113
    debugging (see debugging)

examples from this book,
        downloading, xii
    formatting, 62
        nested function calls, 124
    Perl, 6
    self-documenting, 35
    subroutines (see subroutines)
coding DNA, 70
coding regions, 175
codons, 155
    amino acids, representing with, 156
    stop, 176
    translating to amino acids, 156–163
        testing for redundant codons, 159
columns, PDB files, 252
command line
    calling Perl interpreter from, 104
    counting Gs in DNA from, 96
    input files, naming on, 331
    starting Perl debugger from, 108
command-line arguments, 96–98
    in @ARGV array variable, 98
commands
    interpretation line, 315
    Perl debugger, 108
comments, 27, 33, 316
    importance of, 28
compilers, 6
compiling Perl source code, 12
complementary bases, 3
complex data structures, 304
complex (or imaginary) numbers, 317
computation, algorithms for, 26
computer programs
    defined, 7
    speed of, 8
    (see also programming; programs)
computer science
    biology and, ix
        limits to solving biology problems, 5
        programming, 1
    new trends in computing, 306
    resource materials, 310–312
        algorithms, 311
        general programming, 312
        software engineering, 311
computers, 7
concatenating DNA fragments, 36–40
    join function, using, 67
    print statement, using, 39

DEFINITION field, collecting in GenBank
    annotations, 213–215
definitions of subroutines, 90
dereferencing, 101
designing programs
    input and output, 24
    object-oriented programming, 303
    top-down vs. bottom up, 137
die function, 334
directives, printf function, 291
directories, in different operating systems, 7
disease treatment, protein structure and, 238
divisions, GenBank libraries, 204
DNA, 2
    bases, 29
        counting in strings, 78–81
    coding and noncoding, 70
    coding regions, 175
    concatenating fragments with join
        function, 67
    counting nucleotides in, 70
        global regular expression in while loop
            test, 81–84
        on the command line, 96
        tr function, using, 84
    cutting to insert a gene, 184
    mutations, investigating with
        randomization, 118–148
        generating random DNA, 136–141
        program simulating
            mutation, 126–136
        program using
            randomization, 120–126
        random number generators, 119
        random sequences, comparing bases
            for identity, 141–147
    reading from FASTA files, 166–172
    regulatory elements in, program to
        count, 23–28
    reverse complement of strands,
        calculating, 43–46
    separating from GenBank file
        annotations, 205–212
    sequences
        concatenating, 36–40
        program to store, 32
        representing, 29
        storing in variables, 34
        transcribing to RNA, 40–42

translating into amino acids and
    proteins, 155–180
    reading frames, 175–180
    writing formatted sequence data, 172
DNA computers, 306
documentation
    BLAST, 275
    Perl, 16, 42, 307
        online manuals, 308
        perlop (for operators), 322
        regular expressions, 184
dot (.) operator (see ., under Symbols)
double helix, 2
do-until loops, 67, 123, 330
do-while loops, 330
downloading
    code examples from this book, xii
    Perl, 11
    (see also resources; web sites)
droplet, Macperl application, 33
drugs, targeting proteins with, 238

E

-e (exists) file test, 270
E (expect) value of matches, BLAST
    program, 276
EcoRI restriction enzyme, 184
elements, array
    accessing with subscripts, 51
    adding, using push and shift
        functions, 154
    randomly selecting, 123
    specifying individual, 319
else statements, 326
elsif statements, 327
empty string, 67
end-of-record separator (//), 210
Ensembl web site, use of Bioperl
    modules, 304
Entrez (public database server), 204
enzymes, 238
equal (=) sign (see =, under Symbols)
error messages, 20
    directing to STDERR, 159, 333
    warnings (-w) flag, 34
EST (expressed sequence tag division),
    GenBank libraries, 204
European Bioinformatics Institute (EBI) web
    site, 200

European Molecular Biology Laboratory
    (EMBL), 167
    web site, 200
examples from this book
    protein sequence file, downloading, 47
    web site for downloads, xii
"exclusive-OR" operator (xor), 323, 325
exec function, 270
exists (-e) file test, 270
exists function, 162
exit function, 36, 61
expect (E) value of BLAST matches, 276
experimental studies, in silico, 4
exploding strings into arrays, 70–77
exponential notation, 316
expression, genes, 151–154
expressions, nested, 123
    order of evaluation, 124
extract_HSP_information subroutine, 289
extractSEQRES subroutine, 261
extract_sequence_from_fasta_data
    subroutine, 171

F

false or true value, evaluating with
    conditionals, 57–60, 324
FAQs, Perl, 16, 308
    newsgroup information, 310
FASTA format, DNA sequences, 167
    reading and extracting sequence data,
        main program, 173
    reading and formatting file output, 174
    reading files, 166–172
        subroutine for, 170
FEATURES table (GenBank
        annotations), 224–231
    feature keys
        listing with definitions, 225–228
        parsing, 228–231
fields, GenBank records, 221
    PDB record types vs., 260
file permission modes, DBM files, 233
file test operators, 80, 323
    -e (exists), 270
File::Find module, 304
filehandles, 48, 66, 331
    output, 333
filenames, removing newlines from, 66

files
    ASCII flat files
        GenBank, 200
        PDB, 239
    attributes, testing for, 80
    BLAST output, 277–280
        parsing, 280–290
        presenting data, 290–294
    directing output to, 333
    FASTA format, reading DNA
        from, 166–172
    input from, 331
        named on command line, 331
    naming, 47
    opening, 48, 326
        with system calls, 61
    PDB, 240–266
        format of, 252–253
        parsing, 257–266
    protein sequence data, reading
        from, 47–55
    writing to, 81–85
filesystems, 7
flags, use of, 214
floating-point numbers, 124, 316
flow control, 56–62
    bad code format and, 63
    conditional statements, 56–60
    loops, 60–62
folders
    Macintosh or Windows, 7
    naming, 47
    PDB, 240–248
folding of proteins, 238
for loops, 60, 329
    here document in, 292
    initialization and increment of
        counter, 80
    program using randomization, 123
foreach loops, 60, 76, 111, 329
    $_ variables in, 106
    variable declaration in, 171
fork function, 270
format function, 292, 332
formats, DNA files, 167
formatted sequence data, writing, 172
formatting
    code, 62
        function calls in nested braces, 124

output, 290–294
    format and write functions, 292
    here documents, 291
    printf function, 291, 332
formfeeds, matching with metasymbols, 68
fractions, 124, 317
frequently asked question lists (FAQs),
    Perl, 16
functions
    built-in, 344–346
    nested calls, formatting in code, 124
    Perl, online manual, 309

G

/g (global) pattern modifier, 208, 290
G (see guanine)
gcc compiler, 12
GD and Tk modules for graphics, 305
GenBank (Genetic Sequence Data
    Bank), 167, 199–237
    annotations
      parsing, 212–217
      parsing at top level, 220–224
      parsing FEATURES table, 224–231
      problems with, 200
    desktop workstations, setting up, 204
    files, 200–203
      format specification, web site for, 203
      records, 200
    indexing with DBM, 232–236
    libraries, 203
    library subroutines, testing, 217–220
    separating annotations from
      sequences, 205–212
      using arrays, 205–208
      using scalars, 208–212
gene expression data
    database for, 151
    gene names, data structures for
      manipulating, 154
    hashes, using, 153
    microarrays, studying with, 305
    sorted arrays and binary search,
      using, 152
    unsorted arrays, using for, 151
gene features key, 224
Generate random DNA program
    (example), 138–141

genes
    coding DNA, 70
    computer simulation, studying with, 5
    cutting DNA to insert, 184
genetic code, 149–181
    hashes, using for, 160–163
    reading DNA from FASTA format
      files, 166–172
    reading frames, 175
      translating, 176–180
    redundancy in, 156, 159
    translating codons to amino
      acids, 156–163
    translating DNA into proteins, 163–166
genetic information data banks, 200
Genetics Computer Group (GCG) DNA file
    format, 167
genomes, large-scale studies of, ix
get_file_data subroutine, 170
    reading in PDB file, 260
get_next_record function, 216
global matching (/g), 208, 290
global searches in loops, 194
global substitution, 41
global variables, 91, 342
governmental organizations, bioinformatics
    (web sites), 313
graph algorithms, modelling biological
    networks with, 305
graphical user interfaces (GUIs), 96, 305
    displays for programs, 134
greater than (>), 59
greedy matching, 337
grep function, 271
grouping in regular expressions, 184
guanine (G), 2, 30

H

hashes, 101, 149, 320
    %alignments (BLAST program), 289
    atomic coordinate data, PDB files, 265
    data storage (DBM), 155
    DMM files, using with, 232
    gene expression data, using for, 153
    genetic code, using for, 160–163
    genetic data, use for, 154
    initializing, 150
    PDB character codes, translating, 262
    recognition enzymes, 190
    of restriction enzymes, 185

multiline information sets, GenBank vs.
     PDB, 260
multiline strings
     converting to arrays, 261
     /m pattern modifier and, 209, 290
mutate subroutine (example), 129
     debugging, 134
mutate_better subroutine (example), 135
mutations, investigating with
          randomization, 118–148
     generating random DNA, 136–141
       bottom-up vs. top-down design, 137
       generate random DNA
          program, 138–141
       subroutines for, 137
     program simulating mutation, 126–136
       mutate DNA (example), 131–136
       random position in string,
          selecting, 126
     program using randomization, 120–126
       formatting code, 124
       seeding the random number
          generator, 122
       selecting array elements
          randomly, 123
       selecting array position,
          randomly, 125
     random number generators, 119
my variables, 91, 93, 342
     pitfalls of not using, 94
     removing to debug code, 114

N

n (next) command, 109
\n or \n\n (newlines), 38
N (unknown), 31
names
     filenames, operating system, 66
     PDB file records, 252
     Perl pathnames, 13, 14
     scalar variables, 317
     subroutine, 89
     variables, 101
National Center for Biotechnology
          Information (NCBI), 200, 275
nested expressions, 123
     order of evaluation, 124
nested loops, 147

networks of interacting biological systems,
          modelling, 305
newlines, 38
     matching with metasymbols, 68
     motifs split by, 67
     removing from filenames, 66
     in scalars, regular expressions and, 208
     strings containing, matches against, 290
newsgroups, Perl, 310
next (n) command, 109
next operator, 106
NMR (nuclear magnetic resonance) studies,
          macromolecule structure, 239
noncoding DNA, 70
nongreedy or minimal matching, 290
not operator, 192, 325
     logical negation, 192
NP-complete problems, 5
nucleic acids, 29
     letters representing, 31
nucleotide-nucleotide version
          (BLASTN), 274
nucleotides, 2
     choosing random, subroutine for, 128
     codons, 155
     counting, 70
       global regular expression in while loop
          test, 81–84
       pseudocode for, 71
       tr function, using, 84
     primary structure of, 252
     (see also bases; DNA)
numbering positions in Perl strings and
          arrays, 81
numbers
     array of, sorting, 153
     floating-point, 124, 316
     incrementing, 76
     random and pseudo-random, 119
     as scalar values, 316
     storing in scalar variables, 75
       and printing, 39
numeric equality (==), testing for, 57–59

O

object-oriented programming, 25, 303
octal (base 8) numbers, 317
offsets (see byte offsets)
online manuals, Perl, 308

proteins (*continued*)
DNA, translating into, 155–180
FASTA file, reading and formatting output, 174
homology of, 276
motifs, finding, 63–70
PROSITE web site, 63
organization of, 3
Protein Identification Resource (PIR), 167
RNA, translation into, 156
sequences, 46
reading from a file, 47–55
reading from file with while loop, 60
representing, 29
structure of, 238
(see also Protein Data Bank)
pseudocode, 26
commenting out, 28
for counting nucleotides, 71
DNA regulatory elements, counting, 27
getanswer (example), 27
pseudo-random numbers, 119
public database servers, 204
push function, 101
adding element at end of array, 53
arrays, using with, 154

Q

quantifiers, 336
maximal and minimal, 337
quantum computing, 306
quaternary structures of proteins, 4, 238
query language for databases (SQL), 155
qx// (quoted execution) operator, 270

R

rand function, 124, 125
random number generators, 119
seeding, 122
randomelement subroutine (example), 130
randomization, 118–148, 303
comparing bases in random DNA sequences, 141–147
generating random DNA, 136–141
bottom-up vs. top-down design, 137
generate random DNA program, 138–141
subroutines for, 137

program simulating mutation, 126–136
mutate DNA (example), 131–136
random nucleotide, choosing, 128
random nucleotide, placing in random position, 129
random nucleotide, selecting, 130
random position in string, selecting, 126
program using, 120–126
array position, randomly selecting, 125
control flow, 123
formatting code, 124
making a sentence, 123
seeding the random number generator, 122
selecting array elements randomly, 123
random number generators, 119
randomnucleotide subroutine (example), 128, 137
improving design, 130
range operator (..), using with logical operators, 191–193
rapid prototyping, 8
rational numbers, 317
ratios, 317
raw score (S), BLAST matching, 276
reading
bionet file for restriction sites, 187
DNA from FASTA files, 166–172
FASTA format files
subroutine for, 170
files, 47–55
PDB files, 260
protein sequence data from a file, using while loop, 60
restriction enzyme data, 187
reading frames, 175
ORFs (open reading frames), 176
translating DNA in, 176–180
translating DNA in all, main program, 178–180
REBASE (Restriction Enzyme Database), 185
data file, subroutine for parsing, 190
recognition sites
codes for, 189
IUB nucleic acid codes, translating to regular expressions, 188
(see also restriction maps; restriction sites)

scalar function, 125
    determining size of arrays, 124
scalar values, 316
    assigning to arrays, 319
    assigning to scalar variables, 318
    numbers, 316
    strings, 316
        (see also strings)
scalar variables, 35, 317
    $ (dollar sign), beginning with, 51
    arrays, converting to, 67
    assigning scalar values to, 318
    assignment operator, setting value
        with, 36
    datatypes held in, 39
    GenBank records, reading as, 208–212
    printing out values, 36
    references, storing in, 101
    storing numbers in, 75
    user input, saving as, 66
scientific (exponential) notation, 316
scoping, 91, 93–96
    strict, 95
    variables within while loop, 223
scores and statistics on matches, BLAST
        program, 276
scripts (Perl), 6
search_annotation subroutine, 231
secondary structures, proteins, 4, 238
    predictor program (stride), 267–270
seeding random number generators, 119,
        122
seek function, 216
self-documenting code, 35
sentences, randomly combining parts
        of, 120–122, 123
SEQADV record type, PDB files, 252
    example, 253
SEQRES record type, PDB files, 252
    parsing, 253–256
sequences, 29–55
    alignment methods, 303
    DNA
        concatenating, 36–40
        program to store, 32
    protein, 46
        reading from a file, 47–55
        reading from file with while loop, 60

removing nonsequence data from, 68
representing, 29
similarity, statistical methods to
        calculate, 275
servers
    BLAST, web sites for, 275
    public database, 204
shift function, 101, 154
    taking element from beginning of
        array, 52
similarity as indication of homology, 276
simple data (Applied Biosystems (ABI)
        sequencer output), 167
simulating DNA mutation, 118, 126–136
    program, designing
        random nucleotide, placing into
            random position, 129
        random nucleotide, selecting, 128,
            130
        random position in string,
            selecting, 126
    program (mutate DNA), 131–136
simulating experiments with computers, 4
single line (/s pattern modifier), 209
single step (s) command, 109
size of arrays, 152
Smith-Waterman algorithm for sequence
        alignment, 303
software (bioinformatics), distribution
        sites, 200
software engineering, 311
sort function, 153
sorted arrays
    in gene expression data, 152
    using with binary search algorithm, 154
sorting
    alphabetical, array of strings, 153
    array of numbers, 153
    hash keys and values, 154
source code
    comments, 27
    open source, 21
    Perl distributions
        binary distributions vs., 12
        Unix or Linux, downloading on, 12
source feature key, 224
speed, Perl programs, 8
splice function, 53

subroutines (*continued*)

object-oriented programming, interfacing with, 303

parseATOM, 265

parse_blast, 281, 289

parse_blast_alignment, 281

parse_blast_alignment_HSP, 289

parsePDBrecordtypes, 260

parse_stride, 271

parsing REBASE data file, 190

parsing REBASE files, 193

passing data to, 98–102

by reference, 99–102, 343

by value, 99

random DNA set, generating, 137

random number generator, 119

randomelement (example), 130

randomnucleotide (example), 128, 137

improving design, 130

randomposition (example), 126

reading FASTA files, 170

redundant codons, testing for, 159

return values, 90

returning sequence data from FASTA format, 169

reverse complement, computing, 176

scoping and, 93–96

search_annotation, 231

translating DNA codons to amino acids, 157–159

testing for redundant codons, 159

using hash lookup, 160–163

translating DNA frames, computing indices, 177

translating DNA to peptide, 165

variables in, 91

writing, 88–90

writing formatted sequence data, 172

subscripts, array elements, 51

integer values for, 126

substitution (s///) operator, 41, 68, 327

substr function, 70, 81, 129

supersecondary structures, 238

syntax errors, 104

system calls

checking success or failure of, 61

open and close, 331

open, using with unless statement, 61

system function, 270

T

T (see thymine)

tabs, matching with metasymbols, 68

tell function, 216, 220

tertiary (3D) structures of proteins, 4, 238

text

alignment of, 294

Perl, ease of manipulating, 41

text editors, 15

missing braces, locating, 59

this_program file, 13

3D structures of macromolecules, 239

thymine (T), 2, 30

replacing with uracil (U) in DNA to RNA transcription, 40–42

time function, 122

Tk and GD modules for graphics, 305

top-down program design, 137

tr (transliteration) function, 84

tr/// (transliteration) operator, 328

transcription, 156

DNA to RNA, 40–42

translation, 156

DNA codons to amino acids, 156–163

redundant codons, testing for, 159

using hash lookup, 160–163

DNA in reading frames, 176–180

main program, 178–180

stop codons, 176

DNA into proteins, 163–166

FASTA file, reading and formatting output, 174

translator applications for computer languages, 6

transliteration (tr///) operator, 328

true or false value, evaluating with conditionals, 57–60, 324

tutorial script, Bioperl, 297–301

U

U (see uracil)

undefined values, 324, 341

Unix

directories, 7

installing Perl on, 12

Perl, finding already installed, 10

Perl programs, running, 13

specifying input files on command line, 332
text editors, 15
unknown (N), 31
unless statements, 57, 61, 327
example, 58
unshift function, 53
unsolvable problems, 5
unsorted arrays for gene expression data, 151
uracil (U), 30
replacing thymine (T) in DNA to RNA transcription, 40–42
use, 103
use strict;, 104
use warnings;, 104
user input, getting from keyboard, 66
blank line, testing for, 67, 69
user queries on restriction enzymes, making restriction map from, 194–197

V

values, hashes (see key/value pairs, hashes)
variables, 32
$&, 209
$_, 77, 106
$&, $`, and $´, 197
@_ (see @_, under arrays)
array (see arrays)
containing strings, using binding operator (=~) with, 41
declaring, 75
beginning of program vs. first use, 129, 136
DNA sequences, storing in, 34
global, in subroutines, 91
initializing, 74
interpolating, 39
into here documents, 292
into string matches, 69
in loops, 171
naming, 34
resetting, 123
scalar, 39, 317
assigning scalar values to, 318
scoping
in subroutines, 93–96
in while loop, 223
split function, separating with, 188

in subroutines, 91
symbols denoting types, 101
testing and changing value in loops, 329–330
versions, Perl, 9
for Macintosh systems, 13
viruses, 238

W

-w command-line switch, turning on warnings, 104
W (watch) debugger command, 113
w (window) command, 110
warn function, 334
warnings pragma, 104
variables, finding errors in, 115
warnings (-w flag), 34, 104
web programming, 302
web sites
ActiveState (ActivePerl), 13
bioinformatics, government-sponsored, 313
Bioperl modules, 304
BLAST
NCBI, 200, 275
Pennsylvania State University, 275
for this book, xii
BeginPerlBioinfo module, 103
protein sequence file, 47
CPAN, 297, 308
Ensembl, using Bioperl modules, 304
European Bioinformatics Institute (EBI), 200
European Molecular Biology Laboratory (EMBL), 200
FEATURES table, 224
GenBank, 203
Linux, 312
MacPerl web page, 13
National Center for Biotechnology Information (NCBI), 200
BLAST program, 275
Perl, 307
beginners, 308
downloads, 11
FAQs, 308
latest stable release, 295
online documentation, 16
PROSITE, protein motif information, 63

About the Author

James D. Tisdall consults for Biocomputing Associates of Kimberton, Pennsylvania, which specializes in bioinformatics software development and training.

Jim worked at Bell Labs in Murray Hill, New Jersey, where he programmed computers for the Speech Research Department. While at Bell Labs, he discovered a formal language for musical rhythm and published in structural complexity theory. He also earned a B.A. in mathematics from City College of New York and an M.S. in computer science from Columbia University. He left Bell Labs to pursue a Ph.D. in computer science at the University of Michigan and the University of Pennsylvania.

One of the first people to use Perl in bioinformatics, Jim joined the Human Genome Project in 1991, where he developed DNA WorkBench, a parallel-processing bioinformatics Perl program used worldwide. As a computational biologist at Mercator Genetics in Menlo Park, California, his Perl programs for SNP and haplotype analysis were used in the discovery of the gene for the common genetic disease hemochromatosis. Jim was also the manager of bioinformatics at Fox Chase Cancer Center in Philadelphia.

In his spare time Jim teaches computer music at the Settlement Music School in Philadelphia and publishes the occasional poem. He is the father of three, the son of two, and the husband of one.

Colophon

Our look is the result of reader comments, our own experimentation, and feedback from distribution channels. Distinctive covers complement our distinctive approach to technical topics, breathing personality and life into potentially dry subjects.

The animals on the cover of *Beginning Perl for Bioinformatics* are green frog (*Rana clamitans*) and American bullfrog (*Rana catesbeiana*) tadpoles.

Tadpoles are the larvae of frogs and toads. They are aquatic and when first hatched have large, round heads and long, flat tails. Through a complex process of metamorphosis, tadpoles change from small fishlike creatures to the more familiar frogs and toads. This process can take from 10 days to 3 years depending on the species.

During the first stages of metamorphosis, a tadpole's hind legs sprout, its head begins to flatten, and its tail becomes shorter. In its early life, a tadpole feeds primarily on diatoms, algae, and small quantities of zooplankton. As metamorphosis continues, it stops eating and begins to reabsorb its tail for sustenance while its digestive system changes from primarily vegetarian to carnivorous. During the final stages of metamorphosis, the tadpole's front legs appear, its jaws form, its skeleton hardens, and its gills disappear as the lungs develop. It soon begins to breathe air at the surface of the water. A short time later, the tadpole emerges from the water, reabsorbs the last of its tail, and hops off as a frog or a toad.

Mary Anne Weeks Mayo was the production editor and copyeditor for *Beginning Perl for Bioinformatics*. Matt Hutchinson and Jane Ellin provided quality control. Edie Shapiro, Matt Hutchinson, and Derek DiMatteo provided production assistance. Ellen Troutman-Zaig wrote the index.

Ellie Volckhausen designed the cover of this book, based on a series design by Edie Freedman. The cover image is an original illustration created by Lorrie LeJeune. Emma Colby produced the cover layout with QuarkXPress 4.1 using Adobe's ITC Garamond font.

Melanie Wang designed the interior layout, based on a series design by David Futato. Neil Walls converted the files from SGML to FrameMaker 5.5.6 using tools created by Mike Sierra. The text font is Linotype Birka; the heading font is Adobe Myriad Condensed; and the code font is LucasFont's TheSans Mono Condensed. The illustrations that appear in the book were produced by Robert Romano and Jessamyn Read using Macromedia FreeHand 9 and Adobe Photoshop 6. The tip and warning icons were drawn by Christopher Bing. This colophon was written by Lorrie LeJeune.

Whenever possible, our books use a durable and flexible lay-flat binding. If the page count exceeds this binding's limit, perfect binding is used.